# IN SEARCH OF
# ADVENTURE

## A Wild Travel Anthology

Written and Compiled by:

**Bruce Northam and Brad Olsen**

CONSORTIUM OF COLLECTIVE CONSCIOUSNESS

San Francisco, California U.S.A.

## In Search of Adventure: A Wild Travel Anthology
### 1st edition

National distributor to the retail trade: Independent Publishers Group, 814 North Franklin Street, Chicago, Illinois, 60610 (800-888-4741)

Library of Congress Cataloging-in-Publication Data:

Northam, Bruce and Olsen, Brad
  In Search of Adventure
  A Wild Travel Anthology/ Northam & Olsen
    p.  cm.
  Does not include index
  ISBN 1-888729-03-1 (Pbk.)
  1. Anthology—Travel Book. 2. Travel—Essays.  I. Title
  Library of Congress Catalog Card Number: 98-092915

Printed in the United States of America.

10 9 8 7 6 5 4 3 2 1

**In Search of Adventure**

A Wild Travel Anthology

**Acknowledgments:** Gratitude to our Creative Consultant, Phil Trupp, and for Eric Stamfli's cover design, and to those who provided wise counsel and advice. Love to our splendid friends and family.

# Table of Contents

## Chapter 6: BOY, WAS I A BONEHEAD OR WHAT?
### Misadventures

## Chapter 7: INTIMACY
### Love on the Move

## Chapter 8: INNER QUEST
### The Will and the Why

Chapter 9:  **INTREPID ARCHETYPES**
**They Broke the Mold ...**

Chapter 10:  **TRAMPLED UNDERFOOT**
**The elusion of boredom isn't always a vacation.**

Chapter 11:  **BEGINNINGS**
**Setting Out**

Chapter 12: **THRIFTY TRAVEL SAVVY**
**Cheap Tricks**

Chapter 13: **GOING HOME**
**The Final Hurdle**

# Prologue

*Can a wise Chinaman read another man's future?*

CHEN ENTERED MY LIFE IN 1987, when I was backpacking in the newly "opened" China. He was a multilingual restaurateur and the *unofficial* mayor of Yangzhou. He had a kindly way with backpackers, and one afternoon he invited me to join him on a seventy mile journey in his rickety truck across southeast China's surreal limestone pinnacle landscape.

Enroute we passed a seemingly ancient man and his goat. The man plodded barefoot along the hot, rough road, two immense bags of rice suspended on a long pole across his back.

We passed him without a word, but returning to Yangzhou several hours later, we encountered him again. I suggested to Chen that we offer him a lift. We pulled over, and the old man and Chen had a brief exchange. Chen got behind the wheel, and we drove off, leaving the man in the road.

Puzzled, I asked Chen to translate their chat. He explained that the man wasn't due to arrive in Yangzhou until the following day; if he were to show up in advance, he wouldn't know what to with the extra time.

"You see, my friend, not all of us are in a hurry," he explained.

I asked him to turn back. I wanted to ask the old man a few things. Chen parked and I hopped out onto the road. The old man stopped, balancing on his walking stick, and grinned. We pondered each other—beings from distant corners of the planet, worlds and ways apart.

Chen translated my questions.

"What is the most important thing in your life?" I asked.

The old man looked to his left, made a strange honking call for his goat, but did not reply. Was the goat the most important thing? When the animal arrived at his side, the man looked at Chen and spoke slowly.

"He said that if you can't help people, don't harm them," Chen translated.

I asked, "Why are people hurtful?"

I didn't look at Chen as he translated, but rather stared into the old man's eyes. He was pure human art, more serene than a sleeping cat.

Chen translated, "If you decline to accept someone's abuse, then it still belongs to them."

"Why do we quarrel?" I asked.

"The rise of a man's mind from his scrotum to his skull can be a long haul," came the answer. On that note, the three of us burst into laughter.

The goat bleated. Chen roused me, "Ready?"

The old man and I shook hands, waved good-bye, and the truck rolled away.

I often recall the man's deeply wrinkled face, and I recall that the infuriating fixtures of modern life—traffic jams, rude people, the arrogance of ego—are only options. His words remain a permanent, benevolent echo.

I departed Yangzhou a week later. Chen walked with me to the bus stop. After a hearty embrace, I told him how much his friendship meant to me, and that the old man's words were most likely unforgettable. I thanked him for that, too.

"Use those words to start a book," he said.

"Come on, Chen," I replied. "Do you know how old I'll be by the time I get published?"

"The same age you'll be if you don't," he winked.

\* \* \*

Twelve years, twenty letters, and three books later, I received a birthday card from Chen. I was in for a shock. He confessed that he hadn't faithfully translated the old man's words. Indeed, everything I'd absorbed had actually been Chen's sage advice.

Bruce Northam
March, 1999

# Introduction

*Travel writers fear boredom more than death.*

OF ALL PEOPLE WHO SHOULD END UP as friends and business partners ... we were on parallel missions before meeting in a heated competition. Both of us had quit our day jobs, traveled around the world in our 20's, and then wrote similar books about it: *The Frugal Globetrotter* (Bruce Northam) and *World Stompers* (Brad Olsen) were published in 1996. Simultaneously launching our books, our paths crossed at a Chicago trade show—a New Yorker and a Californian eyeing each other tentatively across a gulf of common pursuits.

Two years later we met again on a press trip to Austria—a spectacular itinerary that took us hiking in the Alps. Concluding the press trip, we opted for a bonus evening in Salzburg that led us into St. Peter's Cathedral for a service spoken entirely in German. Without either of us understanding a single word, we encountered something remarkable, something indescribable. Afterwards, dizzy with inspiration, the ensuing walkabout in Salzburg's Old City gave birth to a brainstorm—the sort of inspiration that relieves, when you truly comprehend what's next—for us, another convincing reprieve from lamentable, typical employment. This book was born on a footbridge spanning the Salzach River.

We envisioned giving this book two priceless attributes: roots and wings. Our roots would be veteran authors, and we felt it equally important to grant up-and-coming writers a deserved forum. Next came the forage for stories, which proved serendipitous and gratifying. Word of mouth, an email blizzard, and chance meetings unearthed a wealth of writing talent, both veteran and rookie.

And now we turn the final product over to you. May this book help you discover your wings.

Bruce Northam　　　　　Brad Olsen
Manhattan　　　　　　　San Francisco

"Brad, have you written your Austria article yet?"

"No Bruce, you?"

"Nope, how can we make it up to them?"

"Mention the tourist office in our book?"

For first-rate vacation counsel on Austria, including their sensational "Hiking Without Luggage" program, contact the Austrian National Tourist Office at (212) 944-6880 or www.anto.com

\* \* \*

Roaming should not be a gene that's out-selected over time. For details on splendid walking vacations, contact the British Tourist Authority at (800) 462-2748. Request a copy of Britain for Walkers and the Walking Wales brochure—or www.visitwales.com

Emotion is created by motion ... "What a Difference a Walk Makes" page 154

# SIMPLY AMAZING

## The Wild and the Wacky

*"I have always been consumed with one desire: to touch and see
as much as possible of the earth and the sea before I die."*

Nikos Kazantzakis, *Zorba the Greek*

# Mongolia: Adventures in You-Cut Hairstyling

**Tim Cahill**

*A popular archaeological theory is that the Mongolian people may have been the first Americans. A dedicated "Mer-ee-koon" sets out, and encounters the yogurt riders.*

THERE WERE A DOZEN OF US, riding the immense central Asian grassland on sturdy Mongolian horses. When I glanced back for a view of the glacier and the sacred mountain we had just visited, I saw two tiny specks inching down the steep windswept hillside, moving in our direction. I turned on my horse, and glassed the hill with a little four power Russian monocle. The pursuing riders were coming towards us at a stiff trot. They were at least two miles back and about 1000 feet above us. Each man held something in his right hand. I could plainly see the glint of metal.

"They carrying," one of the Americans asked.

"Yeah," I said, "both of them."

Bayarra Sanjaasuren, our translator, conveyed the information to the Mongolian wranglers. This was serious: We had yogurt riders on our tail. Again.

"Tchoo," half a dozen men shouted at once.

Tchoo is the Mongolian equivalent of "giddiup." Mongolian horses respond smartly to tchoo, no matter who says it. Guy next to you says "tchoo," you're off at a gallop. We were riding a dozen men abreast because Mongolians do not ride in single file. A defeated army, they say, rides single file. And now, with the dreaded yogurt riders in pursuit, our little party sounded like the whole first grade trying to imitate a locomotive.

"Tchoo, tchoo ...

"Tchoo, tchoo, tchoo ...."

Significantly, there is no Mongolian word that corresponds to "whoa."

We'd been riding eight to twelve hours a day, every day, for a week, and I was fairly comfortable in the old Russian cavalry saddle I'd been given. It was a pair of metal hoops on a wooden frame, covered over in peeling leather stuffed

**18**

with horse hair. The stirrups were metal hoops connected to the frame with rawhide straps. The Mongolians in our party rode ornate handcarved wooden saddles, the best of them festooned with beaten silver medallions.

"Tchoo," I said, and stood up a bit in the saddle so my horse could stretch into his long gallop.

The ground we were approaching, however, was humped up in the marshy tussocks characteristic of soil that is permanently frozen a few feet below the surface. We were only at about 48 degrees north—about the latitude of Seattle—but cold fronts originating in Siberia, to our north, seem to flow down the great Yenisey River, Northern Asia's Amazon, and funnel into Mongolia. Nowhere else in the hemisphere does permafrost extend so far south.

Trees can not grow in permafrost, and here, in the shadow of the mountain called Otgontenger, with bare hillsides rising to 10,000 feet on all sides, we were sitting ducks. We could run, but we couldn't hide. There were no fences, no roads, no trees, no telephone poles, no buildings, no cattle or livestock of any kind. It was just us: a dozen or so men, one woman, along with several pack horses and a string of remounts, all of us dwarfed under the immense vault of the sky.

If our party had consisted solely of Mongolians, it might have had a chance. But there were seven Americans in our group, and—with one exception—we couldn't outpace a pair of determined Mongolian horsemen with only a two mile lead.

As we hit the hummocky marshland, our horses settled into a short hammering trot, which is the gait favored by Mongol riders who want to make time. Mongolian herdsmen churn butter by strapping a jug of milk to the saddle, and trotting for ten minutes. This is the truth. I had a bottle of aspirin in my saddle kit, and it had long ago been reduced to powder.

Every night, as I tried to massage what ever it was that was sore and measured out my dose of powdered aspirin, I thought about this: Mongols have a reputation of being the best horsemen on earth, while their horses have what must be the world's most punishing gait. It was, I concluded, the nature of the land itself that produced this jackhammer trot.

Often the ground was marshy, but studded with grassy hummocks, so that a horse either ran tussock to tussock, or it stayed in equally uneven footing of the marsh. Additionally, there were marmot holes everywhere. In places where springs flowed out of rock walls, the relatively warm water melted the permafrost below, and, on a warm summer day, a horse could sink into mud up to its withers.

The horses knew the land, and they made their way over it in a jouncing weaving sort of way. The short punishing gait—I wasn't the only American who called it "the Mongolian Death Trot"—fit the terrain perfectly. A horse that extended—that stretched out his trot or gallop—was a horse that was going to break a leg, which is to say, it was a dead horse. Mongolia is a harsh land, and only the fittest survive.

Our Mongolian companions, raised in the saddle, simply stood up in their stirrups on legs made of spring steel and pneumatic shock absorbers. The trot was too jouncy for me to raise and lower myself in the saddle, as western riders do. I could stand, like the Mongolians, but for only a few minutes at a time. Sitting, I had the sensation of internal organs shaking loose. When I looked back after an hour, the yogurt riders had halved the distance between our parties.

\* \* \*

Mongolia, sometimes called Outer Mongolia, is an independent country. Inner Mongolia, which borders Mongolia on the east, is part of China and it was the Chinese who coined the what has become a hated terminology: Inner Mongolia is closer to Beijing; Outer Mongolia is further away.

In fact, the country isn't outer to anywhere. Mongolia is set square in the center of Asia, and lies between Russian Siberia to the north and China to the South. It is protected by impressive natural boundaries: the Altai Mountains rise to 14,000 feet in the west; to the north are the dense forests of the Siberian taiga; to the south and east is the Gobi desert, the coldest, most northerly desert on earth, a place where trekkers still find dinosaur bones scattered across the wind shattered gravel-like sands. These natural boundaries protect the grazing lands of the steppes, in the interior of the country. The average altitude is just about a mile above sea level, making Mongolia one of the highest countries in the world.

Landlocked, mountainous, and far the moderating influence of any ocean, Mongolia offers some truly operatic weather: 90 degree summer days, 60 degree below zero winter nights, and 24 hour temperature swings of 80 degrees and more. A European friar, John of Plano Carpini, who visited Mongolia in 1245, called the weather "astonishingly irregular." He experienced "fierce thunder and lightening" that "caused the death of many men, and at the same time there (were) heavy falls of snow." Carpini lived through an absurdly fierce hailstorm, which was followed by such warm weather that the resultant flash flood killed 160 people. He thought the country "more wretched than I could possibly say."

There was a time when geographers, expressing a kind of universal medieval dread, called Mongolia "the dead heart of Asia." The people who survived there, supposedly, were barbarians, nomadic herdsmen with no culture and no interest in agriculture. Every few centuries, throughout the whole of recorded history, these "uncivilized" Mongolians came bursting out of their high cold plateau on horseback to conquer any peoples who stood in their way. Once, in the 13th Century, they conquered the known world.

Mongolians, like many people who live in cold climates, tend to be physically bigger than their southern neighbors, and I imagined them pouring down on, say, the smaller Chinese: Merciless barbarians, armies of huge men on fast horses wearing boiled leather armor, their faces smeared with sheep fat against the cold and wind and sun.

So, thundering across the steppes on a Mongolian horse, in company with Mongolian horsemen, carried a certain savage hormonal rush, like tearing up the highway on a Harley with a pack of Hell's Angels.

But the horses, when I first saw them, didn't inspire confidence. They were small and ratty, with big gawky heads. No animal was of any one single color. They were all about half wild and there was a rodeo every morning when we tried to saddle them up. Flapping rain jackets spooked them. Shadows cast by the campfire set them bucking. A sneeze could start a stampede.

On the other hand, they were fast, and by far the toughest horses I'd ever ridden. They could survive in conditions that would kill any other horse on earth. The animals graze on their own—they are never fed—and yet live through 60 below winter nights, cutting through snow and ice with their hooves for something to eat. Unshod, our horses routinely put in 30 mile days, accumulating as much as 8000 feet of altitude change. And they did it day after tireless day.

The herdsmen inspected their horses for sores or bruises, they doctored them when it was necessary, and rested them when they were tired. They knew each horse intimately—probably saw it born, probably broke it—but they were never sentimental. Mongolians name their horses about as often as Americans name their cars.

And the horses served the same function as cars. They were transportation devices, meant to be kept in superb running condition. Out on the roadless grassland, a horse was the essential link to the outside world: to the market, to the nearest town, or school, or hospital.

Mongolians in the country side literally learn to ride about the time they learn to walk. Not one of them has ever attended Miss Prissy's Academy of Equine Etiquette. They gallop right up behind you and give your horse a smart swat on the backside if they want to race. And, in my experience, they always want to race.

*   *   *

There were seven of us from America, and, for what it's worth, I thought it was a fairly impressive group. Arelene Burns, a well known river guide, had been Meryl Streep's rowing coach in the film *The River Wild*. I believe Meryl does Arlene in that film: I recognized the confidence, the feminine athletic swagger, even the hair style.

Christoph Schork was a pilot and ski instructor in Idaho. He rode his own horse in marathon 100 mile mountain races and was the only one of us who might have had a chance against the yogurt riders.

Photographer Dave Edwards, was working on a photo book about men who hunted with eagles in the Altai Mountains. He guided horse trips out of northern Mongolia to pay his expenses. Jackson Frishman, 18, was the son of a woman Dave had guided with when he worked the Grand Canyon. Jackson had a lot of white water experience and wanted to be a river guide himself. Michael Abbot, a computer networking expert, was an avid fly fisherman who'd spent a good deal of time camping along salmon and steelhead streams in Alaska.

Kent Maiden, of Boojum Expeditions, was our guide. We were all getting a break on the price of the trip because it was an exploratory. Kent had never been to this area of Mongolia before and couldn't vouch for the quality of the horses we'd ride. Or the wranglers who'd ride with us. There were no guarantees. Whatever happened, happened.

What happened was yogurt riders.

For my part, I'd been trying, and failing, to get to Mongolia for over 15 years. In my saddle kit, I had eight plastic ziplock bags, full of human hair—hair cut from the heads of Mongolian herdsmen and women.

It was what I had traveled to Mongolia to get. I am a member of the Advisory Board of the Center for the Study of the First Americans, located at Oregon State University where they believe, fervently, that the earth is a giant hairball.

Although no one knows the absolute average number, humans naturally shed an enormous amount of hair every day. Cosmeticians figure that number at about 170 daily strands. If so, the average human being sheds a little over 3.5 million hairs over a 60 year life span. The figure is significant to the cutting edge of archeology.

Not far from my home in south central Montana, for instance, there are several "early man" sites. One was populated by humans as early as 14,000 years ago. There's a lot of naturally shed human hair buried at that and other sites. Previously, archeologists, searching for the first Americans, discarded human hair in their digs. They tended to study bone fragments and stone artifacts.

There were problems with this approach. The first was cultural: some native American groups saw the exhumation of bone fragments as a kind of grave robbing. Secondly, stone artifacts, such as Clovis points, could be dated by standard techniques, but isolating the technology in time sheds very little light on the identity of the people who embraced the culture. If Clovis points were effective, wouldn't various groups of people adopt them, humans being human. Is someone who drives a Honda Japanese or American, African or Latin?

The study of naturally shed human hair at prehistoric campsites does not desecrate graves and provides important, confirmable information as to the identity of the people who populated those sites. Race can be accurately determined by microscopic and DNA analysis of human hair. That is the work being done by Dr. Rob Bonnichson at the Center for the Study of the First Americans. Field and lab work is focused on the single question: who were the first Americans.

The theory, of course, is that, during the last ice age, when great volumes of water were concentrated at the poles and in various glaciers, the sea level was perhaps 400 feet lower than it is today. The Bering Strait, today a 53 mile waterway separating Asia and the Americas, was left high and dry. It was probably a vast grassland, alive with woolly mammoth, which humans, acting in concert, could kill and eat. They likely used spears tipped with Clovis or other points.

The folks who crossed the Bering Land Bridge were probably Asians. My mission, for the Center for the Study of the First Americans, was to collect samples of Mongolian hair, bring 'em back through customs, and send them to Oregon State University where they could be compared with 10,000 year old strands dug up outside Melville, Montana. It is possible that the ancestors of the people who today call themselves Mongolian—the ancestors of the men I was riding with, of the men pursuing us with pails of yogurt—were "the first Americans."

The air route to Mongolia required a three day layover in Beijing. There, I hired a taxi and drove two hours through the country side to visit a section of the Great Wall, the largest building construction project in the history of the world. It's 1500 miles long, about 30 feet high, with towers rising to 40 feet, and it has everything to do with Mongols, and the fear of Mongols. In the fourth century BC, the Chinese began suffering the attacks of fierce nomadic herdsmen living to the north and west. Almost immediately, they began building parts of what we now call the Great Wall.

The ramparts I saw ran along the razored ridge tops of mountains rising several thousand feet above the rich agricultural lands to the east. There were guard towers every hundred yards or so, slitted windows for archers, and the land to the west—terrain attackers would have to traverse—was little more than a steep talus slope. No way could archers on horseback breach that wall.

Those ancient marauding horsemen—the Hsiung-nu—are thought, by some accounts, to be ancestors of the people who were to call themselves Mongols. The Hsiung-nu, sometimes called Huns, would be the same folks who brought Europe the Atilla the Hun show in the fifth century AD.

Still, in the mid-12th Century, the people living in what is now Mongolia were a fairly diverse group of warring tribes, living rather like the American Plains Indians: superb horsemen, they believed all things possessed a spirit: mountains, rivers, rocks, hillsides. They particularly worshiped the sky, which they called Tengri. Mongolia's continental climate produces 260 clear days a year: the sunniest spot anywhere on earth at that latitude. The sky, a brilliant blue dome, arches over the rolling grasslands of the steppes. It is a felt presence: Asian Big Sky Country, with a vengeance.

The ancient peoples of Mongolia lived in round felt tents, and the archeological record suggests it was a way of life that stretched back to at least 10,000 BC. The clans warred among themselves, engaged in shamanistic rituals, stole horses and women, put great stock in personal courage, and were terrifyingly accurate archers.

It was Genghis Khan, born in 1167, who unified all these feuding tribes— the hunter gathers of the northern forests, the peoples who skied across the frozen lakes on polished animal bones, the camel breeders of the Gobi desert, the herdsmen of the grasslands. In 1206, after years of tribal warfare, Genghis Khan, triumphant, declared himself "the ruler of all those who live in felt tents."

Illiterate and probably alcoholic, Genghis Khan was, according to many historians, the greatest military genius who ever lived.

The people who lived in felt tents probably numbered 2 million. This was the Mongol Horde. The great Khan, directing an army of only 130,000 Mongols, conquered the known world, and established the largest empire that ever was and probably ever will be. Genghis, his sons and grandsons, ruled from southern Siberia to Syria, from the Pacific on the shores of what is now China all the way to the Adriatic sea.

His horsemen sometimes rode 80 miles a day over deserts or mountains others thought to be impassable. In Europe, they were known as "Hell's Horsemen." To the east, The Great Wall was little more than a speed bump on the way to Beijing, where Kublai Khan, the grandson of Genghis, built his Xanadu. He said, "a wall is only as good as those who defend it."

Probably because of the harsh irregular climate, Mongolia, the fifth largest country in Asia, is also the least populated. 2.3 million people inhabit an area larger than England, France, Germany and Italy combined. About a third of Mongolia lives in the capital city of Ulan Baator.

This was a little hard to for me figure out because Ulan Baator did not sing sweetly to the soul. What I saw was a town of rectangular gray cement buildings—Soviet style apartment blocks—with peeling pockmarked facades, all of which appeared to be bleeding to death, the result, I saw on closer inspection, of rusting fire escapes. Packs of starving dogs slunk about in the alleys, cringing and snarling.

Our group had been picked up a the airport by the director of the Mongolian Democratic Party Travel Company, the estimable Batchyluun ("call me Baggie") Sanjsuren, 37, a big hearty man, with big round muscles. He looked remarkably like a Crow Indian artist I know in Montana.

Our translator, Bayaraa Sanjaasuren, was a few years younger: a slender, elegant and highly educated fellow. One of the first things these men taught us how to say was—I render this phonetically—"Mee Mer-ee-koon," which means, "I'm an American." Caucasian people, Baggie explained, were often taken for Russians and sometimes had the snot kicked out of them on the street by roving gangs of angry unemployed young Mongolians. Americans, on the other hand, were highly welcome in Mongolia for a variety of reasons.

To wit: After the fall of the Khans, Mongolia fell under Chinese domination. By 1911, Inner Mongolia was already Chinese. In Outer Mongolia, just after the Russian Revolution in 1917, defeated anti-Communist forces, led by the "Mad Baron" Ungern-Sternberg, took Ulan Baator, then called Urga. The Mad Baron specialized in city-wide arson and mass executions. Mongolian freedom fighters, notably D. Sukhbaatar, Mongolia's National Hero, sided with Russian Communists, defeated the remnant Chinese warlords in Urga and eventually captured the Mad Baron, who was promptly executed. The capital was renamed Ulan Baator (Red Hero), and, in 1921, Mongolia declared itself a communist state, the second country in the world to do so.

Very quickly, Mongolia became a Soviet client, marching in lock step with Russia, and possessed of its own secret service, its own purges, and its own little Stalin, a mass murderer named Choybalsan. Religion was outlawed. For centuries, Mongolians had been Buddhists, of the Tibetan variety. Under Choybalsan, soldiers burst into the lamaseries, marched the older monks out back, shot them dead, and buried the corpses in mass graves. Nomadic herdsmen found themselves members of collectives. They were encouraged to move to towns where they could become industrial workers, striving for progress. Mongolian writing was outlawed, and Russian, "the international language," was taught in schools.

Discussions of Mongol heritage were discouraged. The very mention of Genghis Khan was an embarrassment to Moscow in that the great Khan and his descendants had ruled large parts of Russia for over 300 years. For the last 70 years, Genghis had been a name to be whispered in Mongolia. In 1962, for instance, a party official named Tomor-ochir made the mistake of attending an ill advised ceremony designed to rehabilitate the image of Genghis Khan. The man was accused of "wrong thinking," dismissed from his post, expelled from the Party, and, 18 years later, mysteriously hacked to death in his own apartment.

People had to be circumspect: they hid their Buddhist's beliefs, and they found it expedient not to mention Genghis Khan. Ever. Politically correct thinking was the order of the day. Here, from a 1987 Book entitled *Modern Mongolian Poetry*, is the celebrated Poet, Tsevegmidyn Gaitav (1929-1979), with a stirring effort entitled *Our Party*:

*Radiant,*
> *Boundless,*
>> *Thinking so clearly and*
>>> *with perspective*
*Steering wisely*
> *The state*
>> *and the people*
*Illuminating our road*
> *By the teaching of Lenin —*
>> *Sagacious, meaningful,*
*Daring, straightforward,*
> *You are leading our people,*
>> *Forward, along the socialist road*
>> *Our Party!*

And so on, until the people got pretty damn sick and tired of all that sagacious illumination. The first demonstrations started in the spring of 1990. Many people carried signs reading "morindoo," which means "mount up" and was the battle cry of Genghis and his warriors. The Mongolian Communist Party, perceiving that it was riding a razor edge on the arc of history, voted to dissolve itself.

Soviet soldiers pulled out of the country. Russia cut its subsidies to Mongolia. By 1992, the country was in poor way, unable to feed itself or employ its workers.

Baggie, driving down the muddy streets on the outskirts of Ulan Baator, said the country was grateful for an influx of foreign aid from the US, among others. "We know," Baggie said, "that the money comes from taxes American people pay. Mongolians want to thank the American people."

We passed Sukhbattor Square, where the demonstrations had begun. Baggie and Bayaraa were among the organizers, and both had been active early on in the Mongolian National Democratic Party, which advocated democratic reforms, a free market economy, and, inexplicably, I thought at the time, a national diet that included more vegetables.

Looking out at the street scene, it was clear that the times had changed. Robed Buddhist monks strolled across the Square: a vast expanse of stone where once a statue of Stalin had stood. I could hear, faintly, the tinny sound of someone playing "Lucy in the Sky With Diamonds" on a boom box. The Beatles were very popular in Ulan Baator. Huge hawks buzzed the statue of D. Suhkbaator, and men with ancient cameras took black and white souvenir photos of herdsmen in town for what might be a once in a lifetime visit.

At dinner in a new hotel, one of several springing up around town, Baggie explained how he'd fallen into the travel business. In 1993, as an early member of the Mongolian National Democratic Party, he'd visited the US on an international good will trip. One of the stops was in Bozeman, Montana, where he met Kent Maiden and Linda Svendsen who, through Boojum Expeditions, had been running horseback trips in Chinese Inner Mongolia for over a decade. The couple had even been legally married there, in a Mongolian ceremony. International goodwill led to a business arrangement.

Prior to 1992, only one institution could issue the written invitations necessary to obtain a Mongolian visa. Juulchin, the government tourist agency, was essentially in the business of soaking the capitalists. When I inquired about a visa fifteen years ago, the price of a three week trip was $25,000. Expensive, yes, but you got to hunt and kill Marco Polo sheep among other exotic and possibly endangered animals. I passed on the deal.

By '93, with the demise of the Communist Party, Baggie was free to team up with Kent and issue his own written invitations to visitors. Prices are a small fraction of what Juulchin used to charge.

Before and after and during dinner, we drank toasts to the ordinary American taxpayer, to free speech, to a free market economy, to the Mongolian National Democratic Party, to the American Republican Party which was advising the MNDP on grassroots organizing, and to the new Mongolia altogether, a country finally free to consume more vegetables. The vodka was Mongolian, a popular new brand called *Genghis Khan*.

The next day, we flew from Ulan Baator to a town called Uliastai on a Mongolian Airlines jet. At the airport there, one of seven in the country with a paved runway, a young Mongolian fellow walked toward me, dropped a shoulder into my chest, knocked me back a step or two and kept right on going. Five paces later, he turned smartly and started back. It was a going to be a series of slow motion assaults.

"He thinks you're Russian," Bayaraa explained.

"Hey," I said sharply, "Mee Mer-ee-koon."

"Ahh!" The young man stopped and smiled. "*Saim Bainuu*," he asked politely. How are you?

"*Saing*," I said. Fine. "*Saim Bainuu?*"

And then there was a lot of Mongolian style handshaking in which you grab each other's elbows, both of them, and nod and smile a lot. The guy ended up helping us load our luggage into a dilapidated slick-tired bus. He was glad to help. We weren't Russians. We were Mer-ee-koons.

Presently, the bus was bashing its way into the mountains along a narrow rutted dirt road. We made our way through herds of sheep; and goats; and yaks, which looked to me like fringed Herefords. There are 25 million head of livestock grazing in Mongolia, about 10 times the human population, and according to my Mongolian language tapes, the third thing a polite person says to another—after "how are you," and "how's your family"—is *tania mal saim bainuu*? How's your livestock?

In the pasture lands rising up on the other side of the road, men on horse-back worked the yaks very much the way Montana ranchers deal with cattle. But instead of ropes, the Mongolian herdsmen used rawhide loops set on the end of long poles. The poles, Bayarra told me, serve a double purpose. Stick one upright in the ground, and no one will approach. In this treeless grassland, it was one way for a man and woman to ensure themselves a little privacy. It was also a symbol of virility.

Above, hawks and falcons and huge griffins drifted in great circles, silhouet-ted against Tengri, the sacred sky, which was a brilliant shrieking blue filled with billowing white clouds. A herd of horses galloped across a nearby ridge, their long manes flying in the wind.

Baggie said he approved of my hair styling mission and had always thought that Mongolian people, his ancient ancestors, may have been the first Americans. It is a theory strongly promoted by the Museum of Natural History in Ulan Baator.

\* \* \*

50 miles east of Uliastai, the cruel joke of a road ended in what was an attempt at a hot springs resort, a series of whacked together wooden buildings originally built for Communist Party big wigs. The place looked embarrassed, like a man in a tux at a beer party. All the other habitations in the countryside, without exception, were round felt tents, basically unchanged since the time Genghis declared himself "ruler of all those who live in felt tents." They looked

like white puffball mushrooms and were called gers. Don't say yurt. Russians say yurt.

At the end of the road, wranglers, hired for the trip, watched as we set up our American tents. The men thought our gers were flimsy, but they liked the portability. It took, they said, several hours to take down a Mongolian ger. The wranglers seemed shy, and they smiled constantly, nervously.

In the saddle, though, these same men laughed and sang unselfconsciously, utterly at home on horseback. In Montana, we'd call them "can do cowboys."

Our head wrangler, Lhagra, a lean unflappable man in his fifties, took it upon himself to coach me in matters Mongolian. The wrap around jackets all the men wore were called "dels." The sleeves could be rolled down to warm the hands in cold weather, and the sash that held the garment together was a handy place to stash a knife. The oversized boots with turned up toes were called "gutuls." For the past 70 years, children had been taught in school that gutuls were a symbol of Mongolian subservience to religion. You can drop to your knees so much easier in boots with turned up toes. Actually, Lhagra, explained, the boots are designed to slip easily into the stirrup, and to show respect for the earth: turned up toes don't tear into the ground.

I learned a Mongolian saddle song about a young camel in the Gobi desert, just starting off on his first caravan. It is late in the day, and the shadows fall long across the sands. The camel is leaving his mother for the first time. Here the song breaks into a lot of mournful ululation which is fairly easy to do given the jouncing gait of the horse. The singer then expresses a similar love for his own mother. Mongolian songs never concern death, divorce or unrequited love. Life is hard enough.

We were circumnavigating Otgontenger (Young Sky) Mountain, which was, at 12,982 feet, the highest point in the Mongolia's central Hangay Range. The peak itself was hidden behind other, smaller mountains, and we got our first clear glimpse of it when we topped out on a pass at 10,300 feet. A millennia of tradition required that we stop and pay our respects to the mountain at an elaborate ovoo, a construction of sticks and poles, piled teepee-like on an altar of stones. Tattered blue prayer flags tied to the poles snapped in the wind. There were cigarettes, and bank notes, and pieces of hard cheese piled on the stones. We walked three times around the ovoo, tied hairs from our horses' manes to the poles, and left our offerings.

As we led our horses down the steep slope on the other side of the pass, a cloud passed over the sun, the temperature dropped 30 degrees, and the wind drove a sudden snow fall directly into our faces. It was August, but it felt like winter. Then, maybe half an hour later, the sky cleared and the sun seemed to boom down on us. It wasn't hot, but there was a harsh, unfiltered quality to the light. I could literally feel my face burning.

We mounted up and rode down into an enormous river valley. There were wind sculpted boulders on the ridges of the hills that framed the valley and these ornate rock formations looked like oriental dragons. It was impossible to estimate distance, or to figure the size of the river below because their were no trees or gers or livestock to measure against the immensity of the land. Lhagra said he saw riders moving along the river bank. I couldn't even see them with my pocket telescope.

The riders, two men in their early 20s, joined us for a short time, which, in Mongolian terms, meant two days. We named them for their looks: the Movie Star, and Bad Hair Day, who had about a dozen swirling colicks on his head. The strange style made him look perpetually startled.

The men were out marmot hunting, and would sell the skins for a good price at a market in Uliastai. The Movie Star carried a Russian .22 rifle and a bi-pod strapped to his back. He wore a white sheet over his del, and a kind of white doo-rag hat topped with ludicrous rodent ears. Marmots, I was given to understand, stay close to their burrows and disappear into them at the slightest hint of danger. They were, however, curious, and might stand still for a moment when faced with the eerie specter of a man dressed like the marmot angel of death.

Hunting these buck toothed rodents was a serious business. An animal that was too easy to shoot—one that was slow or stupid—could kill you and your family. The marmot disease was a bad way to go: ten days of delirium, swollen glands, fever, and screaming pain. In the west, the same misery is called Bubonic or Black Plague. In the 14th Century it killed a third of the population of Europe: 25 million people.

The theory is that ship borne rats brought the plague to Europe. But Tim Severin, in his book *In Search of Genghis Khan,* notes that the first European reports of the plague came in 1347, when it broke out among the troops of the Kipchak Khan who was besieging the Black Sea port of Kaffa. The Khan, in what must be the first instance of biological warfare in history, catapulted infected corpses over the city walls. There were Italian trading vessels in the port, and they returned to Genoa. Carrying plague.

\* \* \*

In a book of Mongolian folktales, I found this cautionary narrative:

A hungry wolf comes upon a horse mired in the mud. The wolf prepares for a feast, but the horse asks him if he shouldn't pull his meal out of the mud first. So the wolf performs this chore and prepares, once again, to eat. The horse resorts to sanitary arguments. Shouldn't the wolf clean his food before he eats it? The wolf acknowledges that this might be a good idea, and licks the mud off the horse. Finally, the wolf is ready to eat, but the horse says, "hey, there's some writing on the hoof of my hind leg. Before you eat me, read that please." The curious wolf walks around the horse, who lifts up his hind leg, and bashes the wolf's skull in with a single kick.

The wolf, alone and dying in the mud, howls to himself (and I quote directly from the book here): "I was a blockhead … Am I owner that I should have pulled the horse from the mud? Am I the mother who should have licked and cleaned the horse's body. When did I learn to read and write? I'm stupid and now I am dying."

It seemed to me that much of the etiquette I was learning had to do with never having to tell yourself "I'm stupid and now I'm dying." The Mongolian hand shake, for instance, the grabbing of elbows, assured each party that neither was carrying a concealed weapon. In a ger, a man took his knife out of his sash and let it hang on a long cord, so it was not within arm's reach. Snuff bottles were accepted in the right hand, while the left hand was placed on the right elbow.

And then there was the matter of the dogs. There were always several around any ger, snarling and snapping at the horses' hooves. These dogs, called "Brown Eyes," for the golden eyebrows most of them have, were big German Shepherd shaped animals, with enormous heads, deep chests, and tails that curved up over their backs. When approaching a ger, it is polite to yell, "tie up your dogs!"

A government pamphlet said that this courtesy gives people time to prepare for a visit. Tim Severin thought it had to do with plague: if the people in a ger are infected, they will not answer. That silence, Severin thought, is a signal to ride the hell on out of there. In point of fact, the dogs all wore collars, with a short length of rope attached, and the owners always came out and tied them up. These were not the cringing dogs of Ulan Baator. They were well fed, powerful and protective: dogs that guarded livestock and sometimes fought off wolves. A couple of them could easily kill a man. It was stupid *not* to yell "tie up your dogs."

Our friend, Bad Hair Day, it turned out, had been mauled by a dog when he was younger. I felt a little bad about the name we'd assigned him when he let me examine his scalp, which was a mass of angry scar tissue.

Mongolia is one of the most sparsely populated countries on earth, and we sometimes rode days between gers. The ones we did see were usually clustered in groups of four to eight. There was always a single wooden pole out front, a hitching post brought in from somewhere else where trees grew. A saddled horse was tethered to every pole I saw: the Mongolian equivalent of leaving the car running. Often, handmade ox carts with wooden wheels were parked beside the ger, and sometimes they were piled high with the dry dung of sheep or horses or yaks which is burned as fuel.

**31**

Bayarra and Baggie, mindful of what they'd learned from representatives of the US Republican Party, stopped at each of the gers and talked about the Mongolian National Democratic Party. They used the term "grassroots organizing," which seemed particularly appropriate.

The gers had no windows and a single low door, always facing south. About 18 feet in diameter, the tents were supported by a lattice work wood frame that folded up like an accordion. Woven rugs, always red, covered the floor, and each ger was arranged in precisely the same manner. The man keeps his saddle and tack to the right of the door. To the left are cooking utensils and children's things. The entire family sleeps in the bed against the left wall, children at their parent's feet. The bed on the right is for guests. Against the wall opposite the door are two low chests of drawers, painted orange. On the chests are framed black and white photos: the children at school, the man in his army uniform, the family posing stiffly in Sukbataar Square.

A tin stove stands in the center of the ger, under a flap at the top of the tent that can be opened or closed. A rope drops down from the upper framework of the ger. It can be fastened to a small boulder beside the hearth, to keep the ger from blowing away in the wind.

People we met said they moved their gers two or three times a year. Families tend to winter a couple thousand feet above their summer pastures. Cold air settles in the valleys and it's always warmer higher up.

We tried to observe the household rules—don't lean against the wall, don't point your feet at the hearth—but Lhagra had reason to critique one aspect of American manners. We were always saying "bayarala," thank you, and it was unnecessary. Almost insulting. Every Mongolian has been forced to take refuge in someone else's ger at one time or another. The tradition, then, is one of unthinking generosity. Guests are fed and feted as a matter of course, and there were numerous small niceties in the rituals. The tea, for instance, had to be made in the guests' sight. It contained mare's milk and salt. An acquired taste. The yogurt, on the other hand, was sweet and delicious, the best I've ever tasted. It was thin enough to drink from a bowl.

Sometimes we drank a liquor of distilled mare's milk, and ate salty rock hard cheese formed into medallions about the size of silver dollars. I was never able to leave a ger without accumulating gifts amounting to several pockets full of the stuff. In return, we gave our hosts what gifts we could: extra flashlights, batteries for the short wave radio, tee shirts, bandanas, a few spoons of powdered aspirin. We were down to essentials, almost completely out of gifts, but, by God, we had enough cheese. I could hear it clacking together in my jacket and saddle kit when I rode. It was noisy cheese.

\* \* \*

Every single day, without fail, we consumed two massive meals of boiled mutton.

I can say this: the mutton was always fresh. We'd ride into a ring of gers, buy a sheep, and watch the Mongolians slaughter it. The animal is flipped onto it's back, and held down. A slit is made in the belly, the butcher inserts his hand, punctures the diaphragm, and finds the vena cava leading out of the heart. Hook the finger around the vein and yank. This was said to be the Buddhist way, the most humane way to kill, and, indeed, the sheep was generally dead within 30 seconds.

When Genghis Khan unified the Mongol nation, he established a system of laws, some of which involved penalties for rustling. If a man steals another's livestock, Genghis ruled, he must return the animals, or similar animals, one for one. If he could not, or would not, his "heart" would be "squeezed" until he died.

So the method had the force of tradition behind it.

Mongolians eat every part of the sheep. They crack the bones for the marrow. They boil the head, and make blood sausage from the intestines. The fat, our wranglers said, is the best part. A sin to waste it. Once, when the American contingent cooked dinner, we cut away the fat. The Mongolian herdsmen gathered up the white and yellow mess, put it in a pot with water, boiled it, and drank the results down like a thick tea.

Kent had had the foresight to buy several sacks of potatoes imported from Russia, but most of the Mongolian wranglers said they tasted "like dirt." There was an enormous prejudice against vegetables of any kind. The whole idea of farming was disgusting to a herdsman. Being tied to a single plot of land was no life for a man. In any case, the growing season where these men lived, at about 8000 feet, was about two months long. And much of the ground was permanently frozen a few feet below the surface anyway.

A government pamphlet tried to put the best light on this situation. "Mongolia," it said, "is totally self sufficient in vegetable production."

Some people, it seemed, thrived on the diet. Herdsmen and their wives lead hard, active lives and we met plenty of folks in their 80s. Still, life expectancy in Mongolia is below the world average: 64.6 years for men, 66.5 for women. Which is why the newly formed Mongolian National Democratic Party platform has a plank that essentially reads: "eat your vegetables."

There were ovoos everywhere, at every pass or narrow canyon a rider might care to traverse, and I was leaving huge handfuls of hard cheese medallions as offerings. It was a losing proposition. By my calculation, we were still carrying over 50 pounds of noisy cheese, and we sounded like castanets on horseback.

Michael Abbot, our fly fishing aficionado, was getting grumpy about angling opportunities. There were grayling in the waters above 8000 feet, and lennick—a four to ten pound ugly brown trout looking fish—lower down. Where ever we stopped, however, there was usually some religious prohibition about fishing that stretch of the river: a famous lama had once walked the banks, and we don't fish there out of respect. Or: The river provides water for cooking and washing and drinking so we don't fish as a way of showing our gratitude.

In point of fact, we never saw anyone from the gers fishing, anywhere. Mongolians didn't enjoy fishing as a sport, and they didn't eat fish. They eat boiled mutton and yogurt and noisy cheese. Michael Abbot thought the sacred fishing regulations were a fairly low rent form of religious sacrifice, like giving up limburger for Lent.

He had good luck fishing on the banks of remote rivers, in unsanctified places. But, even then, miles from the nearest habitation, there were sometimes restrictive rules. On the back side of Otgontenger, for instance, at about 8000 feet, we camped at a lake called Doot Nur. It was set in a grassy basin and surrounded by hills rising to 10,000 feet, which hid the mountain ranges beyond. Above 9000 feet, the hills had accumulated a dusting of snow. Michael Abbot stood watching the evening hatch and muttering about limburger. Doot Nur, the Lake of the Voices, was off limits to fishing. In the spring people gathered around the lake, and listened to the ice break up. Sounds echoed in the basin, and sometimes you could hear voices, often the voices of your ancestors.

So you could drink from the waters of Doot Nur, OK, but you couldn't bathe there and you certainly couldn't fish.

The lake was large, maybe five square miles. Christof pointed out several dozen tiny specks moving slowly on the opposite bank and handed me his binoculars. The specks were camels: huge shaggy double humped animals. They moved up through the green grasses and looked exceedingly strange trudging across the snow above.

The camels, Lhagra told me, were domestic beasts, not wild, and were used as pack animals when a family moved its ger. Deduct a few dozen karma points from my cosmic account: I rode around the lake, cut out the lead camel, and spent fifteen minutes frustrating his instinct to get back to the herd. I thought: well, here I am in Mongolia, cutting camels in the snow. Arlene said it looked like a cigarette ad.

And then we went riding up another endless valley that dropped directly down out of Otgontenger. At about 9000 feet there was a huge ovoo, the most elaborate yet, and I saw it as an appropriate place to offer up several big handfuls of noisy cheese.

We rode and walked the horses up a steep rocky slope to 11,000 feet, where there was a small lake at the base of the glacier on Ogontenger Mountain. We hobbled the horses on a level grassy spot. Mongolians ride carrying a long rawhide rope, attached to the bridle. A Mongolian herdsman may fall off his horse, but he never drops the rawhide rope. A man, on foot, in the grassland, is a dead man. The rope is also used to tie a horse's two front feet together, and the hobbled animals graze placidly in a series of festive bunnyhops.

It was about 500 yards over rocky boulder strewn ground from the grass to the lake. There were mini-ovoos every ten feet: a small cairn, a couple of twigs, each of them worth one, maybe two, pieces of noisy cheese. Lhagra advised us to drink from the lake, for our health. The water came from the glacier, which was everlasting. Drink from the lake and live forever.

Ominous clouds moved over the peak above us. A wind rolled down the glacier. It swirled and whistled over the lake. I could hear the sound of distant muttering voices which came, I saw finally, from a series of small waterfalls on the far side of the lake. The sun was setting and the place seemed just a bit spooky to me. One man's spooky, I suppose, is another man's sacred.

We rode three more hours, through the dark, to our campsite, and, naturally, it snowed. In the morning, the sky was crisp and blue, and the sun glittered on the glacier above. The light was very nearly blinding. The wranglers said we must have done OK by the mountain, shown proper respect. Otgontenger had washed its face for us.

That day, we began retracing our route, riding endlessly and wailing in the saddle about lonely camels. The plan now was to top another pass, dump some noisy cheese at the ovoo there, and ride down through the Ider River Valley to the town of Toson Cengel, where we'd catch a flight back to Ulan Baator. Just below the headwaters of the Ider, there was a ring of about eight gers, where we stopped to talk with the people about hair styling matters. Baggie explained the scientific nature of my request. Followed here much murmured intensity among the Mongolians. They didn't want me to touch their heads. Their concerns were a complicated amalgam of Buddhist and shamanistic beliefs, which I didn't fully understand.

But hey, Baggie said, no problem. Or words to that effect. I didn't want to touch their heads anyway. I wanted them to cut a few strands of their hair themselves, using their own knives. Baggie said that I feared DNA contamination, which he attempted to explain. The Mongolians regarded me tolerantly, as if to say, well, there's no accounting for other folks' religion.

So the people cut strands of their own hair, with their own knives, and placed them in separate ziplock bags for me. One of the families gave us a 30 pound tub of noisy cheese, as a gift. The tradition was to give back the tub, filled with our own gifts. We sorted through what was left of our dwindling gear. Give 'em a couple of rain jackets: we only had a few more days and the weather might hold. Give 'em a few flashlights: we would be able to set up our camps by moonlight.

We rode off, my mission accomplished, and our packs considerably lighter. Unfortunately, all up and down the Ider River Valley, the word was out about the strange Mer-ee-koons who worshiped hair. People rode out to visit with us, and they never came empty handed. Generally, they carried metal dairy pails full of yogurt. We stopped, visited, ate the yogurt, rinsed the pails, and returned them full of polar fleece jackets. If it got cold, we could wrap ourselves in sleeping bags.

And then, finally, only a few days outside of Toson Cengel, when we were completely out of anything at all that might be construed as an appropriate gift, I saw a pair of yogurt riders, two miles back, and a thousand feet above. We fled, thundering over the grassland, galloping where we could, and simply enduring where we couldn't. We fled in a deafening clatter of noisy cheese. We fled the smiling beneficence of Mongolian generosity.

When the yogurt riders caught us, as they surely would, we'd give them the shirts off our backs.

# The Doctor

## Michael Kirkpatrick

*Feeling down and out in Taiwan? There is only one person to see
–The Doctor.*

INEVITABLY, PROLONGED TRAVEL BRINGS SICKNESS. The standard fare is some combination of psychological and intestinal distress, as these are the parts of our bodies that actually have to assimilate the foreign worlds in which we've arrived. I had already run the gamut of self-diagnosis and treatment, most of which relied on some combination of plain white rice, Imodium A/D, and imported liquor. At some point, however, the whole body got involved and after several days of fever and fatigue I finally gave in and accepted a recommendation for a physician. This was no simple matter, as the quality of medical care varies in some countries the way the quality of automotive care varies back home. I neither wanted a cursory look that left me untreated, nor a major overhaul that replaced the majority of my internal organs. So I accepted the referral to somebody who was said to speak "enough" English, and who was fabled to practice a Western form of medicine that would not require me to bring clippings of hair and precise information on the time and conditions of my birth. Besides, the place was within walking distance and had a pharmacy in-house, which sounded convenient.

I arrived at a storefront indistinguishable from any other, except for a modest crowd visible in the waiting room through a front window adorned with incomprehensible Chinese characters. I sat down quietly and waited after writing my name for the office staff behind what appeared to be a bank teller's window. An assistant of sorts eventually emerged from the narrow corridor and summoned the only non-Asian face in the room (mine) to accompany her to the doctor's examining area. Not surprisingly, there was only one room rather than a suite, befitting one of the most crowded places in the world; an island with over 550 persons per square kilometer. I was not quite prepared, however, for all that greeted me. The diplomas on the wall were familiar enough, and might have been reassuring, had it not been for the "furnishings." Wisely positioned near a corner where it remained out of view of the hallway was a Dentist's chair, complete with an instrument tray littered with medieval torture instruments. Above the chair was an overhead light with a large reflective dome, reminiscent of the classic interrogation arrangement. The doctor wore one of those mirrors with the hole in the center on his forehead, which I recalled from cartoons and old movies, and a surgical mask obscured his entire face from view except for the very narrow slits of his eyes. Whatever he did to me, it would be nearly impossible to identify him in a line-up.

He asked a few terse questions, all to the effect of "what is your problem?" I told him my symptoms: malaise, fever, congestion, fatigue, and an inescapable need for sleep about 18 hours per day. He wheeled forward on his chair like a spider approaching an ensnared fly. I suppose I was expected to know what would happen, or to obediently accept whatever it was. The general prodding, poking, and peering into my cranial orifices was not unexpected, but the cotton swabs were. Without any statement of warning, instruction, or request, he inserted a long cotton swab—a wand really—into my throat and smeared some greenish muck on the back of my throat. "Ah-ha," I thought, desperately reassuring myself. "He is taking a culture to test for strep," as if there were any hope that he had access to a laboratory that could culture more bacteria than the instrument tray of visibly worn and rusted equipment. Then he drew two more of the swabs and inserted them, I swear I'm not exaggerating, through each of my nostrils, into my skull, and back to the occipital lobe of my brain. Obviously he was performing a lobotomy. I've seen these illustrated in textbooks, performed through the eye sockets or through small bore-holes in the temples. The swabs must have entered the ventral surface of the brain bilateral to the pituitary gland, then extended through the brain stem to the regions they now occupied. If I was left with any consciousness at all, I would surely be blind and, if possible, even more stupid than I had already been to show up here in the first place.

Once both swabs were firmly in place, he turned to make some marks in my file, presumably to indicate the anticipated cause of death. As the tears streamed uncontrollably down both cheeks, I could barely see the very tips of the swabs' wooden handles sticking straight out each nostril about a half inch. I felt a tingling in my throat, which must have been my brains draining down my esophagus. After a few minutes, while the toxin was presumably reaching its maximum effectiveness, he turned and withdrew the swabs from the holes in my skull. It felt as though I had been roto-rootered. As I dried my eyes and swallowed the remaining film of cerebral cortex lying in the back of my throat, he summarily pronounced, "common cold" in comprehensible English and instructed me to get medicine that would "make me feel better." Having some experience in pharmaceuticals (a story that will remain untold until legal consultations are completed), I inquired into the nature of these "medicines." He repeated, "you feel better." I warily eyed the instrument tray and decided it was better to leave him unprovoked.

I left the examining rack and stopped at the teller's window on my way out. There I observed an interesting device that produced sealed, multiple-pill packets, each about half the size of the cellophane wrapper on a pack of cigarettes. Upon retrieving my drugs and paying the nominal fee, I escaped to the street and returned home for an inspection of both my own damage and the goods I'd procured. Once home, I began to consider the possibility that the cotton wands had perhaps reached only into the back of my throat, although I honestly could not recall the anatomical feasibility of such a maneuver beginning at the nostrils. Regardless, I was captivated by the new challenge of trying to recognize the pills by their characteristic shapes, sizes, and colors. Being unsure however, I decided it would be best to pursue the question scientifically. So, in true experimental fashion I quaffed the dozen or so pills that were in the first packet. He turned out to have been speaking quite literally. I did feel better. The sensation was reminiscent of a Grateful Dead concert I'd attended many years earlier. I later successfully identified some of my "medicines." One was an antibiotic, although loaded in doses approximately four times that which would normally be given to large farm animals. At least one of the others I recognized from its broad psychiatric application. The others were unfamiliar, but colorful. After the first night, I become more selective in my dosing.

I did feel better, although I'm not sure how much was due to actual medicinal treatment and how much was due to the physical and chemical modification of my brain. I suppose each might constitute a legitimate "medical" practice. Regardless, upon a return visit months later I was quick to motion him away from the extraction of any neural tissues, and for most maladies I learned to opt instead for cheap domestic beer and white rice. I eventually came around to pursue the more user-friendly traditional practices, whose expensive placebos are prescribed without the probing of bodily orifices. This continues to be my preference to this day, although I have to admit I benefited from a certain prophylaxis induced by fear of further treatment. This in the end has probably been the best determinant of better health, and for that I suppose I should be grateful.

# An Air of Incipient Riot Pervades

## Mary Roach

*Hurling tomatoes at strangers may seem odd at first, but soon you realize it's all good clean fun.*

I HAVE A WEAKNESS FOR THINGS GOING SPLAT. As long as I can remember, I've been helpless to resist it—the puerile hilarity of unexpected glop: ketchup packets underfoot, bird droppings on Grandma's hat, mayonnaise jars dropped on the pavement.

You can imagine my reaction upon learning that each year in Bunol, a tiny town in eastern Spain, 20,000 people turn out to throw tomatoes at each other. It's a festival called La Tomatina, held once a year on the last Wednesday in August. It's not a religious festival, nor is it a tourist event. The tomatoes are hurled for the sole purpose of fun.

Most of the crowd comes from Bunol and the neighboring towns. Only a handful of foreigners are in evidence. Even getting information about the event is something of an undertaking. The Spanish tourism office finally just gave me the phone number of the Bunol Town Hall.

Which is where I am presently, seated beside the small metal desk of Officer Jose Mario Fernandez. I've been asking him about the festival's origins. I had read that the first tomatoes were thrown in 1944, at a local political rally. Fernandez confirms the date but claims the rest is untrue.

*"Es que dos chicos tiraran tomates."* It started because there were these two guys and they threw tomatoes.

*"Por que?"*

*"Por nada."* He lights a cigarette. *"For no reason. Por tirar los tomates."*

My theory was that it was an enlightened and exhilarating way of disposing with the excesses of the local tomato harvest. I run this by Fernandez. He exhales, lowering heavy eyelids against the smoke. Wrong again. They're not throwing local produce. (A good thing, this: Bunol's main industry is cement.) The tomatoes are from Extremadura, a province on the other side of the country. Why from so far away? Are these superior throwing tomatoes? Fernandez slaps at a fly. *"Son mas barratos,"* he says, his R's rolling off the desk and out the doorway. They're cheaper.

**40**

Fernandez gives me a copy of the festival program. In it is a series of sobering warnings: the throwing of bottles and water bombs is absolutely prohibited, as is destroying shirts.

Shirts? Fernandez nods. He asks me whether I have brought extra tee-shirts. I have. "Why?" I ask.

"Because this one will be ripped."

"But it says it's forbidden."

"It will be ripped anyway."

What about his? Fernandez looks down at his blue starched dress shirt. His, he replies, will be fine. "Because I will be inside here, with the doors and the windows locked."

*   *   *

It's 10 a.m., one hour before the fight. Bunol's Plaza del Puebla, where the action takes place, is a typical small-town Spanish square, with stucco buildings and cobblestone and old men on benches in the sun. The shopkeepers on the square are all outside draping plastic sheeting over their storefronts. A team of tellers from Banco de Valencia is carefully taping the crack between the plate glass doors.

Over by the fountain, big-knuckled senoras in white aprons are handing out bollos, loaves of flat-bread with strips of bacon and whole sausages pressed on top like bathtub appliques. A truck pulls up alongside, carting an enormous barrel of fizzy rose. The wine is poured into jumbo Pepsi cups and passed out free to all who care to imbibe, the majority of whom seem to be males between the ages of 12 and 19.

Outside the lock store, someone has coupled a hose to the water main and is spraying a mass of black-haired men, all waving their fists in the air and chanting: "Ole, ole-ole ole! O-le, o-le!" A sopping, tattered tee shirt arcs through the air above the crowd.

An air of incipient riot pervades. What have I gotten myself into? Seeking safety in numbers, I scan the crowd for the photographer who's along to cover the event. I can't see him, but I do spot Officer Fernandez, over on the steps of the town hall. I explain that I've lost my photographer. Fernandez considers this for a moment and replies matter of factly: He has gone with a woman.

This is nonsense. He's working. "You know this?"

He shrugs. Spanish intuition.

I wander over to the crowd to continue my search. A corpulent man in baggy blue shorts is dousing passersby with garbage pails of water. Teenage girls are shrieking, and old men are retreating into doorways. As I duck into the doorstep of a cafe, I feel a hand on my arm. It's the proprietor, grinning from beneath a bristling pushbroom moustache. He leads me into the street. Kind soul, he's escorting me to a safer, drier locale. He is joined by a companion, who takes my other arm. With his free hand, this man whistles. To my dismay, the fat one with the water buckets whistles a reply. Reality dawns. These men are not trying to help me. They're trying to drench me. They lift me off the ground and carry me into point-blank range. Fat Man draws the bucket back and launches the full sixteen gallons at me. My cap flies off, my notepad lands in a puddle by the curb.

My zest for tomato-throwing has acquired new urgency, in the form of revenge. Where are the damn tomatoes? It must be eleven-thirty, half an hour past the scheduled start time. I glance up at the sundial on the church above the square. Oddly, it says ten-something. In Spain, even the sun and the Catholic Church run an hour behind.

The square is jammed shoulder-to-shoulder with loud wet bodies, stomping in puddles and ripping each others' clothes. The chanting has switched from the more lyrical "Ole" number to a driving, monotone *"Tomates, tomates, tomates"*—the sort of thing you expect to hear when the Ramones keep the crowd waiting.

From up the street, a low rumble. An enormous dump truck, the first of three, parts the crowd. Planted atop some 7,000 pounds of tomatoes is a team of crazed bellowing men, firing armloads of tomatoes down at the masses. People are cowering and ducking behind plastic dropcloths.

This isn't how things were described in the program. It said, "The trucks move slowly through the streets to deliver the goods." I had envisioned gentle smiling farmers in open-bed trucks, distributing crates of tomatoes with the munificent air of a disaster-relief crew. Two dozen for you, two dozen for you, two dozen for you, like poker chips before the deal.

Nothing of the sort. This is chaos. This is war. The truck moves with the unstoppable slow-motion menace of an army tank. The tomatoes are hard and small, less like fruit than ammunition. A Spanish man next to me dons plastic lab glasses; his wife adjusts a pair of swim goggles.

"You speak English," observes the man in safety goggles, yelling over the roar of the crowd. He searches for something to say. A tomato smacks his forehead.

"They are throwing the baby out with the bathwater!" he shouts suddenly, as though the thought had been dislodged by the tomato's impact. I have no idea what he means. What I do know is that this man, with his lab glasses dripping tomato slush and seeds clinging to his beard, is the most hilarious thing I've ever seen.

"One good turn deserves another," I shout merrily, scooping up tomato entrails and flinging them up at him.

The hour of splat has arrived. Less than three minutes after the truck passes, every tomato has been mushed. In part, this is because safety regulations stipulate that you squish tomatoes in your hand before throwing them. Five minutes into the event, the curbs are boggy with pulp.

I gather up wondrous mucoid handfuls and hurl them at total strangers, first tentatively, then with gleeful abandon. I'm laughing so hard I don't mind the occasional stinging thud of a whole tomato. This is unmitigated fun. It's the infantile joy of aiming cherry tomato spurt at your grandmother, writ large. Tomato is everywhere, on everyone and everything. One well-aimed orb is spiked on the end of the sundial. Tomato shrapnel flecks the air like soggy red parade confetti. Building walls are spattered and splatted; Banco de Valencia looks like a backdrop in a Peckinpah film. A well-placed quarter-pounder has set off their security alarm.

A second truck plies the route, but this time the ground troops are primed for battle. A phalanx of tomato slingers confronts the truck head-on, backing slowly as they hurl. The wipers smear red back and forth across the windshield, as though the truck had recently passed through a cloudburst of Bloody Mary mix.

Emboldened by the giddy chaos, I make my way toward the water main, seeking Fat Man and his evil consorts. Before I've gone twenty feet, I'm singled out by a grinning man with a dripping handful of tomato gore, a great hideous Sloppy Joe heap. His eyes are on my baseball cap. I had hoped to spare myself the stink and inconvenience of washing dried tomato pulp from my hair, and he knows this. He knocks my cap off, slaps the pulp onto the crown of my head and rubs it around. As I lean down in pursuit of return ammunition he follows up with a second handful. I lob a return volley but he ducks; the quaggy projectile concludes its trajectory in the décolletage of a middle-aged duena. She looks around, flummoxed and besplatted, and fixes a vengeful gaze on her unsuspecting husband. She positions a palm-load of mush just due east of his head and shouts his name. He turns directly into the mess, and they collapse against each other, laughing.

By now the entire width of the street is submerged. It's a river of salsa, seasoned with wayward sandals, wadded tee shirts, wrestling Spaniards and, off by the soupy shoals that have all but engulfed the church steps, a lone journalist groping for her cap.

Up on the balcony above the lock store, a man with a baggie-clad camera is ducking cross-court shots. Like people in baseball caps, people with cameras are prime targets. The harder you try to stay clean, the more hits you take. It's

Danny, the photographer. He is, in fact, with a woman, but she is his assistant, Christina. Christina has made the grievous error of wearing a rain slicker and Aqua Slippers in addition to portering costly, moisture-sensitive camera equipment. A veritable tomato magnet, this girl. Danny motions to a narrow stairway between two buildings. On my way to the stairs, I commandeer one of Fat Man's water buckets and fill it with tomato slop.

I am running short of time. In ten minutes, a large bottle rocket will be set off. At that point, throwing a tomato will go from good, dirty fun to punishable offense. Almost instantly, squadrons of tidy, purposeful Bunolians will take to the streets with hoses and brushes and long-handled push-plows. Two hours later, the plaza will be spotless.

I'm another matter. I've got tomato slop up my nose, in my pockets, down my underpants. My hair is a wet, clotted mass, the sort of personal grooming catastrophe that used to prompt my mother to shake her head and say, "I'm afraid we're just going to have to cut it out." Danny informs me that my ear is stuffed, cocktail olive-style, with a slimy red chunk.

Right at the moment I can't be bothered with it. I've spotted Fat Man in the crowd. He's cradling a private stockpile of unsquashed tomatoes in the lap of his tee-shirt, and pitching them like oblong fastballs, one after another, a human batting-cage machine. I hold off until he moves into range, then upend the bucket. Bulls-eye. Fat Man drops his horde, reels, whirls, and curses his invisible attacker.

I find one last tomato in my pocket and get a good palm on it. But just as I'm about to let fly, the bottle rocket goes off. Now it's just a vegetable again, or a fruit, I forget.

So I eat the tomato and slosh my way back to the car, stinking in the midday heat and grinning like a fool.

# On the Trail of the Hadza

**Eric Seyfarth**

*Chasing food in the Tanzanian bush.*

EVERYWHERE THESE MEN LOOKED THEY SAW MEAT. They saw hide, feather and fang in the hieroglyph of tracks below their feet, in the distant rustle of parched leaves, by the flash of movement across a hillside clearing, and within the droppings that peppered the stratified banks of a dry riverbed.

The five Hadza hunters faced each other, pointed in several directions, and—tongues clicking—talked strategy among themselves. Following a cue that I missed, they set off. All were bare-chested in the equatorial sun. Two wore shorts, the others loin cloths. Their leather sandals were soled with tire treads. Each held half a dozen arrows and a long bow in his left hand as they weaved through a maze of thorn bushes. When they reached the edge of a dry riverbed, the men sprinted and fanned apart. The Hadza are gifted runners. They shoot poison-tipped arrows and often pursue wounded game for hours while the toxin takes effect. The hunters left me behind after the first 10 paces, but I ran after them anyway.

The Hadza, who live in Tanzania's interior, are among the last nomadic hunters in Africa. But their way of life—as ancient as human history—is under siege. Perhaps 750 Hadza still live as their ancestors did for millennia. The number is hard to estimate because their ways defy the very notion of a census. They sleep on zebra or kudu hides placed on the ground under trees. Their possessions are limited to what can be carried as they follow game.

Easier to count are the forces that conspire against them: farming, cattle ranching, aggressive neighbors and a government hell-bent on modernization. Of course, this is all in the name of progress, if for no other reason than progress is measured by such things. And in developing African nations, progress—a deity clad in a European suit clutching a cell phone—reigns above all else. Caught in the sweep of progress, the Hadza cling with one last handhold to the tree of man.

Several minutes after the hunters bolted, I found them under a tree, launching arrows at a francolin, a guinea fowl like bird. When it stopped moving, the smallest of the men climbed the tree to pull it down. He snapped its neck and secured it under a cord at his waist.

The men asked for a cigarette. They passed it around, took epic drags, coughed elaborately, and finished the Marlboro in one round.

They set off again, walking fast and silently. I crashed behind them, alarming meat in all directions. Another wordless cue and the men spread in a choreographed sprint. Red dust flew like psychedelic tracers from their sandals and shimmered in the broiling sun. Well off pace, I finally caught them. They had surrounded a small primate called a bush baby at the top of a tree. After a volley of missed shots, one hunter drew his bow, relaxed his shoulders and released. Bull's-eye. Straight through the chest.

Skewered by the arrow, the bush baby struggled to escape across the top of the tree. One hunter found a long branch, and another fashioned a bark noose at its end. They snared the animal and pulled it toward the ground. The prey was held against a bush and shot again through the chest. In that fatal moment the bush baby grabbed the arrow shaft with its delicate hands.

We hiked back to the riverbed. The hunters gathered leaves and sticks for a fire. They placed the unplucked bird and the unskinned bush baby on the flames. The primate was placed face up, arms spread, head thrown back. Its childlike eyes stared at me. Fur and feathers sent up thick white smoke.

The Hadza pulled apart the animals with their hands and ate the cooked parts, draping the rest on the fire until medium-rare. They ate everything— feet, tail, skin, heads, innards. They offered a choice piece of bush baby to me. I choked down the meat, only a few stray chromosomes from my own flesh. Annihilation is consumption at the most basic level. Soon enough, the primate was transformed into me, amino acids, corpuscles, muscle fiber and DNA.

* * *

After eating, we sat in a silence broken only by the convulsive coughing of the hunters, who had sucked two cigarettes to the filter as if they were the last smokes on earth. The men moved close to one another. They began to sing. One laid down a remarkable baritone, another led with lilting complex phrases, the last three combined in strange and powerful harmony. The moment transcended language, and I knew that the men sang of both remorse and hope from a place deep in history and human emotion. When they finished, we stood up to walk back to camp. Something crashed in the bush so close even I saw it. The brown-red flash of an impala grazed our periphery. The hunters sprang up the riverbank, and I took off chasing them. Then I stopped. Staying with them would be impossible. I had lost the will generations ago.

I was bound for the Land Rover and a flight home, where my possessions were a weight to me like a brick to a drowning man. The hunters remained in a place so free of possession that everywhere they walked was home. My tribe will probably survive for some time. Theirs has about the same chance as a treed bush baby staring down a speeding arrow.

# The End of the Road

**Marybeth Bond**

*Alone on a camel, riding through the remote Indian Thar desert,
things aren't always as they seem.*

I ALWAYS WANTED TO GO TO THE END OF THE ROAD. I had given up my job, and with it the career I had worked so hard to build. I had packed up my house, put all my belongings, including my car, in storage and I took off for a year-long sojourn through Asia. Now perhaps, I could follow a road to its end.

After three painfully hot days on the train from Delhi, I saw Jaisalmer rise out of the flat, yellow Rajasthani desert like a honeycomb. From the humblest shop to the Maharajah's palace, the entire town glowed with the golden color of the sandstone from which it is built. Three centuries ago Jaisalmer's location on the old camel route between India and Central Asia had brought it great wealth. Today it is the end of the line. The air is heavy with the fragrances of jasmine, cinnamon, and sweet curries. Women in flowing scarves and saris of saffron, turquoise, and vermilion glide among camels, sacred cows, and rickshaws in the narrow unpaved streets.

Sipping tea in an outdoor cafe, I was enjoying the sight of three regal Rajasthani men in white tunics and pink and orange turbans when I noticed all eyes in the square were focused on me. Feeling uncomfortable, I gulped my steaming tea and slipped into the tangled maze within the old city walls. Traveling in the summer, in the Indian desert, I thought I had left all Americans or Europeans behind, but at dinner my second evening, I met a French couple from Paris.

Gerard was a professional photographer on his second trip to Jaisalmer. A year before, he had spent a month photographing the desert people. Now he had returned with his fiancée, Nicole, to show her his beloved landscape. Although he was very excited by the idea of returning to visit a friend, Farld, in his remote village in the Thar desert, Nicole didn't seem at all enthusiastic. She had very little to say in either French or English; her bewitching green eyes, framed by long black eyelashes, never stopped scrutinizing me. Gerard, on the other hand, was elated to find an enthusiastic audience for his stories. What excited him about the Thar, he said, was that people still lived exactly as

**47**

they had for centuries. Suddenly, without consulting Nicole, he asked me if I would like to accompany them on their visit to his friend's village. He added, probably without knowing, that the words themselves would tempt me, that it was at "the end of the road."

The next morning at the intersection that served as the bus stop, Gerard introduced me to Farld, then squeezed through the bus's doorway to join Nicole in a seat. The vehicle was so crammed with passengers, pigs, chickens, baskets, and oats that Farid looked at me and pointed to the roof. He formed a foothold with his hands. I caught at an open window and climbed atop the bus, which was piled high with trunks, baggage, livestock, and humans. The only unoccupied space on the whole roof was on top of two filthy, spare tires. Farld smiled and shrugged as we plopped down on the hot rubber.

The bus roared out of town. The blowing sand and grit stung my face and eyes. I put on my sunglasses, and, following the example of the men around me, who used part of their red turbans to cover their mouths and noses, I wrapped my head and mouth with a scarf. The men's dark penetrating eyes were left exposed.

Clouds of dust unfurled behind us as we drove west, into the desert and back into time. Sheep and goats scurried from the road. A baby camel, unsure on skinny legs, looked up from where its mother was guarding it as it ate from a single shrub that clung to a sand dune.

As we traveled deeper into the desert, I noticed that the village men were dressed more and more elegantly. They strutted about with their heads swathed in turbans. Thick black mustaches coiled on their weather-beaten cheeks. The women were no less flamboyant in brilliant, ankle-length skirts embroidered with sequins and minute mirrors that glittered as they moved. They wore tight-fitting bodices and on their foreheads, ears, noses, necks, and arms they wore silver jewelry. Women and children running out to meet their returning men were like joyous visions stepping from Moghul miniature paintings. They came to life with grace and beauty against the parched land and the mud huts. I tried to imagine what their lives were like.

As we proceeded farther and farther into the heat and vastness of the desert, the bus slowly emptied; the road became less and less defined. Upon depositing several men at a cluster of mud huts, where no women came out to greet them, Farid leaned over to tell me: "No marriages have taken place in this village for over five hundred years."

I was startled. Then, not sure I believed him, and not knowing what to say, I stared off into the desert.

"The men in this hamlet never marry. Women who have no dowry end up here to be kept as community property." I glanced at the hamlet, then at him.

He whispered: "Like brood mares." Then he too looked off in the desert as he added matter of factly, "Female babies are suffocated at birth with a bag of salt." I shook my head at his gruesome tale. I wanted to put my hands over my ears.

"Women who give birth to girl babies too often are also killed." The bus started up with a lurch. I didn't want to believe Farid, but I had recently seen the tiny handprints young widows had pressed into the mud walls of the Jodhpur Fort before they burned themselves on the funeral pyres of their husbands. This custom, "suttee," was outlawed in the 19th century. Just a few days ago I had read in a Delhi newspaper about the many "dowry deaths" of young girls. Wives often caught fire "accidentally" while cooking, thus freeing the husband to remarry, and giving him a chance to secure a larger dowry.

We came to the end of the dirt road, not far from the Pakistani border. Ten round earth-colored huts with straw roofs clustered together against the immensity of the desert. Women, children, and barking dogs ran out to meet us. The bus soon turned around, leaving us in the dust. It sped back toward Jaisalmer.

Farid's younger brother, Abdul, greeted him with the hugs and kisses traditional among desert men, and proudly escorted us through the huts to their home. It contained a large room with open windows, several wooden cots, and a table. The jingling of tiny bells from the rings on her toes announced their mother's arrival. Her bearing was regal, and her face was uncovered. She welcomed us warmly with nods and smiles.

Exhausted from our journey, we accepted an offer to stretch out on the cots. During our rest, curious children poked their heads in at the open doors and windows, sometimes giggling, but often just staring in silence. We were more strange to them than they to us. One tiny girl peered timidly from behind the legs of an older boy to assess the strangers. When she stepped into the light I saw a long red scar that ran from the corner of her right eye to her mouth. I gasped. The older boy, who said he was her brother, told Farid that a rat had bitten her.

After a short rest, we were invited across a courtyard to a tiny, unfurnished dining room, where we sat on the floor to eat a hearty lunch of rice, lentils, and curried potatoes. There were no eating utensils so we, as the Indians did, used our right hands.

After lunch, Farid showed us into the family salon for tea. Shelves on the walls held flashlight batteries and empty pop bottles—rare items in the desert.

As Farid's mother served us tea, I noted that Farid and Abdul treated her with great respect. She did not fit the stereotype I held of an exploited Muslim woman. Farid told me his father had been killed in a border skirmish years ago and his mother alone had raised him and his brother. I wished I could talk to her in her own language.

When the heat abated late in afternoon, we went out to have a look around. Cows with ribs protruding from their dried-to-leather hides roamed the dirt paths. Through half-closed doorways I could see women, children, and old men sitting in walled courtyards. Their dark eyes followed our every move.

At dusk, Gerard suggested that we walk to a small hill overlooking the water pond to photograph the village women. Nicole, saying she felt ill, declined to join us.

We heard giggles and laughter before we reached the summit of the hill from which we could see the shiny copper vessels balanced on the women's heads. When they saw us they became quiet and covered their faces with their veils. They filled their vessels with the muddy water and balancing them on their heads, glided back into the desert.

After a dinner in semi-darkness (there were no candles to spare), Farid and Abdul joined us. He told us that, although the India-Pakistan border is officially closed, the desert people do a brisk trade in camels, cattle, goats, and food supplies as well as radios, electronic goods, arms, and drugs.

"Gerard," he continued, "was the first foreigner to come here before you. I doubt any foreigner," he was watching me closely "has ever visited the surrounding villages. Would you," he flashed me a big smile, "like to see them?"

"But how?" My voice was more eager than I expected it to be. "By camel. There are no vehicles," Farid explained, "wheels—wagon, bicycle, or car wheels get stuck in the sand. There are no roads beyond my village."

I turned to the others, sure they, too, would want to go. Gerard was intrigued, but Nicole greeted the idea with scorn. She reminded us how uncomfortable it was even here, and how much more unpleasant it would be riding on a camel and staying in far more primitive villages. Farid said he could arrange for the camels and would ask Abdul to accompany me as guide and translator. That night the thought of a camel trip into the desert wouldn't leave my mind. After hours of pondering the possibilities, I fell into a deep sleep.

Farid woke me with the first morning light, eager to tell me his mother had sent to ask a neighbor if he would be willing to interrupt his plowing and rent his two camels to us. And Abdul, he said, had agreed to come.

The bus, I knew, would not return to this village for five days. Five days would be time enough for at least a short safari. Or would I rather stay here and listen to Nicole complain? Five days! The idea of a solo adventure tempted me.

I was eager to move on, and yet, anxiously, I kept asking myself: Why am I doing this? If anything went wrong, there would be no one to help me. But the more difficult and frightening the journey seemed, the more alluring it became. Though I tried to be rational, I was already caught up in the romance of traveling the ancient trading route that had once been part of the Silk Road.

After dinner, while Gerard, Nicole, and I were playing cards, Farid came in to announce proudly that the neighbor had arrived with his two camels. "And the camel owner," he said, "will accompany us so he can care for his animals."

I laid down my cards. "We've planned out a circular route," Farid continued, "which will take you into some Indian villages as well as others across the border, in Pakistan."

The sun had risen just enough to cast oblique shadows across the morning haze of the desert. I clambered onto the bony back of the camel to settle on a saddle composed of padded cotton quilts and wool blankets. My limited equestrian experiences had not prepared me for riding a camel. As the beast rose, first on his back legs, I was thrown forward onto his neck. Then as he lurched up onto all fours, the ground suddenly seemed remarkably far away. Abdul, along with the camel owner, climbed onto the other animal. They led my camel with a rope attached to a wooden peg, that pierced his nose. Our little caravan headed off into the desert. Gerard and Nicole waved. "Au revoir! Bonne chance!"

Perspiration immediately began to collect under my sunglasses and streak down my cheeks. With every drop of moisture that ran down my neck and chest, a portion of my energy evaporated. Within an hour I was drained and numb. Scant vegetation dotted the barren hills. Each tree or bush or clump of grass, no matter how small, became a focal point for my attention. Abdul and the camel-man rode in silence. From time to time we passed a turbaned farmer shuffling behind a camel and guiding a wooden plow. The desert people grow millet, Farid had told me, which is ground into flour to make the flat chapitis that form the staple of the Rajasthani diet. We passed one shepherd tending a scrawny herd of sheep, a few skeletal cows, and three goats.

As we plodded through the endless waves of sand, the landscape became more and more barren. My enthusiasm evaporated in the excruciating heat, in the unending wind that lashed my face with burning sand. My thoughts turned inward. Memories of sailing off the coast of Mexico filled my mind. Over and over again I imagined cool splashing waves rushing over my body. In reality, on camelback in the Thar desert, I remained an immobile, rocking captive. Minutes seemed like hours. I hadn't worn my watch, nor missed it, since I left San Francisco, but now I urgently wanted to know the time.

*  *  *

Abdul spoke little English, the camel-man none. My situation might have been comical if I had not been so miserable. The sun was directly overhead when we spotted the gass roofs on the horizon. Covered from head to toe in dirt, cranky from the heat, weak from dehydration, I was angry with myself for romanticizing the awful reality of a desert camel trip. This is no fun, I finally admitted to myself as tears filled my eyes and a lump grew in my throat. I was so drained of motivation, and so uncomfortable, I couldn't imagine continuing.

The village was devoid of life. My camel stopped and growled. He wasn't very happy either. As I climbed down, I was so weak I collapsed right into the dirt. Abdul came running. Gently, he helped me to sit up. My legs were stiff, my whole body hurt. I desperately needed to get out of the sun and drink liquids. Abdul led me to some shade and then he went in search of a family who might take us in and provide lunch. I watched him speak to several women. Then he returned and led me to a hospitable looking hut.

Two pairs of colorful leather slippers with turned-up toes sat by the open door. I left my plastic thongs in line with the slippers and entered. Rugs were piled in one corner, and a small fire pit occupied another. Next to the hearth, clay pots three feet high and two feet in diameter stored the family's precious water. The rugs, cooking utensils, clay pots, and two copper jugs for transporting water were the only items on the tidy dirt floor. There were no cans or bottles, no radios or TVs, no pictures, photographs, or books; no printed material at all.

An attractive, perhaps 30-year-old woman, dressed in brilliant red, green, and yellow, fanned the fire in the semi-dark hut. Her head was not draped with a scarf nor was her face concealed. Though her hands were wrinkled and leathery, her face was smooth. I counted eighteen ivory bracelets above one elbow, and thirteen on her forearm. Heavy bone bangles adorned her ankles; her toes were decorated with two silver bells. Her nose stud identified her as a married woman; the tiers of jewelry announced her husband's wealth.

Sitting on the floor I watched her prepare the tea. She avoided looking at me. Neither of us uttered a sound. Across the cultural gap that separated us, however, I felt a kind of acceptance: I was alien but unthreatening. I would provide the family with a little extra income and I would become one of the stories she told to her friends at the well.

Fatigue overcame me, so I curled up on the floor with my pack under my head and closed my eyes. Within seconds I was dreaming of swimming deep under water. When I woke, lunch was prepared and Abdul joined us. We ate rice, curried potatoes, and hot chapatis. We ate in silence. I drank cup after cup of hot, spicy tea to replenish my liquid-starved body.

After lunch I begged Abdul to call it a day, and he, always gentle and kind, agreed. The woman cleaned up from lunch and left. I spent a quiet afternoon alone in her home reading, writing in my journal, and napping. Late in the afternoon I explored the village. As I walked among the mud huts, dogs barked and children hid. The men, I learned, were in the field plowing, and the women had to walk more than an hour each way to fill their water jugs.

At sunset when the woman of the house returned with water, she immediately began to prepare dinner. Her husband, Abdul, and the camel-man joined us soon after dusk, but her four young sons remained outside. The men talked until dinner was served. The woman did not speak. Again we ate rice, chapatis, and potatoes in silence. I was being treated as a male guest, for the woman ate her meal with her children when we had finished.

Later with Abdul's help as interpreter, I complimented the woman on her exquisite jewelry. She was pleased by my attention. She joked with her husband and the men. I didn't understand her words but her humor was evident. She pointed at me and giggled. Abdul said she was teasing me because I wore no jewelry to proclaim my husband's wealth. When I said I had no husband, she indicated that she felt sorry for me. What would I do, she wanted to know, if I had no husband to give me jewelry and no dowry jewels to attract one? With a man for an interpreter, I didn't feel up to embarking on an explanation of American feminism.

What had been my saddle all day became my bed for the night. Abdul helped me spread the cotton quilts on the floor of the hut, and my pack continued to serve as my pillow. Having slept in close quarters with the local people while trekking in Nepal, I did not mind the lack of privacy. However, the lack of washing water bothered me. But knowing that the woman had already walked hours to collect water for a family of six and three guests, I was unwilling to ask for more than the small bowl allotted to me. I stared into the shallow container. Should I brush my teeth? Wash my face? My pits? Or quench my thirst? I dipped my toothbrush in the water, then drank the remainder.

In the morning, I was honored by the woman of the house with an invitation to help cook the chapitis over the open fire in her tiny kitchen area. I was amused to think she was probably trying to show me some useful skills which would aid in catching a husband. We left when the sun was just beginning to rise.

The nasty discomfort of the first day repeated itself, and my fascination with the small mud villages vanished. They all seemed the same. The barren dunes stretched for miles as we criss-crossed the unguarded border between Pakistan and India. I could distinguish the Moslem women from the Hindu because the Moslem women kept purdah—clothed from head to toe in black, hiding from the eyes of all men save those of their families. The Rajput Hindu women, like the hostess in my first village, dressed in brilliant colors.

I thought of the lives of the Thar desert women, the status that jewelry and marriage gave them, and compared it to my determination to live my life on my own.

But alone in the Thar desert with only blue sky and sand and two men more silent than I, I could find no escape from the tormenting truth. As I shifted my aching bones in the saddle, I knew I alone was the one who was responsible for my maddening discomfort. It became clear to me that accepting responsibility for her acts is a rite of passage for a woman. Suddenly I realized this trip across the desert had become my rite of passage. How much could I endure?

When our camels stopped in the village where we would rest the second night, it was already after sundown. With the last bit of my strength, I slid off the camel and stood by myself in the shadows.

Abdul and the camel-man went off to arrange for fodder for the animals and dinner and lodging for us. I sat in the dirt and stared into space. It seemed like hours before Abdul returned. He apologized and said that no one was willing to allow me to sleep in their home. "A single woman," he said, "is suspect." I reminded him that I would pay well for the honor of sleeping on someone's floor, but he told me money was not the object, a family's reputation mattered more.

I settled for the flat roof of the village schoolhouse. Having climbed the primitive wooden ladder, I made my bed for the night by spreading out quilts in a corner. Abdul gave me some cold chapatis he had been carrying with him in the event of not finding food. I ate them quickly to keep the howling wind from blowing sand into my meager dinner.

A tall, powerful-looking man climbed the ladder to our rooftop and spoke to Abdul. They looked at me shaking their heads and discussing some issue of importance, perhaps Abdul had found a husband for me. But when Abdul turned to me he asked if I would like to hear some Rajasthani folk music. And would I care to taste the local "home brew?" If so, he could arrange it through this man, the village elder.

No food in the village, no place to stay, but they could play their music for me. I felt put upon, but I agreed.

Eleven men wearing orange-and-red turbans came to sit in the school courtyard below my perch. One man played a hand accordion, another the sarangi, a violin-like instrument. I learned from Abdul's translation that the melancholy songs were about love and battles. The charm of the repetitious rhythm soon wore off, and the white lightning of the desert, called asha, was too strong for my taste. I crawled off to my corner of the roof to be alone.

The wind began to blow ferociously. A crescent moon stood out in the pitch black sky. The stars seemed to compete with each other for space in the heavens. I was awed by the beauty of the desert night, but pleasure lay shrouded beneath fatigue and loneliness. Despite the suffocating heat, I huddled under my quilt to protect myself from the blowing sand and dust and tried to sleep. The entire sand floor of the desert seemed to be shifting across my bed. I could still hear the village men singing and enjoying themselves as I finally slipped off to sleep.

Danger! I struggled out of sleep. The crescent moon had set, the wind had stopped blowing, the night was dark and silent. I lay dead still, my heart pumping in my chest and a lump of fear rising in my throat. Someone was pulling on my cotton quilt. I smelled alcohol. Then I felt someone trying to crawl under my covers. A big cold hand touched my bottom. Terrified, then infuriated, I kicked backward, hitting the soft part of a body with my heel. At the same time I slapped over my head with one arm and screamed at the top of my voice, "Leave me alone!"

I flipped over to face my assailant. I could make out the shadow of the camel-man as he crept across the roof and descended the wooden ladder. Where was Abdul? Despite the heat and the weight of my quilts, I began to shiver. Don't be hysterical, I reprimanded myself. Forget it. Go back to sleep. I was lucky, after all, that the camel-man was a timid soul, for I was in no shape to fight off a determined attacker. As I kept shaking, I began to pray: "Our Father, Who art in heaven ..."

The camel-man understood my cold glare and cool attitude for the remainder of the trip. Abdul, realizing something had happened, became more conscientious as my bodyguard. No further incidents occurred.

The third day as we entered one more village, where I was looking forward to a little exercise to work out the pains in my legs, only dogs came out to bark. But I could partly see and partly intuit that, as in other villages, eyes were scrutinizing us from behind the almost-closed shutters and doors. As Abdul descended from his camel, a group of men converged on us. shouting "Pagal, Pagal." One old man with a rifle threatened to shoot. Abdul did not utter a word, but, rapidly remounting, he prodded our animals to move quickly out of town. The men followed, screaming insults until we were far beyond their boundaries.

The villagers felt, Abdul spoke softly, that a woman traveling alone could only mean trouble. Such a woman must be either a lunatic or a witch. They wanted no part of me and my bad luck. My mood was such that, I felt it almost an honor, a compliment, to be labeled mad and banished as a witch. I had had just about enough of questioning my own value.

Since Abdul wanted to avoid villages where he didn't personally know a family, we were forced to camp on the sand dunes the last two nights. Before retiring, Abdul scattered raw onion around. "It'll keep the pena at bay," he said. "What's a pena?" I asked. "It's a snake that comes out at night and crawls onto your warm chest. It spits venom into your nostrils and lashes it's tail across your face." Fear of the pena didn't keep me awake. I was too tired to care.

On our last day, I caught a glimpse of two wild gazelle with twisted horns playing spiritedly in the distance, and I saw a single man in an orange turban, his back straight and his head held high, walking behind a camel. Arriving back in Abdul's village, we stopped at the water hole to give the camels a drink. The women, hearing us approach, ran to the opposite side of the pond. They giggled and pointed at me.

Abdul's mother welcomed us with genuine warmth and visible relief. I was happy to be back in the village at the end of the road connected to civilization by motorized transportation.

Beyond the end of the road, despite the swirling sand, howling wind, and overpowering heat, I had come to appreciate the austere beauty of the desert. I was filled with wonder, that, out there, I had discovered serenity in solitude and spiritual peace.

# Itel'men Tribal Harvest Festival

## L. Peat O'Neil

*In Russia's seldom traveled Kamchatka Peninsula, little has
changed. Villagers gather food and live like their nomadic ancestors,
and have a real flair for celebration.*

OUT ON THE TUNDRA, eyes level with the humps of juniper and blueberry
bushes, I crouched and surveyed the horizon. The violet, burnt orange,
purple, and brick red rolled in waves on the fading blue sky. Sunset on the far
eastern reaches of Siberia. I breathed deeply, forcing my body to remember
the fresh piercing scent of the brush 'bagulnik' and cold ground waiting for
the first fall freeze. This is what I must remember of Kamchatka.

I was on the outskirts of Kovran, a hamlet of about 500 souls on the western shore of the Sea of Okhotsk. Siberia had figured in my travel dreams ever
since I'd read Kate Marsden's 19th century narrative 'On Sledge and Horseback
to Outcast Siberian Lepers.' In her search for lepers to minister to—it was the
age of Florence Nightingales—Marsden didn't get as far as Kamchatka, a
peninsula about the size of California lying directly above Japan. Few travelers
of any sort had been here since Vitus Bering in the 1730's and George Kennan
in the 1860's.

Kamchatka's deep wilderness attracts foreign visitors who seek outdoor
adventure. Japanese mountaineers came in search of new mountains to be the
first to scurry up. European and American mountaineers have claimed the
summits of the peninsula's many snow capped volcanoes—Klyuchevskya,
Koryakskya, Avacha, Aag and dozens more. The high-end hook and bullet
sportsmen are plundering the salmon rich streams and game filled forests. It is
to these well-fed, mostly American, hunters that Kamchatka's nascent tourist
industry caters. Unfortunately, licensing and hunting limits are inconsistently
applied; bribes and payoffs play a larger role in the management of natural
resources than sound principles of ecology.

Remote Kovran is an experience in time travel. This is a village with 13th
Century plumbing, hand pumped water and sporadic electricity because of
diesel rationing curtailing the generator. Scruffy dogs forage in the ditches for
garbage and human excrement tossed from the houses. When they bite the vil-

lage children, and they often do, the kids have to go through a painful series of rabies shots at the clinic in Us't Kharoziva, twenty-five kilometers to the south. This is one place where a sign reading 'zlaya sobaka' (mean dog) is a true fact.

The week of fall harvest festivities was just getting underway in Kovran when I lurched into town in a windowless army all-terrain transport truck. During the hour trip across the rutted track and along the high water line of the seashore, I'd been wedged between droopy eyed Koriak and Itel'man tribal people who'd evidently already downed several washtubs of homemade hooch. My backpack was splashed with milk from a beat-up metal urn with a loose lid. The Truck, as it is called, served as local milk run, school bus, airport limo.

There are no hotels; everybody who comes for the festival stays with families in the village. You pay with vodka or coffee, tee shirts, or cassette tapes, whatever you have. The village accountant, Tanya, had seen me on the truck as I was fondled about the face by an inebriated celebrant of the Alkhalalaj festival. Sophie, the moon-faced drunk, told me over and over that I was pretty, as I politely and pointedly returned her handshakes and edged away from her drunken smooches. Alas, none of the handsome young Koriak tribesmen were so forward.

Tanya's daughter Katia had been bitten by one of the starving dogs. They had stayed 10 days in the clinic while the girl went through a cycle of rabies shots in Us't Khairyuzova and were returning home with me on the all-terrain taxi truck. "I asked for you to stay with us," said Tanya, "because you have a good face." Maybe she just wanted a break from the monotony of life at the last stop from nowhere.

Communication was demanding. Tanya knew a few phrases in textbook English and I'd sat through a couple of Russian courses at the community college. Neither of us had learned the phrases for the kinds of topics we needed to discuss. "Where can I wash," I would ask and she'd smile and say "Banya, on Sunday." But Sunday was days away, I'd grumble to myself and splash down the essentials on the floor with a quart of water heated on the wood stove in the kitchen. "Where do I empty the chamber pot" I'd ask, discreetly covering the day's duty with a piece of paper. "Anywhere," Tanya would smile and gesture out the door to the mucky ditch. In the interests of not adding to the problem I buried my offerings, but couldn't help noticing that others in the village didn't.

But we did manage to talk about our families and gardening. Her husband Vitaly hailed from the northern reaches of Russia and was pale blond like a Laplander from Finland. They enthusiastically retold how they met at a Soviet youth camp somewhere on the vast prairie. After a couple of summers together organizing entertainment programs for other campers, marriage was the next step. They hauled out photo albums and I stared at snapshots of their relatives in front of official looking building in various Russian cities. Tanya pointed to herself in front of Red Square, on the steps of several municipal museums, in front of war monuments. I played with Katia and drew a sketch of her which I gave to Tanya.

Tanya served up a full table of cabbage soup, smoked salmon or river fish, along with locally grown potatoes and carrots. Many families in Kovran, including my hosts, have constructed greenhouses of plastic sheeting on wooden frames and grow cucumbers, carrots, greens and dill. I would point to the lettuce, herbs and carrots and explain to Tanya that I grew the same vegetables in my backyard. A couple of times, I joined local folks foraging for blueberries and mushrooms on the tundra and in the woods. And on Sunday, I got my bath in the shed heated with a wood stove that Vitaly had built behind their house. I sweated in the steam, scrubbed, sluiced down with cold water and sweated some more.

During the "Alkhalalalaj" harvest festival (usually the third week in Sept.) Kovran's population nearly doubles with people from the surrounding region who shuttle in by helicopter and the huge all-terrain trucks. The festival is deeply imbedded in the culture of the region's tribes, but during Soviet rule, many of the Koriak, Itel'men, Sunda and other tribes were forcibly resettled away from their traditional fishing and reindeer herding camps and rituals were abandoned. The Soviets plunked them down on the wind burned prairie where it was colder and farther from the sea. Currently, a cultural revival is underway and the indigenous people have begun to reclaim their heritage.

One of the old rituals was a rigorous two-day 22 miles each way hike to erect a carved wooden totem atop sacred Mount Elvel. We were seventeen pilgrims, hiking across the empty tundra of northern Kamchatka. Young villagers and their boy-scout style leaders made up most of the group, along with a couple of foreign anthropologists, myself and the strong, silent Gosha, a villager of substance because he owns horses. He had noticed my struggle to keep up with the hard hiking Siberians and offered his horse to carry my backpack.

We'd hiked most of the day when I found the spoon. I was walking behind Gosha's lumbering beige horse, my heavy backpack roped to its saddle. I happened to look down and found a tablespoon with a pretty scrolled handle embedded in the soil. The spoon bowl faced up. I pried the spoon from the weeds and dirt and stashed it in my pocket, then scrambled to catch up with the group. It would be a while before I learned the meaning of this find.

Despite their rustic and patched gear, the Russians were resilient and animated. They hiked pell-mell across the tundra, heedless of the stragglers. When some of the slower youngsters lost the path up to Mt. Elvel, we had to wait for a couple of hours for them to catch up. The leaders paid little attention to the rest of the group's progress, yet at the camp site, they hastened to build a fire, put on tea to boil and hung sweat-soaked socks to dry. Around the fire at night, eyes bright and alive, they gave impromptu Russian lessons and tried out their English. I wondered if it was this nerve and will and lightheartedness that got the Russians through the wars and putsches and winters?

Also on the hike was an artist who'd studied the tribal folklore. Sergie Longinov Itenmen had carved the wooden totem to be placed on the top of Mount Elvel. Winds at the top were formidable, so while we waited for the teenagers who were carrying the four-foot totem to find their way through the brush up the mountain, I started building a rock cairn to shelter myself and any future climbers who might be stranded up there. Eventually the youngsters arrived, the totem was planted and food left for the mountain spirits, called Kamuli. Salmon is the traditional offering. Then our rag-tag group of pilgrims scrambled down the mountain, broke camp and slogged back to the village through a day of cold steady rain. I guess I can claim title to first American woman and first French woman (I have dual citizenship) to ascend this modest peak, or so I was told by Kovran residents.

During the week long celebration, there were fire dances, drumming, chanting, singing, more totem carving. The festival opened fairly slowly, an evening of singing by school children then some dancing. Consuming the bathtub vodka was the main event. Certificates of purity are displayed by the merchants who peddle vodka on wooden crates in city markets, but when your host offers a toast, it would be bad form to ask where the vodka came from. You raise your little glass and down it, like everybody else around the table.

The festival's cooking competition brought out dozens of variations on themes of salmon, potatoes, berries and gir (bear fat). On another festival day, a seal was slaughtered. I watched, although it was intensely disturbing. After the fat was removed, the inner body resembled an adult human right down to the five-digits on the flippers. The villagers hunkered around the knife wielding butchers, eager to get a share of the meat and fat, carting it away in plastic buckets.

\*   \*   \*

It would be naive to assume that this village is beyond the reach of MTV and other tentacles of popular American culture. When the electricity was running, the television sets would be turned on. A well traveled friend asked "But, how ARE they?" meaning how are the indigenous peoples faring. Oh, I said, they're tribal, very basic—concerned with family relationships, storing up food, drinking, getting laid. Yeah, really different than people anywhere else in the world.

Then there were the idling humm-vee taxis. In the cement duplex adjacent to Tanya lived an assortment of people who enjoyed loud rock and roll of a heavy metal vintage. Anyway, one morning I heard a persistent rumble, like an idling semi at a truck stop. Outside the neighbor's fence, two humvee type all-terrain tank vehicles were idling while the drivers visited inside. The trucks idled for hours, perhaps the empty gas tanks would be evidence that work was performed.

On one of my last days in Kamchatka, I read a recently reprinted edition of Stepan P. Krasheninnikov's "Explorations of Kamchatka, North Pacific Scimitar, 1735-1741" the most detailed authority of natural life on Kamchatka to date. I was stunned to read that when the indigenous Siberian tribes of Kamchatka embark on a hunting trip, they toss a large tablespoon to forecast their success. If it falls so the bowl curve faces up, it's a good omen; when the eating side faces down, bad hunting ensues. I hadn't tossed that spoon I found on the trek to Mt. Elvel, but it came to me eating side up, forecasting good hunting and what was already a luck-filled and successful trip.

# Spoke'n Patagonia

## Anik See

*What is the reward in pain? Why are you here? Surely greener pastures are not much further ahead.*

AY FIVE CYCLING IN PATAGONIA. Fried by the sun and the onslaught to
your senses. One of those days where you're thinking "why do I do
this?" "What am I doing here?" One of those days where you think you're too
old for this, not taking into account the imbalance of your ride thus far—up,
up, up for three days and very little down. But suddenly it all evens out and you
did what in the morning you thought was impossible. You rode against a blasting furnace of a wind, under scorching, white-hot skies, up a 40-mile hill with
a trashed knee and a bike that is so tired that it just creaks under you, up, up,
up, endless caracoles always in sight above you ... struggling not to think about
the heat, the pain your knee shrieks with every push down on the pedal, the
road that is more pothole than dirt. You think of something else. You think of
the two kids you saw playing in a corral the other day, who shouted "Hola
amigo!" when you rode past, and when you answered, there was a moment of
silence and just when you thought they hadn't heard you they shouted back "...
hola am-i-GA!" even louder than before. You think of people back home,
telling you you're crazy to go to Patagonia, let alone on a bike. But they don't
know what you do about Chile, and they never will—a thought containing
overwhelming nostalgia for all of your journeys and experiences here; a
thought that somehow brings all of your exhaustion to the forefront in huge
gulps of emotion, and you feel that the next push of the pedal will probably be
your last, but it isn't, and you think of something else ... you think of what
you're going to do when you get back, what it would be like for you to give up
just about everything you 'have' and live like the Chileans. You think of the
landscape; green mountains crashing into one another with icefields in every
nook, and clouds drifting about at eye level, swooshing over you. You think of
the difficulty of life here, of the 3 or 4 tiny cars that pass you each day, packed
with children, trundling past you at a speed not much faster than your own,
passengers faces pressed to sticky back windows, arms frantically waving a
brief and dusty greeting. You think of someone alongside the road yesterday,
wrestling watermelons from a viney field, seeing you ride by, stopping, waving

and smiling. You think of how you woke up this morning to a rustling outside your tent, and how you peeked out, just in time to see a child running away and a stack of steaming bread in front of you. You think of the farmhouses that will exchange a bagful of that bread with you for a pen or a promise of a post-card from your home.

At lunch you take a break in a village's central square, cooling down, and a man on the edge of the square approaches you and asks where you have come from and when you tell him Argentina, he nods gently. He stares at your bike for awhile and then at you. He smiles at you, and wanders slowly off, clutching a worn, leather-bound book behind his back with both of his hands, and then turns and tilts his head almost at you. "Has it been a good time for thinking?" he asks, and you feel like smiling and crying at the same time.

And in the afternoon, you crest that 40-mile hill and in between two sheer red rock faces is a little window of the oasis below ... a wide plateau surrounded by the greenest of Patagonia's mountains, a cluster of creaky wooden houses and the ever-present two-steepled church ... two-steepled because the land-scape in Patagonia is so lonely to the Chileans that they would never think of building one steeple without building another beside it to keep it company. And you swoop down onto the plateau where all the jacaranda trees are in full screaming yellow bloom and someone is slapping dough between their hands and the kids are running in circles over a dusty road bopping marbles from their fingers, screaming *"otra vez!"* and a serene old gaucho passes you on his horse, bidding you a good afternoon as if he knows you just as well as every-one else in this town. All the warmth of Patagonians envelops you and you know now why you do this and you can't ever imagine going back home.

# Deep Impressions

## Cindy Lee Van Dover

*Journey into the abyss with the only woman ever to qualify as a navy-certified Pilot-in-Command of a deep-diving research submarine.*

WHEN I WAS A CHILD, I thought the entire world was known, the list of explorers complete, species and their habitats cataloged. I thought with envy of the sailors who discovered new lands. I wished I had been the first person to stand at the edge of the Grand Canyon or beside the hot springs of Yellowstone. I wanted to be the first astronaut to set foot on the moon.

Two decades later, I look back and discover I have lived my dreams. I am an adventurer on this planet. I wander in an alien, uncharted realm: the deep seafloor, a place less known than the dark side of the moon.

Reaching the sea floor is a study in understatement. Although the technological feat seems akin to sending humans into outer space, submersibles dive miles below the surface of the sea, day in and day out. There is no countdown, no army of personnel to supervise launch or recovery. From the inside of ALVIN's three-person sphere, the surface of the sea, faceted by shafts of sunlight, flashes in front of the viewports. As the long descent begins, clear water quickly becomes aqua, then a deeper blue-green that has no name, then darker still, until there is no color left at all, only blackness. In this colorless transparency of water, splashes of bioluminescent light pass by like shooting stars; they are the only index of motion as the ungainly little ALVIN continues its plunge. Once on the seafloor, its banks of lights and cameras are switched on; its manipulators unfold like legs of a praying mantis. In this world of inner space, ALVIN springs to life.

To roam the deep sea is to discover a solemn place, mysterious and vaguely sinister, a place of loss, a place virtually unknown. It is a silent world. I have set ALVIN on the seabed and systematically shut down all of its systems. We call it "going dead boat." Silence and darkness are immediate and ultimate, all encompassing and pervasive. I feel the silence more than hear it; it feels cold, oppressive. In the darkness my voice is thin and nervous, insignificant. Never am I more conscious of the crushing weight of the water miles above me. Only when I return power to the boat does my pulse return to normal.

Danger is present in abundance. No one works the seafloor without wondering what it would be like to be trapped, to know that seventy-two hours of stored air are all that lies between escape and a slow, suffocating death. Each ALVIN pilot has been in places we would rather not have been. But once and only briefly did I find myself actually afraid I could die. I spooked myself with the fleet but terrifying thought of being buried alive by a "landslide" as I worked deep in a narrow fissure. My heart raced, my fingers trembled, my imaginings of a slow and hopeless dying ran wildly unchecked. I wanted only to fly up and out of that fearsome crack in the seafloor that only moments ago I had so admired and deftly maneuvered through. None of the submarine's safety features would do me any good beneath a ton of rock. I hit the "up" switch on the joystick and precipitously put an end to my close observations.

The seafloor itself is surprisingly rich in visual textures, a landscape of stark beauty. Where the ocean crust is young, lava flows dominate the landscape; they pool and ripple and swirl in frozen motion. Pillows of lava with elephant hide skins drape the slopes of subterranean mountains like icing run down the side of a cake. Stilled lavas are ripped apart, prelude and aftermath of the violent birth of new seafloor.

I have driven into fissures cut deep into the bottom, deep beyond seeing, and followed them until their steep-sided walls began to close in. Exposed in the cuts are the histories of volcanic eruptions, flows built upon flows. I have used ALVIN's robot arms to pick up pieces of the youngest ocean crust— young measured not in geologic time, but in days and weeks. I have explored sea floor valleys, which run the length of ride axes: raw, tortured topography filled with pits and caverns and tall pillars, with rubble, talus and scree.

Where the seafloor spreads apart and is rent by earthquakes, and where the heat of molten magma lies close to the surface, seawater percolates through the cracks in the basalt where it is heated and reacts with the host rock. Hot and buoyant, the chemically altered water rises as thermal springs within the valleys of the mountains. These submerged geysers easily rival Yellowstone in power and spectacle. Venting water, emerging clear from chimney-like deposits of minerals, quickly become turbulent plumes of "black smoke" as the dark crystals spread.

These "black smokers" stand as cautionary totems of an inhospitable land. Like the undersea volcanoes that drive them, they are born of primal forces, the geophysical engines that control the ever-shifting movements of the ocean crust. I never fail to be awed by them. They first loom as tall dark shadows, black against the surrounding blackness at the gloomy edge of the submarine's pool of light. Maneuver closer and the base of the smoker rises up along the side of a shallow fissure. A fine dusting of minerals cover the nearby flat sheeted lava flows. The stack itself is roughly textured, with irregular walls.

Only a few decades ago, the ocean floor was thought to be barren, lifeless. ALVIN and her ocean explorers have given us an entirely new vision. Among the venting chimneys of black smokers we find animals drinking in the warm seepage of noxious chemicals. They are strange animals, many unknown to science. There are six-foot-high tubeworms and fat Pompeii worms, long spaghetti worms draped in tangled mats, slimy worms with no names. It is a bestiary worthy of a distant planet.

A painted tropical fish can be a lost rainbow among the gaudy carnival of colors in a coral reef; a vividly feathered bird is veiled in the green lace of leaves and twigs. But giant tubeworms are expletives, shouts of brilliance, startling in their vivid simplicity and exposure. Crimson plumes bloom atop long white tubes emerging from cracks in black lava. They grow side-by-side as dense thickets of tubes, nearly all the same size, in parallel array. The growth of the whole guides the growth of one: a chorus of tubeworms.

There is a singular place on the sea floor where I have driven ALVIN along the surreal landscape of the shallow axial valley and seen looming in front of me a tower of tubeworms. Tightly packed, they look cultivated, each a prize specimen arranged in a formal garden just so to present a uniform face of red plumes around the white pole.

Way deep down, there is a beauty to life and to landscape on the seafloor that pleases me. It is life sculpted by extreme and hostile conditions, life that is fragile and all but unknown. It is a world for explorers, and I for one celebrate the fact that this abyssal wilderness is modest neither in measure nor in mystery.

# Burn Gringo, Burn!

## Tom Clynes

*Big fun in Colombia's capital of misbehavior.*

T HE FLIGHT FROM BOGOTÁ TO CARTAGENA took off without a hitch, but landing was another story. "We apologize," the pilot squawked over the intercom, "but there will be a delay. There is an aircraft burning on the runway, so we'll have to circle while the firemen work on it. We have enough fuel for 45 minutes."

In Cartagena, on Colombia's Afro-Caribbean coast, the visitor soon learns that getting off the ground is easy, but coming down is almost always trickier—and often just an afterthought in this fabulously off-balance world of smugglers, beaches and all-night dance parties.

We land—with 10 minutes of fuel to spare—as the city is gearing up for its latest excuse to cut loose: the annual Cartagena Pan-Caribbean Music Festival. This five-day marathon of salsa, soca, reggae and junkanoo cranks Cartagena's normally high level of human folly up to its most extravagant amperage. For world music buffs, the event is a chance to hear bands from Colombia, Cuba, Panama, the Dominican Republic, Haiti and Jamaica. For locals, the festival is a chance to embrace an identity that goes beyond "Colombian" and beyond "Caribbean," back to the happy secrets at the source of most Caribbean music and people: Africa.

Nearly 500 years of ransackings—first by the Spanish, then by pirates, then slave traders and finally drug traffickers—seem to have left *Cartageneros* with a prodigious impulse to have some fun *today*, because tomorrow ... well, you just never know about tomorrow. In the foundry-grade heat the music is everywhere, blasting out of houses, bars, restaurants and the bright, open-sided buses. There's hardly enough power to refrigerate a beer, but everyone seems to have a sound system; most of the speakers seem to have been blown since 1977.

At first glance, Cartagena could be New Orleans' sluttier twin sister. Like the Crescent City, she's a beauty with flowered 16th-century balconies and narrow streets. The seafood's great, and the city's traditions of hospitality and music are legendary. But instead of jazz, blues and zydeco, Cartagena thumps to the tropical rhythms of cumbia, vallenato and mapalé. And here, misbehavin' comes in larger sizes: Soldiers guard against guerrilla attacks. The Hilton has been bombed. Drugs are almost free.

In the evening before the show a breeze rolls off the Caribbean and cools the thick fortress walls of the old city. Travelers gather at the old wharf to drink away any uneasiness with shakes of rum mixed with banana, mora and guanábana. Locals chat and laugh outside their houses, and vallenato (accordion and percussion) bands roam the beaches and streets.

We head uptown to the bullring, where the music is scheduled to get underway at 8:00 p.m. But double-frisking and technical foibles keep thousands outside until past 11. No problem; this bunch can entertain itself. There are portable bars, portable bands and portable soldiers on horseback. When part of the crowd gets rowdy a young policeman tries to "calm things down" by pulling his gun and firing into the air. He sets off a minor stampede.

Backstage, the musicians are laughing it up in Creole, English, French and six or seven shades of Spanish. This year a band from Zaire, Loketo, has been invited in a nod to the music's African roots. Language gaps are bridged by a babel of rum toasts punctuated by explosions of drumming and dancing, and more and more rum.

There's a sense of impending Big Fun, and when members of Loketo leap onstage they initiate a massive boil-over that won't settle down for four days. Immediately, soukous polyrhythms transform salsa and merengue dance steps into freeform delirium. The audience goes ape-shit, leaping up and down in a riotous mosh that jostles the soldiers protecting the stage.

Loketo's front men imitate a "Lucky Pierre" sex act, then invite some local dancers onstage for a hetero version. They play the festival's theme song, and in the bottom of the bullring 10,000 jump and howl along: *"Sí, sí Colombia; sí, sí Caribe!"* Congo lines snake through and some of the soldiers join in, rifles slapping against thighs. A volley of fireworks shoots off overhead; some malfunction and scream horizontally, detonating into the squirming crowd. I'm dancing and sharing rum with a teenager from Bucaramanga. *"Qué locura!"* she yells.

"My head's on fire!" I yell.

The sound quality is phenomenal for an open-air concert. But between bands—sometimes even between songs—local DJs jump on stage and blather away in a Spanish version of Top-40 banality: "Peeeeeerfecta! Número unoooooooo!"

Local cumbia/salsa hero Joe Arroyo comes on with a crackling band that includes about 17 guys on percussion, and you can hear each one perfectly.

Jamaican reggae star Sister Carol declares herself "Motha Culture—the Black Cinderella" but her toasting is lost to the 98 percent of the crowd that doesn't speak English.

At 4:30 a.m. the first-night concert breaks up, and I stagger back to my hammock. Tomorrow there's a symposium on the various Afro-Caribbean religious movements, including Voodoo, Santería, Lucumí and Candomblé. For the brain-dead there's the beach, where dozens of urchins stand ready to fetch you "anything you want, gringo: Beer? Fruit salad? *Cocaína?* A girl maybe?"

All week long, Cartagena is in fiesta mode. There are more wildly erratic fireworks at the colonial fortress, and goofy mock battles between pirates and conquistadors. Most of the "conquistadors" are black, the descendants of slaves who were brought over by real conquistadors.

Colombia's most wanted narco-terrorist, Pablo Escobar, sends a gift—a car bomb—but it's intercepted on the road from Medellín. "I wonder if anyone would have even noticed the explosion," a cabby jokes. "This place is in complete *rumba!*"

Another *taxista* notes the gringo accent in my Spanish and asks where I'm from. "Oh yes, the United States. I spent five hours in Tampa once. Then five years in the federal penitentiary in Tennessee." He laughs hoarsely. "Forty kilos in a Cessna. We took off from right over there, but the pilot got lost. We didn't really want to land in Tampa."

One night I stumble onto a bus with Rara Machine, the Haitian band that has just capped its show with an elaborate fire-dance spectacle. It's 5:00 a.m., and they're chanting and yelling and beating on the bus ceiling with sticks. Voodoo ecstasy? Good drugs? General derangement? When we arrive at the performer's hotel they jump off the bus and go on a spontaneous window-smashing spree.

At the hotel pool the women in Spice & Company, a soca band from Barbados, are jeering at Los Fantasmos del Caribe, a teeny-bopper merengue quintet from Venezuela. The boys look pretty dumb in their G-string swimsuits, and the word is out that their performance was "live" only in the vocal sense: none of them can really play an instrument.

I end up at the beach, where groovy vallenato bands are serenading the dawn. "Sit down, gringo, have a drink with us." We pass around the firewater known as *aguardiente.* By mid-morning I wind up on a boat with some Bogotanos, some Germans and some fellow North Americans. I realize that I've forgotten to sleep.

The destination is a string of islands called the Islas del Rosario, and it's a fine trip. We stop and swim at pristine beaches. We have a fish dinner at an old fortress. We pass the Colombian president's island home. Less than a mile away, we pass Pablo Escobar's island home. "Did you hear about the bomb Pablo tried to send to Cartagena?" the motorman asks.

I sleep for two hours and head back into the South American night. On this final evening of the festival a free show "for the people" is scheduled on the beach. The cab ride is a 15-minute security lecture: "I guarantee the place will be crawling with criminals, and they'll be damn good. They'll slash your camera strap. They'll pick your pockets. They'll steal your underwear without even taking off your pants."

The warnings are moot; it turns out that the mayor has pulled the plug on the show, noting that there's no way to keep out the riffraff at a free, open-air event. "And you know what happened last year ..." he is quoted in the local newspaper, "... too many shootings."

So I eat some fish-and-coconut stew and fly back to Bogotá's chilly smog to initiate a cozy detox. But the Colombian president has declared a "state of internal commotion." The phone company's been bombed and the electricity is down. Dinner with Julio has been canceled, my friend tells me, because his brother's been kidnapped by ELN guerrillas. "And did you hear about the bomb Pablo Escobar tried to send to Cartagena?"

Nice try, Pablito. But if you're still on the loose next year, maybe we'll bump into you. I'll be back in Cartagena, *cierto*.

Clear the runway.

# SO THAT'S HOW IT WORKS

## ... Or Does It?

*"The big question is whether you are going to be able to say
a hearty yes to your adventure."*

Joseph Campbell

# Messenger Extraordinaire

## Simon Winchester

*Where the rain falls hardest, someone is there to measure it.*

RAM KRISHNA SHARMA IS A SMALL, balding and bespectacled man in his early 40s whose job, he admits quite unashamedly, is that of peon. In Western society the word peon has a faintly pejorative ring—but not so in India. Unofficially it means clerk; officially it means messenger, and Mr. Sharma is in a very strict sense a messenger-extraordinaire, since his job is specifically to send important news each day to the outside world from a tiny Eastern Indian village called Mawsyngram.

He has to do so because this village owns the distinction, according to the latest record books, of being with very little doubt the wettest place, the rainiest place, in the entire world. Ram Krishna Sharma is the man who collects and measures all the rain, sends the figures out. Not long ago I set off to see him, on a mission to tell him—chancing that he might not know—just how central a role he plays in detailing the official weather portrait of our planet. I thought he might be amused, and rather pleased.

I had been staying forty miles away in Shillong, the old hill-station that is now the capital of the state of Meghalaya, and the night before I drove down I had become well acclimatized to what seemingly lay ahead: I had been kept contentedly awake for hours by a downpour thrumming pleasantly on the tin roof of the old Pinewood Hotel.

It was then the height of the monsoon almost everywhere in India. Nowhere more so than in India's Eastern states—in both the well-known places like Assam and Nagaland, and the less familiar states of Manipur, Tripura, Mizoram and Arunachel Pradesh—where rain (or snow, in the last instance) seems a near-permanent fixture, seeping out of and into everything. Not for nothing does the word Meghalaya, where I first came, mean "abode of the clouds." It is just steep hills, thick jungles—and thick, dark, rain-filled clouds.

But however much the rain drenches a soggy old hill-station like Shillong, the town is positively arid compared to farther south. I left in that direction the next morning, in a car whose driver asked: Are you sure?, and shivered as he did so. The road winds through thick be-jungled hills towards the frontier with

**74**

Bangladesh, going ever southwards: as it does so it rises almost imperceptibly, and the temperature falls steadily, degree by cloud-making degree.

As both the mercury and (so I was later told by a weather-man) the glass slide down, and as the altitude goes up, so it seems that one is going steadily into the black heart of an impossibly huge cloud, in which it is first drizzling, then thundering, then pouring, then bucketing, all in a ceaseless demonstration of the various manifestations of rain.

The people in these parts of India are called the Khasi—short, sturdy farmers, who have chosen to live all their lives in this unremitting wetness. They put up with it, they shrug their collective shoulders, they look stonily at those vulgar lowlanders who remark that they ought perhaps to develop gills. Some Khasi carry umbrellas almost as an extension of their arms. Most, though, walk through the downpours with boat-shaped wicker baskets hung from their heads and down their backs, keeping the worst of the rain off them. They look like turtles scurrying about on their hind legs, the shells bouncing under assault from the hammering raindrops.

Mawsyngram itself lies at the very edge of the escarpment up which I had been slowly climbing. It is about a mile high, and to its south a great limestone cliff falls suddenly away to the plains of Bangladesh—the cliff being the reason that so much of the world's rain falls here.

It is all very elementary, and obvious: monsoon clouds lumber in from the Bay of Bengal, they sweep majestically (but dryly) over the estuaries and the rice-paddies, and are then suddenly confronted by this impenetrable wall of limestone rock. The clouds rise—remember this from school—in an effort to surmount it, they cool as they try to do so, and then presto!, the rain they have held for so long spills wildly down onto the land below, drenching it without cease for as long as the monsoon winds are blowing.

A few miles from Mawsyngram is a village called Suraj—the British for some reason called it Cherra, and added the Khasi word *punji*, which means village— thus was born the name Cherrapunji, which most schoolchildren have long known as the world-famous record holder for being the wettest place in the world. (Americans, however, like to claim that the Waialeale Swamp on the summit of the island of Kauai, in Hawaii, holds the record for wetness: leaving aside the rather more pleasurably romantic claim—at least to an Englishman for whom India is a second home—of a clifftop in the East, statistics show the backers of Hawaii, close though they may be, are plain wrong.)

Cherrapunji long had ample reason for laying claim to the record. One day in 1876, they say, the village had no less than forty-one inches of rain—enough rainfall to submerge the average Cherrapunji child, and still the wettest downpour ever known in a single day in the history of the world. But now, since Mr.

Sharma has been the peon in charge at Mawsyngram, and has been doing some close observing for long periods of time over there, so things have changed.

That one spectacularly damp Assamese day aside, in terms of unremitting rainfall over a season, the village of Cherrapunji has now been forced to move over. The figures sent down by Mr. Sharma from Mawsyngram are truly daunting.

I found him down at the village Public Works Depot, amid a jumble of rusty buckets and wrecked tractors and broken-down buildings perched on the very edge of the cliff. He was wearing shorts and black rubber gumboots, and he carried a beaten-up umbrella frayed from countless storms (or maybe it had been brand-new that morning, so fearful is the weather here). He was on his way, as it happened, to the rain recording station—a cylinder of aluminum set in the ground and which, during the night, had filled up with rainwater. Small wonder. It was pouring. It had been pouring for hours. It felt as though it had been pouring, unremittingly, for years. The skies were black, the wind gusted, lightning crackled, and water tumbled unceasingly out of the sky. Small wonder, once again, that the little cylinder was brimming.

So I watched a small piece of history being made—as Mr. Sharma picked his way through the mud, drained the water from the tube into a tall glass measuring vessel, and then squinted at the point where the meniscus butted against a number. He yelled it out in Bengali, over the lashing of the storm, to a young boy who sheltering nearby—for even peons have lesser peons, in so socially structured a land as India—who wrote it with a broken ball-point pen into a large and dog-eared blue exercise book.

How much? I asked.

"In millimeters," he replied, "five hundred and ten. Twenty inches. Since this time yesterday. Not too much."

But to an outsider it was a staggering figure, in and of itself. Mawsyngram gets a routine 20 inches in a day: London, damp old London, gets only a little more than that in an entire year. New York gets a little more, thirty-odd inches, San Francisco a little less. But more than one and a half feet of rain for this village, during the hours one fairly unspectacularly ordinary monsoon day?

Maybe this was an aberration, a fluke, something staged for a visitor? How much yesterday?, I called to the damply cheerful Mr. Sharma. He shouted back at me through the storm: 19 inches the day before, 21 the day before that. This whole month—about two hundred inches, give or take. The whole year—maybe nine hundred or so. Let's call it eighty feet. (I looked in the blue exercise book later. It was on the 24th August 1988 that the most rain had fallen recently—530 mm, or 21 inches. 1988 was the year when, with something approaching thirty feet of accumulated rainfall for the year, and Mawsyngram coming in at eighty-odd, old Cherrapunji was forced to move over. It was the day when the keeper of rain gauge up at the summit of Kauai that also makes those occasional American claims, had to realize that he too had met his match.)

And Ram Krishna Sharma was the man responsible. "Well, not for the rain," he chided gently. "I just send in the figures. I send them off to Shillong, then once a year I suppose they go to Delhi, and then I imagine Delhi sends them to somewhere else. London, I suppose. Maybe New York. Whoever is interested gets my figures."

"My figures too," said the small boy, chirpily.

"You be quiet," said Mr. Sharma, and raised his hand. The boy splashed off, laughing.

But, I asked—was Mr. Sharma aware that Mawsyngram now enjoyed, and as a result of his thankless, endlessly dampening work, a distinction above all other places in the world.

"I sometimes hear things. People say I should be famous. But really, I am just doing my job as peon here," was all he said. "That keeps me very busy. That, and trying to keep myself dry." And he put up his ragged old umbrella, went splashing off through the mud, and invited me home for tea. "But no milk, I am afraid" he said. "The milk lorry is stuck in the mud. None for a week, they say. One of the joys of living with all this rain."

# In Gurus' Realm, Pen Is Mightier Than the Laptop

**Anne Cushman**

*A journey among spiritual seekers in India finds that there are higher powers than a PowerBook.*

AT THE BEGINNING OF A FIVE-MONTH TRIP through India to research a guidebook for spiritual seekers, I pictured myself filing dispatches from the Himalayas for Yoga Journal's Web site: I'd just whip out my laptop from its custom-fit pocket on the flap of my backpack, fire up the solar-charged batteries and plug my fax-modem into the jack at the corner of my cave. Or better yet, I'd trot my floppy down to the local Cyber-Chai shop, where my data would flow by satellite to the Net, while I smoked some Shiva-weed with the resident yogi.

Before I left, I spent several productive hours in electronic stores, pondering the problems associated with plug adapters, surge suppression and ungrounded outlets. ("The best thing to do," the salesman advised me when I told him that most Indian outlets are two-pronged and ungrounded, "is to carry with you a seven-foot copper pole.") I then bought a special insurance policy to protect my equipment from the ravages of the road, becoming a bit alarmed to read the list of hazards *not* covered by it, which ranged from "insect damage" to "nuclear accident" to "wars and revolutions"—clearly, someone had thought through the possibilities more thoroughly than I had. But by the time I boarded the plane for Bombay—my computer case lashed with bungee cords to the top of my backpack—I was confident that technology would triumph.

At the very first ashram I went to, I tested the grounding apparatus for my surge suppressor, a custom-made arrangement involving alligator clips and the cold-water pipe in the bathroom. Fortunately, the ensuing electrical fire was confined to the immediate vicinity of my plug; the ashram's main fuse blew, but the Bombay electrician who came to fix it was really quite kind about the whole thing. "Some person," he said, studying the blackened remnants of my surge suppressor, "was not giving you very good advice."

Shaken but still optimistic, I repacked my bags and headed for the bus station, where it quickly became apparent that my load (which had seemed quite manageable when I walked it from my bedroom to my living room back in California) was more unwieldy than I had anticipated. Sure, the main unit was only 3.3 pounds, but throw in two spare batteries, a floppy drive and adapter, power supply, floppy disks and my new and improved 220-volt surge suppressor, and you're talking 10 more pounds to a load already burdened with such necessities as a binder full of guru data, a yoga mat, a six-month supply of contact lens solution and a breadloaf-size tub of spirulina. You're also talking a potential $3,000 loss to worry about. I might as well have been hauling diamond-studded barbells.

I tottered on shaky legs through the heaving, shoving, sweaty, shouting crowds, barely mobile enough to dodge the outstretched leprous arms of the beggars. Resisting the bus driver's entreaties to let him tie my precious pack to the roof, I squeezed it on board, wedged it in front of my seat and rode for 10 hours with my knees folded up around my chin. Looking around the bus, I didn't feel as if my luggage was excessive. At least it didn't cackle, bleat or excrete.

Late that afternoon, I arrived in Pune in western India, home of the Osho Commune, founded by the guru Bhagwan Shree Rajneesh. With my oversize pack bulging out the side of an auto rickshaw, I rode through a thick soup of traffic fumes, watching grim, dingy bullocks dragging their carts through the gridlock. A white horse trotted past, saddle empty but pulling a bicycle with three men perched on the crossbar.

I spent that night in a bamboo hut on stilts, which pitched like a boat at sea whenever the man in the next room rolled over, dislodging a gentle rain of insects and decayed palm leaves from the thatched ceiling. I thought of the images I wanted to record from my day of travel: The glowing eyes of the legless man who pushed himself with his hands across the bus station floor, offering shoeshines. The dog who was run over and bled to death in the gutter near the ticket counter in a sludge of sewage and betel-juice spit, and his mate, who sat by his body, her nose tipped upward, and howled.

But the room, of course, had no electrical outlets. My Powerbook sat in its dusty bag in the corner, as overqualified and useless as a Ph.D. at an orgy.

By morning, I knew it was time to let the computer go. I gave it to an Indian friend for safekeeping and bought a ruled notebook with pages already coming unglued and a picture of beefy, snarling wrestlers on the cover. India, it seemed, didn't want to be captured electronically. She wanted to be scratched and scribbled into increasingly tattered pages, where she would remain illegible, mysterious and largely unretrievable.

Actually, writing by hand wasn't bad, I discovered. There's an intimacy, an immediacy to handwritten words scrawled into a notebook, the shape and angle

**79**

of their letters reflecting the moment and mood in which they were written. As I flip thorough the travel-stained pages, I viscerally recall the places where I filled them. One whole books smells of camphor from the ancient Shiva temple at the foot of Mount Arunachala (a mountain so spiritually potent that even to think of its name is said to guarantee a favorable rebirth). Another's pages are smeared with the sweet peanut candy I ate in an ashram by the banks of a southern lake full of crocodiles, where at night I'd hear the coughing roars of lions.

And occasionally, I did manage to fax in a handwritten dispatch for the Web site, like the one I sent from the holy city of Rishikesh, in the foothills of the Himalayas, where the Ganges River—revered by Hindus as a goddess incarnate—descends from the mountains to the plains. Across from the fax booth, a sadhu (a wandering ascetic) sprawled sleeping in the shade of a wooden mango cart, his beard dyed pink as a party dress from festival celebrations. A cow stood next to him, eyeing the mangoes and dreamily eating the business section of a discarded Times of India.

Before inserting the first page into the feeder, the fax-wallah folded his hands in prayer and made a quick bow of supplication in the direction of the fax machine (a gesture I found alarming, in that it suggested that the notoriously fickle gods were more reliable than the telecommunications technology). When, after six failures, we did get that moon-landing sound indicating electronic contact, the triumph was short-lived. The reassuring digital shriek was quickly replaced by total silence, and a printout informed us that there had been a "communications error"—information for which, like a couples counselor, it presented a bill.

Finally, my fax went through, one tortuous page at a time. With each apparently successful transmission, the machine spit out a receipt printed with "O.K." Unconvinced, I handed over a wad of rupees sufficient to keep me fed and housed in India for a month; then I went into the street and down the steps of the nearest bathing ghat, to sit by the goddess Ganga, swift-running, cold and bottle-green.

An old man with a walking stick descended the steps next to me; with each thump of his cane he muttered the name of Ram. "Feed fish, Auntie?" asked a little girl in a ragged dress, shaking a plastic bag of pellets in my face. "One rupee only?"

A white-haired woman in a faded purple sari tossed a handful of marigolds into the water; she stood with her hands in prayer position, her lips moving silently, then tossed in the plastic bag the marigolds came in, and turned away.

The pink-bearded sadhu, awakened from his nap, came toward me down the steps. "Hari om, Madame," he said, his begging bowl courteously outstretched. "God is everything. You agree?"

# Another Culture Bites the Dust

## Doug Fine

*Suriname opens its rain forest after a civil war, but leaves a journalist wondering, what does eco-tourism really mean, anyway?*

SOME PEOPLE ENTER A NEW JOB BLINDLY, some a relationship. I dove into a Continent backwards and with crossed fingers, having progressed far enough in my admittedly procrastinated background research on Suriname before my departure to hear something about a Native Uprising in the small nation of 377,000 north of Brazil. Supplemental research was provided care of some *New Yorker*-reading friend of the family, who had told my father, and which he had subsequently reminded me daily via voice mail until I left, that "life was cheap" there.

So it shouldn't have been surprising, I suppose, when, some eleven hours after arrival in capital Paramaribo last September 9, our ragtag bunch of travel agents, journalists, and an acrophobic would-be photographer landed, after a single prop flight a few hundred feet over a shockingly undisturbed rain forest canopy, on a grass "airstrip" that had been recently (I received no answer when I suggested the previous day) hacked out of the jungle somewhere in the South-center of Suriname's almost roadless interior. But when we were greeted by an armed and almost naked tarmac crew composed of members of a cultural group known in Suriname as the Bush Negro (or maroon) society, I quickly found my, in retrospect, hastily-arrived at impression that I was into some kind of cushy "Familiarization" tourism industry trip, evolved as if by mutation into "Some Undetermined Thing Completely Different, and A Lot More Real." My eyes were wired open for the rest of the fortnight, my mental "play and record" button fully depressed. At first I was too absorbed in the overwhelming inputs affecting me a few air hours outside of Miami to devote much energy to traveling companions, it was clear even at this early stage, who weren't prepared for a trip to Yosemite.

But then I realized that perhaps more of a journalistic story, if not a culture shock, just one day out of McDonalds range, than the Bush Negroes, was the crew of ours which comprised this government-sponsored, eco-tourism "Fam Trip." It was one which would have put to shame, present company included, I must admit, if in law enforcement rather than the travel business, the Keystone Cops. I glanced around the airstrip, where our photographer (actually a real estate agent from Maryland who had decided that the recent purchase of three Very Expensive Cameras entitled her to bill herself to the Surinamese Government as "*National Geographic* Correspondent,"—she explained to me later she had "contacts," but I noticed she wore glasses) had calmed down a bit after a flight during which she had problems. Pausing only to scream, "no one will insure me!" she had hyperventilated and moaned loudly through the entire flight. While I sympathized with her neurosis and related all-too-well to her perhaps oddly-stated gripe with the health care establishment, I had never seen such a manifestation of symptoms. Even one of our guides, a member of Suriname's Ministry of Tourism, had given me what I considered cause to watch him carefully, ever since those disconcerting moments in the shuttle van the previous evening at the airport when he had to surreptitiously siphon gasoline, orally and despite his three piece suit, from a neighboring Daihatsu, for which he apologized in Dutch when he saw me glancing out the window at him with a Puzzled Victorian expression on my face. He explained something about Suriname's weak and constantly devalued currency that was contributing to a tragic and atypical fuel shortage.

I was immediately grateful for the upturned and clearly not-belligerent expressions on the faces of some of the younger members of our welcoming committee at the airstrip, since I was unarmed, and not one of them, it was clear, spoke Surinamese, Dutch nor, need I add, English. I chose to interpret the smiles as a universal sign of peaceful intentions. (The Dutch colonizers called Suriname's Creole blend of Papiamento, various African dialects, Hindustani *lingua franca* and Dutch, "Taki-Taki," which local intellectuals consider a First World Insult. Herein I refer to the preferred "Surinamese." Suriname's Maroons and Amerindians have their own languages.)

While I helped unload our supplies for the next week in the rain forest, our one guide who did speak the Bush Negro language Sranan Tonga (or this Central Region dialect of it), one of the world's brilliant men and Suriname's Chief Librarian, Stanley Powers, was saying something to a large, be-tattooed man who appeared to be in charge. Both were pointing over at me and the rest of the sensory overloaded group, and immediately after a staccato pronouncement by the Large Man, everyone not fully clothed began to laugh, hard. I broke into exaggerated hysterics as well, as if I understood the whole scam, which seemed to unnerve everybody, especially my fellow tour group members, and one native woman hid her child behind her hip.

"We're off to the Neptune Island Resort," Stanley said in his interesting and unidentifiable accent, careful not to linger on that last word. Everything was happening so fast. "Let's hop into the dugout canoe."

**82**

Despite Stanley's efforts, I couldn't help dwelling on his choice of the moniker "resort." One member of our crew, a travel agent from Missouri named Barry whose behavior since the terminal in Miami had revealed him to be an impressively perfect manifestation of the quintessential Ugly American, was already sweating profusely down his third or fourth chin, madly swatting non-existent mosquitoes in a panicky manner, and asking Sandy, the Real Estate Agent cum International Wildlife Photographer, how he was supposed to "sell hell" to his construction company-owning clients? (She, meanwhile, bundled despite triple-figure heat in her Banana Republic-issue jungle outfit which could have kept her warm above the Arctic Circle on a zero-daylight evening of Northern Lights, was partially stuffing the Very Expensive Cameras into zip lock bags to ensure, as far as I could figure, that if they got wet, they'd stay wet.)

By the dugout canoes, Barry was holding up the proceedings, fishing around in his over-stuffed Army-issue duffel bag for some bug spray or malaria medicine or something, while asking Stanley if there was anything he could do about the humidity. It was 8:15 a.m. Zaftig boxer shorts and several bags of butterscotch candy were strewn haphazardly on the thorny airstrip floor.

Not for the last time I wished Stanley had made the week's itinerary a little clearer a little earlier. Or better yet, that G.E. Mitchell and Associates, the well-respected South Florida travel company that had been granted the "exclusive marketing rights" for eco-tourism in Suriname by the quasi-official tourism agency called METS (Movement for Eco-tourism in Suriname), had used some kind of better, perhaps NASA-approved screening system for the advance team it chose to cut the ribbon on tourism in Suriname, rather than accepting anyone whose company was willing to fork over $450. I had been at *Sierra* Magazine, just out of college, and happened upon the G.E. Mitchell brochure for the trip. Near the part about "opening up the country so the outside world can see some of the warmest-hearted people" or similar phrasing, all the *Sierra* editors had signed off on the offer with notes like, "too close to deadline for me" and "gotta pass: my Aunt's gall stone operation is in September." I scooped up the folder on a whim, asked, and Jonathan King, then the Editor-in-Chief, bless him, looked up from his wine magazine for a second and said, "Hmm? Sure. Go."

Discussing METS' ownership with a member of its executive board is a bit of a dizzying circular journey. METS was originally a government-controlled company which was recently privatized, so says its literature, "according to national policy initiatives" (whatever that means). Suriname Airways, itself partly government-owned, has a strong minority interest in METS. Suriname itself isn't quite sure what kind of government it has.

One conversation on METS financial structure with Amil Gopi, a METS executive, went something like this: I, puzzled, asked, "You still consider your-

**83**

self privatized, even though you're owned by Suriname Airways which is itself a government entity?" "Of course," Emil said, handing me a tall Pina Colada spiked with the fine local Borgoe rum, for which I might soon be the sole US importer. "You see, now the government merely has a majority interest in our organization. They used to own the whole thing, without even bothering with a deed."

I was already learning volumes about the country from the guides. With an area of roughly 60,000 square miles (picture North Dakota without the blizzards for a size comparison), Suriname's pristine environmental situation might actually have, despite the carnage, the country's decade-long internal strife to thank for its preservation. While much of the rest of the tropical world saw a 1980s filled, much like the 70s before it, with the worst kind of short-sighted ecological rape—headlines touted (and tout) the environmental and cultural problems resulting from rain forest destruction in places like Ecuador and Brazil—Suriname was either quietly ignored or looked at as a dangerous investment. The war's international quietness, as you probably have not noticed, since it was ignored by the American media, is likely the result of the familiar no-oil, no Communists, no press situation. Now the presumably stable republic headed by a President Venetiaan arising from the ashes has the unprecedented opportunity to use the lessons of an environmentally and socially bleeding South America to its advantage. Whether it will go to school remains to be seen.

Based on what was proving to be the pleasantly "undeveloped" status of tourism in Suriname, no, of Suriname itself, I decided right on the spot that if there was a "resort" on this Neptune Island, one that even approached meeting Webster's Dictionary Definition of same, I would eat Barry's hat AND believe what the flight attendant on the Miami flight had told me about Lotoya Jackson. It occurred to me that Stanley uttered the "R" word with the same wry humor that the customs man at the Paramaribo airport explained "official exchange rate." I was to get used to that soft-spoken world-wise Surinameses humor. And these were the people trying to convince the American travel industry and journalists (and poseurs pretending to be same) that this was a Destination (to use the industry jargon).

\* \* \*

We cast off, after considerable difficulty loading the human end of the canoe's cargo, on the Gran Rio, close to geographic Central Suriname about 335 miles South of Paramaribo, 1800 miles South of Miami, and 20 light years away from my expectations, heading South.

An hour and a half later our 40 HP Johnson outboard-driven 24 foot dugout "arrived"—the bird-startling engine being the first of many cultural paradoxes which I noted the arrival of tourism in Suriname is precipitating—and cut into neutral somewhere in the Amazon Basin which our second guide, John Goede, Suriname's number one tennis pro and would-be Playboy, told us was Neptune Island. Except for a few palm thatched huts (our resort?) it looked like every other three-acre island we had cruised past during a pleasant morning spent mostly scaring toucans and spider monkeys into frothing neurotic frenzies. But who was I to argue? I wasn't even in possession of the machete, so I squished the lid back on any mutinous thoughts.

All the initial stress—if not the confusion—was soon to permanently dissipate, with some minor gastro-intestinal exceptions, for the remainder of the week. As we emptied off of the canoe unsteadily onto the beach (one Nikon lens had already gone swimming), to a person a puzzled bunch, I couldn't help noticing a sizable red cooler languishing appealingly on a bamboo "bar," inside the closest thatched hut.

"Beer!" a large blur screamed, pushing past me as I tried to help a bleary-eyed, sea-sick Barry off of the canoe. It had been Seth and Craig, who you might call Professional Familiarization Tour Attendees, and who had seemed, up until this point, to linger perpetually at the back of our loud, wildlife-antagonizing pack, except when avians or alcohol came into view: both Vietnam Vet Oregonians were of that strange breed: Serious Bird Lovers. They had horrifying war stories of "ears strung on belts representing each kill" and in Paramaribo Craig informed me I would "get over" my aversion to paying for sex. Over the next eight days, they proceeded to drink, on average (I kept losing count), roughly twenty Heinekens a day, courtesy of a Surinamese Government so poor that we donated batteries in the name of international cooperation at the end of the trip. I'll say one thing for the former-Dutch colony: we may have run low on food, gotten sick, and had run-ins with electric eels and tarantulas, not to mention receiving the Most Bizarre Lecture in the History of Biology, but they kept the Heineken flowing, cold, no matter how deep into the jungle we went. Somebody had hammered home to out hosts a Very Important Point about Americans. About tourism in general. They might just get it right after all.

Spirits were lifting, beers were "phoosh!"ing: we were in the middle of a shady stand of rain forest, a crew of maroon women lined up professionally by the bar, introduced by Stanley as the "Resort Staff." Neptune Island, we were told, was completely owned and operated by the folks who lived in this, well, literally, this neck of the woods. The huts, if sparse, or not up to "resort" standards in the States, were certainly clean, and more than adequate for the purposes of anyone who would travel this far: to view undisturbed tropical rain forest flora and fauna in a sparsely-populated, barely-visited area. I was looking forward to my first evening in a hammock (and have since bought one in a vain to attempt to recapture "The Atmosphere"). Stanley explained that the site is completely self-sufficient and non-waste generating. The two out-houses drain in a pit sufficient for fifteen years use, fifty yards into the forest and away from the water table. Any non-biodegradable waste (i.e., Heineken cans) is to be brought out on a canoe before the next visitors come in.

The site only accommodates twelve people (a big plus), and one hut is specif-ically designated for lovers ...

Stanley was giving his official welcoming speech, about two days late for Barry, but I was trying to listen despite being dazzled, as anyone who has vis-ited the Amazon Basin will understand, by the jungle and its sights and sounds. It really did sound like the mix for a Tarzan movie. I wound up pick-ing up tidbits of what he was trying to get across, which I think qualifies as the "gist of it."

"Welcome to Suriname. Eco-tourism is just getting a start here, you are the first outside visitors to Neptune Island, which was four years in the building. Suriname's last year of significant tourism was 1981, before 'the troubles.' We recognize the potential of this land and we are trying to market it. There is so much space here so far unused, it seems to go on forever."

Uh oh, I didn't like the sound of this. The Amazon Basin, at the dawn of the 21st Century, can no longer be spoken of as "going on forever," not even metaphorically, and this whole marketing talk, while perhaps *de rigeuer* for those in the travel business, made me bristle slightly. Stanley turned out in the end to be as ecologically-aware as anyone I've ever met, and if tourism beats the odds and remains sustainable in Suriname, it will be largely due to his—and a few others'—efforts. He has the government's ear, although exactly who is really in charge in Suriname is not totally clear. Our passports were stamped by two dif-ferent military organizations, but the resolution of internal strife is supposedly indicated by the advent of Venetiaan's republican government.

"We're all here, and we've asked you here, to sell a product," Stanley continued.

"Damn!" Barry flicked at a large fly which had landed in his beer.

"Please, we encourage you," Stanley said again in his hypnotizing accent that made you just listen to the sounds, not the words, "we implore you to make any suggestions you might have as to how we can best market eco-tourism in our forests."

"Good God," I thought, looking around at our swarthy, perspiring group. "He'd be better off getting advice from Gary Hart's 1984 campaign publicity team." Then Something Big started to make sense: is this how cabinet members and CEOs are chosen? From artful, moldable believers? People who could get to Suriname from Missouri, almost for free, with an open bar to boot?

Yes, Barry did bear a vague similarity of facial structure to John Mitchell.

**86**

Sandy, who was snapping endless photographs of tree bark in that deep virgin territory 12 feet from the hut where Stanley was speaking, could, in the right light, be said to resemble Jean Kirkpatrick. I don't even want to think who Seth and Craig reminded me of, but their ideas about truthfulness certainly seemed political: Seth owned a travel agency in Portland. OK, I thought, he qualifies for a Fam Trip solicited from within the travel business. Craig's chief qualification, however, seemed to be that he was Seth's friend. He was a portly and intelligent computer programmer who put down "Audubon Society" on his trip attendee profile. "Hey, I'm a member," he said defensively, pulling out a card in some other name, when I kidded him about it. He kept asking our guides if anyone had yet secured the contract for installing the fiber optics network in Suriname's phone system. I wish I could recreate the looks he received as response. I liked these two guys, for their well-traveled jaded views on Life and Love. Craig, after the "grow out of" ethical problems with "paying for love" conversation, later confessed to four failed marriages.

Then there was Felice, the Septuagenarian travel editor who proudly admitted to not paying her writers (I thought how hungry the piranhas in these parts must get). Also among our crew was the trip leader Phyllis, an environmentally-aware old school Republican (the exception that proves the rule) who, from the quantity of her stories, evidently really loves her grandchildren. She was a genuinely warm lady, who served as the liaison between Gerry Mitchell, the Surinamese Government and ... whoever the hell we were.

I really didn't even want to conjure up the image of the discussions the guides had about us after we left. All of us were, I think it's safe to say, to varying degrees, somewhat unconventional, and several were downright crazy. I wonder what the Surinamese Tourism Bureau was thinking when G.E. Mitchell faxed their office that some "travel business experts" from the States would be coming down to evaluate their nascent projects? I mean, this is a sovereign nation's future we're talking about.

Stanley was still talking, but I missed the rest of the speech as two young kids, children of the staff, had found the life jacket cache down by the canoe and were gesturing me to show them how to put them on. We spent a few hours shooting the rapids in the Awarradam Falls downstream a bit, and I've since written to President Venetiaan, suggesting that this version of tropical body surfing be named the National Sport. With Gerry Mitchell and Associates' skill at creative marketing, will an Olympic event be far behind? Especially in this era of Planetary Sensitivity ...

After a lunch of processed-meat sandwiches, we got our first taste of ecotourism. The "jungle walk" was to last two hours, which, considering the heat even under the canopy, seemed plenty to me, but Craig was complaining that the best hours for birding were those just before sunrise.

Our local native guide from the Neptune area, whose name I don't think I could represent phonetically in Phoenician-derived characters, was quite knowledgeable about the medicinal qualities of the plants (evidently the Amerindians of the region taught the escaped slaves "Flourishing in the Rain Forest 101," from roof-thatching techniques to canoe building). He showed us, via John's translation, an *Aspidosperma marcgravianum* tree, known as "the telephone system of the jungle," whose tubular, ectomorphic bark issues a thunderously hollow resounding sound when struck with a heavy rock, or in these heady days, a machete's blunt side. A useful locator: apparently even the locals get lost in *la selva*. I noticed that John had to keep chastising our guide in Surinamese for taking gratuitous hacks with the machete at plants, trees, and termite nests not directly in our path, and he noticed I noticed. In rationalizing to me behavior which hadn't bothered me, he explained that if the people who live here are going to comprise the infrastructure of the tourism economy, and therefore benefit from the presence of outsiders rather than suffer the usual exploitation and cultural genocide precipitated by the immediate progression through three or four centuries, they'll have to learn about the concept of sustainable practices and low impact visits. "This takes time," he said, adding, "These people have all they need within a mile of their home, with no population pressure. They can't understand why we want to alter the path every year, to allow the vegetation to return." His *ex loco parentis* attitude aside, the comments made sense. I also noticed and didn't know what to make of the guide's Chicago Bulls tee-shirt, however, and made a mental note to keep my eyes open for evidence of, let's call it "McCultural Assimilation," that the presence of people like me, combined with Suriname's desperate need for currency that has a little bit of gold behind it, was inflicting and will continue to inflict upon this basin. It was very difficult indeed, to connect Wall Street realities with the long-term health of the creeping vines, steaming massive palms, lazy electric blue butterflies, more than one type of conscious monkey and birds-of-paradise by which I was surrounded. It did seem to go on forever. I had to keep reminding myself that I knew better.

It took the next four or five days to hash out, and from my interpretation of a nasty conversation between Stanley and the village Chief, I think there might still be payments involved, but I evidently came one dance away from being married to a Bush Negro girl of about sixteen rainy seasons that first evening in the jungle. Evidently three's the limit, but I, of course, had no way of knowing. It had all started off with a spectacularly harrowing dugout canoe ride in the dark from Neptune Island to the maroon village of Kayana some three miles north along the river near where we had landed several lifetimes ago. The ride was one which was supposed to net a view of some river alligators and bats, and which had, thanks to our helmsman's instinct-only avoidance of obstacles like protruding boulders and fallen trees, left Barry muttering and viciously slapping at his leg from his seat in front of me in the canoe. (The loading of the canoe without insult to guests was, I noted, a troubling moment all week for the guides: the weight had to be distributed wisely in the massive burned out tree trunk/river vessel to prevent capsizing. Words were therefore carefully chosen in suggesting where Barry and Felice, themselves plus Sandy's cameras equal to the poundage of the rest of the group and gear combined, should position themselves in the canoe. In any culture, so much of what we say to one another is designed to deceive or prevent either the speaker or listener's humiliation.)

Soon after our arrival at Kayana village, without briefing as usual (which I had to admit lent a pleasantly amusing element of spontaneity to the proceedings throughout the week, especially with regard to people who had never slept in anything less modern than a Sheraton and to whom cultural contact meant room service), the village matriarch, again with Stanley as translator, explained that the women of the place were going to demonstrate *Seketi Ku Mao*, a traditional form of ritualized group dancing. The series of three minute dances featured a soloist postulating on the difficulties of life: a man whose interest wanes after lovemaking, a border guard in French Guyana who won't let her cross to visit family members, you know, the usual. In the background while the lead lady chanted and performed a complicated hip-swaying tap dance, the chorus of women in the back would echo her in dense harmony while bent at the hips toward the ground and clapping to hold the rhythm. Evidently the clapping, Stanley explained, was a form of communication during slave times. Clueless masters would think the ritual mere entertainment, while a certain Morse-code-like sequence would indicate the location of a secret meeting, a tid bit of gossip, or the Previous Night's Letterman Top 10.

Some of the songs still had slave/master type themes. The translated chorus of one of the more contemporary songs stuck with me: "You can shoot a man into space, but you still can't reach God."

Fine so far. The trouble started when some teenage boys brought in the congas and demonstrated a complicated kind of stick dance whereby a young man would surf to the music on a dance floor of two thin horizontal logs held aloft and gyrated three feet off the ground by his friends. The matriarch, whose name was repeated for us over the course of the night, but remained so unpronounceable to me that I couldn't even begin to repeat the first seven syllables of it, let alone jot some kind of educated guess down in my notebook in the dark, could see that the African groove had caught some of us: Phyllis, Seth and I were rocking slightly to the rhythm on our benches. On her command, several young women began to grab first my, then Craig's, then a shocked and paralyzed Barry's hand and bring us onto the ad-hoc dance floor in the middle of the hut.

Suddenly, all hell proceeded to break loose as the rest of the village, which had crowded around the large meeting-hut's three foot "walls," filtered in with a fit of universal commiseration to join the spontaneous party. This, in turn, inspired the drummers to extend and intensify their jams, and the playing got louder. Torches were lit and bodies swayed. Craig was spinning around a support beam by one arm. When he whirled within earshot, I yelled, "I'd pay a $3 dollar cover charge for a bar scene like this in San Francisco!" Any time I tried to sit down for a breather, the same attractive, well-built young woman kept roaring up to me within seconds, beaming, and yanking me back onto the dance floor with an arm strength I couldn't have resisted if I had wanted to. And she danced what I can only determine to be the Surinamese version of "close." After three "songs," in like pattern, some women around the perimeter began to yell what sounded like, from the cackling laughter, encouragement to us. Sensing something, I can't honestly say trouble, I sauntered over in my best nonchalant *Saturday Night Fever* Groove (like Woody Allen in the disco scene of *Play it Again Sam*) to Stanley, who was wrapped up with a girl of his own, to ask him to translate the comments for me. When he heard what the women were yelling, his smile disappeared instantly, and he started rounding up the group quickly for the canoe. "Time to go," was all he would say, in an unusually brusque tone. He clapped three times to get an entwined Craig's attention.

When we had all lumbered down clumsily to the canoe under the stars, Stanley explained to me, a little late, I thought, and thus according to pattern, about the number of individual dances one can share with a lady without giving ... a little more, and we made a Bee-line for Neptune Island, despite my assertion that such distinctions were probably not binding internationally, not without a blood test, and my opinion (a sentiment shared by most of the men in the group, even Barry, who had found a partner of his own, and several of the women), that we should not be such poor guests, and owed our hosts a return to the party at least for a few more dances. Sandy looked over at me from the front of the canoe in a face that, even in the dark, was molded into an "I think I'm funny" scowl, and yelled, "What would mom say, Doug?" I felt like tossing another of her Nikons to the Caymans, in the name of cosmic justice, and had to hold my arm back, literally, from doing so, but I guessed, correctly, that by the end of the week she would manage to damage the bulk of her equipment unaided. That night, my first full one in a hammock (you can do anything in them, a winking John-the-Playboy Guide had told me), I was rocked to bed by a lullaby of haunting howler monkeys, and slept better than I had in months.

Day two proceeded without any new developments, except that a few of us noticed, and John subsequently admitted, that we were already running low on food and would soon have to rely on local fare which, in an Authentic-jungle-experience kind of way, was a change I welcomed. By the end of the trip, I had sampled more than my fill of *Pom*, sort of a Surinamese staple, made from a heavily-seasoned root similar to a potato, wrapped in leaves and baked. Interestingly, for breakfast in both Suriname's interior and the city, people snack on this ubiquitous rolls that look and taste suspiciously like bagels. Sure enough, Stanley the Almanac confirmed that the Jewish minority of the country, attracted to Dutch-controlled territories in colonial times for their periodic lapses in the persecution facing them in Europe and elsewhere in the New World, had introduced the bread to the country, with predictable results.

After a morning swim on Day three, the weather turned menacingly, and soon after we loaded the canoe for the next destination, Suriname's longest-established resort called Kumalu, we were dumped upon by rain spirits that acted as if this was their last chance. Barry was complaining to Stanley that the brochure had advertised this as the dry season, and our navigator was madly baling water with a half coconut shell. By the time we made it the six full throttle-hours downstream from Neptune to Kumalu, we were Truly Soaked, and even a little bit cold, but Craig was happy, binoculars glued to his poncho-covered face, because he had seen a pair of brilliant scarlet macaws. The rest of us weren't complaining either, thanks to an outfit of eight extremely rare giant river otters (who looked like small sea lions), who hissed at us from a log on the river bank before leaping into the river. We also got a mood-lifter care of a double rainbow three fronts away on the horizon as we drifted past the riverside village of Djumu near Kumalu.

I immediately sensed a different pervading ... element of some kind at Kumalu: the locals didn't seem as friendly, but rather more jaded, as we boated past—and they were of the subsistence hard-work lifestyle that seems so shocking to a microwave owner. The women, that is (men of young to middle age were rare, maybe ten percent; more eerie evidence of the until-recently active interior uprising that our guides were avoiding discussing). Perpetually hunched over at the waist, knee-deep in the river despite the rain, were these women, smashing clothes silently against rocks; it didn't look like an easy life.

Rather than the *nous sommes arriver!* feeling I expected as we scampered through the downpour toward the meeting hut at Kumalu (with Barry and Craig in the lead like blockers in a black and white Bears/Packers newsreel), we were instead greeted by a near empty bottle of Johnny Walker Red surrounded by several menacing faces along a bench near the perimeter of the hut. One of these men was the owner of Kumalu, a man everyone called Pappie, from the Asidinhopo Village, and even before seeing the tarantulas, I realized that we had arrived at what Seth later would dub the Chateau Idi Amin.

Although Kumalu did prove to be the least accommodating accommodations we had in Suriname (its unsanitary bathroom had Barry calling it "Uriname"), Pappie, despite his uncanny resemblance to the deposed Ugandan dictator, turned out not to be such a bad guy. Phyllis, Seth and Craig quickly stopped complaining when it became clear our host was going to keep the Heinekens flowing, on government credit, and I was thankful for the interview he had set up the following evening, which turned out to be one of the most fascinating and revealing cultural experiences I've ever had. On the one hand, my universalistic predisposition got a boost (the side of me that thinks Rodney King scenarios are symptomatic of troubling but malleable realities, not inevitable clashes of a hateful species). On the other, some of my worst visions of what "eco-tourism" in Suriname could mean for the heretofore non-McCulturized people in the interior of the jungle were solidified. What is more, the thick of it seems to be that The People Want Nintendo. And who am I to tell them they can't have it? Or shouldn't want it?

It was after sunset and another spectacular performance by the light-pollution-free Academy of Stars was beginning to rehearse when the interview took place. Stanley led us via flashlight through the jungle path to Asidonhopo to meet the Saramaccan Bush Negro elder of this part of Suriname. His title was Assistant Chief. Grandchief Songe Aboikoni was in Paramaribo at the time, for reasons of which I would later become painfully aware. It turned out to be fortuitous, indeed, that we met instead with this Mr. Amoida, a shaman and a man who said he had seen "more than 70 rainy seasons." As we approached the village, Stanley shined his light on a football-field-sized clearing, wherein, even in the dusk, we could see the burnt-out remains of a Dutch-run mission which had been torched "during the troubles." An adjacent Red-Cross hospital, the only intact European-looking building, was operational again after a six-year hiatus, according to Stanley. This was a city, for the Surinamese interior.

A man who—forgive all these celebrity tie-ins, I calls 'em as I sees 'em, and it was darkbore a resemblance to John Lee Hooker, except for the raw cloth robe, carried out an appropriate number of arched ceremonial wooden stools from his hut as we approached (Sandy later bought one from a craftsman in Asidonhopo, insisting on paying twice the price the guy wanted, and effectively flooding the regional currency market out of some kind of intercultural ignorance-inspired guilt). The larger of these domed affairs were reserved for married men over the age of thirty, so there was some confusion as we all shuffled for the socially-acceptable seat.

Several people in the group had questions for the assistant chief. We learned, as Stanley translated his barely-audible, whispered responses, that Bush Negro men were polygamous, and that the culture was made up of six main sub-groups which because of different traditions and the wise genetic mores that often accompany indigenous ritual rarely intermarried. The most interesting response came when Craig asked what the meaning was of the decorations above the doors of Bush Negro huts, both here and at Kayana. These kitchey adornments were intriguing: some looked typically Amazonian, with parrot feathers or canine teeth hung from beads, and the like. But several featured Coke cans punctured by sticks, or a Paramaribo flyer advertising a boxing match, cut into the shape of an ocelot. In translating Mr. Amoida's reply, Stanley editorialized: "He says they're just decorations, but I'd remind you to ask yourselves how quick you would be to reveal to a complete stranger your family's most deeply held secrets on the first night you met."

When it was my turn, I asked the Assistant Chief what he thought about the trickle of outsiders filtering like confused amnesiacs into his world, a stream that was almost certain to increase to a steady flow if tourism caught on in Suriname. I wanted to see if someone who had everything he needed, as John had earlier put it, "within a mile of the site of his birth," grasped the concept of tourism, or if he thought that we were *loco* to be here, such obvious fish out of water, so to speak. His answer and our ensuing exchange under a layer of midnight mist will stay with me for a long time:

*Amoida: I am looking forward to what tourism brings to us, because it means that we can begin to have some of the things that people have in other places.*

*DJF: What kind of things?*

*Amoida: Well, for one thing, I've always wanted to have an ATV quad runner.*

*DJF: Do you think these things will be good for the culture overall?*

*Amoida: Four Wheel Drive Vehicles? I think they will make life easier, more pleasant, and more leisurely.*

*DJF: That they undoubtedly will. I'm not the one to be telling you anything about what is the right way for you to live your life, but I can say that from my experience, the accumulation of these things, which as you may know is something of a religion where I come from, does not as a goal generally lead to a sense of fulfillment when achieved.*

*Amoida: That explains a lot. But would it hurt for us to have more? Do we need to stay frozen in time?*

*DJF: 'Need' is a hard thing to define, but in terms of negative ramifications, I'd look at, say, a car, an off-road ATV. It takes a battery. When it runs out, it gets thrown into the river the way we might throw the bones of a chicken in the river; of course, there's no place else to put the waste. Then the acid from the battery, or ten batteries, begins to poison the fish. You eat those fish, right, even the piranhas, which I've found pretty bony by the way. So, when those fish are gone, what will you eat? You could bring in food, but that means more waste, and clearing the trees to build a road. It's happened all over the world ...*

*Amoida: I understand what you're saying. I even agree. But I still want an ATV.*

*DJF: Who wouldn't?*

As we meandered as a group back to the huts at Kumalu that evening, I found myself humming a baseline by Queen, with alternate lyrics: "Another

Culture Bites the Dust." The most troubling part of the discussion to me had been Mr. Amoida's insistence, at the end of the conversation, that he intended his cultural traditions to stay intact despite whatever material changes the conversion to a market economy might entail. I remember wondering if the burnt down mission would be rebuilt as a Mini Mart. Perhaps accepting credit cards care of Craig's fiber optic system.

The rest of our stay at Kumalu was without incident, save for one near-death during our daytime tour of Asidonhopo. All I know is that most of the group was strolling through the village, and I had joined a tin can soccer game with some naked kids when we heard cackling screams erupting from what was either a very distressed or very diseased larynx on the other side of the village. We all stopped to watch, and suddenly Sandy burst into the clearing, running toward us, and cradling a tripod, a couple of cameras and a zaftig lens, with streams of film dangling behind her and dragging along the ground. A rickety old woman, the source of the cacophony, was close at her heels (surprising agility). I didn't even have to ask. Or rather Sandy should have. When it was sorted out, a renewal of just recently dormant Interior Hostilities was averted, and Sandy was instructed to seek permission before snapping photos in strangers' living rooms.

On the morning we left Kumalu, I noticed the can and bottle-style debris and oil film pollution that the Gran Rio at this mid-way point in its journey already sports from even its thus far limited connection with the Twentieth Century. A tarantula was tight roping on a discarded lollipop stick.

We had to, of course, get the full sampling of what METS hopes will be the resort network that will put Suriname on the "soft" eco-tourism Priority Destination map of the travel business—hence all the free beer. We were all getting our jungle legs, anyway, and, a few upset stomachs aside, we were ready for a new resort called Palumeu, in Caribe Amerindian territory 65 miles northeast by Surinamese military plane along the Tapanahony River. This one promised to be the most undisturbed area yet, in the hardly-explored *terra semi-cognita* which extends in the south to the barely-defined Brazilian border where miners are slaughtering so many of the locals. (Gerry Mitchell called me after I got back and said some exploratory mining excursions into South Central Suriname have showed promise, that the miners expect "a big hit." If that happens, said Mitchell, who has been to Suriname more than ten times, "forget it" for conservation.)

Barry and Sandy by now were under the mistaken impression that our forced proximity was cause for a summer camp atmosphere in which every type of unusual and mostly gastro-intestinal problem was to be shared. By discussing it over dinner, it was kind of full circle for whatever bugs were bothering them and which had somehow spared the rest of us. I found myself asking them one night, "which of this stuff made you feel this way?" But it was useless with Barry, who was a member of the Clean Plate Club nine years running from high chair to Boy Scouts. Of course, starting the next morning at dawn, I contributed about four straight meals to the fertility of the Amazonian soil, in a manner that was described by observing fisherman, through translation, as "projectile vomiting." Ah, but did I feel better afterwards. These dinners, by the way, were also the scene of one or two spontaneous Larium parties. This malaria medication (to which some strains are already becoming resistant, which really makes me think) is a mild hallucinogen, has made several people with susceptible constitutions completely lose their minds, according to my wealthy travel doctor, and we all looked forward to Wednesday, time for the weekly dose.

Palumeu didn't let me down. The palm thatched huts were still under construction and the territory was much wilder. We ran into some anaconda and an ocelot our first morning there, and it was kind of a pre-MTV sight to see two Caribe men with five foot longbows walking across a meadow before the tree line at sundown, each holding a small spider monkey by the scalp—for the evening's soup. I jogged out to introduce myself and have a look. The simians' still-open eyes looked a little too hominid for my taste, but I was in no position to argue. Stanley had reminded some of us, after the Kumalu Photo Incident, about respecting another culture's values, and he later had to put his money where his mouth was when we toured the village adjacent to the resort (the latter owned and operated by the former, probably with some kind of kickback to METS for bringing in the Gringos). A 30-ish woman, as a gesture of friendship extending beyond linguistic differences and camera lenses, offered us a pitcher full of this home brewed, horrible yucca-fermented beverage—local Miller Time. It was clear that it would be rude not to dust the thing off—a Cafe Amazonas happy hour *faux pas*. We each politely took as big a sip (only Seth a swig) as we could muster, leaving Stanley with the alcoholic equivalent of the rest of a keg at a party called extremely early on because of rain. I wish I had photos of some of the facial expressions born that afternoon, only compounded by his attempts to hide them. It was one of the most impressive and genuine manhood displays I've ever witnessed.

* * *

Joining us on this leg of the trip—he just sort of appeared on the transport plane from Kumalu, was a Grinch-looking man who turned out to be Suriname's premiere biologist and expert on bio-diversity, or "beeeodiversity," as he liked to say it (now I say it like that, too, in honor of the man who cared more about it than anyone I've met). His name was John de

Bruin, and he led our jungle excursions at Palumeu. He was kind of a medicinal herb expert, he called them "Power Plants," and was responsible for shutting us all up, so we wouldn't startle the treed ocelot.

It was his herpetology skills, however, which led to, from what I can tell—and I've looked it up—The Most Bizarre Scientific Lecture in the History of the World. Odder than cold fusion. More dubious than Star Wars. Armed with charts, a generator-powered slide presentation, and a small salamander creature we all passed around, de Bruin spent two hours of our evening on day seven lecturing about the *Cnemidopholus*, a female-only lizard from around these parts. "No one can figure out where the males are," he maintained. "Seems not one specimen has every been found." We fired our whole arsenal at him: hermaphroditic intimations, accusations of inept search teams, and politically incorrect jokes rifled the hut, all to no avail. He had an answer for everything. Oh well, the cosmos continues to expand.

For all the cultural and wildlife exposure at Palmeu, the highlight came for me on our final evening as the stars were just beginning to poke through after another smogless sunset (I gave thanks after each one, heretofore thinking them extinct). Seth, Playboy John, Phyllis, Craig and I found a spot a few miles downstream while piranha fishing that served as a kind of natural Jacuzzi. Great place to watch the constellations and patch the bones, until our Amerindian guide started shouting a warning that spelled, in any language, "Get the hell out of the water!" Seems we just missed having our party crashed by a quartet of electric eels. Two particular and perhaps non-sequiturial incidents from that evening also stick out in my mind, for some reason. One is the unbelievably difficult portage we were forced to endure when we tried to get back up a rapids section on the Tapanahony hoisting twelve feet of borrowed hardwood canoe. The other is Seth's odd statement when the guide's keen eyes saved us from the electric eels but woke him from a peaceful doze. While the rest of us were scampering gratefully for cover, the rotund computer programmer was sputtering, inexplicably, almost incoherently, with rage. "NEVER wake a sleeping Croatian!" he screamed. I'll always wonder what he had been dreaming about.

On that last morning in the interior, before the flight back to Paramaribo, I found out we were holding a round table conference intended to address Suriname's eco-tourism potential. Stanley, Palumeu's manager, the two Johns, and, specially flown in for the meeting on the plane that would take us back, METS' Managing Director, all joined in to bend our "expert" ears. By now, it was clear to everyone but the parrots that this was a free trip to South America to a bunch of dubiously-qualified North American travel agents and one difficult-to-understand subversive journalist (what was with all this, "cool, man" "chill out" and "bogus" stuff, anyway? And why had he been so offended that the Amerindians were selling irreplaceable rainforest products to "eco-tourism" visitors?) But when the schedule talks, money-hungry *Homo sapiens* listen.

This is where it is all happening, in terms of Surinamese policy, I thought to myself. It is at a few meetings like this where it gets decided if eco-tourism is going to be truly sustainable or as destructive as logging or oil drilling, both in human and environmental terms. I spoke up officially on the forest products issues and suggested that it might be better if the locals weren't encouraged to hawk rain forest derived products like the non-functional wooden bows with macaw feathers that were offered us the night before at the bar; that on a small scale it was probably no problem, but that should the levels of tourism that METS hope for become reality and the local economy becomes dependent on chopping down trees for souvenirs, it could be problematic and disruptive for everybody (I tried to hit them in the pocketbook).

But Sandy, who considered herself an environmentalist by virtue of working at her local botanical garden, retorted with a week's pent-up bitterness, "Oh, ease up, will you. Nobody needs to hear your arrogant sermons." Two days later as I was about to leave for the airport after a farewell Indonesian dinner, the last thing Stanley said to me was, "Please keep fighting for our land. We're going to need it." I looked around, but Sandy had no more equipment for me to destroy.

The events of the next 36 hours were unsettling. We flew back to Paramaribo, I with thoughts of recuperation from all my relaxing, for a short press conference. It turned out, to my surprise, that this wasn't an opportunity for me to interview government officials and learn some hard facts about policy plans. Instead, the tables were turned: we entered the lobby of the Torarica Hotel (a five-star affair with casino and pool/Jacuzzi while outside the currency was being devalued again), greeted by what was clearly the entire Paramaribo press corps. The two newspapers, some photographers, and the evening news all sent manpower. They gave us an hour to wash up before they wanted to hear about their nation's potential for recovery through jaguars and canoes. Evidently there weren't that many other pressing news stories in Paramaribo that Friday.

At this point, I was still hopeful if ambivalent about Suriname's ecological future. The only catch was, on my way up to my room, I snatched a copy of the hotel newsletter, complete with wire stories and local articles. During some quality time, I saw an article about the Grandchief who was absent during our visit to his headquarters in Kumalu. He was in Paramaribo, at Parliament. You know why? While our trip was being planned, some half a million acres of primary forest in the Western and Central part of the country were leased to an Indonesian logging interest. The whole line they were giving us about preservation-for-cash was a load of bull. I suppose I couldn't have asked them to turn the whole country into a national park, but they certainly didn't mention anything about the impending deal to us.

Later on Amil Gopi tried to placate me by insisting the "development," I love that word, was slated for an area already logged and loaded with plantations. "There's so much space out there," he told me, with a dismissing wave of an arm pointing vaguely toward the ocean and conjuring unpleasant Manifest Destiny imagery.

Consequently, I suppose I lapsed back into preach mode during the press conference, much to Sandy's chagrin. In retrospect, it must've sounded pretty presumptuous (I never got to read the resulting news articles) to stand there telling the national press corps of a country I'd been acquainted with for some nine days how to manage its land, but it was worth it just to see the look of shocked repugnance on the METS hierarchy's faces, next to the smiling countenances of Stanley and John de Bruin, the latter who held the microphone for me the whole time I was pontificating.

Especially in light of the 21 US Air Force "advisors" who were sharing our hotel with us for undisclosed purposes, I left Suriname strongly unsure of whether institutionalized eco-tourism was going to save the country's rain forest ecosystem and native people, and serve as a model for cash-strapped ecologically high-risk areas elsewhere, or serve as yet another empty rhetorical ploy in the losing battle for the planet's body and soul.

*Author's Note:* In case anyone (read: since most of us) acted on at least one occasion in a manner which he or she would rather not have revealed worldwide, the names of the Fam Tour attendees discussed in this feature have been changed.

# "I'm Going to India"

## Jay Golden

*Border crossings using the Jedhi mind trick.*

I'M GOING TO INDIA, I told the boy that led us up a dusty corridor to our room. Behind me stretched the Himalaya, high into the heavens. Ahead lay the vast Ganges basin of India. I had come to Sunali with one purpose: to leave. It was the Tijuana of Nepal, but without the fun. No dancing women or horse racing, only a plethora of Nepali knick-knacks for export across the street. Just one red-and-white striped bar held me back from continuing to India. One red-and-white striped bar, and the fact that I had no visa.

"Indian bureaucracy is thick. You'll need a visa," said Bill, an American travel veteran. Most everyone else agreed. But there was no way I was going back on that day-long bus from Pokhara to Katmandu, just to get a visa. Even if I did go back to the capital, I'd still have another 12 bumpy hours down to the border. "I'm going to India," was my simple response. The windy road to the border landed me and two new friends in the crappiest guest house I had ever seen. We coined it the "Sunali Lodge and Motorcycle Garage," reflecting the shared breakfast/tune-up area. But once I checked in, judgment day was at hand. There was no way I was going back to Katmandu, even if I had to become a motorcycle mechanic.

The border crossing was half a mile's walk. I strode slowly, filling myself with positivity. I was utterly exhausted, but this was no time for fatigue. I recalled Obi-Wan Kenobi's tactics with the "Star Wars" Storm Troopers while entering Mos Eisley. "These aren't the droids you're looking for," he had said. "These aren't the droids we're looking for," they had responded. "Move along," he had said. "Move along," they had agreed.

"I'm going to India. I'm going to India. I'm going to India," I murmured down the dusty street. Gilded busses convened in the great bus meeting place by the border. Bags of stuff passed over to India and were loaded to buses, in exchange for bundles of different things. Bags for bundles, stuff for things: trade in action. "I'm going to India," I repeated, pausing at the red-and-white-striped bar that held the chaos of India from flooding the highlands. I touched the bar, and the stoic gate guard replied with a piercing stare that followed me as I ducked into a small stone hut marked "Border."

Two lines formed under two signs, one that I couldn't read and one that said "Tourist." I joined an international slew that stood waiting with impatient glares. The fatigue of overland travel shone in their shaggy hair and ashen faces, and their colorful garb was worn and dusty. I recalled a guidebook quip stating the most prevalent disease to strike a traveler was neither cholera nor amebic dysentery, rather an ambitious tendency to hippie clothing. A portly man sat at a black metal table stamping papers and passports. On his chest was a shiny metal broach of some sort, marking his official status. His high cheek-bones were reminiscent of his mountain countrymen, though his eyes darted quickly to and fro. Five other men sat at the table playing cards; the dark, crowded room had the air of a small town barber shop. Stamp, ruffle, stamp, made the customs man. Whether German, Dutch, Aussie or Israeli, each of my predecessors had arrived with a pretty orange visa tacked into their passports. I had no such pretty orange visa, but I was going to India.

The stamping was swift, and ten minutes brought me to the head table. I tried to envision myself in India, but I had no idea what India was like. "Hello," I said, matching my face to my passport picture. "I'm going to India." Mr. Border Man looked up for an instant, then back down at his tools of bureaucracy: two hand stamps, a fountain pen, and two neatly arranged stacks of paper. "Passport," he said, without looking back. "Here is my passport," I responded, handing it over. "Visa," he requested after sifting through my passport. "Here … is my passport," I reconfirmed. He looked at me slowly, from my feet up. I reviewed some obvious truths to build my case, "There is my passport. I am American. I am going to India." "You must have visa. You must get visa in Katmandu," he responded, handing me back my passport, looking on to the five-foot English man at my flank. The small man pulled off his gold-trimmed tie-die day pack and shuffled through it. But I didn't budge. The card players hid their hands and glanced up. Behind me, two Dutch women in matching baggy pants halted their banter, as if to mark a casualty of war.

I was not shaken; I knew I was going to India. Some people, like the woman I once stood behind in a Parisian grocery store, rely on raising their voice in a bind. "Breadddd!!! I want BREAD!" She had yelled at the baffled cashier. Staying relaxed, I kept a pleasant grin on my face. "I'm going to India. I'm a student—from America—and cannot go back to Katmandu, because it is not India." How could a person who's going to India not go to India? "It is possible," I reinforced, adding the most universal phrase in the English language. "It is possible" is impossible to deny. The man bobbed his head from side to side and retorted, "It is not possible."

"Ah!" I responded joyfully, beckoning his card buddies to my cause. "As I am a student, going to India, I have an American passport!" I pointed to my name and my picture, confirming with everyone at the table. Nobody could deny that the passport was mine. "It is possible," I said, nodding slowly to the line behind me.

I knew I had him. "It is possible ... to get only a three-day visa," he responded. In an instant, I was sitting with the card players, writing a letter to "The Checkpoint." The rhythmic stamping of passports and ruffling of official documents recommenced. I received my instructions from the dealer, a gaunt, good-humored man named Mantu wearing a faded tee shirt inscribed "Honey Bee of Georgia." The card game, some derivation of Hearts, continued. I was told to explain, in writing, that serious illness made the return to Katmandu impossible, and that I must go quickly to India for medical attention. After completing this ironic task, Mantu placed my letter behind him on a six-inch stack of like documents.

"Visa fee," he whispered, thinking on a number. Baksheesh—Hindi for bribe—is calculated on a scale far beyond my mathematical abilities. "Three hundred rupees." Six bucks. I held back the bargaining reflex, sucked in my belly, and pulled the cash from my belt. I put the money on the table. Lightening fast, as if Mantu had a frog-tongue for an arm, he swept the rupees into his back pocket.

"Do not tell anyone," he said, pulling a dusty stamp from the desk drawer. I wasn't sure if he was referring to the money, the stamp, the visa, or something else entirely. "It is illegal," he finished, peering at Mr. Border Man behind the front desk. He aimed at my passport, and Ka-tong! I was going to India, for medical attention.

# The Blessing Cord

## Margie Goldsmith

*A Bhutanese lama. A special gift. Karmic correspondence.*

I WAS IN BHUTAN, a tiny kingdom wedged in between China and Tibet, about to enter the Wangchuk Hotel. Suddenly a monk stood in front of me, wearing the traditional maroon robe. He had thick black hair pulled back in a pony-tail, and looked about forty.

"Hello." He smiled delicately, covering his mouth with the end of his robe. I wondered if it was forbidden for monks to smile in public or if he was simply hiding bad teeth. Maybe he was shy.

"You are American, yes?" He spoke slowly with a slight accent, emphasizing each word distinctly.

I nodded.

"Are you just coming here to Bhutan?"

"No, I'm leaving tomorrow. I trekked to Jhomalhari."

"Ah, yes." His eyes lit up at the mention of the most sacred Bhutanese mountain in the Himalayas. "Where do you live in America?"

"New York."

"Ah, yes! New York! Would you please mail a letter for me when you return to New York?"

I hesitated. What if there was a bomb in the letter? Or drugs? From a *Himalayan monk*? His request was understandable. Bhutanese stamps are considered a valuable commodity and often are stolen right off letters in the post office.

"Okay" I said finally.

"May I come this evening and bring it to you? You are staying here, yes?" He pointed to the hotel.

What if he wasn't really a monk? What if this was a ploy to rob my room?

After a moment, I nodded.

"My name is Tsultrim Lama," he smiled, again covering his mouth with his hand. "At what time shall I come?"

**102**

"Seven," I said.

He bowed and touched his fingers together. "I come then, here, to the Wangchuk at seven o'clock, to bring you my letter."

Shortly before seven, I was heading down to the lobby for dinner, when the monk came up the steps, holding a young girl's hand.

"Hello!" He smiled. "This is my niece, Phuntsho. I wanted her to meet you."

A girl of about eight years, with eyes like black olives, extended her small hand.

"Here is the letter." The monk handed me a sealed envelope addressed to a Robert someone in Jericho, New York.

"Thanks, I'll put it in my room." I turned, but he put his hand on my arm.

"I have something for you," he said. From his robe he pulled out a necklace made of silk thread. It contained a box-stitched tassel which reminded me of the lanyards we used to make in Girl Scouts—except his was made of twelve perfectly matched red and yellow knots. "Please take this. I have blessed it for you many times. It will bring you good luck."

I put it around my neck. "Thank you so much," I said. "Is it something I should wear all the time? I mean—even in the shower?"

"No," he said. "But when you do not wear it, hang it up high and do not let it touch the ground."

At dinner everyone noticed my necklace. Keysan, one of the guides, had seen the monk leave the hotel. "He came to *see* you?" he said. "That is an honor. People come from all over to study with him. His name is Tsultrim Lama."

I fingered my necklace. "He gave this to me."

Keysan's eyes widened. "You are very lucky. That is a blessing cord."

Feeling special, I wore the necklace to bed, on the flight home and to work my first day back. I mailed the letter along with a note and my phone number, hoping that Robert somebody from Jericho could tell me more about the lama. A few days went by. The novelty of wearing the blessing cord wore off. I hung it high on a hook in my closet.

*　*　*

About a month later, I touched the blessing cord and thought about Tsultrim Lama. That same day, the phone rang. It was Robert from Jericho, calling to thank me for sending the letter. I was amazed at the coincidence. A few months later, one morning I let the silky cord run through my fingers. That day in the mail was a letter with two colorful Bhutanese stamps and a postmark from Thimphu. "Airmail" had been written in red crayon, underlined with a hand-drawn yellow, green, and blue rainbow. I carefully opened the envelope.

**103**

"My dear Margie," it began. "Here comes your friend Tsultrim Lama which we met in Wangchuk Hotel and we together talked each other and I hope you didn't forget me. My niece says hello." He went on to say he thought we had met at another time, in a different life. This was our "before action" or karma. He said he always remembered me when he did his meditation, and he prayed for my health, happiness, peace, and long life. He signed it, "with much love, yours truly friend, Tsultrim Lama."

With this second coincidence, I knew the blessing cord held some sort of magic, even though I didn't know exactly what. I wrote back, and after some time, another letter arrived: "My dear Margie, today I request you if you don't mind for my for help requesting then I would be very much grateful to you. I am doing meditation that way I am really needing some help money by my friends so please could you monthly enclose some money with my letter because it is so helpful for me what you could send me. If you can't send money then no problem. It is very important that we don't stop sending each other lovely letter. Warms regard from my niece, Phuntsho, with much love, Tsultrim."

I called the outfitter of my Bhutan trek and read him the letter. Was it a con? He explained that there are lamas who ask for money for meditation, but also some who make their living requesting hand-outs from Americans, especially New Yorkers. For a long time, the letter sat on my desk. I felt as guilty as when I ignore homeless people on the street. I put the blessing cord around my neck, waiting for an answer, or a sign that this was really a scam. As I touched the silky thread and thought about Tsultrim Lama, I knew what I had to do. I put twenty dollars in an envelope and mailed it. There was no reply. I was hurt because I'd trusted him and now felt betrayed. I took the blessing cord off the hook and threw it into my junk drawer—maybe the colored string would come in handy for something.

Two months later, an envelope arrived from Bhutan with the familiar AIR-MAIL handwritten in red and this time, underlined in green and purple crayon. The neatly printed letter read, "My dear Margie, Thank you so much for your kind help money for my meditation and for my niece also. You are so kindful to us, so that I never forget your kind through my whole life."

I took the necklace from the junk drawer and returned it to its place of honor. Perhaps it really was a blessing cord, after all.

# A Perfectly Reasonable Thing to Do

## Michael Wm. McColl

*A run for your life is never as traumatic as it first seems.*

As I CLIMBED INTO THE RING, it still seemed like a good idea. Here was a chance to really get to know the Spanish people. Not just to watch, but to participate in one of their most important festivals. And maybe to grab a bull by the tail. All in the name of immersing myself in the culture. Sure, it all made perfect sense. At the time.

I was in Zaragoza, Spain for the Fiestas del Pilar, the country's patron saint. During the festivals dedicated to Pilar, huge crowds from across the country pour into town for a weekend of wild partying. My camera-toting friend Juan and I decided to join them.

The culmination of the festival is the Toro de Fuego, quite literally the "bull on fire." While Pamplona's running of the Bulls has gained great fame worldwide, the Toro de Fuego is little known outside Spain.

The Toro de Fuego works like this: Nine bulls, gradually increasing in size and ferocity, are prepared for the event by having small torches attached to their horns. Meanwhile, the young men of the city, along with a few tourists, gather in the center of the city's large bullfighting ring. At the right time, the torches on the smallest bull's horns are lit on fire. The bull is released into the ring, enraged by the flames. And he runs around frantically trying to extinguish them, possibly by burying them in the side of one of the young men.

But do the men seem concerned by this? Not at all. In fact, they try to get as close to the angry bull as possible, to demonstrate their *machismo*. To them, it seems like a perfectly reasonable thing to do.

At the Toro de Fuego, the ultimate act of *machismo* is to grab the bull by its tail. As you can imagine, the bulls don't much like that. Local experts had advised my friend Juan and I to watch the first few bulls, so we could learn how the game was played. But if we waited too long, we would have to face the fiercest bulls.

After Bull Four, we had learned as much as we were going to learn. And the bulls were starting to get pretty large. We climbed over the wall surrounding the ring, and paced across the sandy ground, waiting for Bull Five.

**105**

At this point Juan informed me that he, in fact, would not attempt to approach the bull. Instead, he offered to "sacrifice this opportunity" in order to immortalize on film my act of brazen valor. For unknown reasons, I agreed to this.

From there, events unfolded all too quickly. The gate opened and a huge bull thundered into the center of the arena. "Wow," I thought. "The bulls didn't seem nearly as big from up in the stands." As the bull stomped and charged, some 50 young men, myself included, warily approached. We watched the bull peer angrily through the flames, repeatedly charging at whomever was closest. I edged forward, glancing behind me towards Juan, who assured me that he would look out for me.

As I turned back from Juan to face the bull, I realized—to my horror—that I was suddenly the closest person to the bull. He stared directly at me, and scratched at the sand with one hoof. A mere 15 yards separated me from the beast. Meanwhile, some 50 yards separated me from the safety of the fence.

In a sudden moment of clarity, I understood my error. "How could I EVER have thought this was a good idea?" I thought to myself. "This is the stupidest thing I've ever done in my life!" Could the bull gain 15 yards on me over the course of 50? At just that second the bull charged, and it was time to find out.

Time slowed for a split second, and objects became bigger than they were just a moment before. The bull was suddenly enormous. The length of sand between the fence and myself stretched into infinity. The bull's eyes opened wide with rage. Mine opened wide with fear.

I spun and sprinted for my life. As I approached the fence, I sensed that the bull was very close. I could almost feel his muzzle nudging me as he lowered his horns to gore. No time to stop and climb the fence!

Reaching the fence, I flung myself headfirst over the top and into the stands. A jovial crowd caught me and pulled me in.

Exhilarated by the adrenaline rush that only a run for your life can provide, I turned to look back at my adversary. But the bull wasn't there. He in fact was chasing another victim, all the way across the ring. As the highly amused crowd told me, and as Juan's photo later confirmed, the bull had indeed charged me. But it had stopped after a few yards, and turned to chase someone else.

In my eagerness to reach the fence, I had never actually looked back to see just where the bull was. Oops! So much for demonstrating my *machismo*.

My still-laughing fans, however, complimented me on my fine dive into the stands, and insisted that I stay to help them finish a huge vat of *sangria*. There were several bulls still to come, and I had worked up quite a thirst.

# Campfire Cahoots

## Gail Howerton

*Who's Zoomin' Who?*

WE WERE LOUNGING AROUND THE CAMPFIRE after a day of trekking in the Pokhara region of Nepal. Our stomachs were full with a delightful concoction of spicy chutney, rum cake, and Mustang Coffee prepared especially for our group of four women (Kris, Sharon, Shari, and myself). The aromatic "coffee" distinctly smelled of XXX rum our guide, Keepa Sherpa, had purchased for us earlier in the day. Our 10 Sherpas had ensured our comfort with hot water for our "bird baths," and a roaring fire, which lit up the tent walls surrounding us.

It wasn't long before the singing began. First the men would harmonize in a beautiful, melodic mountain tune which we recognized from the trail earlier in the day. Then we would break out in a sketchy rendition of "Old McDonald," "Jingle Bells," or something from childhood with easy lyrics. So as not to embarrass ourselves any longer; we opted for shadow puppets and skits.

Relying on our camp counselor skills, we showed them how to use their hands to cast shadows of birds or dogs on the tent flap. They were mesmerized by such a new entertaining invention and we received *oohs* and *aahs* as they tried to mimic the motions. Since we were on a roll, we then astounded them with a skit where Kris sat hidden behind me with a scarf over her head and her arms through a jacket which I had on backwards. My folded arms were hidden underneath the jacket while hers wrapped around me to look as if they were my own arms coming through the sleeves. Since our guides had been curious about the daily beauty routine of this all-female entourage, I decided to re-enact my morning ritual of hair combing, teeth brushing, and cosmetics application. We had them rolling off their mats as Kris combed my face, put mascara in my eyebrows, and just missed my mouth with the toothbrush. We received a standing ovation for those antics and I accepted graciously with toothpaste up my nose and lipstick on my cheeks.

Keepa later asked me why I had taken off my rings to do the show. His team had noticed that the hand applying my make-up didn't have on the rings I normally wore. After explaining to them that those were Kris' hands and not my own, they roared with laughter after discovering that they had been taken in by some campfire cahoots. It seemed we had dished up quite a Sherpa surprise.

**107**

# Go Jump in a Lake

**Robert Ragaini**

*A cultural tradition heats up a weary American. But how much can one take?*

W AIT A MINUTE! I SAID. "You can't come in here. There are naked men in here!"

"You first," she said.

I am not a sauna man. I have never been a sauna man. But when you're in Finland, you go to the sauna. Finland has five million citizens and one sauna for every four people. You figure it out.

The sauna there is such a cultural imperative that once a week Finnish government ministers have a meeting in one. They pan roast until tender and then adjourn to an adjacent room to conduct affairs of state. When they reach an impasse it's back to the oven until the obstinacy has been sweated out, and so it goes for a considerable length of time.

Finland has hundreds of thousands of lakes, most of them wrapped in forests of spruce and pine and birch. On the shores you see little red houses or dark log cabins with thick chimneys. This is because the sauna ritual requires not only par-boiling but quick freezing and how better than to jump in a lake in a country where it is winter most of the time.

My feeling is that if God had wanted us to alternately fry and freeze He would have constructed us differently, or at least made us all Finns. But He didn't and I'm not, so when I discovered that saunas were a feature of my tour to Finland and that my group expected me to partake, I was less than thrilled.

Because I'd tried it. I'd been around when it became de rigeur for every self-respecting health club to install a rustic wooden airtight chamber in a corner of their gleaming white-tiled dressing rooms. I'd settled my posterior on red hot slats and gasped fiery inhalations from the genuine imitation sauna stove. And I hated it. As I knew every one else did in spite of their claims to the contrary. Who could like anything so flagrantly nasty?

So why was I the only one with dread in his heart as we drove to the lakeside near the provincial town of Kokkola? It was 7 P.M. and felt like mid-afternoon. It should have been dusk but the sun hovered well above the horizon and showed no intention of setting. For this was the land of the midnite sun. Another Finnish perversity.

We pulled up at a neat little cottage perched on a gentle slope that descended to the lake. Off to the right a small dock poked into water flat and unruffled as the surrounding countryside, flat as Finland itself. Inside, a little buffet had been set up and plenty of booze to wash it down, from big bottles of beer to such esoteric local delights as cloudberry liqueur.

Our host declared the protocol: women into the changing room and then the sauna while the men talked man talk, had a snack, and got mildly lubricated. Women done, it would be our turn, and finally we would all gather for the post mortem. Finland is Lutheran. The sexes don't sauna ensemble.

So off the women went, giving me an opportunity to imbibe a little anesthetic before going into the operating room. I must say it was rather pleasant. While we waited for what seemed an unconscionably long time, we ate and drank and lounged by a huge bay window that looked over the tranquil lake and deep green forest. I suppose this was the Finnish equivalent of a cocktail party back home, but without the obligatory smart talk and sexual inuendo. Not bad for starters.

Eventually we heard some happy feminine voices and saw several toweled bodies trotting to the end of the pier. After a bit of hesitation the towels were dropped and a succession of pearly backs and buns slid into the cold black water.

They emerged—rather quickly—toweled up, and ran back while I waited for them to appear and tell us how awful it was.

And waited, and waited. They were doing it again.

Finally they entered, clothed all in long terry pullovers and lying through their teeth about how invigorating, how refreshing, how ...

Sure.

Anxious to be done with it, I deposited my clothes in the changing room and plunged headlong into the furnace.

Surprisingly, it was not too awful. First of all it wasn't overly hot. When I sat down the skin didn't instantly peel off my buttocks. Tiers of wooden benches rose on both sides of a simple, attractive room—an exact copy of the health club saunas of my recollection—and on the floor sat a square container topped by a layer of rocks.

Our host entered and immediately ladled quantities of water onto the rocks which gave off a wave of invisible, volcanic heat that curled every hair on my body. I scuttled from my perch on the top to the lowest level where the temperature was slightly less hellish while the toxins leapt from my pores.

After an eternity and a half, we applied the towels and staggered outside. At the end of the dock, too dazed to think, I shed my wrapping and took the plunge. Of course this was summer and by Finnish standards the water was warm, which is to say it took several seconds before I began to go numb. I paddled through a thicket of lake grass back to the ladder and climbed into the cool evening air.

Where, wonder of wonders, a strange warmth began suffusing my body. Insulated from within, the sharp exterior chill felt like a revitalizing caress. I stood admiring the lake and the forest surround with a new appreciation, a new clarity of vision. This was very nice.

In our own terry robes we joined the women. I ate, I drank, I chatted. I watched the sun make a heroic effort to touch the horizon, all the time feeling the most loose-jointed physical ease I can ever remember experiencing. And suddenly it was midnight. If there is such a thing as an overnight convert, I was it.

And so we saunaed our way across Finland. We motor-boated through squalls to try a smoke sauna on an island in the Baltic Sea. We went to an opera festival where the sauna was in a beach house on the shore. And at the end, we went to Helsinki where the sauna was in our hotel.

It was there that I was sitting when the door sprung open and a woman stood sillouetted in the frame, gazing impassively at our naked bodies.

"Wait a minute!" I said. "You can't come in here. There are naked men in here!"

"You first," she said.

I looked at my friends who modestly averted their eyes. I looked at the woman. "Botticelli," I thought. Not because of his Venus but because of his name, "little barrel."

"This is nonsense," I said to myself. "I don't have to go with her."

But what does a naked American do when confronted by an elderly woman with eyes of steel and a body like John Belluchi's?

He does what he's told.

She motioned me to lie face down on a table set against the wall. Instantly a hose of warm water played over my body followed by a dousing of slippery liquid soap. Then I felt a rough hand scraping my back with all the delicacy of an electric sander. She had put on a mitt made of loufa, a bark-like material, and was working with a vengeance on removing the top several layers of my skin.

With broad careless sweeps she massaged me from top to bottom, missing nothing along the way. When she got to my feet she gave the soles a swipe that made me jump like a frog in a physics lab. Then she made her way back up, just to ensure that no part of me was left unabused.

When she got to my shoulders she worked them over with her iron fists until the tension that had been harboring there had no choice but to give in and flee in terror. With an inaudible sigh my entire body capitulated. Every muscle said uncle and I lay plastered to the table not caring if I ever moved again.

"Turn over," she said.

Oh no, I thought, please let me stay like this forever, but there was something in her voice that wasn't to be denied. Figuring that what I couldn't see wouldn't hurt me, I shut my eyes tight and rolled over on my back. The woman began swabbing me up and down with the same reckless abandon, a matter that caused me no little concern, but by now I was an acquiescent jelly, the proverbial putty in her hands.

My body was a vibrant tingle and nerveless puddle both, impossible but true. To feel like this I would have followed her anywhere.

I opened my eyes and gazed hopefully, soulfully into hers. In my weakened state she seemed to float over me like a Rubenesque, slightly mature, angel. Was it my imagination or did she seem to look at me with just a suggestion of tenderness, of real caring?

In answer she rested her loufaed right hand on my shoulder. "Okay, baby," she said. "You're done."

# MISTAKEN IDENTITY

## Who (or What) Are You?

"Non sine dis animosus infans. *'An adventurous child, thanks to the gods.'*"

Roman poet Horace

# Mud (Chorus)

## Eileen O'Connor

*A Warning to Casting Directors: miscasting someone could lead to a life of crime ...*

WELL, NONE OF IT WOULD HAVE EVER HAPPENED if I hadn't been cast as mud in a children's play my Junior year in College. Really, it was just altogether too much. I had given a reasonable audition, but there it was, up on the board —EILEEN O'CONNOR—MUD (CHORUS) There was just no way I was going to ooze and squirm my way across some stupid Long Island college stage as mud. I knew I'd get grief for not "appreciating the opportunity to be in a truly ensemble piece" and all that, but forget it. All I could think was that I wanted to get out of town. So I applied to be an "Interfuture Scholar"— an exchange student for a semester.

I was accepted and went to Dublin. Supposedly to study theater. Well, I did a little of that, but frankly there was just too much else going on at the time. I was busy learning to smoke, drinking pints of Guinness and losing my virginity; distractions every time you turned around. So that's how I ended up smuggling hash into Long Kesh prison via my vagina.

I was anxious to shake the dust of Long Island, and quickly made a lot of new friends. We would meet every night in a bar in Summerhill. John, one of the regulars in the bar, asked me to write to a friend of his who was in jail. They had been in the IRA together, and his best friend, Joe, got caught. At first I said no, I mean what was I going to write about? Amusing anecdotes from my Long Island College where they had the poor taste to cast me as mud? But as my friend pointed out, "He's been in 10 years, he got 30 to Life. Anything you write will be fine, he'd just appreciate getting letters." So I did. We wrote back and forth for awhile, and then he asked me to come up for a visit. I was a little scared to go up there, but I said, "Sure."

The night before the visit, I met up with everyone at the bar. Mary, a friend of Joe's, gave me a note to smuggle in. She explained that the prison reads all the regular mail. Then John said, "While you're at it, would you mind bringing a little hash in as well?" I just looked at him for a second. I thought he must be joking "Well, just how do I do that? Someone told me they search you before you go in." "Yeah," he said, "They do. Now, what you'll want to do, see, is wrap it up together with the notes (Mary's one page had grown to four, apparently word got out that I was going and Joe had a lot of friends ...) in plastic, and hide it like a tampon."

Oh, right. Like a tampon. I gotcha. Well, I made no promises, because this trip was getting scarier by the second. I figured I'd better get the hell out of that bar quickly, before someone asked me to smuggle in a pint of Guinness or his favorite bar stool.

The train wasn't to leave until 8:30, but I was up way before then. I found some sandwich baggies and wrapped everything up in one. I went into the bathroom to try it out (It wasn't too comfortable, and I wasn't too comfortable with the whole thing). I took it out again, put it in my purse and went to meet my friend Victoria, who was going up with me. She was going shopping.

We got to Belfast, and it was just like on television. Guards everywhere, even just entering the city. We looked around for awhile, then went to Woolworth's. I love chocolate, so I bought a huge bag of candy bars. As I was leaving the store, I went through the metal detector, and an alarm went off. My heart started to pound and I was freaking out. I thought they must have some sort of equipment to detect hash, and I was waiting for the guard's hand to clamp down on my shoulder, but it never came. I just kept walking out the door and on up the street. No one was following me, but I was shaking. Victoria asked me what was wrong and I told her I had hash in my bag to take up to the prison. She just looked at me like I was a moron. Right then, I decided to take the Woolworth's scare as a sign. I didn't get caught there, but I definitely would if I tried to take it into Long Kesh. I decided to forget the whole thing.

I suggested we go to a bar and have a drink. I was a wreck and needed to calm my nerves. But of course, after three Paddy & gingers, my nerves were so calm that I decided this smuggling business would be a piece of cake. Victoria tried to talk me out of it, said all kinds of horrible things would happen to me if I got caught, but I was sure I wouldn't. I went in the ladies room and put it in.

I said good-bye to Victoria and went to get a black taxi to take me to the Sinn Fein office where there was a van to take visitors up. There were a lot of young women with babies, and I had a weird disconnected feeling like I was watching a movie. I kept thinking of that movie "Papillion" and I wondered if Joe would be all skinny, wasted and wearing stripes. I figured he would, so I was trying to steel myself to not look at him pityingly. We got up to the prison and had to show our passports to two young guards. They took a long time over mine. My heart was pounding too fast again and I was sweating. (I so much wished there wasn't a hunk of hash in my vagina.) I thought, "They know, they know, they're just playing with me here, this is torture." They asked me all kinds of questions about New York, and just as I was about to scream and confess, the guards burst into song. It was "Come on Eileen," by Dexy's Midnight Runners—Oh, they were having a great time with that. I kept wiping the sweat off my face and trying to smile and be good sport. Next I was searched by a female guard and then led into the waiting room. There was a bathroom there, so I went in and had another moment of panic when I could not find the hash ... I mean, Good Lord, where could it have gone?! Eventually I did find it, but it was slippery and with no string, I couldn't get a good grasp on it. I finally got it out, rinsed it off, dried it off and stuck it up my sleeve.

I sat down to wait, and they called his name—"McManus." I got up and was led into the visitor's room. It was a small room with 2 chairs and a guard. I sat down and Joe came in. He was tall, brown hair, green eyes, wearing a leather jacket—he was beautiful. We just stared at each other for a minute. I couldn't believe this was him. He sat down and tried to ask me some questions about my thesis, but I just kept staring at him. So he leaned over and kissed me. I'd never been kissed like that in my life. We kissed for the entire duration of the visit. We had one hour, because he had given up his visit the week before. It was easier to kiss with a guard standing there then it was to talk. If I closed my eyes, I closed out the guard standing 2 feet away, and I wasn't in the prison anymore. At one point I sat on his lap, so I could get the hash out of my sleeve and up his. I just managed it before the guard made me sit back in my chair. The visit ended, we said good-bye, and I walked out. Easy as pie.

I had been one of the first to go in, so I went out to the van to wait for the others. As I was sitting there, an alarm went off, the doors of the prison burst open, and guards and dogs came running out. I thought they had found the hash on him and now were coming for me. I looked around wildly, wondering if I should run. But there was no where to run to, we were in the middle of nowhere. So I crouched down on the floor of the van and crammed all the chocolate I had bought at Woolworth's into my mouth. I figured it might be the last chocolate I'd have for a good long time.

Whatever the reason for the alarm in the prison, it had nothing to do with me. Eventually everyone came back on the bus, and I had to run out to throw up and then we all went back to Dublin.

Still, I imagine the whole experience was less horrifying than playing "Mud" in a college play. And let's face it—definitely less embarrassing.

# The Great Indoors

## Ron Gluckman

*Sun, sand and surf were always on the prescription list for holiday paradise, but, in the south of Japan, they leave nothing to Mother Nature.*

I'M FLAT ON MY BACK IN PARADISE. Perched upon a towel, stretched out on an immaculate white beach, I have turquoise sea in front of me and a cloudless sky overhead. Not a bee, sand fly or mosquito can be seen. The weather is perfect. It's warm enough for swimming in the inviting sea, but there is no danger of sun burn. A cold drink lays close at hand, along with a thick, juicy novel.

Suddenly, a strange haze drifts into view. Smoke envelops the top of a nearby mountain, which begins spitting out sparks of fire. Eruptions can be most annoying, but not here, not in paradise. As the volcano stirs to life, I don't even bother. Checking my watch, I see it's only the half-hour eruption. Returning to my book, I savor a smile. There is still another 30 minutes before the mountain blows its top.

Paradise proceeds with clockwork precision inside Ocean Dome, Japan's unique, sometimes surrealistic, but utterly updated version of the Garden of Eden. Inside a huge dome that could house six football pitches, the world's largest artificial sea washes over the biggest indoor beach, fringed with fake palm trees and other eyepopping innovations that have given a holiday makeover to old Mother Nature.

This evocative 21st Century resort shows that even paradise has room for improvement. In Ocean Dome, once every hour, on the hour, the surf is always up. Every afternoon is a carnival. Mechanized parrots squawk from branches of the dome's ingenious rain forest, which remain lush and tropical without rainfall or humidity. Best of all, in Ocean Dome, you can lull for hours on crushed marble pebbles without a worry about beach vendors, bugs or sun burns.

Instead, perfectly-timed waves whip equally well-groomed surfers along in 28-degree, chlorinated, salt-free water to the sanitized shore where they drip-dry in Ocean Dome's perfect climate, which remains a delightful 30 degrees, day and night, 365.25 days each year.

When the Beach Boys grow too old to remember the Good Vibrations of the faraway California shore, they could hardly do better than to be dispatched here, to this safe, self-contained beach paradise, where the sun never sets and the fun never stops; provided you have sufficient beach cash—specially-designed Ocean Dome payment tokens in the form of computer-coded plastic tags.

God didn't dream up this beach; the Japanese did.

Perhaps the best designed beach on the planet sits inside a massive dome measuring 300 by 100 meters, about 1,500 kilometers south of Tokyo in Miyazaki, on Japan's southernmost Kyushu Island. A heated ocean with a width of 140 meters sends 13,500 tons of salt-free water sweeping across 600 tons of polished marble chips that constitute a 85-metre long shoreline, ringed by a three-story promenade of shops.

Every fifteen minutes, the volcano smokes to life. Every hour, on the hour, it spews fake flames. Like seismic chimes, these pseudo-eruptions sound a "surf's up" that signals a new level of excitement at this indoor Beach Blanket of the Bizarre.

All of a sudden, the artificial ocean turns tubular, thanks to Ocean Dome's enormous computer, which commands 10 large vacuum pumps to start sucking in sea, then spitting out a series of cool crests. Teams of professional surfers provide entertainment as they ride 3.5-metre waves, then lifeguards arrange squads of Japanese tourists toting boogie boards on either end of the "sea." They even point out the perfect points for catching these utterly predictable curls.

After a few minutes of orderly mayhem, the excitement abruptly ends. The staff clear the "ocean" and water jets jutting from the sides of a pair of "islands" squirt powerful spray to tame the rare uproar at this otherwise tranquil indoor sea. Calm quickly returns to the brave new world of Ocean Dome.

This prepackaged holiday vision of the future is part of an enormous $2 billion recreational complex called Seagaia. The name itself is an odd concoction, melding the English word for the sea with "Gaia," an ancient Greek word for the Earth. "The name of a true paradise expresses the admiration for the perfect combination of sea and earth," explains one brochure from Seagaia, which ends: "This is a place where we can feel that we are part of nature."

Yet natural elements are kept to the minimum in Phoenix Resorts' masterplan for Seagaia, of which Ocean Dome was merely the first entree. The plan includes a wide assortment of other amusements, shopping centers, hotels, tennis courts and golf courses. It's a bold leap into the future for a local corporation that started its business life much more modestly, by renting seaside cottages to honeymoon couples in the 1960s.

But that was then, and this is now. Seagaia has taken a Space Age splash with

Ocean Dome, which comes complete with all kinds of high-tech thrills and frills. A series of waterslides circle Mount Bali Hai, the volcano with the quarterly hourly eruptions. On the other side of the beach is the plastic rainforest of Lost World, where guests can take a ghost train ride amongst holographic sea pirates, demons and packs of Jurassic-era creatures.

There are also water cannons, beach bars and boutiques, and statues that look like a strange marriage between Cambodia's Angkor Wat and New Mexican pueblo, all under a 200-metre long retractable roof, which makes those at football pitches seem mere car sunroofs. Like everything else at Ocean Dome, the world's largest retractable roof is only pulled back at predetermined points of perfection when the confluence of wind, sun and temperature meet the dome criteria.

Still, sunshine is no factor when you want to stage a beach carnival in the world's biggest party dome. Every afternoon, scores of dancers and musicians in Caribbean costumes provide a festive beach flavor. Every night, there is a spectacular stage show, performed upon the indoor ocean with aquatic performers. But that is long after darkness has descended outside the dome. Only then, when the last of the indoor surfers have stowed away their boards, are the indoor lights lowered, and the laser lights sweep across the artificial sea.

And, setting new standards for indoor beaches of the future, is Ocean Dome's exhilarating rafting trip down rugged Phoenix River. The Water Crash ride is rated Class Five, but there is no real danger despite scary-sounding chutes like Shark's Tooth, Devil's Staircase and Satan's Plunge. The rapids aren't real, and neither are the spills. Forget genuine chills, for this is all simulated. There's no river.

However, the raft shakes and spins, and water splashes over the crowd, in five wet-and-wild minutes of virtual-reality rafting.

"It's right silly, when you get down to it, mate," confides an Aussie worker in straw hat, as he guides guests to safety from one of the water slides. "It's kind of surreal, but the Japanese love it."

Indeed they do. Along the beach, men cover their eyes with washcloths, even though the sun is safely sealed outside this beach Bubbleland. Nonetheless, the smell of tanning lotion remains brisk amongst the fake breakers.

"It's clean, modern and safe," says one pleased visitor, Rie Takeda, a mother of two from Kochi prefecture, in Shikoku. She praises the predictability of everything at Ocean Dome, even the hourly waves. "And, I never have to worry about the safety of my children or sunburn."

Yoko Yamada, 22, visiting Ocean Dome with her boyfriend, enthuses about the "wonderful illusion." Several other Japanese visitors described the blissful release from that oppressive feeling of infinity imposed by mean old Mother Nature.

"When you look out on the horizon, you know that feeling you get, how things can go on and on, forever," says one. "You look out and see to infinity. It makes you feel small and insignificant. Here, things are confined, more peaceful."

Whenever one tires of the immaculate weather or the chlorinated indoor ocean, you can always take a stroll down another simulated beachfront delight—the boardwalk. There, scores of shops offer the latest in beach tongs and a wide range of cuisine.

Customers pay a single price for admission and all fees are deducted from the computerized barcoded tag dangling from each guest's wrist. The tags are color-coded according to price, which may be another modern improvement on beach culture of the past. Now, the snobs can instantly separate the have-somes from the have-everythings, without squinting to read bikini labels.

All this indoor beach excitement can be expensive. Admission runs about US$50 for adults, with rides running $5-10 more. Add $10 for two hours with a boogie board, or $5 for two hours of inner tube rental.

Perhaps the oddest thing of all about this artificial environment is its location. Adventurous guests can step outside Ocean Dome and gaze out at ... the REAL beach. From the third floor of the enormous dome, beside rows of eateries like Marco Polo, Buena Vista and Key West, doors lead outside to a balcony and a view of the age-old, unimproved beach, just the way God intended, a mere 300 meters away. It clearly holds little appeal to most visitors.

One afternoon, while the marimba bands churn out cheerful beach muzak and the fake Hawaiian dancers shake plastic grass skirts, I slip outside for some genuine fresh air, unfiltered and quite possibly polluted. I make my way to the ocean and find it utterly deserted, even on a sunny day. Maybe it's the strange juxtaposition so close to the simulated seaside nearby. But the sand between my toes feels so sensual, in ways that crushed marble never could.

Still, even skeptical observers are bound to experience a certain sense of awe upon entering Ocean Dome, like the first sight of the opening scene of a new generation of "Star Wars" films: even if the plot doesn't appeal to your tastes, you have to marvel at the special effects. In some ways, it's like seeing a giant draft board of a software firm, which is designing the recreational virtual reality microchip of the future. Someday, perhaps, office workers need not even abandon their desks. They will simply watch a destination tape and swallow a vacation tablet.

In the meantime, we will just have to struggle along with the next best thing; recreations of the Great Outdoors, set inside sanitized domes. With sand.

# Questioning the Answer

**Andrew Bill**

*Sometimes the most unsuspecting strangers provide the most relevant answers.*

I'LL SAY ONE THING, it didn't happen in the usual way. I was always brought up to believe that enlightenments were delivered in blinding flashes of light. Like Saul's on the road to Damascus. Or whispered by a Sufi, lotus-legged on the stoop of his sacred cave. But my moment of clarity—the time I learned the secret of travel and, by extension, of life itself—occurred in a bar so run-down; calling it a "dive" would be paying it a compliment.

Where it was is almost unimportant because it could have been anywhere. But, at a guess, I would say it was a hole-in-the-wall in Cairns, Queensland, known as the Pirate's Pub.

The lighting is so poor that, stepping inside, it takes a few minutes to make out the details. The bar has been hammered into place so inexpertly, long nails protrude to catch unwary knees. There are a half dozen tables cobbled together into the essential shape—three or four legs and a reasonably flat surface. The glare of day knifes through the swing doors whenever anyone enters or leaves. Dogs scratch themselves under tables. The cosmopolitan cocktail of beer, cheap cigarettes and resignation taints the air. Low conversation is punctuated here and there by a slap of cards, a table-ring of laughter, the scrape of a chair. A shout.

I'm sitting at the bar doing what I usually do when I'm in a new town. Sucking it up along with a couple of slow beers, I'm exploring the underbelly of my destination; listening to it digest. And I'm chatting, or half chatting (because he is doing all the talking) with this fellow that happens to be on the next bar stool. He was something once, which I can't put my finger on. English perhaps. But now he is a road-man, one of those people who went on vacation once and never stopped, because going on was easier or less painful than going back. Now he has forgotten who he was when he left. To me these nomads are as intriguing as any "Danger" sign on the side of the road.

Losing the flow amid the unsequential chapters of his life, I stop him. After spending more than half his life in near constant motion what, in his opinion, is the secret of travel? He is silent so long I wonder if, by cutting his momentum, I have lost him as well. But his rheumy eyes are open and locked as if searching the back wall of bottles for inspiration. Then he stiffens out of his two-elbow slump and swivels to meet me. Carried across in a mist of old beer and other things I have no wish to identify I catch words crushed together that, when separated in my mind like tangled fishing line, came out like "Vindaloo and ice-cream." Couldn't be. If it *is* Cairns, we are a thousand miles from the nearest Indian restaurant and a hot curry. I make him repeat it, but each time the words lose their edges. As distant from their original shape as rags.

I file his beer-sodden words in my brain, cross-referenced both under "lunatic ravings" and "things to be considered at a later date." The first file is simply an extension of the "trash." The second is already crammed into confusion with such big-byte items as all modern art after Picasso went blue; all music recorded after 1985; most of the Rubaiyat, James Joyce, chemistry, and all women. I don't expect to see this culinary tit-bit again.

So I am surprised when the words stay with me and grow, over the next twenty years, more and more defined until I not only know exactly what my beer-buddy meant, but I agree wholeheartedly with his answer.

At its most pure, travel is an effort to explain life, not just from the familiar perspective, but from every perspective. To understand it fully, you must look to its extremes and taste them side by side. You must know the feathered luxury of a five-star hotel and the simple pleasure of sleeping in a tent on a beach miles from the nearest light-bulb. You must understand both the duet of fine filet mignon with vintage claret, and you must know what it's like to go days without food. You must experience riches and poverty, the mountains and the plains, the hot and the cold.

# Henry Miller's Nephew

## Tom Miller

*Eager students who let their minds wander can imagine virtually anything.*

THE DOLLAR IS THE IMPERIAL CURRENCY, not just in international trade but in the smallest *víveres* outlet as well. No matter how well acquainted you are with a Latin-American town and make friends with its people, you still symbolize the gringo dollar. No one hesitates to ask about the United States. Everyone wants to know: What is your income? How much does a watch cost? A television? A car? A hat? A plane ticket between the United States and Ecuador? During that pause suspended between the question and the answer the inquisitive *mestizo* comes one tiny step closer to that material world. He imagines himself, for a moment, directly in touch with the dollar and all that it represents.

"What is it like to teach in the United States? Do you think we could get jobs there?" These questions came from students at the Universidad Estatal de Cuenca, whose class in Culture and Civilization of the English-Speaking Countries I visited once again. The previous day classes had again been suspended for a political rally, virtually guaranteeing a day free of disruption. On my way over I had stopped to browse at a bookstore, struck by the wide range of books from Argentina, Mexico, and Spain. The few domestic offerings included *The Responsibility of the United States Government in the Territorial Mutilation of Ecuador,* published at the University of Guayaquil.

Most of the students aspired to teach English, the imperial language. They had just finished discussing the relationship between Herman Melville and Nathaniel Hawthorne, and they asked about contemporary United States authors. "Do you know Norman Mailer?" My last name was close enough for them. They were especially interested in Saul Bellow. "Do you like John Steinbeck?" They were familiar with *Grapes of Wrath*, often compared to their own novel *Huasipungo*, by Jorge Icaza, about the horrific treatment of Indian chattel in the Ecuadorian highlands. "Are there any of our authors well known in America?" I counted on the fingers of one hand the Ecuadorian writers whose works had been translated into English. They felt better when I described the upsurge in interest in Latin-American literature brought about, in

**123**

part by Gabriel García Márquez winning the Nobel Prize for Literature. Imagine, a South American writer—a neighbor, no less, who writes about life along the Pacific Coast!—recognized with the world's foremost literary honor.

"Well, we want to know about the decline of American morals. Is it true?" "Is *what* true?" I replied. "You know, that you have no values left in the States." Shot. Kaput. Bankrupt. Another grand experiment down the drain. My answer, an awkward and uncustomary defense of the United States, was overrun with further questions. "We have heard of the environmentalist movement. How big is it?" "We've been reading about Indians in US history. Are they well treated now, or is it like our Indians here?" "What difference have you noticed between family life in America and in Ecuador?" "Are Eastern religions very influential?" "Why do you have so many vegetarians?" "What happens to the Mexicans and others who get caught coming into the United States illegally? For the ones who don't get caught, what sort of treatment can they expect?" "Do you think John F. Kennedy's brother will run for president?" "What do Americans think of our president?" I fudged that one; in truth, of course, only a handful of people north of the Panama Canal can locate Ecuador, much less identify its president.

They were keenly interested in United States domestic politics. "You have a two-party system in a country of two hundred million. Do you have any minor parties? We never hear about them. Here we have fewer than ten million people but we have seventeen political parties." "What is the difference between the Republican party and the Democratic party? From here they look so similar." They don't look a whole lot different closeup, I confessed.

*La Fuerza del Cariño (Terms of Endearment)* had just opened at a local theater. "Is America really like that?" "Well parts of it are, yes," I said warming to my advisory role. "Actually that'd be a good movie to see. It shows some subtleties of American culture you don't find in many films here." "Oh, we know all about American culture," a student replied. "Yes," another followed, "We watch *Dallas* all the time!" "*Dynasty* too," another chimed in. "We learn about your culture that way."

The next afternoon I was invited to sit in as three professors grilled an English major on her senior thesis—"Thomas Hardy: Harbinger of the Screenplay." She planned to leave Cuenca the following fall to attend an exclusive New England college to complete her education. Her family threw a graduation party for her that night. Fellow students mingled with faculty, relatives, and family friends. Servants brought out terrific food, and we toasted her success with Chilean wine. The elite of Cuenca gathered once again to celebrate another passage into their ranks.

"Excuse me," a man said as he introduced himself. "But are you related to

**124**

Glen Miller?" Older Ecuadorians remember the band leader from a visit to Salinas on the coast, where he entertained United States troops during World War II. Not in the slightest disappointed that Glenn and I were not related, he returned five minutes later, smiling. "Ah I know. You are related to Henry Miller, the author. I just heard it."

Since my earlier visit to the university campus, a rumor had circulated that I was Henry Miller's nephew, in Cuenca to conduct interviews. The few times I was confronted with the story I denied it, which of course gave it more credibility. Now it seemed that half of the faculty at one of the country's most prestigious universities was convinced—nay, honored—that the nephew of the well-know American writer had graced their campus. I was, after all, of the same name and profession, and I was writing about life halfway between the Tropic of Cancer and the Tropic of Capricorn. Did they need further evidence? Nothing I could say would dissuade them.

"Well?"

Chitchat around my corner of the room suddenly ceased as the guests awaited my reply. Being Henry Miller's nephew wouldn't be such a bad gig for a while, I thought to myself. Surely no one here knows anything about his real nephews, if indeed he had any. If I play my cards right, I could probably dine out on Uncle Henry for months. First I'd spend a few weeks in Cuenca perfecting my ruse, then take my show on the road all over the continent—Lima! La Paz! Buenos Aires! Rio! Caracas! Bogotá! I'd stay one step ahead of the US Information Agency, which would put its junior-most officers on my trail. What finally convinced me to forego my celebrity status—all in the space of five seconds—was not so much conscience as caution. I had only a passing familiarity with Henry Miller and his works. I hated to disappoint them.

# Un Favorito, Por Favor

**Robert Young Pelton**

*Beware, looks can be deceiving. Even a thug can dress up.*

COLOMBIA IS BOTH A SPECTACULAR TROPICAL VACATION AREA and a dangerous war zone. Somewhere in the middle is the hard-edged business of drugs that keeps the rich, the wealthy and the poor, destitute. I spent quite a bit of time on a tropical island breaking Americans out of jail, diving, and getting a tan. I also got to know the locals very well.

I had agreed to go out with the official's daughter. She was coming into San Andreas tomorrow from Cali for Holy Week. To decline the social request would not be a wise idea. I watched in amazement as this distinguished gentleman was able to piss in the sink at the same time he was washing his hands. We were in his hotel suite, which served as his full-time home. He was a very high level government official on the island. Instead of wallpaper, he had cases of Mumm's stacked up from floor to ceiling, creating a pleasing but somewhat industrial pattern. His choice of music was limited to one or two AM radio stations on the island—he used a state-of-the-art quadraphonic stereo system to blast out Julio Iglesias. Like most of his possessions, they were "gifts" or leftovers from customs inspections of travelers.

He explained how he made his money. He has a group of three to five "beach boys" who sell coconut oil on the beach to tourists. Along with the golden fragrant oil in old beer bottles, they offer hash or marijuana to unsuspecting tourists. As the sun goes down, they turn in the money they've made and carefully point out each and every person who bought drugs that day. During the night, the doors of the surprised victims are crashed down and they're trotted off to jail at gunpoint. They pay the judge, the lawyer, the DAS, the F2 and, of course, the Aduana dearly for their freedom. In fact, they even have to pay for meals while they are in jail. As he adjusted his evening clothes and carefully combed his hair, I thought he looked rather dashing for a thug.

# AT&T, the Serpent's Shadow and the Dreadlock Gringo

## Antonio López

*In spite of corporate sponsorship, Bohemians get cosmic.*

C HICHEN ITZA, LOCATED IN THE HEART of the Yucatan peninsula in Southern Mexico, is where I discovered AT&T had gotten into the ritual business. This ancient Toltec-Mayan city has become a popular destination spot for the Equinox ever since a local guide discovered the image of a serpent climbing down the limestone steps of the Castillo, Chichen's central grand pyramid. The illusion simulates a serpent crawling towards the Cenote, a huge sinkhole located opposite the pyramid. For the Maya, it represented the return to Madre Tierra by the sacred feathered serpent, Quetzalcoatl.

Peso-less, I had hitchhiked to the ruins with a longhaired Spanish photo-journalist. Primavera, the Mexican name for the first day of Spring, is com-memorated as a national holiday. Can you imagine a European country being so Pagan? All the banks were closed, and most bus lines were jammed with tourists eager to catch the Mayan spectacle.

When we arrived in the town near the ruins, I noticed immediately that some-thing was amiss. This was the third time I had visited the site in the past month, and I had never seen so many tourist buses and cars packed along the road. The young Mérida-based reporter, who had picked us up in his white Volkswagen bug, let us out near the entrance. The scene resembled the opening gate of Woodstock or a Dead show. Venders thronged the side of the road selling every-thing from roasted corn to tie-died Grateful Dead tee shirts, creating a funny mix of Indian entrepreneurs and New Age hippies.

As we entered the main field, girls dressed in freshly pressed Girl Scout uni-forms handed out program notes printed by AT&T. I passed under a banner commemorating the phone company overlord. Today was free, thanks to the Northern corporate amigos. Mexico's state owned telco, Telemex, was eerily absent, perhaps relegated to sponsoring less important solar movements, or only Christian holidays. Either way, it was a blow to Mexican state-run industry and a boon to the neo-liberal internationalists who brought us NAFTA.

**127**

Once we entered the main field in front of the Castillo, it was our goal to search for my friend's Czechoslovakian sweetheart, who we found among a group of anarchist squatters and dreadlocked gringos. Echoing throughout the pyramid complex was the lonely voice of some administrator who told the story of the Maya, the Equinox and the serpent shadow. I could barely hear his voice above the catcalls of the mostly drunk spectators, numbering around 50,000 people.

Most of the attendees were chavos, young Mexicans happy to have the day off work. The Mayans were smart, I realized. They got all these people here—hedonists, drunks, lovers, Catholics and New Agers—in spite of themselves. For most people, the spectacle itself didn't mean much, but being there was somehow important.

A strange group ritual emerged from the noisy crowd, suspiciously derivative of something I saw in a cheesy Latin variety TV show. When ever a man was sighted with his arm around a woman, a large group of chavos would jump up and provoke the couple by chanting, "be-so, be-so, be-so." Kiss, kiss, kiss. As soon as the couple consummated, everyone cheered, much to the dismay of pyramid watchers. Hey, wasn't there an Equinox happening?

At 4:30, when the frustrated MC failed to get a moment of silence from the crowd, he announced that the shadow had officially crawled to its destination. The crowd dispersed rapidly, somewhat confused and disappointed that this much-touted ancient ritual was just some boring shadow that took three hours to form and then unmiraculously dissipate, as it did for hundreds of silent and boring years. So much for geological time and cosmic ritual.

Before the climax, I searched the crowd for something more meaningful than a lover's shooting gallery. I wandered over to a dark-skinned women with short hair and a perfectly clean Zapotec-white outfit. As she faced the pyramid, she held up a purple crystal triangulated between her fingers. She chanted in a lovely voice; a number of disciples in similar garb surrounded her. When her voice tired, she begged in Italian accented English for her comrades to join her. I decided to chant along. I closed my eyes, and fell into inventing my own incantation, which came out as some kind of North American Indian pow wow song. I uttered something like, "We go to Disneyland, Disneyland, hi-ya, hi-ya. Micky Mouse, and Goofy too, there are movie stars, at Disneyland, hi-ya, hi-ya" repetitively.

I fell into a soothing trance until loud whistles rang my ears to the point of total distraction. I opened my eyes to discover about 50 French and German tourists standing around us in an arc, snapping pictures with little disposable cameras. They clapped when they realized we were done singing our cacophonous prayers.

I should have passed a hat.

Behind me were a dozen riot police blowing whistles, wearing blue jump-suits, black helmets and carrying 3-foot long wood batons. They swept the field with a large forearm sized rope, herding us out of the archeological complex. It was a strange moment to be trapped between scary looking cops, New Agers and gaudy tourists.

Meanwhile, another small group of white clad New Agers had scratched a diagram into the ground with a bunch of stones and crystal surrounding it. As the riot police dragged them away with the rope, they rushed their prayers, panting, trying to beat the law. I could feel their souls wrenched by the quick destruction of the pilgrimage they had traveled so far to complete. These cops just didn't give a fuck about Quetzalcoatl, crystals or the so-called coming Age of Light.

I regrouped with the anarchist crowd; my Spanish friend informed me that we would stay in the "hippie gruta" tonight, a nearby cave where a bunch of the Bohemians were staying the night. I had no money, so this would work, saving me from hitchhiking back to Mérida in the dark.

The forest shrouded cave was only a couple hundred yards from the ruin site, just off the main entrance road. Inside were close to 50 people; a diverse crowd that rivaled the Rainbow Gathering or a downtown LA street scene. The 2,000 square foot gruta was filled with the dreadlocked gringos, lesbian skinheads from Germany, some Brits, a young Mexican brujo and his clan, a Japanese long hair who spoke perfect Spanish and several others who I didn't have a chance to meet. A fire was built, and the prime camping spots were taken. I was relegated to my jacket and a rock for a pillow. When an older Mexican woman curled up next to me, I cuddled with the hope of staying warm. She, or I should say, her hands, had other designs. Eventually I snuck away from her, lodging myself between a dreadlock gringo and the brujo.

At some point a large group exited the cave, which gave me a chance to jam on a lone guitar. When the dreadlock gringo came back, we tried to play together, but he got mad when I told him I didn't play songs. He was intent on improvising two chord reggae jams. But free jazz? It was a moment of truth: the Canadian pot dealer had warned me, people with dreadlocks take them-selves too seriously. Never offer to do anything that will free their minds. I was happy that the German lesbian and I at least had a good tune going; she was singing rap-style about comets in the sky, while I droned out in some open-tuned Indian raga.

Later, after I fled the lusting Mexican woman, I ran outside to pee in the bushes. When I looked up at outer space, I was astonished. There, burning through the dark, early morning sky was a comet the size of my fist, with its tale shimmering and melting into the darkness. I fell to my knees: I thought the mothership had come, then I remembered the skinhead woman singing about comets. What the hell was this? I heard of no comets. You'd think that you'd be informed about such things by the cosmic authorities, the paper. Still, there it was, a truly beautiful, awesome sight. However misinformed I was, I was happy to see it, a sign from the Great Whatever.

I made a small prayer, feeling satisfied that I had fulfilled my spiritual pilgrimage to Mexico: to initiate the next phase of my life at the pyramids, during the Equinox, in a private and personal way.

And I smiled, because I knew that this moment was not, and could never be, sponsored by AT&T.

# The Hitchhiker

## Carla King

*In a country of 1.3 billion people, 95% of whom are Han Chinese,
one rider speeds up the journey.*

"OOHWHAAAH!" THE HITCHHIKER IS YELLING IN MY EAR. And just in case I haven't heard him, he shouts again.

"oohWHAAAH!" he shouts when I ride in the middle of the lane.

"oohWHAAAH!" he shouts when a truck jumps on the highway ahead of us.

"oohWHAAAH!"

Occasionally, the hitchhiker thrusts his pale bluish finger into the air in front of me, inexplicably reaching for the ignition button and nearly knocking my hand off the throttle. He has been doing this repeatedly since we began, for some reason I cannot comprehend. Still, I am grateful for his strange company, and that he is guiding me through all the little villages, away from the roads that dead-end at a field or the river. It takes precious extra hours for me to navigate these places alone, but he knows down which alleyway to turn, how to extract oneself from a crowded marketplace and of the shortcut between two huts which leads back to the main road to Yinchuan, which is where I want to go. I am late, and this is the reason I agreed to take him with me, though I'm not sure of his motivation.

The motorcycle, its sidecar full of my traveling gear, thumps over the potholes and fallen bricks and around bicycles and slow-moving three-wheeled tractors that clog the curving road that follows the banks of the Yellow River. This guy behind me barely adds 100 pounds but makes driving harder as I can feel his extra weight in my shoulders and back, especially now, after dark, when the icy air whips through kinks in all my layers of clothing, even underneath my leather jacket, wool scarf and full-face helmet.

"oohWHAAAH!"

As the darkness comes on, the patchwork of bright-green fields fades to textured gray squares and the wide river full of silt that in daylight, true to its name, is yellow, melts to pink, and finally shines with an eerie dead glow. The night is soon pitch black and the road is so dark that even the drivers who are sure that they can conserve gasoline by keeping their headlights turned off, turn them on, and then the truckers start their sadistic little light-game power-trip.

"oohWHAAAH!"

I have no idea why they're flashing their brights at me. If I have the lows on, they flash their brights. I am blinded. So I flash my brights. They flash their brights back. Then I keep my brights on until they get close and then dim them, and they flash their brights. When I careen past a ghostly, lampless tractor, I forget to dim my brights at all, and get blinded again. Driving here in the dark is like driving under a strobe light.

"oohWHAAAH! I'M SORRY!" shouts the voice from my back seat. I picked him up from the roadside where I asked directions in an industrial town where the Yellow River turns south toward the silk route at the Gansu corridor. Yinchuan, my destination, was turning out to be farther away than the map would have one believe. HE wanted to go there, too, he said. Desperately.

It was a four hour ride away at 6 p.m. I was lonely and tired of navigating villages, dodging fugitive hogs, getting lost repeatedly, all while watching for obstacles such as handcarts of cabbages or sticks that often overturned into the road. This guy looked okay, just like every other Chinese guy, only a little more nervous, maybe. It would make a nice change for me to have some company. I had picked up truckers before, who had been traveling from Beijing to the Tenger desert. I came upon them standing beside the road, staring morosely at their bent axles or fallen trailers, and had taken them on to the next town to call "The Company." They never tried to talk to me, only smiled widely and shook my hand when I let them off. But this guy can't shut up and he hasn't stopped jouncing around since I met him.

First of all he makes me understand that he needs to stop by his home so that he can collect some things. The place would have been impossible to find without him, located as it is in a cluster of a dozen identical six-story apartment buildings which are encircled by a huge factory that has exposed conveyor belts and hoppers attached to buildings with large, sheet-metal covered sides that hide mysterious inner workings. Itself almost a life form, all this industrialism is eerie after all the desert and farmland I'd passed by on the northern banks of the Yellow River.

At the apartment building my hitchhiker literally runs upstairs, then downstairs again to make sure I am following, like a dog whose emotions are shredded by a simultaneous urge to gallop the 1000 yard dash and to wait for its beloved master. I try to hurry, but I'm loaded down with my helmet and leather jacket, and I haven't climbed a staircase for a month. The building smells of dust and burnt grease and exotic spices. He doesn't stop until we reach the top floor and a doorway where there's a pile of bricks on the stoop. If something really weird happens, I think, I could use a brick as a weapon. Suddenly I am paranoid. Maybe he's one of the highway robbers that I've heard about. The excitement that seemed charming before is now obviously agitation, which makes me nervous, and I have very little way of finding out what's going on with him. So, before I look around the apartment, I thumb through the phrase book, and point to "hurry" and "trouble." He gives me the thumbs-up at "hurry." Being careful to smile widely, he gives me the thumbs-down at "trouble." Grabbing the phrase book from my hands, he finds "friend" and "guide" and "no money," and pats my shoulder in the most companionable manner. His hands are shaking.

I am surprised that the neat modern apartment looks much like a small two bedroom apartment in the US I use the flush toilet which is a novelty for me after my weeks of squatting in fields and over holes behind the straw and mud walls that serve as latrines in most of China.

When I emerge, he is dashing around in a frenzy, but slows down long enough to hand me a cup of hot tea, then trots into a bedroom. Running back, he holds his driver's card up to his face, inviting comparison. The photo could be of any man in China. He's probably Han Chinese, as is 95% of the population, and I cannot, even after a month here, pick out an individual from the crowd. Then, trying to hurry everywhere at once, he turns in circles a couple of times, jumps into a bedroom to scramble through a dresser, throwing out items of clothing and junk until he finds a pair of black leather gloves, which he runs out to push into my hands. They have fur linings, he shows me, and makes me try them on while he finds a pair of red cotton gloves to add to my collection of gifts, which soon includes two tins of tiger balm and, after more scrambling, a tiny green bottle of cologne.

Muttering in Chinese he runs to a desk and takes out a plastic model of a race car, comes back to where I am sitting on the couch with my green tea and races it through the air in front of my face, making hilarious sounds that must be the Chinese version of "vroom vroom."

Laughing in glee he hustles over to open the door of the second bedroom, which is tinted rose inside by the sun shining through sheer red curtains covering the window. I hear more noise of drawers being shoved in and out before he emerges, as though he has been physically ejected by some unknown force, to refill my cup with hot water.

I decide to allow myself the luxury of the modern toilet again, and when I emerge he has for me a large black magic marker and a leather key ring, which are given with the explanation, "JAPANESE! GOOD! CHINESE! BAD!" and runs back into the bedroom.

On the living room wall is a poster-size wedding day photo. His bride's happy beautiful face is framed by the high collar of a red lace wedding dress. Her head is tilted, touching his perfect hair, his smooth face and precise features made more precise by his wedding-day pancake makeup, mascara and lipstick which is part of the costume of all Chinese grooms. I am studying this carefully, trying to decide if I should go collect a brick when the phone rings. After a hasty conversation the hitchhiker shouts, "LET'S GO!" In case I haven't understood, he gathers my driving gloves and helmet and the gift gloves and the balm and the perfume and the other things and shoves them into my hands and my pockets, then runs in circles a couple of times for good measure before he pulls me out the door by my arm.

Finally on the road, he leads me through villages and past roads I would have mistaken for the main route, and helps me through a detour around an accident between a couple of big blue trucks, which are apparently the kind that he drives. We stop for gas once, during which time he walks between the office and the gas pump at least ten times before the tank is full. I offer him the gift gloves, as it is cold outside, but he refuses.

We ride in the dark for an hour or two before I have to pull over to stretch and to let the engine cool. We are both freezing, and for a second time I press him to wear at least one pair of the gloves, but he shouts "GIFT!!" with a double exclamation mark, further emphasized by his eyebrows which are arched high on his forehead. The subject is closed. He lights a cigarette and walks in circles, pulling me with him, jabbering in Chinese with the occasional English word until I am made to understand that his truck is in Yinchuan. It is not supposed to be in Yinchuan. Hurry.

"Vroom vroom!" he then says again, in Chinese. Then "Borshe! Fellalli! New Yok! Vroom! Good!" He is a hyperactive race car fanatic, and I am glad he's not driving.

A dog barks outside a hut that we hadn't seen in the darkness. The hitchhiker looks me in the eye, decides something and pats the front of my leather jacket until he finds the little green bottle of cologne. He opens it under my nose and I jerk my head back. It smells like a mixture of menthol and turpentine. This is when I finally get it. My hitchhiker is amped on amphetamines. I've picked up a speed freak trucker who probably did some black-market deal gone bad with goods he'd picked up from Lhasa or Dali and now his truck is stuck in Yinchuan, for God knows why. He will be eternally grateful that he found a ride from someone who doesn't know him. I am his savior.

The dog barks urgently now, smelling a foreigner. The lights go on and the family comes out, straining to see us in the dark.

"LET'S GO!" says the hitchhiker, in a stage whisper. He is incapable of talking softly. As he pulls me by the arm to the motorcycle I hear the engine still pinging in the chill air. Nevertheless, I climb on the bike but the hitchhiker stands there until I turn the key to ON. He presses the ignition button and jumps when the engine turns over.

"YESSSS!" he shrieks. "YESSSS!"

He runs around to the other side of the bike and pushes the horn button.

"YESSS!" he shrieks again. Now the dog is in a frenzy and the family is edging toward us, but the hitchhiker has jumped on the back and now are off and running, bearing down on a three-wheeled bicycle which swerves toward the middle of the road, its back platform loaded down with bricks. I beep the horn twice.

"YESSSS!" shouts the hitchhiker, in wild delight. The rest of the way I beep at every tractor, bicycle, and pedestrian I see.

"YESSSS!" he yells. I beep my horn at a pothole. Then I beep my horn at nothing, just for the hell of it.

"YESSSS!" he shouts, as if he were summoning God, and then he takes hold of my shoulders, kneading them hard through the leather and all my layers of clothing until he reaches the sore muscles that have been bugging me for a week.

"YESSSS!" I scream through my Plexiglas face shield. The hitchhiker follows with a chop-chop back massage. We are both laughing with glee. We have finally understood.

# My Secret Is That I'm Green

**John Ferguson**

*When adventure finds you.*

I'M LUCKY.

Life is a string of beach parties, pool halls, army base recreation halls, Harley-Davidson bars, surfing, weddings, barbecues, dance clubs, nudie bars, schools, hospitals and jail. Love that sun. Wherever I go, I'm a babe magnet. Women assemble, 98% say hi. Nobody believes I'm real.

I steal attention from my friends, but they catch the ride with me.

I fit in everywhere, as tranquil a spirit you've ever met. Kids are amazed by my coolness. They can pet me, even hold me. Come to think of it, I act like a child myself. If I want something I take it, If I don't, I throw it. Happy while out on the town—left alone, caged in, I snap. To picket my abandonment issues, I once ate five grams of lead that hung in the base of some old curtains. Nearly bought it. Yeah, I mess with everything—whoops: gnarled the seats in the brand-new boat. How about the time I was lost for days until my mate found me on the railroad tracks?

I sleep standing on one or two feet. When annoyed I tuck my head under my wing. When I'm cold, I puff up to insulate myself. I sneeze when I'm cold too—stuffy nose.

A few years ago two pitbulls attacked me. Afterwards, all I could manage were groggy moans. I was saved and hand fed after a surfing accident too.

Man, I'm neon green. I even poop green. Bewitching the gals is swell. I puff up when they come around too. And I'm not a bad-mouthing parrot—don't even get in trouble when I whistle "nice ass!"

Don't dislike me because I look cool while wind surfing. I have bad days too: I was once nearly killed by a drunk. Drunks are no longer allowed to hold me. Always watch where you leave me, some people want to steal me.

I reflect your mood. I know when it's time to sleep, wake up, eat and surf. Wallowing in pool halls, I always get a great seat on your shoulder.

My 12-year-old Black Lab friend, Zeus, doesn't mind when I cruise the beach on his back. I also sit on Apollo's head while he swims. You oughta see us together. I'm a parrot, they're dogs. No big deal. Green is keen.

All of my days are adventures. See you around, look for the flock of babes.

\* \* \*

Lucky is a stouthearted Yellow Nape Amazon Parrot who was found on McLellan Air Force Base.

# SERENDIPITY AND FRIENDSHIP

## The Kaleidoscope of Personality

*"Free your mind, and your feet will follow."*
Anonymous Proverb

# Strangers

## Linda Watanabe McFerrin

*The allure of strangers is the allure of travel. There is no thrill like the first wicked little tongue of flame.*

I WAS LEAVING ANTWERP BEHIND. The rail car rocked and rolled on its carriage, shaking me up. Outside the train windows the landscape rushed by, rain-soaked and dark. Antwerp had been gloomy, the weather bad. Peter Paul Rubens' rosy nudes seemed to sulk, petulant under a murky pall. Lawrence and I had ventured out under big black umbrellas until the damp and cold crawled under our clothes, spreading icy hands over our flesh. But, the weather drove us indoors. We retreated to the warm cocoon of the hotel room, to the ministrations of kitchen and staff. We spent two days between sheets, until they were thick white ropes, twisted and knotted; days punctuated by the gloved knock of the bellman, platters of smoked eel, delicate wines, pastry crumbs.

"This rain won't let up," Lawrence said, leaning into his arms, his weight against the window casement.

I was watching the hard line of his back, ass and thigh, the way muscle bunched and stretched with each movement, the white sheen of bare skin.

"I'm leaving for England tomorrow."

He turned towards me.

"Why?" I asked, "Can't take anymore?" Fingertip to my breasts, I traced each nipple, watching it rise and harden under my touch.

"Hardly," he said, leaning over me, replacing my hands with his.

"Maybe I'm not finished with you yet," I said.

"Maybe not, but I've got to work."

"Fine," I murmured into his neck. "I'll take the train."

I took the train. Antwerp to dreary Oostende—I leaned back into the train cushions' dingy velour plush. Most of my body ached. The chill had finally weaseled its way into my core. My limbs thrummed in exhaustion. Part of me craved still more attention. That morning I had noticed how my nipples had darkened, become deeply russet. Other changes—breasts and lips swollen. A delicious languor filled me. I was leaking sex.

**140**

Thunder? Or was it the train roaring along its track? The low rumble rose, not in the distance, but beneath me like a flapping sheet of metal, noisy and grim. On the shape-shifting horizon, an arrowhead of tiny black birds shot heavenward. A cuckoo nest looked cockeyed, balanced precariously, high in a tree. The cows never looked up from the high grass that they'd settled in. Ramshackle houses. Rail tracks criss-crossing. Rust rail on rust. Fat bundles of sheep buried deep in grass. And the grey curtain of rain draped over all.

A long-haired young man walked down the aisle past me, back tracked, hoisted his bag up onto the rack over my head. His jeans brushed my cheek when he did this. He smelled of vanilla and bay rum.

"You don't mind?" he asked in English.

"Oh, no, not at all," I replied.

He sat across from me, right ankle resting on left knee, pushing his long brown hair behind his ears. I looked back out the window. His gaze followed mine.

I'd left Lawrence in Brussels. Apprehensive, I was having one of my panic attacks—my heart racing like a featherweight stockcar, slapped with its decals—old memories, old wounds. Even now, anxiety stabbed with the thought of Lawrence standing, strangely alone, two suitcases and his briefcase stacked neatly beside him. I reminded myself that I'd see him again, in England. Sudden and vivid, the recollection of our dinner at a restaurant in Antwerp—champagne cocktails, a golden Sancerre, much wine. I saw Lawrence's white business card, illuminated in his hand, like some auspicious and mysterious sign in a Cocteau film. The card looked luminous in the shadowy dining room, a ghost object, something drawn from another world or from a magician's hat, like an egg or a live, kicking rabbit.

"So, where are you headed?" the young man asked.

"Huh? Oh, Oostende. I'm taking the ferry to Dover."

"The ferry? That's a long ride."

"I mean the hydrofoil," I corrected myself. "I'm meeting someone in England."

"Someone?" he asked playfully.

"Yes," I mumbled. "Someone."

Outside, the cows huddled in one corner of rainy field. They were red-spotted. Their large pink noses quivered as the train clattered past them. I saw my own brown eye flash past, reflected in the window on a background of clay and white houses, the protective coloration of the collective. My eye looked dark and mysterious, an inquisitive brown orb sliding thoughtfully over the landscape, over farm and hamlet alike. The young man's visage was reflected in the window, somewhere behind mine—his face, curious and attentive, his hair, softly umber—a cloud in the back of my mind. I had seen Lawrence this way, in the train window, reflected on rivers and castles along the Rhine. I had drawn him twice, once as an Egyptian with kohl-rimmed eyes, because I saw the suggestion of this in my own eye and in the deep creases that crawl from the corners of his. I told him that I would begin to draw him then and that I would draw him 8000 times. He told me that would take thirty years, at one image a day. I have thirty years; but I drew him twice, thinking to make it fifteen.

"I'm getting off at Brugge," my compartment companion announced. "Have you ever been there?"

"No," I answered, looking at him closely. He had a handsome face, tawny lips, beautiful white teeth, a compassionate smile.

"It's like Venice, very romantic," he said.

"Really?"

"Yes, you could even have lunch there," he added. "My treat."

His invitation, the sincerity of his voice, kindled a response in me. I felt its pull—the stranger's desire to connect.

"I don't think so," I said. "I'd be late. I have to meet someone."

He nodded and smiled. "I see," he said.

The train pulled into Gent. A line of shabby buildings sagged mournfully on either side of the track. The black-trunked chestnut trees with their tattered, rust-tipped leaves provided only a partial curtain. The train pulled out. The brick became modern. We passed through secluded coverts. Trailers nestled in them like little white eggs—more clay and white houses, clay and white cows, and the ominous grey of the sky.

The young man, whose name was Michael, told me about his career as an ecological engineer. He was exuberant. He was full of fire. He asked me, again, about lunch. I was hungry. I'd had nothing to eat but a cookie and coffee at around 6:00 in the morning. Again I declined. But I liked the way he would smile out the window and watch me from the corner of his eye. I regretted my rush.

One cannot, of course, see much of Brugge from the rail station—wet streets, shiny asphalt, more cloud-covered sky. It didn't look much like Venice, but it was charming, a city of very old houses. Michael got off there. Reaching up for his bag, he looked down at me.

"Last chance," he said.

I smiled and shook my head "no."

I missed him at once. The rail car seemed empty and forlorn. I sneezed twice.

*Damn this cold weather,* I thought. *I'm catching a cold.*

Outside, the landscape was flattening—Oostende, dirty Oostende, opening onto the channel, the crossing to England.

The ferry terminal was not attractive at all. Was this what one was to expect crossing over? Everyone looked equally bad in the urine-yellow light. I had yet to purchase a ticket to Victoria Station and another from Eustace Station. There'd be a cab ride, too, in between. I had no idea of time. I changed money. A certain criminal air hung over everything. After the efficiency of the trains, the ferry operation seemed tardy and mediocre. Not so bad, I supposed, if one had only to do this once, this second class sort of steerage, as if large herds of cattle were daily shuttling back and forth.

*It's a long way to England,* I thought. *Red Rover, Red Rover, send my lover over to Dover.*

It was clear, almost immediately, as they announced the first movie, that I had boarded the wrong vessel. I was not on the high-speed hydrofoil. I was on the ferry—the slow boat to Dover. Too late to turn back, the seamless grey of channel and sky stretched before me. I sulked in the cabin, pressed around by large families, by children running about. I read for a while. I slept fitfully. Roused by my hunger, I got up from my seat and foraged, found nothing to my liking in the cafeteria. I bought Belgian chocolates, for gifts, at the Duty Free Shop thinking I'd eat some of them. I got wedged into a line. Someone was shoving behind me—a young man in a black leather jacket.

"They're pushing behind me," he explained. "Cut it out," he yelled over his shoulder, hazel eyes full of laughter. I considered the broad backside of the person in front of me and decided to hold my line. Still jostled, I paid for the chocolate with large bills and made my way back to my seat. He followed and took the seat next to mine. He had a guitar. He had a small knapsack on his back. Six gold hoops of diminishing size glittered on the lobe of his right ear. I would have guessed him to be nineteen, but the fifth of vodka that he'd bought at the Duty Free Shop suggested that he might be older than that.

"Name's David," he said. "Wanna play cards?"

I looked at him, at my book, at the featureless horizon outside the window, at the vodka, and said "OK."

We played a childish game. We played War. He snapped up my cards with a wide grin and gusto. Occasionally, he'd take a pull from the vodka.

"Do you play the guitar?" I asked.

"Yeah," he said, taking a break from our card game to plunk out a few notes. It sounded nothing like music. "I'd play a song for you," he said. "I'd play a song for you, because you're so pretty."

**143**

He placed his hand on my thigh and leaned toward me. The thick brown curls of his hair smelled of sweat and dust. A silver chain swung from his shirt. It had a funny charm on it that looked like a boot. His breath smelled faintly of vodka, vodka and the Belgian chocolates that I'd bought. I reached out to touch each of the tiny gold hoops that gleamed on his ear. He rubbed his jaw voluptuously against the back of my hand. I was surprised at how soft it was.

When we disembarked at Dover, David hovered protectively at my elbow, using his body as a barrier between me and the crowd of other passengers. The guitar on his back made him dangerous. The night was rainy and black. The famous white cliffs of Dover were ash-colored ghosts hunched in darkness. We stood in long lines under fluorescent lamps, waiting for passport stamps and instructions. We all boarded a bus to the train station. David sat next to me.

"I've missed my train," I said.

"We're both going to London," he said happily. "We'll keep one another company."

"Yes," I agreed. He scooted closer to me on the seat. "Yes, that'll be fine."

Once at Dover Station, we found that the last train would leave in ten minutes. It would let us off at Victoria Station. We'd both need to catch cabs or the Underground to Eustace Station to get on with our journeys, but there would be no trains out of Eustace until the next morning. We could not stay all night at the station.

"We can share a cab," David insisted, showing me the paltry cash that he had on hand.

"And a room?" I asked.

"Well?" he smiled shyly, his fingertips stroking the back of my hand.

I must have smiled sympathetically, because he grabbed my hand quickly and said, "Come on. Come on, now, the train will be leaving."

"Wait," I said. "I have to place a call."

"Not now," he insisted.

"There is someone waiting for me," I said.

I found a telephone booth and stepped into it, trying to figure out how to use it. I hadn't enough change. David loaned me twenty pence, his face worried as I made my connection.

Lawrence's voice: "What happened? You weren't at the station. No, don't risk the hotels in London. Stay where you are. Find a place for the night."

We talked on and on and David faded, a ghost, a waif drifting reluctantly off to the last train. I didn't even see him leave. I heard the train pull out and knew

I must find a place for the night in Dover.

The station was deserted. It had a sorrowful, funereal feel. David's puppy-like zeal had been comforting. I felt lonely. The station master grew kinder as the crowd thinned. At last, he pointed toward an embankment on the hill above the station.

"There'll be bed and breakfast up there," he said. "Or, you can check out the Priory, right across the street."

Yearning for charm and intimacy, I climbed the steps to the street above and crossed it, dodging puddles and a sudden couple of cars, to the line of tall, narrow buildings, each with its sign, "Bed and Breakfast."

Selecting one, I walked hopefully up the front stairs. A florid, bleary-eyed women met me at the door. She had on a thin cotton robe that came to her knees, white socks, and slippers. Knots of varicose veins, purple and green, marbled the stone-colored flesh of her calves. A bonnet of curlers and pin-curls capped her head.

"Oh, yes," she said in answer to my questions, "I'll show you the room, then."

She climbed the cramped stairway with great difficulty, her slippered feet catching often on the frayed, floral carpet. The room was dreadful—dirty and drab.

"I was also thinking about the Priory," I said, turning to where she stood in the doorway behind me, hands on wide hips. "Do you know it?"

"Oh, yes," she remarked critically. "I don't think you'd like it. New owners and all. You can still smell the paint."

"Well, I need to check it out," I replied. "I'll probably be back."

I was back on the cold street, the promise of new paint my sole comfort.

The Priory was a crowded matchbox of warmth. Rosy faces, glowing in firelight, turned toward my entrance. I found the manager, a thin dark-haired man, and explained my situation to him.

"Been to the hill, have you?" he laughed. "Well, we'll set you up. Jeffrey, show this lady one of the rooms."

Jeffrey or Jeff, who was serving beers at the bar, was fair and muscular. He had spiky blond hair that stood up from his head and seemed to ignite in the firelight. A faint golden stubble covered his jaw. I followed him up a meandering staircase, past other landings, to a small white door. The room was small also, but crammed with a large pine armoire, antique table, and chest drawers. The four-poster bed was nearly buried under a down comforter covered with a delicate rosebud pattern. The room had a clean porcelain bath and the smell of fresh paint—white trim, soft aqua walls.

"It's perfect," I sighed. "How much?"

"Twenty pounds," was the prompt response.

"I'll take it." I was elated.

Jeffrey walked into the bathroom. "Lovely bath," he said proudly, "right in the room. You'll probably want that."

I wondered, for a moment, if I now smelled like David—sweaty and faintly alcoholic. A vague nostalgia stirred.

"Can I pay you now?" I asked. "I have to catch a 4 a.m. train."

"Course," Jeff answered. "Hardly worth sleeping. Come on out back, and I'll show you how to leave in the morning. There'll be no one up at that hour."

He led me downstairs and took me out back to a little, fenced garden where a prim, white gate opened onto the street. It was windy and wet. Leaves and blossoms, whipped to a frenzy, released a sinuous fragrance—the foliage dripping, the night bitter cold.

"This'll be it. Would you like me to wake you?" he asked. His blue eyes held something behind them: chaos, the first sign of a blaze.

"I don't think so," I said. "But thanks, anyway."

We were turning to leave when I stopped him. "Listen," I ventured, "I'm starving. Any chance of some food?"

"Sorry, no," he said. "The kitchen's been closed for hours. Maybe a package of chips." Disappointment edged his voice.

"I'll pass," I said glumly. "How about some white wine?"

"That, I think I can do," he responded shortly. We both went inside.

As Jeffrey did not come up with the wine, I hopped into the bath. "Probably pissed off at me," I thought. The bath was a luxury, after the arduous day. Blowing my nose into toilet paper, I knew that I really was catching a cold. I coddled myself, admiring my body in the herb-scented water. I took my sweet time. I was just getting out when I heard someone knocking. In mild irritation, I put on a robe and opened the door. Jeffrey stood in the hall with a large service tray. He had untied his tie and unbuttoned his collar. His eyes twinkled with merriment. On the tray was a platter of toast, chicken liver *paté* in a big, clumsy bowl and two glasses of white wine. He smiled gallantly.

"I've put something together for you," he said. "Hope you like it."

I looked ruefully at the two glasses of wine.

"I've changed my mind," I said. "You can wake me at four."

"Great," he exclaimed. "Let's drink to it."

"Oh, alright," I surrendered. "Come on in. But remember to wake me at four. I have someone waiting for me."

# The Invisible Jam

## David Redhill

*For a musician on the road, some of the best conversations have no words.*

HEY THERE!

The voice was American, the accent Southern, with a trace of teenage redneck. I looked around. A sunburned, crew-cut face grinned from the back seat of the bus, surrounded by other sunburned, cheesy grins. He pointed brightly to my guitar.

"You play?"

I could see it coming. They were probably singers themselves, and of the chipper college-gospel ilk at that. "The Celebrant Singers," he confirmed. "We're playing in Colombo tonight. We're gonna share some *joy!* Hey, why don't you come on over?" An extra big grin: "Maybe yew could sit in with me an' the team!"

My last day in Asia: seven countries and a year on the road. Jungle ruins, coconut mountains, gliding sikharas and chattering children. The guitar had held out nicely, notwithstanding the odd fall from an elephant's back into a river—and the tumble down that Himalayan hillside had done me more damage than the fretboard. It had been worth it, if only for the night playing to children in a Thai village, the jam in a Rangoon street with surly police looking on, or the late night session in the Rajasthani villager's hut, trying to follow his weird rhythms. Leading to six lost months in India, and a week in sad, war-torn Sri Lanka.

"Say, is that an *Aws-tray-lian* accent you're talkin'?"

The monsoon had broken that morning, and the palms at the side of the road were lashed by a violent gale as we rumbled up the road, with dirty water streaming along the bus floor. I was due to catch a flight for London early the next morning, and had one night to kill in the capital. The bus groaned over the last few potholes into the depot and expired. We all filed out into the rain, the singers whooping as they ran for cover. "We'll be stayin' and a-playin' at the Wah Em Cee Ay," hollered the grin. "See ya laterrrrr ..."

I did not stay at the YMCA.

I stayed at the Sri Lankan Ex-Serviceman's Club, a venerable, scruffily elegant establishment permeated with the dignity and pathos of the declining Raj. My room was classic Asian dog-box: mottled walls, a narrow iron bed and two feet of floor space. It was the last of a row, with communal showers on the other side. I prepared my bag for departure the next morning, had a smoke, and sat down with the guitar for one last time. It could barely be heard over the splashing and yelling from the showers, the shouts and echoing Tamil laughter all but drowning a Bach suite I had been massacring for months. Again and again; I could not get it right. I put the guitar down and lay back. And froze.

In the next cubicle, a violin was tentatively plucked. It wheedled, coughed and began playing a tune I knew: the Bach. It was taken all the way through, all six parts. Perfectly, ethereally, like silk and spun glass, swimming up and spilling over the gap between the wall and the moldy ceiling, cascading into my own room and flowing into my ears like honey.

Was this really happening?

Now for a bit o' the blues; I wondered if this virtuoso could, er, relate. More fool I. The violin swept in on the fourth beat, wailing into a wrenching solo as the Tamils showered, oblivious to the Dog Box Blues. That violin had lived through some pain. I strung together a solo of my own, swung through a few more choruses, and we faded out together.

Silence.

Then it began again. This was Eastern, however, and unmelodic: the bow sawing away at the bottom strings, a demented drone punctuated by staccato jabs off the top. And then back West it went, a raunchy stomping fiddlin' hoedown; I chimed in on the gee-tar and we took it through several scattered rounds before collapsing in a disheveled mess.

Of course, I was bursting to know. I had heard laughter from the violinist at one of my more audacious trills, and from this, the only sign, I knew my companion was male. But who? How old, how young, how serious, how crazy? And from which country? Less than two yards separated us; it would have taken but a few steps to knock on his door, to meet face to face, and share a smile. This was, after all, the best jam session of my life. Yet something inevitably held me back, as I'm sure it prevented him—there was a great deal more at stake. There was, anyhow, no time to wonder, for now came another toccata, now a Gaelic dirge, now some rock and bloody roll. The guy was unbelievable. Everything I played, he embellished with the maestro's touch. He spun mellifluous circles around that doss-house like a magician, and I never saw his face. Or knew his name. For that was our unspoken agreement; it could only be perfect that way. Such moments are to be shared singly. I shall go to my grave with the exquisite pleasure of remembering.

We kept at it until dawn, when I got up, packed the guitar, and left for the airport. It was drizzling. Asia was over.

# Sleepless in Siena

## Don George

*So you think you've had a lousy night's sleep? When you least expect it,*
*expect it.*

IN TWO AND A HALF DECADES OF WORLD-WANDERING, I have found myself
in some pretty strange beds, from a back-stabbing rough-straw pallet in
Jakarta to a concrete slab in Luxor, a fuel-perfumed sleeping bag on the deck
of an Aegean ferry to the mother of all U-shaped sagging-spring mattresses
on the Caribbean island of Carriacou. And I have shared sleep—or the lack of
it—with a wild range of comrades, from crazy nightmare-muttering Eastern
European poets in a youth hostel to prim, pent-up, nervous-giggling Swiss sec-
retaries in a train compartment. And of course I have spent my share of hours
with companionable mosquitoes, rodents and cockroaches.

But the strangest place I have ever slept was on the first of my miserable
nights on the road.

So let me take you back to December 1976. I have recently graduated from
college and am in the midst of a year-long fellowship teaching English at Athens
College in Greece. It's Christmas vacation and so I have set out on an exploration of Italy and Austria—footloose, penniless, experimenting with the world.

I have been blessed by the pope—a velvet-shrouded third-story speck—on
Christmas Day in St. Peter's Square, and spent days gaping at the Sistine Chapel,
the Pieta and other treasures, awed by the convergence of skill, faith, courage
and perseverance.

In this epiphanic mood, I have missed one train to Siena and so have gotten
on a later train, a train that arrives in that dazzling 16th century town at 11 at
night. This is when I discover that 16th century towns go to bed early. I wander off the train platform toward the information booth, where I am accustomed to finding a room for my stay. Closed. I look around at the last few
passengers scurrying into the black, cold night. No fellow travelers; no sympathetic locals.

I take some frayed *Let's Go* guidebook pages out of my backpack and find a
few pensiones near the station. Shuffle down the street and knock on the door
of the first one I come to. The door opens a crack and quizzical eyes peer

around it.

"*Scusi, una camera ...*" I begin to say, when a voice barks, "*Completo!*" and the door slams shut.

Three more doors, three more "*Completo!*" Around midnight on an end-of-December night, all of Siena is completo, I am sure. So I wander exhausted over the in-other-circumstances charming cobbled streets of the town until, brain-weary and bone-cold, I come upon an elegant old apartment building. On an impulse, I push the door, and it opens.

Alice in Wonderland: I step into a marble-and-chandelier foyer, dark and deathly silent. A wide polished stone staircase spirals in front of me. For some reason I walk up and up and up, until on the sixth floor I find a hospitable-looking door stoop with a welcome mat for a mattress. There, almost numb with sleep, I unroll my sleeping bag and slip into a stony repose.

The next thing I know light is slivering my eyes—the Siena sun! Well, no, it's light spilling through the door that has just opened above me, barely illuminating the astonished eyes of the Italian gentleman in the silk bathrobe who was expecting to find his morning paper. He stares at me, unable to speak. "*Scusi,*" I say, stumbling over my tongue. I wave a wan hand in the air. "*Tutto completo,*" I say. "OK, OK," he says, and closes the door quickly but carefully.

I lie back, trying to recollect who and where I am, then number the creaks in my body and assess the gray whirl in my head. In my 23 years I cannot remember hurting so much, in so many places. I am cold and sniffling and creaking and all I want to do is pull the sleeping bag over my head and discover it's a dream, but then I think about the old gentleman dialing the Italian police and figure I'd better get moving.

So I coil my energy, preparing to leap out of my sleeping bag, roll it up, stuff everything into my backpack and get walking before I am conscious of the cold. As my frozen fingers are stubbing my sleeping bag into its sack, the door opens again, and the man reappears—with a roll on a china plate and steaming coffee in a gold-rimmed cup and saucer. "*Prego,*" he says, setting it on the stone hallway with a small smile. "*Efkharisto,*" I say in Greek, because I suddenly can't remember the Italian word for thank you. He nods and shuts the door firmly.

Suddenly that spare, sixth-floor stoop feels like a sumptuous sitting room, and I stretch my legs on the stone floor, sipping and chewing in Sienese grandeur, and silently saying "*Grazie*" to a welcoming wooden door.

# The Khan Men of Agra

## Pamela Michael

*Taxi-wallahs in India may surprise and bestow the ride of your life.*

ONE GOOD THING ABOUT MONSOONS: they sure keep the dust down, I thought to myself, peering out the milky window of the Taj Express. I surveyed the approaching station from my uncertain perch between two lurching cars, ready to grab my bag and disembark purposefully. Despite the early hour, the platform slowly scrolling past me was packed with people.

Of the dozen or so bony hands struggling to wrench my suitcase from my grip as I stepped off the train at Agra, perhaps two were porters, four or five were rickshaw drivers, three or four were taxi drivers, and maybe a couple were thieves. The sudden rush of mostly barefoot men in states of [un]dress ranging from rags to britches brought me face to face with the difficulty of "reading" a person's demeanor or intentions in an unfamiliar culture. What to do?

I already knew from my few days in New Delhi that I would have to choose one of these men—not because I didn't want to carry my own bag, but because I would be hounded mercilessly until I paid someone to do it for me. It's a defensive necessity, and an effective hedge for women traveling alone who must rely on their own wits and the unreliable kindness of strangers—the taxi-wallah as protector and guide. In Delhi, though, the competitive tourist market is based more on ingenuity and charm than intimidation. Many of the drivers had developed very engaging come-ons, my favorite being the rickshaw driver who purred, "And which part of the world is suffering in your absence, Madam?"

My reluctance to hire anyone apparently was being interpreted as a bargaining ploy. Several men had begun to yell at each other and gesture toward me, ired by the low rates to which their competitors were sinking for the privilege of snagging a greenhorn tourist fresh off the train. Not wanting to see the end result of such a bidding war, I handed over my bag to the oldest, most decrepit-looking of the bunch, deciding I might be able to outrun (or overtake) him if I had to and also because he had an engaging (if toothless) smile.

Triumphant, he hoisted my bag on top of his turban and beckoned me to follow as he set out across the tracks. For the first few minutes the old man

**151**

had to fend off a persistent few rival drivers who thought they could convince me to change my mind by casting aspersions on the character, safety record and vehicle of the man I had chosen, whose name he told me, was Khan, Kallu Khan.

Half-way through the station, in a particularly crowded spot, Kallu handed my bag to another (much younger and, I theorized, more fleet-footed) man. "Hey, wait a minute!" I protested. "My cousin Iki," Kallu assured me. "So, what's he doing with my bag?" I asked. "Helper," I was told. I went into red-alert and quickened my pace to keep up with Iki and my luggage.

As we reached the street it began to rain again, part of the deluge/blue sky monsoon cycle to which I had become accustomed. Over my objections, Iki put my bag in the trunk of their car, a battered Hindustan Ambassador that was unmarked except by mud, no reassuring "Agra Taxi Company" emblazoned on the door. "Thief might steal suitcase in back seat, Madam," Kallu explained. I acquiesced—the dry shelter of the "taxi" looked inviting and I was worn down by the ceaseless demands on my ability to communicate, decipher, make decisions, find, respond, protect, etc. that travel entails, even in a four-star situation, which the Agra train station was decidedly not.

Once underway, my relief at having escaped the crowd and rain was somewhat dampened by my realization that I was on a rather deserted road with two men who were probably making the same kind of un- and misinformed assumptions about me that I was making about them. I peered out the rain streaked window to my right to get my bearings and to take in some of the sites I had come to India to see. I was also tentatively toying with escape options.

All I could see was a blur of red, towering overhead and as far into the distance as I could make out. This was the Red Fort, of course. I had done my homework, so I knew the walls were 70 feet high, surrounded by a moat. On my left was a long stretch of sparse forest, separated from the roadway by a crumbling, low iron fence.

Suddenly, Iki pulled the car over on the left and stopped alongside a broken place in the fence. Kallu got out of the passenger side and opened my door saying, "Now I show you something no tourist ever see, Madam." "That's all right, let's just get to the hotel. Tomorrow is better," I demurred. "Please Madam," he insisted and, sensing my concern about my suitcase, he added, "Don't worry, Iki stay here with your bag."

I was already chastising myself for being so naive and trying to decide how much real danger I was in when I looked—really looked—into Kallu's eyes for the first time. They were kind; kind and bloodshot, but kind.

In an instant I made the sort of decision that every traveler has to make from time to time: you decide to take a risk, trust a stranger, enter a cave, explore a trail, act on intuition and experience something new. It is this giving oneself over to a strange culture or environment that often reaps the most reward, that makes travel so worthwhile and exhilarating.

As if to affirm my decision, the rain stopped. "OK, Mr. Khan, you show me," I said. We walked down a muddy path through a stand of stilted trees, leaving Iki behind, smoking a bidi. My courage faltered a couple of times when I caught a glimpse of a spectral, loin-clothed man through the leaves, but I said nothing and slogged on, hoping for the best.

It came quickly and totally unexpectedly—an enormous mauve river, its banks aflutter with river-washed tattered clothes hanging from poles and vines—work in progress of dhobi-wallahs, the laundry men. Directly across the river, luminescent in a moisture-laden haze, was the Taj Mahal, seen from an angle that, to be sure, few tourists ever see and shared with affection by a man who clearly derived great pride from its grandeur. The monument's splendor was all the more striking, its manifest extravagance even more flamboyant in contrast to the faded homespun garments flapping rhythmically in the humid monsoon breeze. We could only stand there and beam at each other on the shores of the mighty Yamuna, the Khan man and I. I like to think it was a sweet kind of victory for us both.

# What a Difference a Walk Makes

**Bruce Northam**

*A Welsh wildflower welcomes wondering wanderers.*

MY FATHER AND I WALK TOGETHER A LOT. Last summer, we undertook a 180-mile trek across Wales, coast-to-coast along Offa's Dyke—the grand earthwork project conceived in the 8th century by King Offa to separate England from Wales.

En route we befriended Erica, a Welsh woman who was clearly oblivious to the beck and call of stress. We joined her for fifteen miles atop the long, curving ridge-boundary of Brecon Beacons National Park. At dusk the three of us encountered an elderly lady and her beagle hiking toward us. Teetering along on a walking stick, she wore a motoring cap and clutched a bunch of wildflowers. I said hello and asked her where she was going. She replied in Welsh, "Rydw i yma yn barod." We looked to Erica for a translation.

"She said, 'I'm already there, I'm already there.' "

They continued their placid conversation in Welsh until the old women carried on. As she faded into the distance, I declared my envy for her philosophy. "Let's catch up with her, there's something else I'd like to ask." We spun and caught up with her. She walked a few more steps along the trail, traded her flowers into the other hand and raised an eyebrow. We scrutinized each other for a moment, beings from different eras and opposite sides of an ocean. I marveled at her vibrancy, she contemplated our shift in direction.

Erica translated my question, "What's the secret to a long and happy life?"

She directed her answer to Erica. "Moments." There was a quiet pause.

Then the old woman smiled, squinted at my father and spoke slowly, "Moments ... moments are all we get. A true walker understands this."

Moments. Yes, the significance was not lost on me. A year before this trek, I got the news that my father was seriously ill. A long moment that. No more walks, no more calls, no more ... moments. No more golden sunsets concluding a day of long distance hiking. Well, he was seventy. But a moment is all it takes to change your direction, take a singe step, then another. Soon the distance is met. Open-heart bypass and back surgery. Miraculously, one year later we're savoring Celtic wisdom.

After a silent, timeless minute, we all clutched hands with the old woman, hugged and waved goodbye. Just before she faded into the horizon, I looked back at her, plodding on with eternal poise and bearing. I sent a smile to my father and, together, we treasured that one moment—she's right, that is all we get.

# In Search of Connection

## Linda Packer

*A continuum of spirt spans a generation.*

I'T'S HARD TO SAY WHEN I FIRST FELT THE CONNECTION to my father slipping away. He had been dead for well over a decade, and the fog was overtaking the memories, turning them into fading, sepia-toned snapshots. I wanted to touch him again, touch his life, and in some way make him real.

And so it was that I began to think of finding Pierre Coulon.

It was a name I had grown up with, a figure of mythical proportions. My father had met Pierre Coulon nearly half a century ago, during World War II. Dad had been a navigator in the Army Air Corps; a kid of just 23, he was on a mission to bomb Frankfurt and had been shot down over occupied France. From out of nowhere came the French Resistance, who took him to a tiny town called Bulles some kilometers north of Paris, where he lived for several weeks in a big red brick house with Pierre, his wife and their two young daughters.

I had heard the story every year on the anniversary of the day he was shot down—the only time my dad would talk about it. It became an annual dinnertime ritual: I'd sit across the table from him, fork immobile, listening to the story about his plane being shot out from under him, about the struggles to open his parachute, about landing in a country whose language he didn't understand. He was checked over by a doctor and then taken to Bulles and sheltered by the Coulon family. One day there came a knock on the front door. It was another member of the Resistance, who gave my father a false uniform and passport, led him on a walk through back roads and minefields to a train, and sent him off, in a car full of German soldiers, to freedom. And this part I knew best of all: When the knock on the door came and he had to leave quickly, he took off his watch and handed it to Pierre. "I will never forget you," he said in English, and the Frenchman squeezed his shoulders tightly. They never saw each other again.

\* \* \*

I searched for the little town of Bulles for several months before stumbling upon the detailed maps of the French Government Tourist Organization. No wonder I couldn't find it; apparently it had more cows than people. I asked the

**155**

woman helping me if she could tell me how to contact the town's postmaster—the one individual who, in small European towns and villages, seems to know the whereabouts of every generation of every family who had ever touched the village soil—and I sent him a letter. "I am the daughter of Paul Packer, a navigator in the United States Army Air Corps," it began, "and I am looking for the family of Pierre Coulon. I know that he lived in Bulles during the war, and that he harbored American fighters. My father was one of them."

Within a week I had a response. "Pierre Coulon still lives in Bulles," the postmaster wrote in French. "His wife died many years ago, but his daughters Colette and Denise live nearby. Here is his address," and this was soon followed by another letter. "I am Denise Soulier, the elder daughter of Pierre Coulon," it said, also in French. "We heard about you from the postmaster. We remember your father quite well; please write and tell us about yourself."

Denise had been 15 when she met my father, and her memories were still vivid. We began to correspond, she in French and I in English, and with a dictionary by my side I read how my father had tried to teach them a few words of English, how her little sister Colette had followed the American stranger from room to room. I learned there had been other Americans, eight or nine in total, and that they had slept in the attic. She told me how they hid when the Germans came to search the house ("I am just a simple carpenter," Pierre had said). She told me her father was 82 years old. And I began planning my trip to France.

* * *

Denise, her husband Serge and their basset hound Bibi picked me up at my hotel on the Ile St. Louis. I was going on sheer adrenaline; I had barely slept for two nights, partly from excitement and partly from the fear that, having no common language, we would all spend the day in silence wishing we were somewhere else. Denise seemed to feel no such concern. "Welcome," she said in English, wrapping her arms around me and kissing each cheek twice.

We piled into their car and began the drive to Bulles. To this day I'm not sure where it is or how to get there; I couldn't ask and they couldn't explain. But we used our dictionaries and I figured out that they had never been to America; that they had a daughter Annie and two grandchildren who lived nearby; and that Denise knew things about my father's aborted mission I had never heard from him. I learned there had been three other men with Dad, all from his flight on the Flying Fortress, and that Dad was the only one of the four to write to them. And then, so simple it seemed almost dreamlike, we were in Bulles, driving up to the driveway to the red brick house I had heard about my all my life.

The car stopped, and a young man came strolling up the driveway. Denise smiled broadly. "Letter," she said to me; he was the postmaster, who had come to see the moment he'd made possible. And then we were surrounded by people. First was Colette, tall and blonde and pretty; then their mother's sister; then Colette's husband Roland; then Roland's tiny mother.

And then, suddenly, there was Pierre. He came out of the house all straight and proud, with white hair and thin shoulders and eyes that were gray and blue and liquid. Later in the day those eyes would start to water as I told him he was the reason I'd come to France, and mine would water when he told me my father was the first American who had ever been in his home. He kissed me twice on each cheek and hugged me, and when he did I felt like he was hugging my whole life and everything that had brought me to that moment. He touched his chest and said, "Papy," meaning "grandfather."

We went inside and I sat at the kitchen table while Colette and Denise puttered around making lunch. Pierre disappeared, and when he returned he had in his hand a worn certificate from General Dwight Eisenhower, praising the allies and thanking them for their bravery. It was the first of the many items they wanted to share. They brought out a doll Dad had sent to Colette 40 years earlier. A photo of him in his uniform. Pictures he had sent of my aunt and uncle and cousins. A letter he had written just before Christmas of 1946 in which he had asked the dress sizes of Denise and Colette, and said he'd like a picture of the Coulons for his Christmas present. It was signed, "Your firm friend, Paul."

We gathered around the dining room table with our French/English dictionaries and sat for hours, eating and drinking and taking pictures and eating and drinking and eating again. They toasted me, I toasted them, and we all toasted Papy Pierre, who sat at the middle of the table, looking at all of us with his eyes shining. Denise leaned over and whispered that he hadn't slept for two nights because of his excitement. Pierre and I: co-insomniacs.

As night fell, we prepared to leave.

"Un grand fete," I heard Denise say quietly to Serge, and he nodded. I walked over to Papy Pierre, dug into my bag and pulled out a tissue-wrapped bundle, a pair of cufflinks that had belonged to my father. I touched his arm and said the only French I knew, the phrase I'd been practicing for days. "Ces sont de mon pere; c'est certain qu'il le vous voulait." *These were my father's; I'm sure he would want you to have them.* The whole group was silent, possibly trying to understand my fractured French. But Papy knew. He touched his wrist and said something to Denise. "Your father, he a watch," she translated, and I smiled inside and nodded my understanding. "Merci, Linda," Pierre said quietly. Then he handed me roses from his garden, kissed me on both cheeks, and we left.

\* \* \*

**157**

That was the only time I saw him; he died not long afterward. Denise sent me the death notice from the paper. It said:

### Monsieur Pierre Coulon

Ancien menuisier

Ancien combattant 1939-1945

meaning,

Former carpenter

Former serviceman, 1939-1945

and with it, Denise had written, "Until his last day, he remembered you, Linda, who came from far to meet him in the memory of your father."

And so it goes, I thought, the fragile strands of connection. From father to daughter, from stranger to stranger, one touch building upon the next until we are all, inextricably and eternally, woven together.

# Desiderata

## Unknown

*I met a soft-spoken poet in the Mojave Desert who also kept a travel journal. We shared some of our favorite maxims, such as the poignant passage: "He who knows, does not talk. He who talks, does not know." After exchanging a few quotes, he showed me "Desiderata," which made a deep impression. The passage was written by an unknown author and discarded in Baltimore's Old St. Paul's Church. Passing on from person to person for centuries, it was reprinted in San Francisco's famous Oracle paper in 1969. Timelessly appropriate, Desiderata dates from 1692— reminding us that people devoted to peace, religion aside, have walked the earth since the dawn of thought.*

—Brad Olsen

GO PLACIDLY AMID THE NOISE AND HASTE, and remember what peace there may be in silence. As far as possible without surrender, be on good terms with all persons. Speak your truth quietly and clearly, and listen to others, even the dull and ignorant; they too have their story.

Avoid loud and aggressive people, they are vexations to the spirit. If you compare yourself with others, you may become vain and bitter; for always there will always be greater and lesser persons than yourself. Enjoy your achievements as well as your plans.

Keep interested in your own career, however humble; it is a real possession in the changing fortunes of time. Exercise caution in your business affairs; for the world is full of trickery. But let this not blind you to what virtue there is; many persons strive for high ideals; and everywhere life is full of heroism.

Be yourself. Especially do not feign affection. Neither be cynical about love; for in the face of all aridity and disenchantment, it is perennial as the grass.

Take kindly the council of the years; gracefully surrendering the things of youth. Nurture strength of spirit to shield you in sudden misfortune-but do not distress yourself with imaginings. Many fears are born of fatigue and loneliness. Beyond a wholesome discipline, be gentle with yourself.

You are a child of the Universe, no less than the trees and the stars; you have a right to be here. And whether or not it is clear to you, no doubt the Universe is unfolding as it should.

Therefore be at peace with God, whatever you conceive Him to be, and whatever your labors and aspirations, in the noisy confusion of life, keep peace with your soul.

With all its sham, drudgery and broken dreams, it is still a beautiful world. Be careful. Strive to be happy!

**1692**

# On the Road to Friendship

## Steve Zikman

*A string of synchronous encounters leads the way ...*

SLAP! "GO AWAY! GO AWAY!" Slap, Slap! Both arms waving madly, I race around in circles, in and out of the shade, trying in vain to lose my flying stalkers.

"Leave me a-looooooooone!" I bolt down the road, fifty, a hundred, two hundred feet. Stop. Look around. Nothing. I think I've done it. They're gone. They're really gone! I don't hear them. I am rid of those little bastards. Relief, finally some relief!

Zzzzzzzzzzzzzzzz ... They're back! Zzzzzzzzzzzzzzzz ... "Okay, okay ... I surrender." I return to "my spot" and squat down on my backpack.

My third day by the side of the road—waiting, waiting, waiting, on the edge of the Okavango Delta. How could it be that nobody, absolutely not one single vehicle, is heading up to this narrow quirky piece of the jigsaw puzzle that is post-colonial Africa. Only fifty miles to the Caprivi Strip and nothing. Nothing but a festival of flies and a solitary quiver tree sheltering me from the relentless sub-Saharan sun.

Back in the refreshing spray of Victoria Falls, the thought of hitchhiking my way to this sounded irresistible. After all, it looked close enough on the map. But distances on this continent are deceiving.

Suddenly, in the rippling horizon—a reflection, clouds of dust. Something's coming. I scramble up and into the middle of the dirt track.

It's a motorcycle ... no, two motorcycles, no three. I wave my hands wildly in the air. "Stop! Stop!" They're not slowing down, not in the least. And they're driving right towards me. I spring to the side of the road and watch in disbelief as my rescuers zoom past ... and wave. "Shit!" I turn around.

Another dust cloud approaching? A 4x4? No ... two ... a Jeep and a Landcruiser, caked in brown ... and they're stopping! There's an Italian flag on the hood of the Jeep. The driver motions me in. I grab my pack.

\* \* \*

"Ein Kaffe." Dressed in her traditional Prussian garb, she carefully pours some aromatic blend into her finest Bavarian china. Her black hand is weathered, tired. Her warm smile is welcome.

That one fortuitous ride and twelve days later I'm sitting with Annette and Linda from Johannesburg, sipping coffee in a quaint cafe in deepest, darkest Germanic Africa.

And three little candles. A bright red butterfly. A yellow and black polka dot bowtie. An orange and blue clown with earmuffs.

And streamers, streams and streams of green and purple streamers.

"Ach, blow them out, man ... quickly!" Linda's energy is always pushing us forward.

"Not yet! He needs to make a wish first." Annette can always be counted on for the divine. I close my eyes.

I wish to be in this moment forever. Who else would I share my thirty-first birthday with than this duet of determination and love. Only one week and we've already cultivated a rich and magical connection. From wind-whipped shipwrecks off the Skeleton Coast to the spirited sand dunes further south, we have mined the lunar landscape of our wandering souls. Dusty and delicious discourses about everything and nothing, affinity and passion, truths and untruths. In a blink of time and the magnitude of many miles, the three of us have become friends for life. It's strange how we meet people along travel's path, the twists of fate and circumstance which allow our lives to converge. I feel a grin forming from within as I float back to the slivers of synchronicity which brought us together ...          *   *   *

Vincenzo and his compatriots pull off near a thirsty riverbed for lunch. As I set out my hundredth can of Simba-brand spaghetti (with meatballs), he invites me to join them. We stroll to a shaded area, towards a table covered in a red and green tablecloth. Cutlery, plates and wine goblets are smartly placed. Spinach linguine is being served.

He explains that, being Italian, they had their necessities shipped in the Jeep directly from home—prosciutto, fromaggio, loaves and loaves of bread, bottles and bottles of homemade wine. A slicing machine is running off the vehicle's battery preparing today's Afro-European repas. An Italian aria wafts from the Landcruiser. I don't need to be persuaded to partake of this sumptuous feast.

"Salut!" We clink glasses. I breathe in deeply, fully and savor this surrealistic fling of my faring fortune.

I continue with my Italian contingency for three days on their journey to a game park in northern Namibia. I wasn't planning to head there but I decide to take this culinary excursion as far as it will go.

On the evening of our third day, we arrive at the main gate. A small herd of elephants and some Burchell's zebra form a wondrous silhouette against the setting orange-red sphere. A commanding "Beau Geste" fortress overlooks our campsite. Makatoni palm trees and umbrella thorn acacias abound. We waste no time pitching our tents. It's fettuccine tonight along with the usual appetizers I've quickly grown to crave. There's noticeably little chatter around our campfire dining room. We're exhausted and soon we are fast asleep under the joyous brilliance of the Southern night sky.

A few hours later, awakened by a rustling sound just beyond my tent. I listen carefully and assume it's the wind or a warthog scurrying home for the night.

Moments pass. I hear it again, a little closer, towards the back of my tent, nearest my head. I lie still. The tent material flutters, slightly. Something's out there—or is it a desolate breeze? My hand wanders over to grace the tent. Slaaaaaaaaash! The cold desert night air whooshes in. Adrenaline rush. Impulsively, I spring to the far end of the tent in primitive fear and flash my eyes back towards my pillow. The tent is split wide open. I glance four angry paws. In an unrestrained frenzy, I cry out, "LION! LION! LION!"

"What is it? What is it?," shouts my Italian savior.

I'm panting, "Can you see anything out there? Anything? A lion?"

I hear a zipper opening, cautiously. Silence. More silence. "No, nothing ... nothing."

My fellow campers step warily towards my ravaged tent. I creep out the gaping hole and look up at their aghast expressions. We survey the scene of the crime. The tracks look too small for a lion. What was it?

Eventually, the others return to their slumber. I remain semi-dormant, huddled in a fetal position at the closed end of my tent, my backpack pressed firmly against the exposed area.

In the morning light, I decide to stay behind to repair my mangled abode. My desert deliverers will have to continue without me. While they need to be on the coast in a few days, I have no deadlines and only one tent. They offer me some of their cheese and vino. We exchange wishes for a safe journey. We hug warmly and, in a glint, their convoy disappears into the shimmering silvery white textures of the immense shallow pan.

I'm alone again. I pause to draw some air. If it wasn't a lion, what was it? What will I do about my tent? I'll ask the rangers. I start towards the park office past the other campsites. I notice two women preparing tea and some breakfast.

"Excuse me, would you happen to have some duct tape I can use to fix my tent? I was attacked—"

"Ach man, are you kidding? Do we have duct tape? We own a camping store in Jo'burg ..."             * * *

I lean forward, blow out the festive fire, and, slowly, I open my eyes. I gaze gratefully at my two South African companions, thankful for the grand adventure of our chance meeting, the trail of serendipity's generous gifts—a barren desert track, ten well-fed Italians and one very rabid black-backed jackal.

# Ubuntu

## Bridget Henry

*After South Africans dissolved apartheid, forgiveness and reconciliation*
*hopes to follow. One beautiful word describes it.*

AFRICANS ARE NOT A VENGEFUL PEOPLE; the guiding principle of their traditional culture is ubuntu, a concept only roughly translatable into English, but one that embodies charity, forgiveness, generosity and an essential humanity. Archbishop Desmond Tutu, a great proponent of ubuntu, once explained it like this: 'We say that a human being is a human being because he belongs to a community, and harmony is the essence of that community. So ubuntu actually demands that you forgive, because resentment and anger and desire for revenge undermine harmony. In our understanding, when someone doesn't forgive, we say that person does not have ubuntu. That is to say, he is not really human."

You must first realize that the transition to democracy in South Africa can be called nothing short of a miracle. After over forty years of apartheid, South Africa negotiated the peaceful transition of a black majority government to power. This transition included the 1994 free elections. However, the new nation lacked a constitution since the 1994 elections had been held under an interim one.

The South Africans, ever intent now on achieving the impossible, gave themselves two years from the 1994 elections to develop, draft and ratify a constitution. The Constitutional Assembly (CA), the group which wrote the constitution, was tasked to create a constitution that truly represented the complexity of the new South Africa but most importantly was participatory.

The CA undertook educating the populace and guiding the negotiations that led to a new constitution. In the two year operating time, the CA received over two million submissions about how people saw a democratic South Africa taking shape. These submissions might take the form of a letter to the CA by an individual or a mass petition by an organized group. The final document that took shape was the product of hours of round the clock negotiations that were completed on time. In the end, a diverse nation of almost 40 million people saw 11 languages officially recognized, international human rights enshrined in the constitution, the role of traditional institutions protected and the equal status of all races mandated.

**164**

My sister Lori and I went to South Africa to visit our brother Patrick who is currently in Johannesburg working as a consultant to the South African government. I was looking forward to the trip to see firsthand the aftermath of apartheid. At what level did racism still persist? Was there really a dramatic difference in the lives of whites versus the other ethnic groups—coloureds (those of mixed blood who shared the white Afrikaners language, religion and cultural rituals), Indians and blacks? Could the people of South Africa really forgive and could they rise above their hatred that I assumed was inbred?

One Friday evening in Cape Town we were invited to a party hosted by some Canadian and English journalists. Most of the conversation centered around politics. Nelson Mandela's spokesperson Parks was there, as well as spokespeople for other Members of Parliament, lawyers, and PhDs—all of whom had fought to demolish apartheid regardless of their color.

As they relived stories of imprisonment, torture, death, victory and finally the building of the new South Africa, I was amazed at the lack of anger and that no one demanded revenge or retribution. Americans have a tendency to demand compensation instead of granting absolution, so it was difficult for me to understand the exoneration shown to the apartheid regime. One black friend, Mpho, tried to explain it to me. He did not need a public apology via the Truth and Reconciliation Commission (where apartheid tormentors confess their crimes and are then granted amnesty instead of prosecution) from the prison guards who had brutally beaten him when he was 12. Instead, his revenge, or vindication, was the ANC's victory in the elections. Mandela was president and Mpho was now free to pursue his dreams. He wanted to focus on the future and to help create a strong economic South Africa, in which people of all colors could prosper.

\* \* \*

Early the next morning, eight of us trekked up Table Mountain. You can take the cable car but I highly recommend the 2 ½ hour hike to the top. It actually isn't too difficult and well worth the view. From the top you can see the beautiful sprawling Atlantic coast, the shanty towns, the city and waterfront area of Cape Town and Robben Island, where Mandela was imprisoned for over 20 years. You actually feel like you are on top of the world and can accomplish anything.

Here I was on top of Table Mountain with my brother and sister, blacks, whites and coloureds and the significance of my climb slowly started to dawn on me. I now understood how vital forgiveness and reconciliation was to South Africa. I realized my group represented the new South Africa. These friends were incredibly enthusiastic about their country's future and were willing to work hard to help it achieve prosperity. Their ability to forgive is enviable and will move their country forward more quickly than anything we've ever tried in the United States—If only we could import some ubuntu.

**165**

# All's Fair in Love and War

## Randall Lyman

*The extra electron made a simple threesome radioactive at a time when scorn hath more fury than bullets.*

IT WAS NOT YET LATE BUT ALREADY DARK when the three of us located the youth hostel in Zadar, drove our rental car through the high, gated fence into the enclosed yard, and unexpectedly found ourselves amidst a platoon of soldiers wearing camouflage fatigues and bearing rifles.

"Uh-oh, I think we made a wrong turn," at least one of us said, abruptly less concerned with spending the night than with simply surviving it.

To our relief the soldiers didn't seem alarmed by our arrival and didn't surround us with guns aimed through the windows. One casually approached the driver's window, we said we were just looking for somewhere to sleep, and he explained to us affably that his unit had taken over the hostel as a headquarters, but there was a large hotel nearby, and he'd be glad to take us. Quickly he rounded up three comrades into jeeps—and so a few miles from the front in Yugoslavia's civil war we got a military escort to a five-star hotel on the sunny Adriatic coast.

By now my two female companions and I were marveling at our luck. The soldiers were most hospitable. When we cut our engines in the nearly empty parking lot, our host approached us again and suggested having a drink in the hotel bar. Being journalists, we leaped at the invitation, and the soldiers let us mock drill with their rifles and Tommy guns in the lobby while we interviewed them over red wine about the two-month-old war that was tearing up their country. They were not regular army, but local national guard volunteers defending the city where they lived. Angelo, our host, ran his own jewelry boutique by day, and by night wore a hunting knife tucked into his bootstrap. Their new, still-creased fatigues and our worn denim and tee shirt ensembles contrasted uniquely against the hotel's plush blue armchairs.

It was mid-August, the height of tourist season along one of the most touristed coasts in Europe—yet Taryn, Jennifer, and I were among only 13 guests that night in the 620-bed Hotel Pinija. The war had virtually destroyed Croatia's tourism industry (about 80 percent of its economy), and in a kind of Swiftian modest proposal, the government was attempting to fill the coast's empty hotels with what it now had in abundance: refugees. Zadar housed 2,250

**166**

already. While the children enjoyed the sunny beaches and cowered at the chopping sound of passing helicopters, the women listened to their radios from early morning until late at night for news of their homes and husbands.

I'd recently met Jennifer and Taryn in Berlin during a workshop on foreign corresponding. Jennifer and I had been participants, struck up a friendship, and decided to administer ourselves a mettle-testing final exam by heading into the war zone. She was blonde, sweet, attractive, mid-20s, and in love with the Bible she always carried—the kind of girl who can turn the single guy's usual quest into a theological brain-teaser: scoring with her would be bliss, but sacrilege. I decided not to risk testing my Maker's sense of humor, since I might well be meeting him in a few days. Taryn, a reporter stationed in Berlin, had been a guest speaker at the workshop and asked at the eleventh hour if she could join us, just for the adventure. Jennifer and I looked up to her experience and welcomed her along.

Though I knew Jennifer better, Taryn and I shared a fluency in the German language and a reckless streak in our spirits that bonded us quickly. On our final afternoon in Croatia, for instance, we went swimming in the Adriatic, and while Jennifer dangled her feet in the water and tried not to look, Taryn and I went skinny-dipping. But there was nothing sexual or even flirtatious in my relationship with either of them; had there been, at least I might have understood the later course of events. On the contrary, finding me a "Yugoslavian babe" became a minor occupation of theirs. No, our attentions were focused on the war: covering it and, hopefully, returning from it. But I was about to learn that, like a certain hydrogen isotope, the extra electron was what made a simple threesome radioactive.

We rented a compact car in Berlin but made the mistake of revealing our profession to the rental agent, who immediately typed "Car may not be taken into Yugoslavia" on our contract. That gave us pause. But only pause. As if to punish us—or maybe still save us—the car tore up a fan belt a few miles from the Yugoslav border, forcing us to get it fixed in some Austrian road stop town while we spent the night debating whether to continue, since car trouble in the Yugoslav countryside would make us not only sitting ducks for snipers, but international fugitives from Hertz.

The border ran along the natural line where the Austrian plain bent sharply up into the mountains of Slovenia, and the car bobbed through the hilly terrain like a rowboat in heavy seas. In a valley we crossed a railroad track and found there a fire-gutted boxcar flipped onto its side, and we could still almost hear the flames crackle and feel the ground shudder with the hard landing—as if the battling armies had rushed past just moments before, like trucks leaving invisible turbulence in the air.

We spent the night in the Croatian capital, Zagreb, where we conducted interviews and got situation updates in the press room at the Intercontinental

**167**

Hotel. The next morning we headed south for the coast, following a serpentine road through sylvan hill country broken up by vineyards and fields of haystacks, corn, and sunflowers. Only two weeks earlier the trees pressing close upon us had played home to Serb snipers. In front of roadside *gostionica*, pigs turned slowly on spits in open brick ovens. Our discussion turned to the subject of religion, and Jennifer lectured me and Taryn on the proper way to pray.

The lush woodlands fled abruptly before the sun-silvered coastal mountains, an imperious ridge of stony molars and bicuspids, the lower teeth of a world-dragon whose upper jaw might be a coastal range continents away. We passed almost no other cars, and the seaside resorts all lay empty, their currency exchange booths closed, their hundreds of rental boats languishing against the docks. Between towns we saw low stone walls undulating over the slopes below the road, outlining the large oblongs of ancient Roman military camps.

By afternoon we'd reached Zadar, a fortified city dating from the Roman Empire, still intact, rising in white limestone walls from streets of pale, polished marble. The city's outskirts had been struck by mortar fire the week before, and armed guards manned checkpoints all along the roads. We conducted some interviews and around sunset stopped to rest and eat at an outdoor table at the Restaurant Dalmacija, on whose multilingual menu all the Serbian dishes had been whited out. A few yards away, a soldier patrolled the front door of Radio Zagreb, pausing to chat with a married couple pushing their baby in a stroller.

It was at the restaurant that Jennifer inexplicably began to grow aloof, and during the interview with Angelo and the other soldiers—which Taryn and I conducted in German, since they spoke no English—she became downright sullen, refusing to take notes on what we were translating back to her. Afterward, as we were checking in for the night, Jennifer and Taryn abruptly began tearing into each other verbally at the reception desk while the astonished concierge and I looked on. Jennifer seemed to be angry at me too, but for some reason I got spared her vituperation. Finally Taryn shouted, "I can't go on with this!" and stormed outside into the night with her backpack.

The remaining two of us were still checking in when Taryn returned a few minutes later, muttering about why should she be the one to spend the night out in the street, and so the three of us, instead of rooming together like good budget travelers, checked into separate adjacent rooms, mine in the middle.

My confusion escalated into alarm. The two women seemed to understand perfectly the source of their discord, but I had no clue. We were in a war zone, hundreds of miles from safety, with one car to which Jennifer had the only keys; and she informed me, after I cautiously knocked on her door later, that she was planning to get an early start, with or without us.

I saw no recourse but to embark upon a mission of shuttle diplomacy, and I seriously considered sneaking outside and taking the car's spark plug wires for negotiating power. I visited both camps that evening to determine their opening positions. Jennifer was feeling like the odd-person-out, complaining that Taryn and I were pursuing our own interviews at her expense. Nor did she like Taryn "ordering" her to take notes during the interview with Angelo. I explained that we'd actually needed her help then, since it's difficult to interview someone in one language while taking notes in another. Taryn had simply grown fed up with Jennifer's childishness and sanctimoniousness: that lecture on the right way to pray, for example. I presented Jennifer's injured feelings as sympathetically as I could. All this, of course, was merely the tip of the iceberg.

I didn't get much sleep, having sneaked outside but deciding to trust to fate and leave the spark plug wires, and as soon as I heard my companions stirring the next morning I resumed my shuttle diplomacy. I'd reached a decision, and laid it out to them separately. We'd agreed at the start of our trip that should any one of us ever feel his or her life in danger, that person could unilaterally call off the whole trip, and the others would abide. True, we'd meant danger from some trigger-happy army, but splitting up would be life-threatening too, since we'd be not only separated but stranded. Here was the plan: Jennifer and I both had morning interviews scheduled, so she would drop me off at mine, go on to hers, and then we'd all meet and head back to Berlin—only half a day early, but early nonetheless. With a little negotiation of logistics, they agreed.

I spent two hours with Zadar's director of tourism and his daughter (my "Yugoslavian babe" at last, we'd later joke), but when I returned to our pre-arranged meeting spot, I was astonished to find Jennifer and Taryn chatting and giggling like high school girl friends. "What happened?" I asked.

"You wouldn't understand. It didn't involve you," Jennifer said.

"It's a girl thing," Taryn cleared things up. "We had our fight and now we're better friends. You can't really be part of it."

Oh, gee, thanks, I thought, a little disappointed to be left out. On the other hand, I'd been spared their hostilities. That was the trade.

For several days we'd been attempting to understand, as best we could, the reason a vicious civil war had broken out in eastern Europe's most advanced post-communist country, and the answers always came back invoking centuries-old grudges and long-lost empires, something we foreigners, everyone assured us, could never really hope to understand. Women may be right to consider war a "guy thing," virile and therefore incomprehensible. But now I saw that the causes which drove women to war and peace could be just as mysterious.

It was better to have peace than answers. Our car ran smoothly as we took our time driving back up the rocky coast. While it was still light we pulled off the road to go swimming in the warm waters of the Adriatic, beside the summer sun plunging hotly toward the cool, blue horizon.

# GLOBAL ISSUES AND VIEWPOINTS

## Lost (and Found) Idealism

*"The growth of the mind is still high adventure,
in many ways the highest adventure on earth."*

Norman Cousins

# A Fistful of Rupees

## Jeff Greenwald

*Coping with begging on Third World trails.*

S EVERAL YEARS AGO, on a solo trek in northern India, I was joined by an
eight-year-old boy wearing a tattered red vest. He greeted me with a phrase
in perfect English:

"Excuse me, sir, but what is your hobby?"

Startled, I uttered a brief but incomprehensible reply about astrophotogra-
phy. The boy was utterly unphased by my gibberish.

"Very good," he recited handily. "Mine is coin collecting. I collect coins of
every country. Please, sir, you will give me a coin of your country. Any coin of
your country. You will give it to me *now* ..."

This ingenious gambit was but a new angle on what has become one of
the most common and frustrating dilemmas faced by travelers. Children (of
all ages) in India, Nepal and Tibet—as well as Africa and the Americas—
have come to see begging as a lucrative and entertaining form of trick-or-
treat. Nor are their demands limited to cash. Returning tourists tell of being
hounded for color film, batteries, even Motrin. Young porters in Nepal's
Helambu region have been caught soliciting Walkman batteries; it's only a
matter of time before trekkers into that ethereal realm are assailed by schoolchildren beggaring phone cards, or high-density floppy disks for their
PowerBooks.

(In Hindu and Buddhist cultures, of course, begging for alms is a well-estab-
lished custom. It supports pilgrims and monks while giving lay persons an
opportunity to practice generosity. Such spiritual mendicants, however, are easily distinguished from four-year-old urchins who cling to your shins and allow
themselves to be dragged along for miles.)

There's a kind of chicken-and-egg question about begging and giving on Third
World trails. Which came first? Some people argue that impoverished locals, confronted by invading hordes of affluent tourists, were the first offenders. This
makes little sense. People are unlikely to demand something they have never
received before—and expectations of winning coins, candies or "school pens"
from transient strangers were not conjured up by children in remote villages.

**172**

The problem started, more likely, with the first tourists and trekkers to visit these hamlets. Surrounded by raggedy children, and lacking any other means of explaining themselves, they began doling out money and sweets. Such behavior turns kids into beggars faster than you can say "one rupee"—as future travelers to those regions soon discovered. Even a used Bic is a rich prize to a kid whose parents make forty cents a day. In no time at all, anyone wearing rip-stop nylon became a potential mark.

*  *  *

Generosity isn't a habit we want to be cured of. Despite our sometimes better judgement, we will give things away. The trick, of course, is to do it without promoting greed or tooth-decay. It isn't difficult. With a bit of imagination and planning, gift-giving can be one of the most pleasurable parts of a trip—and a great way to forge connections with local children and families.

The first thing to remember while packing for a trip is that generosity doesn't have to mean giving away things. Sharing a bit of yourself, opening a window into your own world, is a good place to begin. During my years as a travel writer I've learned that people around the globe, from Bali to Belgium, have one thing in common: they all want to know about my family, and see what my home looks like.

For the oddest thing about Westerners—from the Thai or Malian point of view—is that we tend to travel alone. Our apparent solitude is incomprehensible to people who have lived in one village, within an extended family, for generations. The quickest way to break the ice is to pack along some family snapshots, and a few dozen postcards of your home town. Such evidence places you in the world as a legitimate resident, and creates a foundation for dialogue and friendship.

Dealing with children is not much different. They, too, are acting out of a natural curiosity: a desire to make contact with the bizarre-looking aliens tromping through their villages. Begging is a simple form of communication, and the possibility of a reward makes it all the more fun. But what these kids really want (like kids everywhere) is to be entertained. If you know how to juggle, do string figures or play the harmonica, you've got it made. If not, a few simple props will do. Cornered by a troupe of 10-year-old beggars in Delhi, I pulled out a small, inflatable world globe. What started as a feeding frenzy quickly became a geography lesson. The kids immediately began matching bits of news they'd heard on the radio—about Russia, Japan and the US—to the appropriate countries, and argued heatedly about why India was pink and Pakistan blue.

A plastic magnifying glass, strong enough to burn holes in a dry leaf, seems miraculous to kids seeing it for the first time (but don't leave it behind; especially in a village of grass huts). Any toy store, or an outfit like the Nature Company, can supply you with cheap but astounding objects like gyroscopes,

**173**

holograms and magnets. When I stop for a lunch break—and find myself sur-rounded by a bunch of kids with outstretched palms—I'll hand out colored pencils, and let them draw in my sketchpad. It's great fun, and their uninhibited sketches of mountains, flowers and beefy tourists in blimp-like parkas are among my most prized souvenirs.

Though I demonstrate things like kaleidoscopes and prisms, I rarely give them away. The kids don't mind; their natural appetite for engagement has been satisfied. Sometimes, though, at an unusually hospitable lodge, I'll befriend the owners and want to offer a token gift to them and/or their chil-dren. For these situations, I offer two rules of thumb.

First, it's unwise and irresponsible to give away money or candy (unless you're planning a follow-up visit with a dentist). There are other gifts more genuinely expressive of one's personality. Picture postcards, mentioned before, are light and cheap, but are always cherished—and displayed—by the people who receive them. Ball-point pens, folding pen-knives or 'disposable' lighters (they're refilled all over the Third World) are also appreciated. Don't get too exotic; my friend Mary once gave a Moroccan woman a little green flashlight, and she chucked it into her stew.

Kids are easier. I recommend balloons, tops (stock up on those little Hanukkah driedels before your trip), magnifying lenses, prisms, little rubber dinosaurs or those cool hologram stickers sold in card stores. These are fun and educational presents that kids can share, and that might help them unlock a few secrets of the Universe to boot.

Second, avoid giving gifts directly to children. Give the present to a parent (or an older sibling) and let them make the actual presentation. Such a gesture is a sign of respect, and reinforces the endangered notion that family mem-bers—rather than wealthy tourists—are the ones to turn to for gifts and rewards.

* * *

There is another, very different kind of begging, much more poignant and disturbing than requests for bon-bons or coins. Quite often—especially along major trekking routes—children and adults appeal to the traveler for basic medical supplies. First-aid items like aspirin, antibiotics or iodine are hard to refuse, especially when the person making the request substantiates their claim by clutching their head, doubling over or displaying a gaping wound.

It's a tough call. But playing doctor can sometimes backfire, with terrible results. What if the child is allergic to penicillin? What if blind faith in a tem-porary treatment (applying iodine, for example) keeps a villager from seeking further care?

**174**

My sense is that it's best to help however one can—short of dispensing drugs. I won't leap to the aid of anyone with a bruised elbow, but if a situation looks threatening I usually try to deal with it. In a few cases I've found out where the nearest health post was and given a relative (or local porter) enough money to take the sick or injured person there. This kind of behavior risks casting Westerners as cure-all philanthropists, but watching people suffer isn't much of an alternative. Again, there's nothing inherently wrong with giving; problems arise when people give compulsively, without regard for the consequences.

Although I've portrayed myself as something of a saint, let it be known that I've left the imprint of my Vibram sole in more than one kid's rear end (the Indian coin-wallah being a prime example). I've also denied help to people who probably had legitimate claims on my good will. What to do? The issue is confusing, and every encounter is different.

As with so many other situations, though, a little mindfulness goes a long way. Before I give away anything to anyone, anywhere, I find it useful to ask myself a few questions. Will what I'm doing improve this person's life, or degrade it? Will it promote greed and dependency, or foster some small degree of autonomy? And finally: how will fellow travelers to this place—tomorrow, next month or ten years from now—be affected by my actions? For unless we can find a way to stop the cycle, what is now an irritating habit will become, for many Third World residents and their children, a way of life.

This frightening prospect became vividly clear to me two years ago, after I'd dragged an unusually persistent Limbu brat affixed like a leech to my leg all the way to his packed-earth house on Nepal's Naudanda Ridge. I deposited him on his doorstep, rapped on the door and began lecturing his mother. My name, I told her, is not "One Rupee;" she might try teaching her kid some manners.

She gave me an apologetic look, and extended her hand.

"One rupee," she demanded.

# In the Wake of Adventure

## Richard Bangs

*As promising as adventure travel is as a tool for environmental conservation and cultural understanding, travelers—even the most well-meaning—have an undeniable impact on the places they visit. The key is to insure that the impact is minimal and more conscionable than the alternatives.*

NOT LONG AFTER I PUBLISHED A BOOK on adventure travel in Indonesia I received a letter from a solo European traveler who had made his way to the interior of Kalimantan, on the island of Borneo, to the village of Long Ampung on the Kayan River. It was his second private tour of this hidden vault of wilderness. The first time, a year previous, when he hired Dayak porters to carry his gear to Long Uro, about a four-hour trek, they wanted $1.80/person for the enterprise. In the interim an adventure tour company had arrived and paid the same porters $3.00 each, and now that was their asking price.

The letter-writer was incensed. He couldn't believe that others might follow in his footsteps on an organized tour, and that they might pay more for what he received so cheaply. Once more, he complained, tourists of this type would corrupt the local culture, and ruin the experience for true explorers such as himself.

This is at once a specious and elitist conceit, imperialist in its assumptions, and anti-evolutionist in its expression. The ersatz moral ping that courses through the minds of the mobile rich visiting the inert poor is rarely based in reality. All politics is local, and inevitably the locals want to decide how and when they change, and tourism, more often than not, offers an alternative, a chance to change, to evolve. Later in the same letter, the irate author talks about the high infant mortality rate of the region, the absence of medical aid, and comments that a nurse or doctor visits but twice a year. The nexus is missing, but inductively it would seem that if adventure travelers began to arrive in significant numbers, and paid for local services, then monies might become available for hospitals, schools, and social services. It has worked in Nepal with ACAP (Annapurna Conservation Area Project), which exacts a fee from every foreign traveler, and the monies are then turned over to the locals to not only supplement a miserably poor economy, but to help in construction of ecologically sound lodges, and to buy kerosene as a fuel substitute, so fewer trees will

**176**

be cut. Economics is the most potent coin in adventure travel, and to wistfully wish that nobody follows in the privileged footsteps of an explorer so that the less-advantaged remain so, and will entertain lone visitations for obscenely cheap prices, is a shameful fancy. Yet, it may be equally shameful to allow the ungraceful degradation from the relatively small numbers of adventure travelers to the call numbers of slash-and-burn mass tourism. The challenge is to find the balance, while defending the wilderness from other so-called nonsustainable industries, such as logging, agriculture, petroleum extraction and mining, which tend to destroy whatever they finger in a sort of reverse Midas-touch.

Cultural issues aside, without economic incentives, habitat preservation will prove an expendable luxury in the increasingly desperate non-developing world. Adventure travel draws much of its potential from a dichotomy of riches: The industrialized world is flush with cash, but the tropical world has the lion's share of the planet's animal and plant species. Adventure travel is a plausible way to apply some of the financial wealth of the developed world toward protecting the biological wealth of the developing world. Sound adventure travel practices that provide such a currency flow have already proved their worth in a number of noteworthy examples. At the Tangkoko-Batuangas Nature Reserve in North Sulawesi, much of the wildlife, including the rare black macaque, has been poached almost to the point of extinction. But recently tourists have begun hiring local guides from the village of Batuputih to show them the animals that previously were killed for food. The guides' daily fees provide enough incentive for the villagers to stop poaching, and even to join Indonesian park service patrols to reduce poaching by others.

That's an inspirational tale. But, let's take this to the next step, and look at the visitor, not the visited. The word gets out that travelers can now call on this piece of paradise, and see endangered wildlife in the raw. They seek out the Edenic myth, and soon an hibiscus-covered resort is built, with dancers in the lobby, cheeseburgers and imported wine on the room service menu.

Now, as many of these visitors do not realize, the resort, with its capacity for hundreds, has paved a piece of wildness, and created a facsimile utopia that not only upsets the balance, but spawns a set of problems stickier than rotted pawpaw. The bloodline of these problems is entwined in Western history, snagged in its culture, in the concept of packaging and selling "paradise," when the inconvenience is that paradise ceases to be when too many pad its trails, when too many dip in its waters.

Though the marketing of Paradise as a construct of adventure travel is a young art, merchandising Eden has a rich legacy. Consider the government tourist officials of the Dutch East Indies during the period between World Wars I and II, whose brochures and magazine advertisements attempted to

**177**

lure world cruise travelers to the "Tropical Garden of Eden." This Paradisiacal myth is deeply implanted in Western tradition, with roots in both classical and biblical soil. It was kept alive in the Middle Ages by Cartographers, who customarily showed the authentic locations of this antediluvian promised land as in the Orient, between the Tropics of Cancer and Capricorn. The romancers of the Age of Discovery had little difficulty in placing Elysium in the exotic lands that curl through the equator, which they would people variously with noble savage, lost tribe, or superior human being. The early explorers—Columbus among them—gave open support to this kind of thinking. And it is this mind set that persists today in the expectations of tourists who flock to the islands of Indonesia and other "wildernesses" today, searching blatantly for Paradise.

The tourists' impact, as should be expected, more often erodes than preserves the acreage of Paradise. Resort tourists, even the ones who believe they have registered with an "environmentally correct" property (one that separates the trash), too often see what cannot naturally occur, an idyllic insulated retreat with all the amenities of a Beverly Hills hotel. It is for these deep pockets that the resorts are built—trees felled, swamps drained, rivers dammed, and villages shoved aside to preserve the "natural feel" of this contrived Paradise. Even more sadly, the villagers themselves may find their traditional livelihoods as fishers, farmers, and artisans supplanted by a resort economy built around touro-dollars; they can find work only in the white smocked service and support industries, learning new words for new skills, and new vices. The end result of this type of tourism is all too often pollution, both environmental and cultural, and the damage is too frequently irremediable.

The adventurer traveler, however, is generally a kinder, greener visitor who immerses himself in the trackless travel experience and comes back deeply connected, wiser and concerned, educated and motivated. These travelers are the ones who accept what they find, learn to appreciate it on its own terms, and become passionate enough about the magic and magnificence of a place to join in the effort to preserve its life forms, cultures and ecological systems. The true adventure traveler seeks out locally-owned inns and eateries, uses native guides, visits natural areas, and chooses low impact transportation, a raft rather than a cruise ship, walking rather than a tour bus. And, perhaps most profoundly, the adventurer traveler minimizes the foreign exchange leakage, (and this is as true for the Huli wigman of New Guinea as for the Hopi of Arizona) spending a significant portion of his vacation monies in the local economy, purchasing goods, services, even authentic art directly from the source, giving indigenous populations incentives to preserve.

There are some other key distinctions between conventional travel and adventure travel. To a large extent, in conventional travel, the standard of excellence is a predictable, uniform experience ... "the best surprise is no surprise" epistemology promoted by the chain hotels and restaurants. Adventure travel, on the other hand, celebrates diversity, and the goal is discovery, enlightenment, and all manner of personal challenge—intellectual, physical, cultural, and even spiritual. This embracing of diversity represents a positive evolution towards a higher consciousness. The first principle of the science of ecology is that uniformity in any system is unstable and unhealthy, while conversely, diversity is the singular attribute of a healthy, stable system. Seeking out and fostering diversity in the natural world and among human cultures is a most significant characteristic of adventure travel. The best way to instill an appreciation of the wonderful diversity of this planet is to experience it first-hand. Then, the appreciation becomes more than just academic, but rather emotional. To someone who has truly gained such an appreciation, it is not necessary (or sufficient) to justify protection of wild spaces or endangered archeological sites in term of discounted net value of revenue flows from tourism versus those from natural resource exploitation. The non-material benefits of protecting these special spots may be intangible (in a material sense), but they are very real—and they are priceless and irreplaceable.

Related to this, conventional travel advocates an ethnocentric, one-way community connection versus the two-way approach of adventure travel. In the case of adventure travel, hopefully the relationship between the visitor and the visited is such that as each learns from the other and neither is forced to conform to the standards or expectations of the other. It is mutually deferential, without the tarnishing and trivializing that were once the calling cards of the ugly American. And there is encouragement to not just respect the foreign or unfamiliar, but to regard its link to everything on the planet, and to fathom the interconnectedness and interdependence of all things, to know that when a dragonfly flaps its wings by the Columbia river, it affects the weather in Kyoto. Also, adventure travelers are active versus passive, in that the traveler takes an active role in creating the experience, rather than just collapsing on a beach or the barstool and being waited upon. In most cases, just getting there requires active participation, such as rafting, hiking, or kayaking. And the active traveler is the traveler most likely to act, to take an issue position once being exposed to a threatened environment, and to dedicate time, energy, money and voice to saving what now has personal meaning. Such is the moral imperative behind adventure travel. With firsthand experience comes appreciation, acknowledgement of worth and respect, and a desire and a reason to preserve the Earth's bounty. The Colorado River still flows through the Grand Canyon, the salmon still run up the Rogue; Walden Pond still reflects, the wildlife of Tanzania still roams, all in part because of the softly stepping visitors who liked what they saw and experienced, learned about the issues, and subsequently got involved. Where and how we travel is our choice, our vote, and then our opportunity.

# Puppy Chow

**Bryan Clayton**

*Good things can happen when you wander into an area "not recommended for travel" by the US State Department.*

I JUMPED ONTO A RANDOM BUS (jeepney) leaving Manila and ended up in a remote Northern Luzon village. I got lost hiking to a mountain summit when the sun set. Above the clouds, I had no food or shelter. A circle of tribal Filipino men invited me to join their dog-on-a-spit barbecue. Not wanting to be rude, I said "I'll just pick," but then I ate a lot. I slept curled up by the fire, waking once to snack on another bowl of puppy with rice.

It was more fun than being "kidnapped by Communists."

# The Price They Pay for Our Cuppa Joe

**Kathryn Gardner**

*When traveling, we are oftentimes confronted with painful issues—some that sting at first, then resonate with compassion.*

IT'S THREE O'CLOCK IN THE MORNING. Movement can be seen in the mass of people as they begin to stir. Groaning, they open their eyes and groggily search for their clothing—a colorful array of course woven fabrics that brighten the darkness of night. Someone lights a lamp and the shadows of a few women can be seen, already in the makeshift kitchen preparing food for the day. A baby, sick with diarrhea and poor nutrition, wails in protest of being disturbed from sleep to be bundled up in a tala and tied to his mother's back.

Soon the people gather their baskets, burlap sacks and tools and begin a long walk into the fields. It is harvest time in Guatemalan coffee plantations and these are the *trabajadores*, a ragtag group of peasants who live in the country but find themselves toiling their way on wealthy estates to earn a meager living.

But what price are these people paying to bring foreign coffee lovers their morning brew? Does the production of Guatemalan coffee, destined for North American and European markets, benefit the workers as it does the economy? After all, coffee accounts for 30% of the country's income. Sadly, the answer is no.

Seventy percent of Guatemala's productive land is in the hands of 2% of the (wealthiest) population. While the rich get richer, the poor struggle to put food in their bellies and shoes on their feet—a struggle indeed.

Despite modern technology, workers still find themselves toiling on hands and knees, sifting the soil between their fingers to remove rocks, sticks and foreign debris before the coffee seeds can be planted. Later, healthy seedlings will be transplanted to fields where they will be weeded, pruned and harvested—all by hand.

For all of their hard labor, the workers receive no more than $3.00/day (less if they are women), a wage that has not changed since the 1980's, despite the legal minimum wage of approximately $46.00 per week. Paid on a piece-meal basis, the harvesters suffer in a valiant attempt to earn whatever they can to help sustain their families. "Unfortunately," explains a wary foreman "the scales used to weigh the coffee beans are usually incorrect—not in the worker's favor."

The pay, or rather lack of it, is but one of their problems.

Having left the cool climate of their highland homes to work in the hot humid valleys, the harvesters find their heavy woven clothing (the only garments they own) uncomfortably hot; daily downpours of rain saturate the fabric making it so heavy that work is virtually impossible. To combat this problem, the people rise at 3:00 am to make the long trek into the fields. They slave until the rains begin, and then return to camp.

Imagine having to get up in the middle of the night to go to work because something as mundane as your clothing literally prevents you from working in the rain!

While working conditions are difficult, living conditions are shocking. On large plantations, up to 75 families may share a concrete platform, sheltered by nothing more than a tin roof. Could you share a platform the size of a tennis court, a makeshift kitchen housing only a concrete sink and a campfire, and a pit toilet with 375 other people? What if your employer offered no more than a thin tarp sheltering a patch of dirt? Claustrophobia would be the least of your problems; sickness and disease compounded by family feuds, promiscuity and prostitution permeate these environments.

While these people are laboring in the dirt, earning less than half the minimum wage, the landowners rake in extraordinary incomes exceeding $470 million dollars in the mid-nineties.

Rarely visiting their remote properties to view the conditions for themselves, most of the plantation owners live comfortably in Guatemala City, housed in large airy homes that are surrounded by manicured gardens and protected by ornate but fortified walls.

Who are the owners? Very few of them are Guatemalans. In 1871, when Guatemala's primary export commodity of natural fabric dyes fell prey to synthetic dyes, the president forced the country people to give their land back to the state under the guise of the *Law of Liberal Reform*. While their land was auctioned off to a handful of highest bidders, primarily Spanish, Italian, German and other foreigners, Guatemala's poorer citizens were relocated to small parcels of arid, virtually useless land often far from their homes and families.

Large, diversified plantations capable of greater exports, they were told, would stimulate the economy and create employment opportunities. It almost sounded reasonable.

By the mid-nineties 1% of the total number of coffee plantations, produced almost half of Guatemala's coffee. A handful of plantations remain in the hands of the Catholic Church and the military, but in essence, Guatemalan citizens are toiling under virtual slave labor for the benefit of foreign bank accounts.

Why do the people accept these insane conditions? In a word—poverty.

More than three-quarters of Guatemala's population live in poverty; more than half of whom cannot afford the most fundamental foodstuffs. Understandably, they would do anything to feed their families. Eventually, however, the harsh conditions become too much to bear.

Guided by the "Unidad de Accion Sindical y Popular" (UASP), workers are quietly organizing themselves into labor unions, indigenous, and human rights groups. When negotiations break down, the workers operate *tomas* where they literally take over the estates and stand on strike in attempts to regain their human and employment rights.

Union leaders, government human rights liaison officers, estate owners and the military soon find themselves in head on confrontations that may lead only to further bloodshed, death threats, arrests and "disappearances."

While Guatemalan Union members believe that the people must continue to fight for themselves, others believe that improved education and health will provide other, long term avenues of hope. Is it plausible even to speculate that if enough people completed their education and were able to work elsewhere, that the coffee magnates would be forced to improve the pay and living conditions for those who do enjoy plantation life? Will there be jobs available for the educated?

What about the short term?

Gourmet blends of Guatemalan coffee may be identified by their regional origin of *Atitlan, Antigua* and *Huehue* (pronounced way-way) but how do you know if your cup came from a so-called bad plantation or a good one?

Large coffee retailers and cafés usually purchase their beans through brokers or importers, who in turn may have purchased from thousands of estates. Tracking the origin of these coffee beans may be next to impossible. Smaller, independent shops, however, may be involved with specific plantations where it is known that workers are treated fairly. Sometimes proceeds from sales go directly back into community projects like clean water and education.

So the next time you fancy a cuppa joe from your favorite café, side on up to the counter and inquire from just where their beans come and who benefits from their sale. If you cannot get a definitive answer, perhaps you should look for a new shop to haunt. And while you are searching for coffee, why not take a moment to learn how you can help the coffee workers in Guatemala. Contact Amnesty International, 322-8th Ave. New York, NY 10001. Phone (212) 807-8400.

After all, is a cup of coffee really worth all their suffering?

# Across the American Southwest Without a Clue

**Bill Shein**

*What crazy shenanigans can transpire between Santa Fe and Oklahoma City? Two determined comics find out, and give hilarious State of the Union commentary.*

ONCE AGAIN, MONTHS OF ADVANCE PLANNING paid off for the "Buzzsaw Across America" cross-country road trip. We arrived in Santa Fe, New Mexico, a town known for its arts community, on Monday, the day when all of the town's museums are closed. If word of this mistake gets out, I may lose my license to be a travel writer, which I got a few weeks ago by cheating on the travel writers' proficiency exam.

Michael and I had spent Sunday night at the misleadingly named "Luxury Inn" motel on the outskirts of town, and had to drive about five miles to get to the plaza in the heart of Santa Fe. The road we took, Cerrillos Road, translates from colloquial Spanish as "Ugly road filled with industrial parks, auto repair shops, strip malls, and cheap motels." So far, Santa Fe didn't seem to be the quaint mountain town we expected.

But as we got closer to central Santa Fe, we began to see the adobe buildings characteristic of the area. We saw adobe homes, adobe stores, adobe office buildings, adobe cars, and a number of adobe people. Wanting to fit in with the locals, I pulled over and bought myself a nice adobe suit.

In case you don't already know, adobe is a brown building material made from mud and grass that's used to build inexpensive, well-insulated structures. But then again, it could be made from cork and blueberry jam; I'm not certain, and I don't have much research assistance out here on the open road. So please, don't try to build a home from mud and grass—or cork and blueberry jam—using only the details I've included here. It could be a recipe for disaster.

Nestled in the mountains north of Albuquerque, Santa Fe is the kind of town that gives writers that rare opportunity to use the word "nestled." During our brief visit, I sensed that Santa Fe offers a livable pace and good quality of life, though I'm not sure I could live in a city that attracts thousands of tourists who fill the streets and gape at the sights all summer long. That's why I choose to live in Washington DC, a town with little tourist appeal.

Santa Fe has a permanent population of about 60,000 which doubles during the summer with an influx of tourists and young people. Based on my observations, many of them come to Santa Fe to avoid wearing shoes. There are dozens of shops and vendors selling authentic Indian jewelry and various arts and crafts produced by local artists. Or perhaps made in massive factories far from here by armies of child laborers, and passed off by Santa Fe merchants as authentic local trinkets.

All around Santa Fe, there is a lot of art that depicts "Kokopelli," a mythical traveling flutist that local custom calls a "despoiler of women, seducer of wives, and gambler." For fun, I soon adopted that as my trip's new subtitle and my personal mantra. Well, at least the "gambler" part.

Indian tradition also says that Kokopelli is a symbol of fertility, which I learned only after buying my girlfriend a beautiful silver bracelet adorned with his image. While I love kids, I'm not quite ready to add the cost of a Little Buzz to my list of expenses. Perhaps when I don't view children in purely financial terms it will mean that I'm ready to have some.

While we waited to have lunch at the popular Shed Restaurant, we spent some time in a shop called "Santa Fe Arts & Kokopelli Gallery," managed by the lovely Rose family. Located next to The Shed, the shop is an old adobe building, which explained its extremely small doorways. Adobe buildings have small doorways and windows for insulation purposes, I was told, rubbing my forehead after smacking it yet again into a "Watch Your Head. Low Doorway" sign.

As usual, we hit the road late in the afternoon, many hours after we had planned to leave. In fact, there has not been even one day when we've pulled out of a town as early as we planned. We drove out of Santa Fe and across New Mexico's beautiful landscape, enjoying the stunning vistas. The storm that we had fought our way through a day earlier had followed us, and we were once again driving through a hard rain and lots of lightning.

As we drove across the Hopi and Navajo reservations in New Mexico, we saw many fields filled with grazing cows and bison. Reminded of the film "Dances With Wolves," we decided to give each other new Indian names that described the essence of our being. So for the rest of the trip, Michael's name was "Annoying Like A Gnat," and mine was, "For the Love of God, Shut the Hell Up Already!"

Clearly, the strain of the trip was beginning to show.

* * *

**185**

And On Into Texas

As the sun was setting on another day of driving, and I struggled to come up with more travel-related cliches, we crossed the border from New Mexico into Texas. To save time—as well as to avoid running out of fuel in a remote location where we'd survive only by eating rattlesnake for weeks on end—we chose to cross the Lone Star state at its narrowest point on the Texas panhandle. This would take us through Amarillo, Texas and get us to Oklahoma by midnight.

About 50 miles into Texas, we passed through the town of Bushland, which may have been named after the famous Bush family of Maine. It reminded me of the dozens of e-mails I've gotten during the past week suggesting that we stop in towns with odd names: Toadsuck, Arkansas; Bucksnort, Tennessee; and others. Because what would a cross-country trip be without stops in places with funny names, right?

Unfortunately, we didn't have time to stop in any of those places, but to those of you considering a drive through odd-named towns, here's what I imagine it might be like:

Me: "Wahooo! We're in a town called Bucksnort! What kind of silly name is that!? Bucksnort! Ha! This is great! So, what should we do?"

(Long silence)

Me: Well, okay then ... let's get back on the road.

As we crossed Texas on I-40, we saw dozens of signs for "The Big Texan," a restaurant that offers a free 72-ounce steak to anyone who can eat it in under an hour. Otherwise, it's fifty bucks. Though no one at the restaurant could confirm this, I believe the steak is 72 ounces because that is the precise weight of Texas oddity Ross Perot. Even though the place is a major tourist trap, we figured it would offer some decent food and have some high-fat comedy potential.

Not surprisingly, the extremely large menu was filled with a wide variety of meat options: Sirloin meat, rib eye meat, tenderloin meat, and super-meaty meat. You don't want to go to a place like "The Big Texan" and say: "Do you have anything, you know, without meat? A nice healthy salad? Grilled cheese? Or maybe a small, fluffy piece of quiche?"

By the way, if you choose to take the 72-ounce challenge, you get to sit on stage in the middle of the restaurant where other patrons can watch you stuff your face before you cough up fifty bucks for the privilege of making yourself sick. While we were there, two kids no older than 12 were each trying to consume the monstrous steak. Neither of them succeeded, but not for lack of trying; by the end, one of them was actually sweating Au jus.

We both ordered 10-ounce sirloin steaks complete with mashed potatoes, salad, and vegetable soup. Though far, far smaller than a 72-ounce steak, the meal was just big enough to make us ridiculously tired before heading back out on the road.

With Oklahoma City our next stop, we were both approaching record-setting levels of fatigue. While I wrote, Michael drove and did whatever he could do to stay awake. I realized that he was just about at his limit when at 1:00 a.m., in the middle of Oklahoma, he suddenly jammed on the brakes, slowing from 80 mph to 40 mph, and turned to me with glazed, sleepy eyes. "Whoa! Did you see that? It was the disembodied head of Sam Houston singing an Abba song. That was really weird."

Pray for us.

# Pardon My Country

## Carolyn Durkalski

*Is it too much to ask that when we travel, we at least attempt to acclimate ourselves to local customs?*

SOMETIMES WHEN TRAVELING in foreign lands, I get a strange feeling when I see other Americans. It's sort of the same feeling you get when someone scratches their nails across a chalkboard.

This larger-than-life wife got on the bus and whined (in English, of course) "How much is it? What?! Where's the beach?"

I felt like saying "Lady, you're on the coast of the Sea of Cortez! It's all beach. Now sit down and shut up."

Yet I say nothing as she and her husband sit next to me.

She inquires "How much did you have to pay?"

"Five pesos" I reply, sending her into delirium that they had to pay three times as much.

I didn't share with her that greeting and asking politely in Spanish may have had something to do with it. Some people just don't get it. The bus driver got it.

# No Futuro

## Antonio López

*Not all Mexicans take American Express. In Mérida, for Mayan punks, the only plastic they'll accept is a scratched Sex Pistols record.*

IN A SMALL COLONIAL PLAZA, nick-named Parque Fantasia by locals after an adjacent cinemateque, a small group of caifanes—punks—gathered under a dim light post, slapping hands and punching fists. The theater's late show of "Seven" was letting out, while a three-piece marimba band played their loopy, monotone repertoire in front of an outdoor restaurant. Among the white-painted metal love seats occupied by young lovers and foreign tourists, these chavos hovered in their usual spot—a stairway leading to a large, central statue of General Cepeda Peraza, a 19th century governor of Yucatan. To the punx, or "punkes" as it is pronounced in Spanish, this frozen figure doused with bird shit has as much relevance as the current PRI government.

Given the unreality and theatrics of Mexican political and economic life, I suspected "Fantasia" was more than just a name of a theater. Crowded below the monument, with small amps and guitars in hand, the punx clearly had more on their minds than Mexico's post-Colonial political heroes. A joint, electricity to juice an amp, an ax to jam on and band practice were the most real things to expect in a world gone haywire.

There was nothing fancy about their clothes—jeans, an occasional black, heavy metal tee shirt, a discreet tattoo. No Doc Martins, no fancy leather jackets, no slick jewelry or patches. Watching them bum cigarettes from the tourists, I realized that punk can't be bought in Mexico. There are no trendy shops with spiked dog collars and stickers. CDs cost around $25, and a broken guitar string could mean the end of a band.

Anyone seen with these kind of accessories can easily be pegged as a chilango—someone from Mexico City. Most of these kids just wore simple clothes, slightly off-color from the normal preppy, conservative dress of average local youth.

The thought of capitalizing on the counterculture just doesn't exist. When I suggested, for example, finding a way of networking the punks on the Internet, Ruben, the singer of a local hard-core band called "Sub-Urbanos,"

**189**

dismissed the future project.

"No, Antonio," he said, leering at me with his usual stoned, sad, bloodshot eyes. A nose ring and tattoo circling his wrist was the only indication that he was some kind of freak. "No hay futuro. No futuro."

No future: not the mindless echo of a rich suburban punk from LA. This was for real. With hyper-inflation, guerrilla warfare, staggering unemployment, and a worthless currency, many Mexican youth hold an apocalyptic view of their economic plight.

For these Mayan young people in Mérida, the capital of the Yucatan in Southern Mexico, punk is not about clothes or what you can buy at the mall— It's about power chords, speed, attitude, and being pissed off.

It's about being punk.

\* \* \*

On the Yucatan Peninsula, the boot-shaped part of Mexico that looks like its going to kick Florida in the balls, "underground" has many connotations. If you ask people about the "underground," they will reply two ways. First, you must be talking about the extensive cave network that cuts through the limestone plateau. Second, you must mean revolutionaries making bombs or organizing a clandestine army. In some historical cases, the two have converged: during the Caste War in the 1860s, when Mayans rose up against the central government and temporarily drove them back to Mexico City, rebels had to hide out in the caves of their ancestors. To this day, you can still see the defensive walls they built when you visit the grottos.

These days, when "underground" is just another catchy metaphor to describe the counterculture, in Mexico to be countercultural, you often have to be underground, in defiance of the state and dominant conservative culture.

Mérida is widely regarded as the post-colonial, Mayan capital. Located within half a day's bus ride to Chichen Itza and Cancun, destination of frat boys and rich, gringo tourists, Mérida is a grand colonial urban center modeled after classical Spanish cities. Filled with large stone churches and high-ceiling buildings painted in a variety of floral colors, Mérida resonates with history, and is not much visually different than when John Lloyd Stephens' featured it in his famous 19th Century travelogue, *Incidents of Travel in Yucatan.*

Since Stevens' time, however, things have changed quite a bit: there has been a modern industrial revolution in Mexico; technology has invaded, with cell phones, Internet, satellite TV and smog choking cars and buses everywhere; silver coins have been replaced by electronic currency and worthless paper money, and traditional society is being wiped out by pop culture and NAFTA.

Enter the punx. These are hardly the tourist friendly venders hocking hammocks or Panama hats. As they rove the local parks for dope or cigarettes, these are not model youth the Church or government rewards with the promise of a consumer, domesticated life. Instead, they face an outsider status, regularly scandalized by their family and neighbors.

Arlene, a petite chava with an ostentatious sun tattoo on her inside forearm and heavy combat boots, decried my fascination with traditional Mexican culture. While her parents' generation mamboed to live music on the Zocalo, I commented on how sweet I thought it was that the community gathered on Sundays to socialize, court and bring the kids out to play.

"Just a bunch of gossip and assholes," she sniffed.

Rebellion is universal. You've got to hate what ever your parents like.

When kids in Mexico gather, dress a certain way and hang out at a regular spot, they often fall into a loose category called chavos bandas—"youth bands." But chavo is slang for youth or teenager, and "banda" has the implication of a tribal band. There is no word for gang.

In Mérida, the clique of countercultural types is small and isolated enough to come across as a kind of chavo banda. But among these kids, social organization is less defined. What matters is what band you play in.

And just like most kids around the world, many of these Mayan youth are bored, they don't relate to the society, they get stoned, tattoo themselves, are broke and idealize about the "revolution" (the Zapatistas, as you can imagine, provide endless inspiration). In many ways they are like US or Canadian punks, although there is a much deeper sense that something is wrong. Signs of violent political repression are everywhere, and a real armed insurrection is only a one-day bus ride away.

On the Zocalo, beneath the shade of tropical trees, one can see bulletins protesting government repression against union and political activists. On the street, it is well known that anyone can get wacked for $50, and it would never be investigated. Unlike the illusion of safety provided by the democratic system of their northern neighbors, in this part of the world, no one doubts who the powers-that-be are: drug lords.

Consequently, people are often killed for political and economic reasons. To speak one's mind, protest a new golf course development and oppose the ruling party in Mexico can lead to death. Being a rebel is not taken lightly.

While these youth desire something beyond mainstream Mexican culture, I suspect that some of the chavos privately desire an easier life. I have noticed the punx stare off at Latin MTV over pizza and beer in the trendy district, mouthing lyrics to the Red Hot Chile Peppers, with TV's sexy imagery reflecting off their glassy eyes. The day-to-day battles of Mérida to scrape out an existence is a far cry from lives of easy credit and convenient strip malls. In spite of an efficient bus system, vehicles are rarely affordable, limiting access to the outside world. Most Méridians haven't traveled beyond their municipality.

Although the city possesses its own self-contained universe, which is connected to a vast history spanning thousands of years, I suspect that consumerism, if at all attainable, represents an escape hatch for many of the punx.

Still, skepticism of the "American way of life" is ample. Juan, handsome with a deep voice and classic Mayan profile, was certain that we Norte Americanos have no history, and hence, no culture. Sitting across the street from Burger King, a grim reminder of my home turf, there was little argument against that symbol of cultural imperialism. In this sense, he possessed greater sophistication than your average North American punk: Juan has roots to something as deep and ancient as the pyramid cities covering the Yucatan peninsula. And he knows exactly what to hate.

"We have a past, a heritage," he raved. "What do you have? Fast-food!"

Indeed, perhaps North American punks have little to focus on, just roving angst. There is not much history available to the average suburban punk—just existential rage.

In an effort to be self-sufficient, a small but vibrant alternative culture persists, with fanzines, bootleg cassettes, heavy metal tee shirts and homemade clothes. There is little decent music equipment to be found, but that doesn't stop any of the chavos from putting on shows. Mayan punx in Mérida actively participate in public cultural events, always setting up their own alternative stages during the constant calendar of festivals that fill a typical Mérida year.

Most shows are held at rented club spaces, typically costing 80 cents to get in, with beer served to whoever pays. None of these kids, who mainly live in Mérida's impoverished colonias, have cars, so shows start early enough to close down in time to catch the bus home. According to the fairly strict social rules of Mexican society (a heavily class-based culture), rich and middle class kids would not be caught dead at a punk event, although some of the Bohemian, artist adults (who tend to be foreigners) patronize the punx.

Of the hundred or so people that go to these shows (in a city of 600,000), there are about ten women. They mosh together, and huddle protectively in the face of a mostly male dominated scene (I did not witness a single female band member of the ten groups I saw play live; although women musicians are more common in Mexico City). Again, according to tradition, women should be married with kids. Most of the countercultural girls are barely out of high school so it is not surprising that punk girls are considered sluts and druggies.

In Mérida, the punx have music classification down to a science. Sub-genres are often hybrids of the English name. Death Metal, for example, is called Det

Metal (Gren De, I discovered after much confusion, is Green Day). Other genres include noise-core, hard-core, speed-core and so on. Unlike the US or Canada, there is no distinction between music and fashion. Long hair, short hair, ripped clothes or ethnic clothes, people are not attacked for liking one brand of music and dressing a certain way. This reflects the egalitarian nature of a scene that is more united by poverty than anything else.

A lot of these punks like to bitch about "American" culture, and consider theirs superior to ours. Yet discussions about music often become contests of who knows more bands than the other. One night I found myself out-done by Mario, a male prostitute, on band names from the US and England. In the end, many were openly envious that I had seen a lot of their favorite bands in the States.

Popular among them was a Basque-separatist hard-core group from Spain, Mano Negra from France and a slew of groups from Latin America emerging from the Rock en Españiol movement.

But as we sat in Fantasia park, Ruben made a point of letting me know where Norte Americanos stood in his mind. "I hate gringos," he said. And then he smiled, knowing that I understand the difference between gringo and me. Later I learned, after spending a whole month trudging through bad Spanish and hanging out with him, he knew perfect English, and more slang words than I have ever heard.

"Where did you learn these words?" I asked on my last night in Mérida.

"Beavis and Butthead. Where else?"

* * *

As I stood behind the mosh pit watching Sub-Urbanos rip into a cover of "God Save the Queen," the crowd roared like a quake. The awesome power of that song finally transmitted through. It had been 18 years since that anthem first moved me to ditch my Led Zep albums, but it had not resonated the way I saw it reverberate among the Mexican punx.

While Ruben chanted "no futuro" through the mic, I zoomed back into time, back to when I was a punk in LA during the early '80s, and how my reality was so radically different than what these kids face today. I can say I was a punk because I dressed a certain way, got hassled by the police and published a fanzine, but in no way did I face the economic uncertainty of these youth. Never did I have to prostitute myself, nor did I have to worry about my next meal. This is part of the day-to-day reality of Mexican youth.

It was uncanny to stand there, 15 years older than the average mosher, as a tall, light-skinned pocho witnessing the one cultural export I shared with pride. As the mosh pit pushed against me, I realized that these were puro punx, pure punks.

In Mérida's counterculture, there are no poseurs.

# Earth Freaks

## Mur

*Follow one of the original intercontinental overland hippies as he envisions a planet teeming with Earthpeople.*

MY EARLY TRAVELS THROUGH EUROPE and Asia accelerated my spiritual evolution, such that in 1971, at the age of 24, I legally renounced my American citizenship at the American Consulate in Madras, India—to become an Earth man.

A few minutes before the renunciation procedure, I recorded my state of Spirit. The following passage is an except from that writing.

\* \* \*

Let's put free water wells through every parched land, utilizing helicopters. I mean NATION MONSTERS are flying around a lot of helicopters right now to kill the Earthpeople in Laos, Cambodia, and Vietnam.

So, why can't we EARTHFREAKS get an Earth fleet of choppers together for a peace offensive? You know, everything absolutely free with each act, a gift and an offer to keep it flowing towards equivalence, AT ONE WITH that 'other' force, that 'other' part of you, your Self?

And this trip is simple, because there are only two very different ways TO GET IT TOGETHER.

The inferior, old-fashioned method is to use your mind, to analyze everything to death, to run it through the computer, to distinguish how different we all are—to weigh, to compare with, and to kill. This ruinous route always leads to 'the buffalo over the cliff,' dualistic, stupid self-destruction of our species.

The superior path TO GET IT TOGETHER is to use your spirit—to identify, to unify, to empathize with, to be at one with.

And this is where you see a beggar on the train station platform in India with his rags, leprosy, and lice, and you do not distinguish between you. He is you. That's your Self looking at yourself. And if he's hungry, you are hungry.

Like, Ghandi was not on a goodie-goodie ego trip. This giant Earthperson realized that subtle cosmic law that he is everybody on Earth, and before he can get it together ABSOLUTELY, before he can be free, before he can be fully fed—every BODY on the Planet has to be enjoying that at the same time.

Ghandi realized the law of the one. With this enlightenment comes the understanding that all 'external' violence is essentially a kind of Self suicide.

That's the truth that powers the Peace Movement.

So, the joy of this trip, what's making me ecstatic about it, what's making me do it—is that in a few minutes, I shall merge with everybody on Earth.

I am Earthpeople.

There are no more Yankees, there are no more Russians. There are no more 'foreign' people anymore for me. Oh, it's so nice to be Human again.

\* \* \*

Flash forward to 1999 ... I have enjoyed celebrating my life as a stateless person and World Citizen without any nationality or national passport for the last 28 years—as laughing proof that we Earthpeople don't need nations anymore.

**195**

# BOY, WAS I A BONE-HEAD OR WHAT?

## Misadventures

*"A travel adventure has no substitute. It is the ultimate experience, your one big opportunity for flair."*

Rosalind Massow

# A Turkey in Istanbul

## Steve Millward

*10 hard-earned lessons how to avoid trouble on the road.*

I REALLY WISH THIS STORY WAS ABOUT SOMEONE ELSE. I'm not proud of it, but I learned some hard lessons fast on my first non-business solo trip off the continent. I'm hoping that by sharing my boneheaded story, it may help other travelers avoid repeating my blunders.

Somehow I had escaped my green grass life back in Raleigh, North Carolina, in exchange for the medieval Istanbul, Turkey. Suddenly I was on my own, on foot, on the strange city streets. A long sleepless night in the grungy, dank Hotel Lark made me laugh in spite of myself. I had to get out of that dive for a good look around this ancient gem of a city. My first goal was to catch a boat on the Bosphorous.

A clean cut Turkish man named Mehmet saw me studying the huge unreadable schedule and explained that the next boat to my intended destination was not due for a couple of hours. Then he asked where I was from and offered to buy me a soda at the kiosk there. I gently refused the offered drink, but upon stronger insistence I accepted. **Lesson One:** I wish it wasn't so, but you've got to be extremely wary of anyone who interprets for you or offers you unwarranted favors—if your gut says find a way to shake someone, act on it fast.

The thirty-ish guy and I sat for a few minutes as he generally led the conversation. He said he was an airport cop and wanted to practice his English. Lots of questions came my way: what's my name, where am I from, how long have I been in Istanbul, where else have I traveled? Since my truthful answers painted me as a rookie sap freshly loaded with cash, any would be rip-off artist would have been licking his chops. **Lesson Two:** It's okay to casually lie (let's call it acting) when it's to protect yourself from being taken advantage of on the road—use your imagination to invent potential identities with suitable life stories. At least play your cards extremely close to your chest!

Since I actually believed the boat was a few hours from leaving, I accepted his offer to walk awhile with him to sightsee. Of course, I questioned his motives. He said he was doing this more for himself, because he was planning on visiting his father in New York soon and he really needed to practice his English. Knowing New York pretty well, I asked him a few questions about exactly where his father was. He marginally passed my test. **Lesson Three:** Even if you really want to believe someone's story, assume it's false and keep testing for validation.

Despite inklings of impending doom, I enjoyed our banter as we strolled the span across the Golden Horn headed toward "New" Istanbul. Mehmet suddenly got the idea to hop into a taxi and show me the road along the west side of the Bosphorous. I claimed to not have much money, but he said it's cheap and he'd pay. I hastily figured that everything would be fine in a taxi with a potential witness. **Lesson Four:** Don't make snap decisions that steer too far from the conservative, especially in situations where you give up significant control.

The sunny drive was nice along the winding street through the more affluent coastal neighborhoods. I diligently paid close attention to landmarks in case I had to find my own way back. He told me about a great restaurant up the road where we could stop for lunch then return to downtown. All the while he became more animated and inquisitive. He also used the word 'friend' way too much. **Lesson Five:** If someone you only recently met is very friendly, he probably will never be your friend. But you are in a likely position to let him become your enemy.

Upon reaching the restaurant, the quiet taxi driver was convinced to join the meal. While waiting for our food, Mehmet became gung-ho about having a few glasses of raki (a licorice liquor like sambuka). Despite my opposite intentions and aversion to morning alcohol consumption, somehow he convinced me to have a few myself. I think he used some lame, typical male logic. **Lesson Six:** Alcohol on the road can be a big mistake unless you're in an extremely 'safe' situation with sober people you can trust with your life.

If I wasn't already loose-lipped enough, the strong sweet intoxicant didn't improve concealment of my road naiveté. Through his seemingly innocent and clever weave of believable self-revelations and questions, I somehow shared information about the valuables I had brought on the trip and how I'd safeguarded them. Yeah, I know, what an idiot! Just wait, there's more.

Although I'd had a few drinks, I felt like I was still in complete control: we were in public in broad daylight, a witness was present, and we were ready to head back to town. I even felt better when we had talked about the expense of the lunch and the taxi fare (which were approximately equal). I offered to pay for the meal so I didn't feel like I was running up a debt with this guy. **Lesson Seven:** Carry enough money to pay any foreseeable expense in an accessible pocket, completely separate from other valuables. If you have to remove your money belt to pay up, find a rest room to extract extra cash. I learned this lesson the hard way, too.

As we headed back toward town, Mehmet suggested that we visit a Turkish bath. I told him that I wanted to visit one but probably not my first day in town. His purported connections as a airport cop gave him special access to a great nearby bath, he claimed. Becoming more suspicious, I boldly asked him to show me his ID to prove his identity. He reacted with great disappointment in my lack of trust—after all we'd been through! I held my ground so he grudgingly showed me his card and even wrote down this name and address in my journal. Foolishly, this eased my right-minded concern.

**Lesson Eight**: Just because someone has a photo ID doesn't mean it's real, and the more official someone's occupation sounds, the more likely it's bullshit. Moreover, special access claims often indicate ulterior motives. He explained that upon entering a Turkish bath, one puts his belongings in a safe. In fact, he said, the normal practice is to list one's valuables to ensure they're all returned. Foolishly, I followed his lead by listing everything in my daypack: a camera, binoculars, etc., then the contents of my money belt. To determine exact amounts, I took it off and listed them: $1,400 in traveler's checks, $200 cash, 10 airline tickets, driver's license, passport, a credit and ATM card. Being naturally suspicious, I held on tight to everything and still felt in absolute control.

**Lesson Nine:** You've got to be a complete moron to reveal all your valuables to a total stranger! The temptation of such a sight could convert a nun into a thief.

As we neared downtown, Mehmet's curiosity peaked, tinged with intoxication and even a little forcefulness. His raised intensity made me very uncomfortable, but his apparent inebriation made him seem harmless. He claimed to never have seen an ATM card and asked me how it worked. He practically pleaded for me to show him how.

At this point I was very wary of his intentions, but in his reduced state, I agreed to demonstrate at a very visible public ATM on our way. I quickly punched the keys and extracted $20. He was miffed that I wouldn't show him my PIN. That's when I became absolutely positive that he would rip me off if he could. I calmly planned my escape as we got back in the taxi. As soon as I was positive where I was downtown, and we stopped in traffic in a well-populated spot, I'd step out and ...

He beat me to my own plan! Stopped in traffic at a crowded intersection, he casually slurred in Turkish to the cabby, who nodded (as he did a dozen other times). Before I knew it, he opened his door and snatched my money belt laying just inside my daypack on the floor between my legs. In just seconds he'd fled through the crowd into the twisting alleys. I gesticulated frantically to get the driver to help me catch him, but the language barrier delayed his realization as the precious opportunity flew by. We searched in vain as I spewed obscenities while my panic gave way to desperation. He was gone and I was screwed!

I proved on the very first day of a 2-month trip how foolish one could be. I was so demoralized that I very nearly turned back home. How I got back on my feet is worth sharing.

After getting back in the cab, I used a pocket dictionary to convey that the guy was a thief who just stole all my valuables. The cabby was pissed-off at the slime too, so he turned off the meter and raced around the block a few times trying catch him. As I calmed down, he was heating up.

Mehmet had convinced the cabby that we were friends and that he needed to step out to make a phone call. Knowing I'd paid for the meal, he realized he'd been stiffed on a $30 fare. I told him that I'd pay him as soon as I could recover some money. Having studied the Istanbul map the previous night, I had an emergency plan—the nearby American Consulate. I figured they'd pull more weight than the local police would.

My pitiful sucker story drew head shaking from the seasoned Consulate guards. I profusely thanked the cabby and asked him to return the next day to pick up his fare. As he ranted about the thief to the Turkish militia, I was ushered through the fortress into a little chunk of the USA.

An investigator named Mete had to be called in to officially question me. He was surprised at both my stupidity and my unusual preparation for this misfortune. In fact, at first, I think he even suspected I had fabricated the story. Taped directly into my journal were items ensuring my nearly complete recovery in just a few days. Most importantly: photocopies of my passport and plane tickets, records of traveler's checks, and credit card company and bank telephone numbers. **Lesson Ten:** Keep a photocopy record of all your valuable documents and the valuables themselves in two separate places amongst your belongings.

From the Consulate I called a friend, American Express, and my credit card company. The Citizens Services and the airline office personnel were impressed with the proof I possessed, and reissued my precious documents easily. In the meantime, Mete assured me that I could travel anywhere in Turkey with my passport photocopy, and backed it with his 24-hour phone number. The Consulate even gave me 500,000 lira ($15), and set me up at the nice Hotel Monopol across the street at 40% regular price (on credit).

Don't get me wrong—the red tape, legwork, emotional anguish and embarrassment humbled and frustrated me nearly to wit's end, but the preparation I did before leaving home saved me from ruin. American Express delivered traveler's checks in less than 24 hours on a Sunday morning! I had a new passport Monday morning, and reissued plane tickets from 3 airlines by Tuesday. My credit card was unused and reissued that week, too.

Believe it or not, the rest of the trip in Turkey, Nepal, Thailand, Hong Kong, and the Philippines went without a hitch. The Day 1 shocking incident prepared me well to safely enjoy the next couple of months. Every now and then I wonder who's using my passport identity ... Too bad for him it expired in February 1999!

# Cracking Wise with an Immigration Officer

## Eileen O'Connor

*A cautionary tale of a bad haircut and drinking too much.*

IT ALL STARTED WITH A BAD HAIRCUT. I was 22, living in London, and wanted desperately to be sophisticated. (I wasn't—not by a long shot.) My friend Patty and I were working as bartenders there and had saved enough money for a trip. We chose Malta, because it was the cheapest. I went for my sophisticated haircut the day before we left. The haircut was a disaster. I remember stepping out of the salon and the sun behind me cast my shadow on the sidewalk. My head looked like a little pea rolling around on my shoulders.

Thank God for floppy sunhats—I managed to have a very nice time in Malta. However, on the flight coming back to London, Patty and I got drunk. I went into the bathroom and stared blearily at my reflection. Aided by the alcohol and a squint, I decided from certain angles that it wasn't really all that bad. In fact, in the light of the bathroom, I suddenly realized I looked a lot like Clark Gable. Problem is, I'm a woman. Well, no matter. I got out my eyeliner and drew a little moustache on my lip. (To be honest, I kind of turned myself on a little bit ...) I knew this was just going to kill Patty. I wove my way back to my seat and Patty and I collapsed in a convulsive heap of hilarity.

The plane landed at Gatwick, and we went rolling through the terminal. I got up to the desk and handed my passport to the immigration officer. He looked at it for a long time, then eyed me for longer. "All right, Ms. O'Connor, when are you returning to New York?" I said, "Um, I'm going home for Christmas." He demanded to see my ticket. I said, "Well, you can't do that, I don't generally travel with tickets I don't need." I looked around for Patty, but she was in another line. "All right, Ms. O'Connor," he said, "come this way."

I suddenly found myself in a room of illegal immigrants. Hmm, well, this was kind of strange. I wondered what the mix-up was all about. I wasn't too concerned. I tried to find out what was going on, but no one else spoke English, so I took out some paper and a pen, and started writing a letter to my friend Denyse in NY. I said I was sitting in a room of illegal immigrants, but

**202**

that I didn't know why. Then, (because I was still a little drunk ...) I proposed that maybe I was there because some eunuch of an immigration officer couldn't grow a moustache and was jealous of mine. I reflected that you just never know what makes people tick. Then the officer came in, grabbed me by the arm and escorted me to the baggage area to claim my luggage. I thought it was over then, but it was just beginning.

He then took my luggage and me to a little room where there was a female officer. Together, the two of them went through my luggage, item by item. I had a few Christmas presents that I had picked up in Malta. These were broken in the flurry of getting everything out of my suitcase. They even tore apart a box of tampons. "What are you looking for?" I was getting really exasperated and was still not quite sober. The immigration officer barked at me not to speak until I was spoken to. (Yeesh.)

I started to get a little inkling that this was not so hilarious anymore.

They took me to a tiny, windowless room, leaving me with nothing but my cigarettes and a comb. They kept everything else. I was in that room for hours, and to cheer myself up, I took the cellophane off my pack of cigarettes and played "Yellow Rose of Texas." on my comb. I was just trying to keep myself from crying, but he put a quick stop to that. He opened the door, yelled at me to stop, grabbed the comb and left.

The officer came back in the room holding a letter to me written by a friend in Long Kesh prison. That's when my heart started to pound. Here come the dreads. This was two weeks after the Brighton Bombing in which the IRA had tried to blow up Margaret Thatcher. I had nothing to do with the IRA, I just kept up a correspondence with this guy in prison. Whoops. Here we go. "Now, Ms. O'Connor, I see here you have a friend in Long Kesh Prison. Tell me, Ms. O'Connor, what is your friend doing in prison?" "Well," I said, "He's studying French and Philosophy." Long pause. "Interesting, Ms. O'Connor, now why would your friend be studying French and Philosophy in prison?" (If he's going to get snippy with me, well, two can play at that game ...) "Well," I said, "He wants to better himself and grow intellectually like everyone else." This officer is really hating me now, and I get the feeling that if I would just break down, cry and beg, it would probably be okay. But I couldn't do it. I just couldn't. He kept going out and coming back in again with more questions. He wanted names and addresses of everyone I knew in Dublin. I had spent a semester there the previous year, which is how I came to be writing to a prisoner in the first place.

My mind was whirling and I just made up names and addresses. I started thinking of the movie "Midnight Express." I suddenly realized that being American wasn't really going to help me here. The officer was talking about sending me back to Malta as he left the room. That would be horrible—I'd spent all my vacation money and was broke. Not even a credit card. That's when I almost cried. But instead, I picked my nose and put a booger on his chair. I knew it was feeble retribution, but it was all I could do at the time. He had my passport, my belongings, my fate—everything. But at least he'd also have a booger on his butt. So there.

He came back in the room, sat on the booger, and said "All right, Ms. O'Connor. We've decided to send you back to New York. Oh, and Ms. O'Connor?" he smirked, "This has nothing to do with the fact that I can't grow a moustache."

"Yeah, I'm sorry about that," I said. "Oh, not that I wrote it, but that you can't grow one. It does wonders for a weak mouth."

And really, you know, I'd had enough of London. It was time for me to go home.

# Goofus and Gallant Travel Tips

## Becky Youman and Bryan Estep

*Remember going to the doctor's office when you were a little kid and getting stuck reading Highlights magazine? Recall Goofus and Gallant? The authors always related to the disheveled Goofus, though Gallant waltzed through life while Goofus stumbled.*

THE AUTHORS RECENTLY TOOK A TRIP TO BRAZIL with Goofus and wished they had traveled with Gallant.

### Goofus

Goofus doesn't talk to the locals as soon as he arrives in a new spot. He'd rather have a 3 a.m. test of wills with the cab driver over whether or not he is going to pay double the meter fare because it is after midnight.

### Gallant

Gallant learns loads from talking to the locals. He gets the real scoop on things like tipping practices, taxi rules (yes, it's more after midnight), and how to strut on the beach in a weenie-bikini.

### Goofus

Goofus is restaurant impaired. He walks into the first one he sees, orders a bunch of food, and is shocked by the $102 bill. He is so numbed that he does not check the total and ends up tipping the waiter twice. He continues to pay a lot for food "because it's Rio."

### Gallant

Gallant knows it's hard for any fare to taste good when it's blowing his food budget for the week. He is also aware that there is always something tasty and cheap even in countries with overvalued currencies. In Copacabana it's beer, beans and bum.

### Goofus

Goofus runs around all day and gets crabby when his blood sugar level hits bottom. He sulks when his partner wins in cribbage.

### Gallant

Gallant knows that after surfing, biking, or exploring he is going to be hungry. He makes sure he always has portable food. He's not perfect. He sulks too when his partner wins in cribbage.

### Goofus

Goofus reads his tour book as if it were the Bible. When he gets to the beach that his book says is pristine and finds fecal matter floating in the water, he stomps his feet.

### Gallant

Gallant realizes that even the best guides aren't completely current by the time they are published. He uses his to get near undeveloped beaches and then continues 15 miles down the road for unspoiled paradise.

### Goofus

Goofus wastes time running around looking for ropes. Then his stuff, poorly secured, falls off his car and carpets the highway with dirty underwear.

### Gallant

Gallant carries bungee cords and carabiners. He uses them to secure his pack to the top of the bus, tie his surfboard to the rental car, and entertain his girlfriend at night.

### Goofus

Goofus doesn't bring eye-patches or earplugs so he gets no sleep when his hotel room is above a samba school. That makes him grumpy with his travel friends.

### Gallant

Gallant, with his earplugs, sleeps soundly through an insane woman playing Yatzee outside his window from three to five a.m. He is chipper in the morning.

### Goofus

Goofus goes home saying Brazil sucks.

### Gallant

Gallant goes, sees, does, enjoys and becomes an honorary *carioca*.

# Norwegian Ice Toast

## Susan Parker

*Even a noxious drink has its time and place.*

I DON'T DRINK BRANDY. Don't like it, never have. The smell alone can induce an instant hangover—a nauseating *deja vu* of a college binge. But I had the chance to try it again under different circumstances. On July 4th, when most Americans are watching fireworks and enjoying family picnics, I was standing on a pristine Norwegian glacier with my boyfriend Bruce, our guide Sverre, and three middle-aged Poles. We were all glacier-hiking neophytes and the very first tourist group to venture onto the newly opened Kjenndalsbreen. Afterwards, Sverre commemorated our premiere with a brandy toast. A fine gesture—I didn't want to be a party pooper.

Jostedalsbreen, the "roof of Norway," is the largest glacier on the European continent. Forty miles long and fifteen miles wide, it is the heart of an awe-inspiring national park. More than 25 extensions or icy *arms* drape off of the mother glacier and reach out into the surrounding lush, green valleys. The iridescent blue color, a result of the way light refracts through immense blocks of ice, makes the environs a perennial magnet for world adventurers. Kjenndalsbreen, an arm of Jostedalsbreen, was previously considered too unstable for exploration. This mighty appendage had grown and thickened enough in recent decades to now sustain trekkers. Our expedition pioneered the coniferous mountainside path to the glacier. At the frozen, jagged edge, I bundled myself in winter clothing, strapped on boot crampons, secured my hard hat, tied myself to Sverre and the others and walked onto blue ice—forever changing Kjenndalsbreen's destiny.

I felt as though I stepped into a Georgia O'Keeffe painting; a panorama of erotic concaves and hollows. For several hours we negotiated the glacier's sensuous white and blue facade—ice-picking our way up luminous hills, crawling through opalescent tunnels, and leaping across crevaces secretly winding to unknown places.

In glacier hiking, you're only as safe as your weakest link. I had doubts about our Polish contingency. The two women were both heavy smokers who gasped for air while climbing up the mountainside to the glacier. On the ice, Sverre lead and placed Bruce and I at the back of the human chain to help balance

**207**

any deficiencies. At one point, we almost lost one of the women when she nearly slid into a crevace. Sverre quickly instructed us to pick up any slack in the leash that bound us together. Simulating a game of tug-o-war, she was quickly pulled back into the fold. I had to swallow my fear and remain focused as nature continued to take command of my senses—the cool wetness of the ice, the warmth of the wind, the constant thunder of the surrounding waterfalls, and the echo of falling rocks and ice. The glacier was alive.

At the end of our journey, as a late afternoon fog rolled in, Sverre produced a bottle of Courvoisier from his backpack along with some paper cups. He asked each of us to gather and place a small handful of the 1000-year-old ice into our cups. He served everyone a liberal dose of the elixir and offered a toast to Kjenndalsbreen for giving us a few hours to create a lifetime of unforgettable memories. Responding with a hearty group *skoal*, I decided to take a small nip and secretly pass the rest off to Bruce. Whether it was the spirit of the moment, the primitive environs, or the bond of a maiden voyage—I finished my cognac without ill effect. I still don't drink brandy ... but I haven't had it with 1000-year-old ice again either.

# Sweet Tooth

## Ruth Halpern

*Think you've had a pre-trip dilemma? Try an aching black hole leading straight into the brain.*

LATE LAST NIGHT, I was chain-popping mint-flavored Mentos at San Francisco International Airport as I waited for the 11 p.m. departure of a multi-stop flight to Roatán, Honduras. My mother and grandmother were waiting for me there so we could begin our first ever nine-day three-generational adventure. I had the roll of candy in my jean jacket pocket as I wheeled my carry-on suitcase-cum-backpack through the art exhibit at the entrance to the international departure lounge. A series of tall Plexiglas cases displayed confectionery from around the world. I fed myself the mints in quick succession as I drifted from the case full of architectural Italian marzipan (candy facsimiles of the cathedrals of Rome), to the sky-scrapers of pastel-colored Japanese rice candy, to bouquets of Chinese New Years treats wrapped in lucky red paper.

Each time I squished out another plump white disk I tore off more of the flattened paper tube that contained them. My fingers sifted and squeezed the scraps of wrapper that littered my pocket, ensuring that not a single disk escaped uneaten. I had an endless appetite for chomping down through the crunchy crust and burying my teeth in the chewy middle, drinking the flood of peppermint that suffused my tongue. I kept count with my fingers, squeezing the ridges in the roll to see how many disks were left. By the time I reached the display case of American classics—the brilliant orange square of the Reese's cup alongside the paler orange rod of the Butterfinger bar—I was down to the third-to-the-last Mento, wondering whether I should eat the remaining mints more slowly or buy another roll before the gift shop closed. Then it happened.

I bit down on a Mento with my right molars, and felt more than the usual crunch. The candy pinched my gum savagely and then pulled away with an almost audible crack as I opened my jaw.

On the second chomp, I knew something was terribly wrong—no Mento should be as rigid as stone, as smooth as polished steel, with pointy edges like sharp prongs. In the dark instant that I held the chewy mass balanced on my tongue, I recognized the subtle fracturing sensations in my upper jaw which I had been ignoring for the past month:

My gold crown had just wrenched free of its cement foundation and gotten masticated into a Mento.

Gagging with horror, I spit the gleaming pulpy glob into my palm, lifted out the little gold cup, and tossed the twice-bitten Mento into the trash. A hole. My entire jaw felt like a gaping aching black hole leading straight into my brain. The first breath I gasped howled through the gap like a glacial wind, forcing me to clamp my lips shut and press my tongue against the naked fang where the tooth had been whittled down to fit inside the crown. My head had split open. Evil spirits would whirl up into my skull, corrode my brain, rot my central nervous system. Could the people slumped around me hear the wind whistling through the gaping chasm?

I panted in panic as I reviewed what I knew about the situation. When a limb is severed, you have to pack it in ice and take it with you to the emergency room. When a tooth gets knocked out, you can sometimes get the nerve to re-attach if you insert it back in the gum fast enough. But what do you do for a false tooth, a cap of gold?

It was 10:55 p.m. The steward's voice came over the PA system, announcing that anyone with more than two carry-on bags would have to step forward and check them now. As soon as all the excess baggage was checked, the boarding process would begin.

I scanned the packed lounge. It was the week before *Semana Santa*, Holy Week, and the lounge was full of Central Americans going home to celebrate with their families. Judging from the size of their cardboard boxes, it seemed that all of them were bringing color televisions home for the holidays. The few children who were still vertical were wobbling around the edges of the lounge like wind-up toys winding down. A few people shot shy, sympathetic glances at me—they could tell from my wild eyes and ragged breathing that something was wrong—but I saw no one dressed in a white lab coat with a spit-sucking tube dangling from the pocket.

I wanted to shout, "Somebody help me, there's a hole in my head! My tooth is rotting! How can I go to Honduras?" but I was afraid that if I opened my mouth wide enough to yell, an icy gust would whip in and freeze my brain. Instead, I wheeled my suitcase over to the white courtesy phone and dialed the airport medical clinic. "Josh" answered on the first ring.

"Josh," I said, "I've got a really bizarre problem."

"Oh, good, I love bizarre problems. I'm ready."

"OK, try this on for size: my gold crown just fell out while I was eating a

Mento, and my flight to Honduras is scheduled to leave in five minutes."

I heard the sound of pages flipping, and then Josh began to read.

"Save the appliance."

"I've got it right here." I had zipped it into my money belt and tucked it safely into the waistband of my pants. I patted it every few minutes to make sure that pressure from my gut hadn't squashed it flat.

"Reinstall the tooth or appliance as soon as possible. Preferably within 30 minutes."

Thirty minutes? Where could I get to in thirty minutes that would re-install my appliance? I'd be lucky if it didn't take thirty hours. My heart raced.

"But Josh, my plane is leaving!"

"That's about it. I've read you all there is."

"But Josh, what should I do? Brainstorm with me here for a minute, Josh, think creatively. It's practically midnight and my plane is leaving. What can I do? How can I go to a remote island where they have no phones with a gaping hole in my mouth? What would you do, Josh?"

"Well, I guess I really don't know. I've read you everything in the book already. Do you want the phone number of a 24-hour dentist? We've got a list here ..."

I wrote the number down on edge of my magazine, hung up the white courtesy phone, and trudged over to the bank of pay phones.

On the first phone in the bank I dialed the 24-hour dentist's automated paging system. I punched in the number of the pay phone, pressed pound, and hung up. Could these pay phones even receive incoming calls?

I moved to the second phone and dialed my boyfriend. He had just dropped me off at the airport two hours before, but I knew he'd be sound asleep—he had a strict 10:00 bedtime. I discussed my predicament with his answering machine. Should I take the flight? Should I skip the entire nine-day trip? What would he advise, if he were awake? What did he think my mother would say I should do? Would he hear my voice rambling on through his dreams and wake up? He didn't.

The first phone rang, and I snatched it up. A friendly-sounding woman introduced herself as the dentist's answering service, and asked what seemed to be the problem. Her lighthearted yet informed tone suggested that she was experienced at handling this kind of medical emergency, so I described my situation. I had two choices, she said. I could spend $200 on the emergency dentist, who could meet me in 20 minutes at his office somewhere in South San Francisco. How I got there was my problem. Or I could take a taxi home and go to my own dentist in the morning.

A taxi home in the middle of the night—that would be at least $50. Plus at least $100 for my dentist to reinstall my $500 crown. Plus the distress of my mother and grandmother, who would have no idea what had happened to me when I didn't step off that plane tomorrow. But far worse than money or my family's anxiety, how could I face my dentist after this disaster? This was the same dentist who, two years ago, had dropped a different gold crown down my throat as she attempted to install it. Maybe I should call her and ask her what to do. But no, even if it was her faulty crown-gluing that had gotten me into this pickle, I've always been reluctant to tell her when I'm dissatisfied with her services, because I'm afraid that her unconscious anger will cause her to do something even more disastrous to my mouth in retaliation. I've had that fear about dentists ever since the punitive flossing lessons I got from my terrifying childhood dentist, Dr. Wasser, whose whiskery nostrils, German accent and relentless, pointy-tooled probing made me associate dentists with the worst kinds of war-time sadists. Was there a dentist anywhere I could trust?

Sick at the thought of some half-asleep emergency dentist prodding my fang, I thanked her and went up to the check-in desk to see if the steward could help me with my predicament.

"I don't think I can take this flight," I announced to him. "I'm having a medical emergency." I pointed at my tooth and grimaced to indicate where the problem was.

He studied my ticket. "You will not be able to fly on a weekend," he said, "Your fare does not permit it. You will not be able to leave San Francisco until next Wednesday, a week from today."

Next Wednesday! Two days before I was scheduled to return! My eyes flooded with tears and the crowded lounge went dim. I labored to speak around the cold hole in my jaw and the thick fear in my throat.

"My mother and grandmother are expecting me in Roatán tomorrow and they're staying at a place with no phone. How am I supposed to contact them?" Sniff. "It's a medical emergency, how can the airline hold me to that fare? They must make allowances for special circumstances."

He looked at me with the detached compassion of somebody else's guardian angel—he only had a little pity to spare for a *gringa* with a bad tooth who was falling apart in front of him.

"I'm sorry, that's what it says on the ticket. Would you like to call the reservations line and see what they say?"

As the steward waited for my answer, a short middle-aged *gringo* shouldered up to the desk and asked whether the steward thought our flight would get to El Salvador in time to make his connecting flight home to Roatán.

**212**

"Ah, Madam, this man is going to Roatán as well," the steward said to me, "Maybe he can tell you about dentists down there, so that you can take the flight tonight."

"Oh yeah, absolutely," said the man, when I described my predicament, "They have great dentists in Honduras. I know *gringos* who save up their dental work to have it done down there, because it's so much cheaper. I've got some friends who could recommend 2 or 3 dentists in La Ceiba, it's just a 20 minute ferry ride from Roatán. Don't sweat it, you should definitely take the flight."

I looked from the steward to this gregarious white man. They were both nodding. They thought I should get on a late plane, my tooth in a zipper pocket, fly all night to a third-world country, get off the plane not having eaten or drunk anything but water, take a long taxi ride to our hidden condo, and promptly announce to my managerial mother and grandmother that I had a medical emergency, which I'd come down there in spite of, and would they please accompany me to La Ceiba by boat or by plane? These men could probably guess just by looking at me that I only speak enough Spanish to *comer* and *comprar*, and they still thought I could get my ducks in a row and my tooth in my mouth?

I didn't have many other options: the closer *Semana Santa* got, the harder it would be to get on another flight. Would I rather waste a couple of days lying limply in my dentist's chair, gazing reproachfully at her forehead while she glued in my crown, or just get to the beach and deal with it there? Maybe I could use a piece of Doublemint as a temporary adhesive.

The *gringo* picked up my guide book, which I'd been thumbing fruitlessly for medical references, and showed me on a map how close it was from Roatán to La Ceiba. He lived on Roatán part-time, he said; he was a real estate developer; he probably knew someone who could get a message to my family. He smiled at me with the wide-eyed conviction of a veteran insurance salesman.

The steward patted my arm.

"It seems very bad right now, but I think you should take the flight anyway. This problem with your tooth will work itself out. Your family will be waiting for you."

\* \* \*

The plane finally left San Francisco at 1:00 a.m. All that night I lay back in my narrow seat, swaddled in the tight dark of my sleep mask, chewing on nightmares. In the black night, the shrill of the plane's engines wound up to the whine of a dentist's drill and every time I accidentally breathed through my mouth, the icy chill and cranial horror woke me up. The 6 a.m. sandwich service threw me into despair. How long would it be before I could eat or drink again?

We reached San Salvador 20 minutes after our connecting flight to Roatán departed—the next one was the next day. At the airline's 3-star hotel, I went directly to the front desk to plead for help. I was hungry and desperate—I had to find someone to glue my crown back in. The desk clerk made an appointment for me with his own family dentist, hailed a taxi, and gave the driver detailed directions to the office. A uniformed guard stood in front of every shop we passed, hands braced on holstered hips. Since the CIA stopped doing battle here, the soldiers had to find other work. How many of them had become dentists? And what about all those Nazis who emigrated to Central America after World War II?

I recognized the dentist's office by the picture of a papa tooth, a mama tooth, and a baby tooth painted on the door. Inside, it seemed I had walked back in time directly into Dr. Wasser's basement of horrors: same sharp smell of antiseptic; same low acoustic-tiled ceiling and medicinal green walls; same long-necked chrome fixtures, now corroded with 30 years of tropical humidity. The hairs on the back of my neck prickled. No one in the entire world knew where I was. How many 9 inch needles might this Salvadoran dentist insert, how many crowns and fillings might he extract, before abandoning me to wander in a nitrous oxide daze through the streets of San Salvador?

Just as I was gathering my few words of Spanish to hail another taxi and flee, I heard movement from the back of the office. A shy 15-year old introduced himself as Juan, the dentist's assistant and translator, and showed me into the treatment room. The dentist bowed and offered me a seat on the cracked burgundy leather of his examining chair. I lay rigid, flicking my eyes across the tray of gleaming gougers balanced beside me.

The dentist opened my jaw gently, explaining each step so Juan could translate it for me. He rotated the crown into position over the fang, and without a syringe or a spit-sucker or a single criticism of the state of my gums, he glued my *corona linda*—pretty crown—back into my mouth with a cement that Juan said was good for 100 years. Which is exactly how long it's going to be before I eat another Mento.

# In the Absurdity of the Moment

## Sam Khedr

*Why all the fuss over the Mona Lisa? Was she truly Leonardo's poster child of the Renaissance, or just another product of media hype?*

I ENTERED THE ROOM THAT HOUSED THE MONA LISA, as I suspected, there was a happy-horde of tourists hovering about. Mona's popularity has grown so large, she needs a museum all to herself. I was, however, determined to catch her on film. I politely asked the horde to step aside. No one budged. After considerable effort and flawless timing, I finally had her within clear view of my scope.

The flash went off like an alarm setting off a cacophony of oohs and ahs followed by one oops ... mine. I had thrown myself into the center of attention. I suddenly remembered the abundance of signs warning "NO FLASHES." Next to actually stealing a painting, it seemed I was now in violation of the museum's highest commandment.

In the absurdity of the moment, I noticed a peculiar but somewhat relieved grin on the face of a guard (his mindless hours of standing and scrutinizing was not to be in vain. And he wasn't alone, their moment had come. With one flash, I had justified their fraternal existence. Three guards zeroed in on me. I had never heard French growled as such; they were furious. Zooming in for the kill like blood-sensing wolves, their fangs protruded, and although I don't speak French, I thought I heard the word guillotine. It was too late for a discrete escape, I had already run amok, leaving me with no other option but to run for the door. Hoping the guards would lose interest; I slipped out of the room, but as I turned the corner, the growling pack followed. The chase was on.

Getting lost in the Louvre is unavoidable. That's fine when you're leisurely viewing great works of art, but not when you're being tailed by three man-eating monsters clad in French civil servant uniforms. Nonetheless, I wasn't about to let a chase get in the way of experiencing ... I mean glimpsing the most celebrated collection of art. I darted past French Impressionism, dashed through the Neoclassical period, and scooted by Rococo. I even stopped to take a picture of a Dutch couple embraced in the foreground of Delacroix's *Liberty Leading The People*. Thinking of my own liberty, there at the end of the corridor,

**215**

I saw the Keystone Brigade fixing me within their sight. I handed the camera back to the Dutch couple and resumed my part in the chase. Fun as it was, it was time for my exit-stage-left.

As I descended the elegant marble staircase I momentarily stopped to pay homage to the sculpture of *Nike*, the Greek goddess of victory. "Just do it, just do it," I imagined her saying. So, with a hop, jump, and a stumble I made my way out the door. I heard the sound of whistles. By now my headhunters had eliminated the possibility of my being just a "stupid American tourist." In their minds, I imagined, I was either some evil drug dealer, or a treacherous terrorist on the run. Surely, by this time, even a dimwitted American tourist would have thrown in the towel. Instead I justified their conviction by knocking aside a thug who attempted to block my exit. Caught up in the excitement of the chase, I fell into a total lapse of reason.

Outside, I tried to dissolve into the countless tourists spilling out from buses. But it was too late, the guards' incessant whistle blowing had doggedly followed me outside. I can imagine this must have been the most fun they had in years (truly a story to share with their families over dinner.) As the guards closed in, the police arrived. The chase was over.

I gave myself up to the peaked hat policemen. Sitting handcuffed in the back of the police car, I heard the guards' rant and rave. Their flustered state may have been warranted for a criminal with evil intentions of overthrowing the French republic but certainly not for a tourist whose camera flash had gone off. Luckily the two policemen were more rational. As one was taking notes, the other took a long look at me and suddenly began to laugh. I would live. I was driven to the station, interrogated, searched, re-interrogated, and then locked up in a cell.

Six hours later nothing was happening. I was on a one-day kamikaze bus trip to Paris with Dad. Regrettably, my visions of discovering the magical beauties of Paris had not included imprisonment. Now my only concern was to catch my bus back to Germany.

Clang! The cell door opened, I was "free" to go. I was escorted back to my bus by two peaked hats who did not want to miss an opportunity to see me leave their country. Imagine the expressions on the passengers' faces, notably my father's, when the police car rolled beside the delayed bus to deposit me.

Though Paris was not to be, Dad chuckled for hours about my imprisonment. "Will the picture come out," he wondered?

… It did.

# INTIMACY

## Love on the Move

*"Strong as the desert,*
*Soft as the sea,*
*oving like the wind,*
*Forever free."*
Lee Clark, *The Traveler*

# Manihi

## Phil Trupp

*The legend of early explorers in the South Pacific descending upon
an earthly paradise still entices travelers today.*

MARIE-JEAN LIKES ME. I can tell. In her smile a spark, a familiarity. She
places a lei of flowers around my neck.

*"Maeva,"* she says. "Welcome."

We are speaking a jumble of French and Tahitian and English. Standing with
her on the little wooden dock where I have just landed, I tell her I am glad to
have found Manihi. It is so perfectly remote, so isolated—the Pacific of my
dreams.

Marie-Jean has not traveled beyond the Tuamotuan Archipelago of which
Manihi is a part, and so she makes a habit of awaiting the arrival of visitors.
Today she has dressed for the occasion in a traditional pareo. A white Tiara
Tahiti is tucked behind one ear, a signal of her availability.

I wonder if perhaps she is a student. No. At sixteen her schooling is long
over. She has settled into the little Kiana Village resort where she serves in the
dining pavilion. Her brothers and sisters also work at the resort.

"What work you do?" Marie-Jean asks.

"Journalist."

She makes scribbling movements on her palm. "Writer? What you write?"

I tell her about my love/sex/death/race themes as we drift into the shade of
the pavilion.

"Oh, *nehenehe* (beautiful). You like Hinano?"

Sly and conspiratorial, she slips behind the bar, unlocks the double glass
doors of the alcohol locker, and hands out a sweating bottle of beer. The first
and best drink of the day.

She excuses herself. There is work to do. We will meet again, yes?

I retire to my little bungalow with its blue tin roof. Here, set out over the
lagoon in deep silence, I ponder the image of French Polynesia as the islands
of desire, a legend which began in 1768 when a bare-breasted *vahine* paddled

out to a French ship anchored in the Sea of the Moon, off Tahiti. She mounted the deck, dropped her pareo and stood smiling in front of sailors who hadn't seen a woman in months. Captain Louis-Antoine Bouganville wrote in his diary, "I thought I was transported into the Garden of Eden ... The abode of Venus."

Is this idyll real? I have been trolling my curiosity through the big islands, Tahiti and Moorea, and into the outbacks of Riatea and Rangiroa. Mostly I am greeted by shyness. Marie-Jean will prove an exception. Will she take me to a secret Manihi, to a life described centuries ago by Captain James Cook? An Englishman who detested exaggeration, Cook wrote in his 18th century *Account of a Voyage Around the World*: "There is a scale of dissolute sensuality (to) which these people have ascended, wholly unknown to every other nation whose manners have been recorded from the beginning of the world to the present hour, and which no imagination could possibly conceive."

Europeans were at first skeptical. One critic insisted it was natural for seamen to glorify the women they'd met in exotic places. But other explorers confirmed the visions of Bouganville and Cook. The French naval officer Max Radiquet, in his *Le Derniers Sauvages* (1860), wrote: "(Polynesian women) are of middle height, and their outlines often molded with a purity hardly ever seen in France except in statuary ... Their development never exceeds the limits fixed by the laws of beauty ... Few women anywhere else in the world have more grace, at least in their attitudes if not in their movements."

Now comes Marie-Jean—hardly a great beauty. Like many Polynesians, she appears to be on a perpetual junk food binge. Spam, Cheez Balls, potato chips, candy bars, sweet soda drinks are consumed between more fulsome meals of fried bananas, fried pork and oil-rich Polynesian hush-puppies. She has a wonderful loving face and almond eyes, and even if years of Cheez Balls bounce on her hips, she possesses an allure, an air of knowingness.

I ask if she finds Europeans attractive.

"What mean attractive?" The word is not part of her vocabulary. "Is like beauty? Ah, not like *vahines*." Besides, she goes on, *vahines* know more about what men want. She casts a sweetly wicked glance. "Soon maybe I tell."

Mornings I wander through Kiana Village and the seaward fringes of the atoll making pencil-sketches of the traditional *fares* which have all but disappeared from the major islands. Tiny Manihi, with fewer than five hundred natives, is part of a fading South Pacific, a time warp away from modern Tahiti.

It is on one of these excursions that I meet Allison, the American wife of the local French dive master. I come upon her hanging wash outside her *fare*. Fresh-faced and with a halo of chestnut hair, her athletic shape hugged by a traditional pareo, she moves with the insouciance of her *vahine* neighbors.

(Marie-Jean later describes such presence as "a scented breeze.")

She and her husband Guy have lived here for six years. Allison says she only occasionally misses her former life in Southern California.

"At night it seems so far away. And then I long for something familiar."

They are raising two boys and have enrolled them in the French-speaking school on the far side of the lagoon. Guy ferries them to a one-room class aboard a petite pirogue and brings them back at noon. I have seen the boys and their father in the mornings and remark how pleasant it is, this image of the children, book bags tucked into the bow of the little craft, skimming over the lagoon past the black pearl hatcheries.

"To the kids, it's life as usual," Allison says. "They've grown up here."

She has settled at Manihi by a circuitous route. Guy worked as an oil rig diver in East Africa and later migrated to Martinique. Seeking a deeper solitude, they tried Tahiti. He detested Papeete. Manihi appealed to his reclusiveness. "The aloneness of the place," Allison says. "That's what sold him."

What about the boys?

"Of course the school isn't the best. We'll have to deal with it eventually."

I ask about the romance legend.

"Probably the kinky stuff was true at one time. Maybe it still is. I don't know. These people are—" She pauses, choosing her words carefully. "They're precocious."

Precocious but not promiscuous in the American/European way. We encourage sexual exploration, pretend it is of little consequence. In the end we are Puritans. The French are engaging and teasing and less hypocritical than Americans. But Polynesians are intensely serious. Sex suffuses almost every aspect of society.

"Their courting is different," Allison says. "It's matriarchal, and this colors it."

Yet a pulp fiction quality haunts Western accounts of Polynesian love. Often we find conquering heroes surrounded by uninhibited women who fondle, cradle, and at last seduce with a powerful concoction of lust. If the real islands of desire do exist, how much is grafted onto the culture by the romantic foreigner?

Several days after my arrival, a little sloop anchors near my bungalow. At noon a young couple rides a dinghy to shore where they purchase food. They return to their boat and disappear below. Apparently they have been making their way through the Tuamotus, though I can not imagine them taking on the sea beyond the lagoon.

"Lovers," Marie-Jean informs me.

"They'd have to be. It's a very small boat."

One morning I discover the couple out walking on the beach. They might have been brother and sister: wire-thin, sun-stunned, both with the self-absorption one expects from yatchies. They are disillusioned by a world they left behind. It is irredeemably corrupt. And they've sailed thousands of miles from Nannes to Manihi only to drop anchor in the French nuclear test zone!

"Kiana Village is finished," the woman tells me. "I am French. And I can say honestly we have no instinct for colonization."

I wonder how long they will drift through the Pacific. Soon they will evolve unaware into middle-age. They will be overwhelmed by fears of ruin and a return to a life once scorned. I ask if they are married?

"Why should we?" the man replies, slightly indignant. Marriage is too ordinary. Expats are proud of their nonconformity; it is what they have the most of.

Later that morning, with Marie-Jean, I watch them motor back to their sloop, the man fast at the rudder, the woman steadying a basket of fruit. We wave. They pay no attention. Marie-Jean is sad.

"What is it?" I ask.

"I see *moana* (deep ocean) ... See end of dream."

\* \* \*

Marie-Jean is clear: in matters of sex, one is practical. Sex is a shared communal pleasure, more commonplace than courtship or feelings of romance. And because sexual activity is a communal art, almost everyone is expected to be a skilled lover. Learning begins at home.

"Parents teach," Marie-Jean beams.

She takes me into the *fares*. They consist essentially of a single room. A few have little screens which afford scant privacy. No wonder the Europeans were scandalized. To them (and to us) it is a bit disconcerting to contemplate children watching their parents engage in sexual intercourse.

Both genders are expected to develop strength and endurance. Typical love-making begins with the women. A ritual known as "rotation" is begun, with the women assuming various positions. The male, inventive and flexible, finds ways to fit in.

Europeans believe we are all the same size in bed. Marie-Jean laughs when I tell her this. A woman of her generous proportions demands an equal or greater life-force. Over and over she emphasizes the importance of physical strength.

"When make love, we eat lime gourd, tobacco, betelnut (a potent stimulant) No food," she explains. "It is shameful—food and love. Man say he want me. I say I want ... Put legs on his hips, maybe elbows. He do this ..." She poses in the typical male position. I am reminded of a baseball catcher behind home plate, hunkered down, knees bent, body slightly forward. "Sometimes on side. Put one leg around man."

Did she ever make love to a white man?

"One time. Polynesian better. They no press down." She squeezes her palms together to illustrate a body-to-body crush. "White man make heavy. When man heavy, woman can not move."

Proper sexual etiquette in the West allows the woman to reach *ipipisi momona* (orgasm) before the male. It is the same in Polynesia. This is a fine point, and there is a distinction between male and female orgasms. Male orgasms are called *isulumomoni*, indicating ejaculation. Women have *ipipisi*, a metaphorical word indicating a less obvious response. And talking while in the act—this is imperative.

"American women talk? What they say?"

Sometimes both men and women are content just to make sounds, I tell her.

"Ah, many sounds. Like birds. Like animals. You like woman sounds?"

Yes, I am found of a sonorous bedroom.

"Magic medicine," Marie-Jean winks, now darkly wicked, the confident huntress loving it, visualizing perhaps some past encounter, a joining of souls in the blood. I know she might easily have her way with me. She moves closer, sensuality coming off her like body heat. "You see now?"

I barely lift the sound of my voice out of my throat. "Yes. Yes, I do."

The following morning I stroll with her past the flimsy "dance houses" built by young Manihians as lovemaking shelters. Boys and girls interact in a happy, carefree manner. They fondle each other. Some are dancing, the boys waving arms above their heads, feet pounding the sand. The girls appear indifferent, but in reality they challenge the boys to do something special. Occasionally a couple disappears into one of the dance houses.

I wonder if it is expected that a man will have many women. Yes, Marie-Jean replies. It is encouraged; and the women, too, pursue many lovers.

"We are flower of village," she says proudly.

*  *  *

Evening. Kiana Village prepares to shut down its main generator. I am alone in the dining pavilion. Marie-Jean greets me. She is wearing a saffron-colored pareo. A Tiara Tahiti is tucked at an angle behind her ear.

"You work all day?"

She makes the scribbling-writing pantomime on the palm of her hand. She knows my appetites and has prepared a dish of rice, onions and spicy peppers. There is warm fresh bread and mangos in a wooden bowl. I break the bread and inhale its warmth.

"*Maruuru.*"

"*Maururu roa.*" She makes a little courtsey.

She disappears into the kitchen. I nibble the food and sketch the Papua New Guinean war canoe which dominates the pavilion. Its long narrow hull is dark with age and detailed with elaborate carvings. An outrigger provides balance. A carved dragon snarls from the bow.

Marie-Jean reappears. Her clingy pareo, dark eyes, thick black hair, the white flower—she knows she is getting to me. Again she makes the scribbling motion and laughs. She is a *potii*—a young girl whose laugh makes her appear older and wiser. I feel lonely in the empty pavilion, so I ask her to bring the coffee to my bungalow.

I wait. The tide moves seaward. My body flows with it. A flood inside me, a sea rising to the moon. Soon the entire island will be dark and I will be wide awake.

I settle on the little open deck. Sharks create trails of phosphorescence in the dark water.

A tapping on the door. Marie-Jean enters with tiny steps. She carries a thermos of coffee and a jar of coconut milk. She studies me with her huntress gaze. What to do? A Western visitor does not entice a Polynesian woman to cohabit his bungalow. Manihi is a long way from anywhere but there are rules. She reads my mind, smiles and tip-toes back into the night.

*   *   *

There is another woman at Manihi who excites my interest. Annette is very tall, uncharacteristically thin, almost willowy, with high cheek bones and an aquiline nose. Her black hair falls nearly to her waist and she is seldom without a Tiare Tahiti. There is a worldliness about her, a face of secrets less revealing than Marie-Jean's. Her complexion is smooth and pale, a mix of Polynesian and European blood. She moves like a Frenchwoman—focused but never forgetting her sex.

Annette works at Kiana Village Resort's dreary little pub. I try to speak to her but she is gloomy, ignoring my attempts to converse in Tahitian. She will speak only French, and only very little. She had married a Frenchman, one of the Black Berets, and is recently divorced. She has come to resent Europeans and is embittered by the annual "July Festivals" when the French parade their military through the streets of Papeete—this to celebrate the day in 1880 when the Polynesian King Pomare-V, for a pension of a few thousand francs, sold out his empire. Annette watched as her husband marched and sang of "blond beauties" in a nation of dark-skinned people. Conquered and the vanquished: seldom a happy co-mingling.

Marie-Jean says love has made Annette a little crazy. "White love make all crazy. But she say she not go back to old ways. European man hurt her. She want him anyway."

We are talking about it in the bungalow. The morning sun glares on the surface of the lagoon. I notice scratches on Marie-Jean's smooth face. When I asked about them she is coy, a slight blush filling her cheeks. She holds out her arms. Long red lines cover her shoulders. She's been with one of the young men in the glade behind Kiana Village. The scratches are a sign of erotic success. She is proud of them.

"The man, do you mark his face?"

"Yes, like this." She runs her fingernails lightly over my cheeks. It is not an unpleasant sensation.

She tells of encounters in the *bukumatula*. For a long time she and her lover lay side by side, their bodies intertwined. She is very specific. They rub noses, then cheeks. Their lips meet, but not in a Western-style kiss. Polynesians allow their lips to play over the face and body, hardly stopping long in any one spot. The tongue is sucked, the lips bitten, skin deeply marked. If there is blood they lick it; this is considered extremely sensual.

Women write the rules of sex-play. I have noticed fingernail markings on women and men, but the men are more visibly raked. The answer to the ubiquitous Western post-sexual encounter— "Was it good?" —is etched on the skin of Polynesians. The markings are a source of pride, signatures of passion and conquest.

Marie-Jean points to her eyelashes. "When very good we bit here." A revelation. No wonder so many of the young people have stumpy eyelashes. They have been chewed by eager, lustful teeth. If the early European explorers wrote the script, the natives supplied the raw material. Bouganville's *New Cytherea* was the "abode of Venus." Not the Venus Aphrodite rising from the sea in Ionia, but the flesh-and-blood reality living in Rousseau's land of the "golden age."

Marie-Jean, in an inspiration of trust, chants a once-secret tone poem sung by a Tuamotuan woman named Kurataukiapu during a liaison with a Tahitian chief, Hono. She chants in Tahitian, which I later translate.

*The everlasting wind was blowing from the east*
*When I yielded to him, overcome.*

*Like a mountain fern*
*He bent over me*
*And whispered sweet words.*
*A mountain fern was he.*
*Hono's passion was satisfied and he found peace,*
*For I resisted no longer, overcome.*
*My lover's passion awakened my own desire anew*
*And again I let myself be taken like a dove, overcome.*

As she sings I sensed the power of her words, the luxurious ancient rhythm. Sweet and unaffected, the tonalities a mix of innocence and desire.

"Marie-Jean must like you very much," Allison remarks when I tell her about the song.

"Am I getting in too deep?"

"Don't worry. Women control things here. She'll let you know if anything's wrong."

I flash on visions of a Polynesian goddess, Ruuruhi-keerepoo, an ogress-cannibal, fond of decapitating the victims upon whom she feasted. This goddess reflects the markings on Marie-Jean's body, the prideful display of blood. Perhaps blood is the true and ultimate message.

\* \* \*

For several days there is no sign of Marie-Jean. I have grown used to her; her absence is unsettling. I keep to the routine of rising early and finishing my writing by noon. I wander into the empty dining pavilion. The carved warrior outrigger with its dragon bow has become a living presence, defiant in its captivity.

I grow impatient and ask after Marie-Jean. I am greeted by shrugs and shyness. Then I catch myself: *You're breeding suspicion.* Perhaps rumors have already spread. I make no further inquiries.

It is pleasant enough to lounge on the deck of my bungalow and watch the sharks. Their long gray bodies make rippling shadows on the sandy bottom. They circle the deck, make for the pier, buzz the love-boat, return to swim beneath the deck. A pattern old as the planet, ancient as primal passion.

A cold drop of rain. Where did it come from? The sky is cloudless. More rain. Cold rain blowing over the horizon. I move inside, open my notebook and write:

*This is only a hint, drops of rain from a sky without clouds, a sky where there should be no rain at all. The sky lies.*

*A dull haze lifts over the horizon. Ripples on the surface of the lagoon become whitecaps.*

**227**

*Wind is mounting.*

*Now a gray band overtakes the blue emptiness. The lagoon churns white. I can no longer see the horizon. I am suddenly cold.*

*Rain. Icy pellets sting the surface of the lagoon. It is a hungry rain.*

*The sun is consumed by the squall. A high wail of wind is squeezed into a scream as it rushes through the coral passes, the scream lashing through the rumble of thunder. I hear the anger of big seas exploding on the reef.*

*There are sustained howls and pockets of silence. A strangely human sound. The rhythm of the wind and the silences, the lover's sloop pitching, the trembling final seizure of the squall has come and vanished in a few minutes.*

*Silence. The sound of spent fury. Slowly the horizon appears. White combers accent the lagoon. Clouds part and there is blue and tissues of cirrus. The squall seeks a new conquest.*

Later I walk the beach. The sand is scarred by the storm as Marie-Jean has been marked by passion.

*   *   *

The morning of my departure I find Marie-Jean in the dining pavilion. She leans against the warrior canoe, her face shaded beneath a straw hat. After an absence of several days I am cheered to see her. She smiles brightly as the day I arrived. She removes her hat. Her face and shoulders are freshly scarred. Her lips are swollen. Teeth marks line her neck and chin.

She senses my concern and squeezes my hand.

"No, no. Is okay. It is from *bukamatula*. I go with *Here Hoe* (main lover)."

She tells me everything in explicit detail. By now I understand that her descriptions serve both as truth and metaphor.

She places a lei of Tiare Tahitis around my neck. We saunter out of the pavilion and into the sunlight. My bags are piled onto the tap-tap.

"I will miss you, Marie-Jean."

She looks away, tracing little patterns in the sand with her toe. A voice in my head whispers: *Tonight you will sleep in Papeete. And in the morning you will push off into the sea and sky which separates our worlds ...*

We wedge into the shade of a coconut tree. Marie-Jean reaches beneath her pareo and hands out a folded pandanus leaf. I open it and stare at two exquisite cowrie shells, tiny glistening nuggets. The shells carry special meaning. They had once served as a form of exchange, and receiving them as a gift counts as a serious invitation.

"I give one. Annette give one. Time pass. You come back."

I am startled. Annette, to whom I'd hardly spoken, has thought to give me a shell. Marie-Jean reads my mind and suggests I will find her waiting in the pub.

Annette has her back turned as I enter. For a long moment I study her slender lines, the shining hair, her natural elegance. Slowly she turns to face me.

"Thank you for the shell."

A faint smile. "You go now?"

"Yes."

"Next time is better. I was afraid."

It is best not to ask why. Besides, it has nothing to do with me. All Europeans frighten her a little. We stand there in the dim light, ill-at-ease, and I feel Manihi passing out of my life. It is disconcerting, this clear sense of passage.

"It is not easy." She gives me a look. "Next time will be different. You will see. Goodbye."

Marie-Jean is waiting outside. She is talking to the driver of the tap-tap. We embrace. A little kiss on each cheek. Slowly, carefully, she turns and skips away into the shade of the pavilion. Like that!—she is gone.

*  *  *

The little turbo-prop plane waits at the aerodrome with its engines idling. The runway of broken coral is dead-white. A few passengers mill about languidly beneath the thatch that serves as a shelter. Pretty Polynesian women place more leis around my neck. A wonderful tradition, this giving of flowers upon arrival and departure.

Moments before boarding, a hand comes to rest on my shoulder. I turn expecting to find Marie-Jean. To my surprise it is Annette. With that faint, slightly hurt smile of hers she hands me a scrap of paper folded to the size of postage stamp. I start to speak. She shakes her head.

"Say nothing. You take." She presses the paper into my hand and walks away.

The plane yaws over the runway. The tiny atoll of Manihi flashes against the sea. There is a circle of green and a final glimpse of the blue-roof bungalows standing out over the lagoon. I strain to see the island one last time, but we are climbing fast and it is disappearing behind us. There are only the scattered motus and the sea and the whitecaps lifting, falling, vanishing.

Carefully I unfold the paper. In a stiff, almost childlike hand, Annette has written:

*Oceans embrace green islands/In our soul is one hidden Manihi/Go not far/Thou canst return.*

I sit back, pull the shade over the sun-filled port, and I sleep.

# The International Mile High Club

## Bridget Henry

*Sex in the stratosphere is an enticing proposition. Wanna join the club?*

I HAVE ALWAYS WANTED TO BE A MEMBER of the "Mile High Club." Unfortunately, none of my boyfriends have been that adventurous. On a recent trip to South Africa, I learned there is another "level" to the Mile High Club, an even more prestigious one—similar to the difference between a green and platinum American Express card. This upgrade is the International Mile High Club.

At JFK airport, I met a crew of interesting people: Luke and Cecil were from Botswana, Roger from Pretoria, Steve from Al Gore's Secret Service advance team (residence unknown) and Jen from New York. Since our conversation was more interesting than the movies offered, we decided to drink our way across the Atlantic on the 14 ½ hour flight to Johannesburg. The flight attendants soon tired of serving us so they opened one of the beverage carts and told us to serve ourselves.

At one point late into the night, I noticed two members of our party had disappeared. I couldn't figure out where they had gone until Luke informed me that Jen and Roger were being inducted into the International Mile High Club. I had never heard of this Club and wanted to know the initiation rites. Apparently to achieve international status, you must 1) "do it" on an international flight 2) with someone you just met and 3) you must have sex in the seats (any class will suffice), not in the restroom. Evidently, the five middle coach seats with the arm rests pushed up are the place of preference and though you may try this with your significant other or spouse, that encounter will not get you inducted into this particular club.

Eventually, the missing two members of our party returned with sheepish grins on their faces. I'm not sure who is responsible for issuing the International Mile High membership cards, but based on the noises coming from coach class, they had obviously earned theirs! And to think I was ready to settle for the restroom on a domestic flight. ...

# The Scent of Communist Perfume

## Anonymous

*Blame it on gringo naiveté, blame it on bad judgment. Blame it on pot,
blame it on rum. Or better yet, blame it on Ernest Hemingway. After all,
the bar was his stupid hangout.*

A T THE CORNER ENTRANCE FROM THE STREET, I saw her fight the swinging
doors. When we had entered, the doorman—black pants, white shirt,
employed by the state—never gave us a second look (because he knew we were
Dollar-baring turistas). Since Cubans are not allowed into their technically public owned establishments, this striking mulata was repelled by the Party doorman. But when it came to dollars, everyone owed a favor or two, and got a kick
back for what ever deal went down. Knowing the right code, and the right
friends, you can get in.

At some point she pointed and said the right thing. Triumphant, she swag-
gered past the doorman, oozing her way by the other gringo and me.

"Que bonita," Doug, a fellow traveler, said. Hunched over the counter, he
pointed his eyes towards her.

She stopped, flipped cheap plastic sunglasses up her forehead, locking them
beneath a sprout of bleached, frizzy hair. Beneath a one-piece, blue pock-
adoted dress with thin shoulder straps, her breasts and ass flowed naturally as
she moved with innate, academic precision back towards us, artfully balancing
on special clogs, which I later learned, were a special sign as important as a
Free Masons' handshake.

Seating herself next to me, she crossed dark, clean-shaven legs. I offered her
a drink. Before the libation arrived, she grabbed my head and pulled it close so
she could whisper in my ear. Her words hot and breathy (for real!), I melted
inside my swirling world of pot and rum. In Spanish, she told me I was attractive. Did I want to go to her place? She had her own flat. My fantasies got the
best of me: I had no doubt that I would go, and that within half-an-hour, we
would be fucking our brains out.

My partner shrugged his shoulders and egged me on. "Only in Cuba," he
said. "Have fun."

He paid for our drinks, toasting us as he became a blur while the beautiful chava dragged me out of the bar, pulling me by the hand.

Because of the lack of cars, expensive gasoline, and infrequent public transport, most people travel by foot or on Chinese bicycles. One couldn't find rush hour on the street, but the sidewalk was another story. Suddenly I felt gobbled-up by the thousands of pedestrians waiting in line, or traveling to where ever people go on a typical Havana afternoon.

She moved quickly, a good sign, I thought. She really must want me. Then we stopped for a moment. Could I buy her a sandwich? This was common. No one had money, and you were expected to buy Cubans food, drinks and cigarettes if you wanted to hang out with them. As a foreigner, if you wanted a companion, it was your economic imperative.

I gave her a couple of bucks (Green, mind you. Nothing happens in Cuba without US Dollars). She pecked me on the cheek and resumed dragging me through the crowded sidewalk.

Like most Spanish colonial cities, Havana has narrow streets lined with tall, multi-colored, paint-layered buildings with some degree of decay. The difference in Havana is a post-nuclear war ambiance. The bullet holes in the wall aren't patched-up, and nothing looks restored since the time they were built. Havana has been occupied by one corrupt casique after another (always some strong heroic figure/savior). But the money never seems to trickle down to the masses. These days, things have changed a bit. The Spanish, Italians and Canadians are investing heavily into the tourist trade. Ironically, the Spanish, who were traditional enemies, appear to be the saviors against the US sponsored economic blockade. One can see soldiers, who make $3 a month, ripping out old buildings and remodeling them into tourist-friendly hotels. Things were especially colorful with the sun's golden, late afternoon wash hitting the upper stories of the monstrous structures.

Suddenly, she pulled me into an open doorway. We passed through a long, windowless corridor with people milling around in cavernous darkness. We turned a corner, emerging into a brightly lit courtyard. Several men sat around in wife-beater undershirts. Children ran across our path. Scowls shot like Howitzers towards me. I was soon relieved to find ourselves in a small apartment with two older woman folding laundry. The room was no bigger than your average kitchen, with a loft and small wood ladder on one end. This was a far cry from the apartment I fantasized that would be full of books, artwork, colonial furniture and a well-stocked bar. Beneath the loft we sat in the only furniture: two weathered green vinyl chairs with a Santeria figurine sitting on a small light stand between them. If I stretched out my foot, I'd hit the refrigerator. If I stretched my arm, I'd hit the wall. Five feet from us the two women smiled at me, as if they knew something I didn't. My new friend Lola spoke in rapid fire Cuban, which could be called Spanish if you slowed it down to 33 rpm. Cubans also have the tendency to drop off the last syllable of every word, so it really sounds like mumbling to the untuned ear. She looked at me, and informed me her "other" place was occupied by her cousin. Could I give her mom ten dollars so she could buy medicine? I was easy. I took care of mom, and my liberal conscience, with the dwindling pocket money I had left.

After finishing their laundry chores, the two elderly women left. I asked for a glass of water. Lola poured me an ice cold glass from a lime '50s vintage refrigerator. She closed a curtain, which constituted the front door. Then She walked towards me, lifting up her dress so I could see her brown, pointy breasts with over-sized nipples, and tight black bicycle shorts. Like a belly dancer, she shook her pelvis, and ran her hand from her crotch, to her belly button, and then stuck her finger in her mouth.

She asked: "How much would you pay for this?"

I shot out of my body.

A Jinitera! Shit, oh fuck. What do I do?

Now I was hanging below the ceiling, watching myself sit in front of her, my invisible mouth hanging wide open. I had my fancy $100 Italian hiking boots, green shorts and turquoise, French cut tee shirt. My blue REI bag with my camera, journal, Professional Walkman and assorted papers sat hunched on the floor next to me. I fell back into my body, drowning in the chair like a sinking ship. I had two choices: cut my losses, act totally outraged, grab my bag and storm out of there. Or finish what I started. This was Cuba, the dark seething, shadow boxer of US imperialism. I was illegal and loving it. Besides, Dear Old Hemingway had put me out of reach from reason. I could screw a prostitute and get away with it. I was far away from the feminists, liberals and generally nice people I call my friends. This was one lifetime curiosity, for better or for worse, I would explore.

"Ten dollars," I said. She almost slapped me. Then yelled at me.

"That's how much my little sister costs. You want her, I'll go get her. Now how much?!" The dress had dropped back down, her right hand was on her hip, her other was palm out, jabbing at me.

"How much?" She remained indignant.

"That's all I have, really." My mouth was dry. I asked for more water.

"Empty your pockets," she demanded. So I did. Nothing came out except a few pieces of lint, gum wrappers and crumpled paper. Then she felt around my back pocket and pulled out another five.

She smiled with clenched teeth. Then she grabbed my bag and ravished it, pulling everything out, including my small camera and $300 tape recorder. My prized photos were in there. Please don't take them ...

"How about a gift for me?" she asked, changing her tone. Perhaps if she were nice, I'd give her more.

I grabbed the money from her hands and started the negotiation. Now this was business. I would behave accordingly.

"I want three hours or I walk," I told her, playing the tough guy, though I was still scared shitless.

"OK," she said, grabbing the money back from me.

"Con amor," I added. With love. Yeah, right.

She commanded me to disrobe. I did so, somewhat awkwardly, feeling filthy, both physically and emotionally. I wasn't used to the tropical heat, and I was sweating profusely from the negotiations. She examined my penis, which was slightly hard, because, in all honesty, I was excited. I was being really bad. My feminist friends would never forgive me. She seemed to approve, but I think it had to do with the lack of any visible sores rather than with any aesthetic considerations.

"Take a shower," she demanded. Looking around, I shrugged. Where could there possibly be a shower? Out there among the nasty looking men who might kill or rob me? Would I be left to run naked through the streets of Havana, stripped of my former identity? Was this the moment of truth, a shamanic death that would launch me into my next, terrifying life as a stateless outlaw? No, wait, the passport was back in my room at the apartment I was renting. I could breath easier.

Tucked in the corner of the room was a small cement stall with a shower curtain. Pointing at the corner, she practically shoved me into the wall. There were several metal buckets full of water by my feet. No running water.

She thrust a bar of soap into my hand and watched me as I bathed myself with cold water, making sure I used the proper bucket to rinse. Then she smelled my armpits. Shaking her head, she demanded that I wash them again. So I did, and we went through the test again. Finally she handed me some under-arm deodorant and made me apply it. To her, I must have smelled like a beast.

Through all of this I maintained a small erection. Something about being "bad"; it was a surreal turn on. I had never dreamed I would be doing anything with a jinitera, let alone in Communist Cuba. After all, Fidel had said "at least Cuba doesn't have prostitutes."

She stripped down to large, oversized grandma white underwear. She crawled ahead of me up the ladder to the loft. I could see her butt crack and her cheeks swish in front of my face. In her nakedness, she had became egalitarian, un-exotic. A normal girl. My desire waned a bit.

When we reached the loft, which was so close to the ceiling you couldn't even sit up, she clutched my confiscated condoms. In her continually pushy way, she demanded that I remove her underwear. Soon she had me inside her, and we went through emotionless robot movements that some could call sex, but I would say was less exciting then masturbation. I tried to get into it. I kissed her nipple, but when I got to her neck, she cringed, as if my lips had acid on them. She pushed my head back down to her breast. I asked if I could kiss her lips. She said no, her teeth hurt too badly.

I got a small concession from her when I asked her to change positions by getting on top of me. Then she got annoyed when she hit her head on the ceiling. We went back to the missionary. I took my time. I had three hours.

Then she asked, "Leche, leche?" Milk, milk?

"Que?" I replied.

"Are you done yet?" she asked in a form of Spanish that was easier to understand than Cuban.

"Three hours," I held up three middle fingers. "I'll take my time."

With both hands she thrust me off of her and started her business mode again, speaking extremely fast. "I have family that needs to use this place. There will be no three hours. You finish up right now."

With that, she delivered the final blow to my plans of at least a tiny bit of fun. I mechanically did my job, trying as hard as I could to at least get that so-called "pay-off" shot. It was the hardest orgasm I ever had to work for. I fought for it, but it was Pyrrhic victory. She faked a few moans to help me along, and finally it happened. I achieved my anti-climax.

Within two minutes she had me down the stairs, not before I disposed of my wet condom by her bed, where I discovered another freshly used one. It was one last reminder that, in spite of anything I hoped for, I was just another trick.

Thankfully my bag was still there. Here in the heart of my fun ride in the Late-Twentieth Century Communist Theme Park, things would remain somewhat civilized.

She led me out the door and into the street, everything blurry, the bright light attacking my dilated pupils. She asked what I was doing for the rest of the day. The question seemed rather trite after everything that had just happened. I didn't know what to say. I just shrugged my shoulders.

As we stood in the promenade of the large Spanish colonial building, a steady stream of people flowed around us. She squeezed my hand, and politely kissed my cheek. I could see she felt sorry for me. It was the only moment of humanity I got out of the whole experience. Or perhaps everything was all too human. After all, I wasn't like one of the older, fat Russian guys. In my wildest fantasy, I thought she actually might have liked me in an alternate life, like in New York or Miami. But not here. I was a tool for survival.

I turned to the street, trying to locate where I was. In my earlier, lusting haze, I failed to keep track of where we were going. For all I knew, I could be in the equivalent of some really bad neighborhood in the Bronx.

When I turned back, she was gone. I felt like I had been pushed out of a truck going 50 miles per hour. Suddenly, I was flattened, demoralized, totally blown away in the middle of Havana. And all my money was gone.

Her lipstick had a cheap, perfumery smell, which lingered and stuck to me like poisonous fumes. I rubbed my cheek really hard, but I couldn't get rid of that damn smell. The horrific experience would live with me, physically, for the rest of my stay. No matter where I went, I would smell that Communist perfume on me, like I was tattooed for life. Every prostitute in Havana would know me, know I was a sucker. I was marked.

Then I thought of Hemingway. Goddammt it! It's all your fault! Why did you hang out at that stupid bar anyway?

# Paris in Pink

## Katya Macklovich

*What a difference a dress makes.*

IT WASN'T SUPPOSED TO BE THIS WAY. Me sitting alone at Les Deux Magots trying to make glass after glass of *vin ordinaire* fill the expanse of a hot September afternoon. I was supposed to be in Paris with Tim, the man I had been living with for the last two years, the man who had hinted for months that he was going to ask me to marry him somewhere in this city of romance. We had planned this trip together for nearly a year. We had made lists of all the places we would see. For months I had imagined accepting his proposal and the moment I would be transported forever out of the dungeon of spinsterhood.

Instead, one night three weeks before we were to leave for Paris, Tim told me that he didn't love me anymore, wanted me to move out as soon as possible, and I could have the tickets to Paris, he had other plans. His other plans were SooZan, the former wife of his best friend: a woman as pretentious and phony as the spelling of her name. She called. Tim ran to her. I got booted.

I have very little memory of the next three weeks. I truly don't know how I managed to pack, to get on the airplane or even how I got to the Hotel du Quai Voltaire, the small, antique-filled hotel we had chosen because it had sounded so romantic: all its rooms had French windows opening onto the River Seine with the Louvre as backdrop. All I do remember is my friend Debbie telling me that if I wanted to regain my confidence with men, I needed to parade myself down the boulevards of Paris, *toute suite*, and let the men follow after me like poodles in heat.

"If you stay home and wallow in self-pity, you'll find that by the time you're ready to get back out there you'll have become ITM," she warned me. ITM was Debbie-talk for "Invisible to Men," a state of perennial spinsterhood and a purgatory of the worst kind.

So I went to Paris alone, a sad, frowzy thirty-five year old. I dragged myself down the Champs Elysees, the rue de Rivoli, and the other boulevards. I scanned the city from the rooftop cafe at La Samaritaine, paraded myself through the corridors of the Louvre, the Musee d'Orsay and L'Orangerie, and took bus tours to the Eiffel Tower, Napoleon's tomb and Sacre Coeur. Not a sniff. Not even a leer, or a wink. Nothing. I had indeed become ITM, a truly unpleasant state in a city that was certainly God's prototype for Noah's Ark.

For five nights I lay awake weeping. I left the windows wide open to let in the breeze off the river. But the open windows also let in the light and noise of the *bateaux mouches*, the boats that plowed up and down the river until well past midnight, playing music, displaying silhouettes of lovers embracing along their rails, and periodically shining spotlights onto couples kissing along the river's walks. I was being smacked hard with reminders of what I had lost. I had never been to Paris before and now the city would be so associated with these lonely memories that I didn't think I could bear to ever come back.

I had been sitting at this prime sidewalk table for hours, determined to get drunk. Instead all that I was developing was a ripping great migraine from the lethal combination of strangling heat, the rivers of vin rouge I had been consuming, and the incessant chords of an accordion player on the corner, who swayed rhythmically while producing noises like frogs being passed through a sieve.

Meanwhile, my waiter was trying to mentally levitate me away from this famous cafe and across the boulevard St. Germain to some other establishment at which he collected no tips. I started crying. My face got red and wet, my nose ran.

"Madame, Madame," my waiter said, shaking his head sympathetically at me. "Thees man you cry for ees not worth it." And then he handed me a napkin to blow my nose in. I nodded, thanked him, paid my bill and went back to my hotel room. How did he know? How embarrassing!

I decided to leave Paris, to take a train somewhere else for a few days. I found the number my friend Michael had given me for his old school chum who lived in the Hague and worked for NATO. The Netherlands, perfect. Perhaps he was someone with whom I could have a drink, share a meal, speak to in English? I dialed the number and a voice richly burnished by years in an English public school confirmed that he was indeed, Neville Darnay. I told him that I was a friend of Michael's, presently in Paris but thinking of traveling up to the Hague. Could we get together for a drink, perhaps? In a voice as smooth and creamy as caramel, he told me that he was going to be in Paris the next day for a meeting. If he finished early enough, perhaps we could have that drink in Paris? He took my hotel number and promised to call either way. Traveling out of Paris seemed pointless.

The next morning I felt better for some reason. Perhaps getting drunk really did help? Perhaps it was the prospect of sitting and talking English with a native speaker, even if it was only for a few hours? I decided that I would pam-per myself, treat myself to some new clothes from Le Bon Marche. I bought three clinging summer dresses, all in different shades of pink.

"Je deteste rose," I had protested to the saleswoman.

"Oh but pink, eet ees Madame's color, and eet shows off Madame's figure so well," I had been assured. I was talked into a pair of pale pink sandals as well.

I wore one of the dresses out of the store. It was cooler and lighter than any clothes I had brought with me. As I walked back towards the hotel, a man on the street smiled at me. "Ca va?" he said. I smiled back. Then an old man doffed his cap at me and smiled a toothless grin. I smiled. "What was going on here? Was it the dress? Was that all it took, a skimpy, thin, pink dress?" I wondered. But it did seem as simple as that. Suddenly, men of all ages were nodding, and smiling and acknowledging my presence as I swished past. I decided to go completely mad, and spent the afternoon having the gray in my hair replaced by the reddish highlights I had had as a child, a shorter haircut, a manicure, a pedicure, a massage. By late afternoon I was poorer, but pinker and perfumed.

At the hotel, Neville had left a message to meet him in the bar at the George V Hotel at 5 o'clock. I decided to take my time and walk slowly across the river, through the Jardin de Tuileries, and along the Champs Elysees. This time I saw men's eyes follow me, undress me. I walked slower, exaggerated the swing of my hips. An old man with brown teeth offered to buy me dinner. I declined politely. By the time I got to the hotel bar, I was feeling as sexy as I had ever felt, and then I saw what had to be him: a handsome man in a pale blue shirt, pale linen suit and large brown briefcase. He looked crisp and English. He had graying hair and a moustache. I froze for a moment. He was too good-looking!

"Neville?" I inquired.

"Katya?" he replied. I smiled, and he stood up, held out his hand and escorted me to a chair.

We ordered some wine and talked. First about Michael, then about nearly everything else: our work, the theater, movies, books, politics. I saw nothing in that room but him. After more than two hours I asked him when he had to leave. He asked me if I was hungry. I nodded.

He made a telephone call and then we took a cab to the restaurant, Campagne et Provence along the Quai de la Tournelle. The food had the full-bodied flavor of the south of France. His voice had the rich romantic tones of the actor, Ronald Colman. We drank champagne. I smiled a lot. I had that light-headedness of falling in love. I have no recollection of the restaurant's decor or the other diners. I only saw him across from me.

Dessert was a tarte tatin served with a dollop of lavender ice cream, fragrant with the scent of the pale purple flowers. He scooped some ice cream onto a spoon and beckoned me to lean forward and open my mouth. He fed me. He fed me some more, and then he leaned across the table and kissed me hard, his tongue sharing the taste of apples and flowers with me. I felt the tiny hairs on the back of my neck rise. My heart beat so wildly I was certain he could see it through the thin fabric of my dress.

"Let's go," he whispered. I was powerless to refuse. I didn't want to refuse.

We walked along the river. The sky above the twin towers of Notre Dame was lapis blue streaked with deep pink. A full moon was rising. He took my hand, then he slipped his arm around my waist and pulled me to him. I had the chills, I was shaking. We stopped. He pulled me closer and we kissed, at first slowly, just lips, then our mouths began devouring each other. His hands teased the small of my back, while my hands found their way under his shirt. My temperature rose wildly and I felt my nipples harden, my crotch pulse. A *bateau mouche* slipped past us on the river, and suddenly we were bathed in bright pink light. From the boat came whistles and applause.

"Oh my God!" I shouted. "We're making love in public."

"Hmmm," he said while nibbling the cradle of my neck.

And then the boat moved on. He held me against him. His heart was beating as fast as mine. I was melting into him.

We climbed back up to the street. At the foot of the boulevard St. Michel, a young man was playing a tarantella on the accordion. People were strolling about. It was a warm, calm night. Neville let go of me and I momentarily thought that I would crumple. He dropped some coins into the man's hat, whispered something; the man nodded. With a flourish, the man started playing "La Vie en Rose," a song made famous by Edith Piaf, a song I had always thought downright sappy.

"Do you know this song," he asked me. I nodded. It was the story of a woman telling how, when her lover held her close in his arms, all of the troubles of life disappeared from view and for that moment life was beautiful, pink and rosy: la vie en rose. "I asked him to play it for you," he said. Then he kissed me gently. I trembled.

I listened to the music as Neville pressed me to him. He stood behind me encircling me with his arms. I had been wrong. It was a lovely song. The accordion was a lovely instrument. Everything was lovely. Then the song ended and I was back in reality with a thud.

"Don't you have to leave?" I asked.

"I don't have to be back until Monday," he answered.

"But, aren't you married?"

He nodded. "She's decided to stay in the Algarve another few weeks," he said.

I didn't need to know anything else.

We went back to my room and made love by the pale pink light of the moon. Then we ran the bath and slept in each other's arms in the cooling water. We spent the next three days together: eating, making love, sitting in cafes staring into each other's eyes, holding hands. We wandered about the bookstores of the Left Bank, and bought each other tiny gifts from the *bouquinistes* along the river. At night, I put on a new pink dress and we would dine elegantly, drink fine wine musky with the taste of French earth. And afterwards, we would find a seat and snuggle in some place with a view: the steps of Sacre Coeur, the top of the Eiffel Tower, the tip of the Ile St. Louis. We synchronized our breathing. We found secret places to make love while Paris winked her glowing pink lights knowingly in our direction. And then we'd go back to the hotel and make love again. They were the most perfect three days I had known.

Early Monday morning I rode in the taxi with Neville to the Gare du Nord. We stood on the platform entangled in each other until the train started to leave. He ran on board, and then poked his head out a window and blew me a kiss. I stood on the platform watching until his train disappeared. That was the last I ever saw of him.

I have been back to Paris many, many times since. I always wear pink. And I always stop and secretly smile whenever I hear "La Vie en Rose."

# The Floating Jukebox

## Hank Rosenfeld

*The stars who inspire us are termed such for a reason. The proof lives aboard the Peace Ship.*

DECEMBER 8TH 1980, I was driving up near the old train yards west of Syracuse, listening to Marianne Faithful on the car radio, she was singing that song by John Lennon, "WORKING CLASS HERO," that goes: "You're still fucking peasants as far as I knooooow ..." And then later that night, I heard John Lennon got shot.

So the next weekend I'm with my girlfriend Susan heading to the Lennon memorial in New York City, coming down the Mohawk Highway in a snowstorm and every radio station is playing Beatles up and down the dial. On the AM side too, all these songs like snowflakes, Susan says, sung by John sent down from heaven. And we get to the city and go to Central Park for the gathering, thousands of us sitting on the cold grass with Yoko, singing "IMAGINE." And there are choppers overhead like a war is on and we're losing, but if we keep singing together long enough we could win, right? And after, it starts snowing in the park and that feeling. The next morning we wake up on 114th Street and go down and our car window's been smashed and everything we had with us driving down from Syracuse is gone: our clothes, jewelry, records, our writing from the entire semester, everything. I'll never forget it.

A year later, I've left Susan, I've left the country, and I find myself in the Middle East in the middle of the Mediterranean Sea, working on a ship and playing records on the radio. Pirate Radio. The Voice of Peace: "PEACE IS THE WORD ... AND THE VOICE OF PEACE IS THE STATION ... 24 HOURS A DAY." From a tiny hole down below deck, the studio microphone swaying with the slightest swell, I'm playing rock-and-roll peace music for Israelis and Egyptians and Lebanese, and they say at night we can reach Crete.

The following are excerpts from a pirate's journal:

**DAY 1.** I'm here with nine other "peace sailors" aboard this 45-year-old hunk of rust and wax. The Peace Ship is really an inland cargo coaster, built for sailing through canals. Rotterdam to Paris was its big run. Then self-proclaimed peace-nut Abie Nathan bought the 400 tons, and with the help of supporters in Holland, had it towed to New Jersey and rehauled. In 1973 it cruised into the Mediterranean with two studios aboard, a library, and transmitting equipment featuring a hundred-foot antenna tied to the rear mast.

Our captain is an old Dutchman living in semi-retirement in fine wood-paneled quarters below the bridge. "The sea, she looks good today," he grinned at me over his teacup this morning. It was my first shift and a nice welcome. Then he told me how he was on the very first ship ever to sail up the St. Lawrence Seaway to the Great Lakes. Amazing. I've got a feeling I'll be hearing this story again.

**DAY 2.** We're rotating on our anchor here, six klics off Tel Aviv, broadcasting in English, French, Arabic, and Hebrew. The commercials are in Hebrew, station IDs in all four tounges, and the other three deejays are Brits. They take their tea strong and their music weak, which fits the format. Most of the day is pop-full of Cliff Richard and his ilk, but at night we get to vary from classical to jazz to country to straight ahead rock around midnight.

I'm anchoring the Twilight Time late afternoon slot, which consists of two Paul Anka's an hour with some Mills Brothers and Shirley Bassey thrown in for excitement. This is Abie Nathan's favorite show. "Don't you know," the engineer on board told me today. "We're Abie's private jukebox." Wherever Abie is, in the Tel Aviv office, in his car, even in his bed—he can reach us via his shore-to-ship Motorola. He might call in the middle of a program: "Hello Peace, Hello Peace ... come in ... and please ... I want you to stop playing that record. Yes? I want to hear more Edith Piaf please ... Hello Peace, Hello Peace?"

Each announcer's air shift is six hours, seven days a week. We are allowed to talk for seven seconds in between records. We are not allowed to mention Israel, the Middle East, politics or religion. Abie has been upset in the past by deejays who blabbed on an on about peace and love, or about how awful the food was out here. Right now we're short a cook, so the captain's been serving up his "Moby Dick" stew: boiled potatoes and meat leaning toward the blubberish. How did I forget to stock up on chocolate and sunflower seeds before I left shore.

**DAY 4.** I feel sick. Why didn't anyone warn me it would be winter out here? I thought I was in the Middle East, but last night I helped batten down the hatches as a storm ripped through. I was up all night in my freezing little cabin, tossing like a baby on a cold damp bough, "The Wreck Of The Edmund Fitzgerald," haunting me from our hellish playlist. Storms make records slide off the shelves of our narrow little library. Coffee mugs keep slamming into turntables. The tone arm rides steadily enough though; in fact the entire studio, half a meter below sea level, has been built to survive these swells. The announcer chair is nailed to the floor and the turntable switches are mercury-weighted so they won't flip off as the ship lurches. The microphone tends to run away from the mouth however, creaking side to side, word by word.

Buck, our chief engineer, said half the antenna broke off and fell into the sea last winter during a storm like this. I'm starting to miss the dry land of Israel.

**DAY 6.** The crew has finished the last of the motion-sickness pills. Two crew men have lived on soup all week. We have one real seaman aboard, from Ireland. He hasn't been off the ship in four months, and I saw him pacing last night below deck muttering to himself "Hello Peace ... Hello Peace ..."

**DAY 15.** Abie came on the air today from his office. He spoke about a fund he has created, to heat the homes of old folks in Jerusalem. As crazy as everybody out here says he is—they say he has spies listening 24 hours to make sure we don't goof up—Abie Nathan does brilliant, marvelous charity work. He's taken trips to help disaster victims in Nicaragua, Biafra, Lebanon and Cyprus. He helped bring the first Vietnamese boat people to Israel. He would love to put the ship up on blocks as a tourist attraction in Tel Aviv. Two years ago he shut down and threatened to take the ship to Kuwait where he'd gotten a million-dollar offer to broadcast anti-Khomeini programs. He's always threatening to take us up to Belfast or Beirut. Tensions are boiling between Syria and Israel, and Abie says he will sail us up to Syria to bombard them with peace messages so they don't attack.

**DAY 18.** Tonight was my International Showcase program. We nicknamed it "Internal Hemorrhage:" three hours of Javanese gamelan, Guatemalan pipes and any other music donated to the Peace Ship Fund. I wonder who's listening. I played an entire side of Nubian guitar, hoping some Sudanese might have their transistors tuned in. Then some Cretan bouzouki and a few Balkan favorites. The last hour I turned off the studio light, lit a candle, and put on an LP called "Tibetan Ritual and Magic Music," and tried meditating between bank commercials.

Last night during this revolving time-slot, I had to play "Drop Kick Me Jesus Through the Goalposts of Life." Yes, the Voice of Peace babbles in many tongues. Weirdly enough, except during specials, Abie allows us just one Israeli song per hour.

**DAY 24.** I'd like to get back to shore in time for New Year's Eve. Andy, a former BBC-TV Technician just told me that "people who worry on large seagoing vessels can become impotent." He suggested playing James Taylor's "The Secret O' Life is enjoying the passage of time ..."

But I think I'm depressed out here. I played ten Joni Mitchell's in a row on Siesta today. The ship has been riding another swell for two days. Can't get any reading done. I spend most of my free time searching for something to sit on that will not move away. Other quality time is spent holding my head. The ship creaks, the body aches. There may be few things that feel as sick as lying on your back hearing Gershwin's "Rhapsody in Blue," with nothing but potatoes and pita sliding side-to-side inside you. I tried making a huge pot of chicken soup last night, but it sloshed all over the deck. I guess this is called learning to respect the sea. And learning to hate it.

**DAY 25.** I had a dream last night there was an Arab radio station out here, floating next to us. We played peace tunes and they listened and wanted to borrow them. So we sent records over on our dinghy. Eventually we began to write little peace notes on the album covers we sent. Was it possible to change their attitudes this way? This thought came: music doesn't make the mood. Music IS the mood.

**DAY 28.** Stayed up all night. The moon's up too, and the sun beginning to pinkburn its way over the eastern lands. I had my best broadcast on the Voice of Peace last night. Naturally—it was my last. I put on some fun songs for children, as a Hanukkah holiday special. Suddenly I heard Abie bellowing "Hello Peace ... Hello Peace ..." through the two-way. He said I was playing too much Israeli music. We got into a shouting match over the Motorola.

"And who gave you permission to play children's music?"

"The holidays start tonight Abie." "I think Woody Guthrie and Pete Seeger and Kermit the Frog fit your format of music that speaks of peace, love, and human understanding. Don't you?"

"I want you out of the studio immediately," he said. "I will send the dinghy for you tomorrow and you will come off the ship. Am I understood?"

**DAY 30.** On land, again. Oh, the humanity! Abie continues the good fight. We part amicably; we both believe in peace. He sent chocolate bars to the children of Warsaw, ambulances to Beirut. He held a music festival in Tel Aviv. And every evening at sunset, the Voice of Peace leaves the air for a minute of silence, followed by Abie's taped voice wishing everyone peace by playing, "I WISH YOU PEACE," a song by the Eagles. It is a small, wonderful radio moment.

The best moment I had aboard was December 8th, 1981. We were playing Beatle records all day as a year-gone Lennon memorial, and I got to deejay the last couple hours. I played "WORKING CLASS HERO," and that long "#9 DREAM," and finished up with Side 2 of ABBEY ROAD, where all the songs run together like a sweet dream. This ended exactly at midnight, a perfect sign-off, so I thanked all the listeners and the spirit that is John Lennon, and then I climbed out of my hole and went up top to the deck of the ship, to sit for a spell in the warm night air. Just staring out over a calm Mediterranean ... until suddenly just like that: the greatest shower of shooting stars I ever saw, off the starboard side, there must have been fifteen of them, all at once like streamers dropping into the dark and sparking back up off the sea. I looked above me, and thinking of those snowflakes a year earlier coming down the Mohawk highway, I shouted through my tears: "Glad you liked the show, John!"

# Santorini Style

## Abby Sinnott

*Seduction has a very strong appeal to the traveler.* Mighty, in fact.

OLD WOMEN, BACKS HUNCHED OVER, faces like the landscape—sun-cracked, bumpy, difficult, consistent. These women, always dressed in black, spend their days and nights in perpetual mourning.

Young glossy men, soaked in olive oil. Finger nails long, black jeans hug tight asses. They look at my male friend, not me every morning when we go to drink the thick gunk, Turkish coffee. Show themselves on shiny white motor bikes, flash smiles even shinier.

Ruins older than my own country, caves, temples, churches dedicated to Her. Windy narrow paths for streets with no names to trick the soldiers. And of course, the beach.

Missed the ferry each day to go to a different island. How long have we been here? My ticket home is expired and this, in a land of foreign light and smells, comforts me.

The same bus, hot, smelly, jammed-packed, drops us off at the end of the road; it can go no further. We forgot our shoes, do we have shoes? We walk anyway, leaving all of the other passengers behind with their cameras, straw mats, sunscreen, bathing suits. We walk for hours and hours, lost in a muddy pit. Towering dry plants scratch at my face, at my legs; I am bleeding all over. But alas, someone calls us; our names crack the still air. She invites us to come and sit by her from now on.

We sit on our bums, slide down the steep dune, land on a golden floor. He pulls my ripped dress over my head, stares at my naked body and smiles. He has already kicked off his shorts and we grab hands and run into the sea like a wet rainbow. The fairies twinkle above us and I can see them flying over the surface as I come up for air.

Thank you, we tell her. Thank you for soothing us with your cool fingertips. Thank you for letting us taste your salty blood.

We slither back on to the beach. The sand fine and sweet; I roll around in it, sugar coating myself.

Yum, he tells me he wants to taste me.

"Taste me then, tell me if I am sweet or salty." Starting at my ankles, he drags his pointy tongue all the way across my body until it slips between my lips. Without saying anything, his mouth tells me that I am both sweet and salty, but he does not know that I can taste bitter yet.

We make love on the beach, all day and the next and the next. Each day until the sun goes down and we start to walk back through the mud pit and mean plants to catch a meager dinner at the hostel we are staying at. Finally, we decide never to leave the beach. From now on, we will sleep here, I say.

The next morning we are shocked by the site of another human. How did that creature find us? We wait anxiously until we can see the man, long hair the color of clay braided down his back, sage eyes I've never seen since.

He tells us he is from France. He speaks English very well and says he does not dislike Canadians. But we are Americans and know better than to make the correction our passports disclose so often.

"I come here every year," he says. "How did you two find this place? The bus stops nearly five kilometers back."

"We walked through a sinking pit with plants as sharp as blades," my friend says.

"Sharper," I say, pointing to a particularly ghastly looking cut on my left forearm. "Plants as sharp as witches' tongues."

The Frenchman lightly touches the skin around my cut and says, "Since you young lovers have already discovered this beach and suffered for its beauty, I find no harm in showing you the easy way in and out."

"But we are never leaving," I say. "We decided this yesterday."

"Nonsense. How can you stay here forever? How will you eat, how will you butter your bread, cork your wine?"

My friend and I look at each other for an answer, both of us having never considered the Frenchman's obstacles before.

He continues, "Ah, you are young and in love, so you think you can just feed off of each other. But if you do that for too long, you will become shells. You cannot isolate yourselves forever."

We remain silent.

"You two look like you need a good meal, a place to get out of the sun for a while. Come, I'll show you to my small house where I will offer you wine as light as," he pauses and lifts his head and arms up to the jagged sun. "As light as le soleil."

We follow him down the beach for about two miles and none of us talk because we are all listening to the sea speak to us in her different voices.

After a while, the Frenchman looks at us and nudges his head to indicate that we should change our straight path. We turn away from the sea and climb a steep dune that unfolds beneath us every time we take a step forward. At the top, there is a scratchy rope attached to an old sun bleached tree. The Frenchman goes first, grabbing the rope easily in one hand as he swings across the earth's open mouth that stretches between the dune and a small patch of grass. A huge cliff towers above us when we get to the other side where we are told to climb a narrow set of wooden stairs snaking from the rump to the crown of the cliff.

When we finally reach the last rickety step, we see a modest white cement bungalow, typical of the other houses on the island, sitting quietly, welcoming us. Bright pink and purple flowers surround the house and scale its cool soft walls. A small round metal table and four lounge chairs are stationed outside for drinking wine and admiring the heavenly surroundings and liquid sunsets. In the distance, a volcano occupies the middle of the view—cold, lonely, ash gray. Looks rude and intrusive with the graceful ocean on all sides. White seagulls cruise the edges of the canyons layered in different hues of red, purple, orange and yellow. I can't stop staring it is so beautiful. I feel so high I am like one of those easy birds. If there were clouds in this sky, I swear I would ride them.

My friend has fallen asleep on one of the lounge chairs; the drink the Frenchman compares to the sun conveniently wipes him out for the hours to come. The two of us continue to share wine and laughter.

"You know," the Frenchman says, "you have the loveliest shoulders I have ever seen."

"Thank you," I say, because I know that it is a waste to be modest around this man. And perhaps he is telling the truth; I haven't had a mirror in weeks now so I forgot what parts of me look like. He puts his hands loosely around my neck and with ten fingertips drags them over my shoulders, all the way down until ten meets ten and twenty collapse on each other.

Keats would be disappointed, this time the woman is not a hand stretch away. I shudder. The sun is still hot on me but I get goose bumps all over anyway. The Frenchman notices this and I can tell that it makes him feel proud.

"You have little bumps all over your skin, but this part, on the insides of your thighs is still smooth and soft," he says as he rubs them, generating more heat and bumps. He continues to stroke the insides of my thighs. "This part of you is milky, the sun did not get this part of you. You are like my favorite desert, *crème brulé*. You are the color of burnt sugar on the outside, and the inside of you is creamy white and sweet."

**248**

"Thank you."

"You have sad eyes, lovely shoulders and sad eyes," the Frenchman decides. "You like to read sad tragedies, am I right?"

"Flaubert maybe," I respond sheepishly.

"Aha, Madame Bovary had dangerous eyes, so dangerous that she went blind. But no, your eyes are not dangerous, they are sad. I can see that you feel other people's sadness."

"Is that bad?" At this point, I cannot speak fully, so I utter a whisper.

"What is said to be bad may be good, but one thing is for sure, *je ne suis pas desolée maintenant,* so your eyes won't have to drink my sadness."

"Thank you." But I am thanking him for more than that. His large square hands on my body feel better than my own hands, he can touch so well.

He removes his hands from my thighs, wet now from his petting and grabs one of my limp arms and leads me inside as if I am sleepwalking to a small mattress covered with an earth colored tapestry that sits on the floor by a large circular window with no glass, allowing the sea's scent and sun's touch to caress us even when a rooftop separates us from the sky.

We lie down and his full slow lips brush up against mine a million times before our nimble tongues touch and then he licks my teeth with his pink tongue. It leaves my mouth and I wish he didn't do that until I feel it someplace else. It circles around and around, licking, dancing, singing, until I feel dizzy. I arch my back and go further into his mouth. The urn crashes. I shudder. I tremble for some time afterwards and he does not let the pleasure wane. I forget where I am for a moment, until his fingertips come back, this time running down my spine, tracing my pronounced ribs.

Some time later, still rubbing my bones, he offers me a cigarette. He then stops for a while so he can smoke and we lie on our backs, shooting rings into the air like horseshoes. We stamp our butts out and the smell lingers above us, mixing with sea salt and wine. He closes those moist sage eyes and his braid lies across my chest. It all looks so pretty—his clay tail, my burnt sugar breasts and raspberry nipples—that I remain still trying to keep things in place for as long as I can.

# INNER QUEST

## The Will and the Why

*"The moment the slave resolves that he will no longer be a slave, his fetters fall. He frees himself and shows the way to others. Freedom and slavery are mental states."*

Mahatma Ghandi

# Geographical Cures

## Abby Ellin

*Along the way you have invented and reinvented yourself into the traveler you have become.*

FIRST THERE IS THE EMPTINESS, which you have spent a lifetime trying to fill. Then there is the restlessness, which gnaws at you like a giant dormouse. It always has. As a child you identified with Amelia Earhart, Joy Adamson. You recall spending your entire allowance on a book about *Born Free*, flipping through the photos and imagining a life in the wild.

But it is the lay-off which pushes you, the lay-off which shatters your self-esteem even though you loathe writing small-city news and have been planning your departure for months. That, and the fact that your most recent lover is leaving town, the classical pianist whom you have gotten used to the way you are used to the blackened mole on your left shoulder, the mole which will one day be removed and then tested for malignancy.

As he packs his belongings into his little red Civic (you hate the word "civic," it reminds you of "civil," which you aren't), you fold your arms across your chest and do not offer to help. You do not even blink when he slams the hatchback and says that his leaving has nothing to do with you, that the word "love" is simply not in his lexicon.

Once he leaves, you waver between relief and anger and despair. You pen pathetic lamentations. You are glad you are unemployed, so you can lie in bed and eat Mallo-cups and watch *Rhoda* reruns. When Rhoda almost misses her wedding, you break into a fit of hysterics, even if Joe is a creep who will eventually discard her like week-old pastry. When for some inexplicable reason the next day's episode covers their divorce, you compose a memo to the TV station. *At least*, you write, *let us enjoy the illusion of a relationship that lasts longer than 30 minutes.*

After reading the memo aloud, your friend Lorraine gently suggests you sleep with a random stranger. Your friend Jonathan enrolls you in an African dance class. Your mother hands you copies of the Help Wanteds and the Singles Directory. You ignore them. Instead, you do what comes naturally: you call American Express to inquire about student travel vouchers, praying they

**252**

don't realize you graduated four years ago. When the friendly representative says the computer says you are no longer eligible (in your confusion and insecurity you wonder if its been in touch with your former lover), you indulge in a tirade about the failings of modern technology. Instead, you cash in on your frequent flyer miles, which you've been saving for an emergency.

As you stuff clothes into a backpack, Lorraine says, "Don't you think it's time you stopped doing this?" Jonathan just sighs. "Again?" Your mother suggests you are running away from your problems, but you do not look at it that way. You have always prided yourself on your ability to pack up and go; you think of this trip as a step forward, toward a tangible and necessary goal. You tell her the word "escape" is simply not in your lexicon. "Denial," on the other hand, might be.

When people ask how long you'll be gone, you shrug and flip your palms. You tell them you are a continental drifter, that "road" is your middle name. You ignore newspaper clips detailing the plight of American women in Third World countries. You think of Beryl Markham, and Margaret Bourke-White. The issue is not whether you can do it alone, but why you feel that you must.

At the airport, Jonathan shyly hands you a pocketknife, the one his cousin Irv the gangster gave him at his Bar Mitzvah. Lorraine slips you a 34-pack of Trojans. She has wrapped the package in newsprint from a supermarket tabloid, and you can make out the words "cellulite" and "yoga" and "sex." Your mother, terrified that you will fall in love with a dashing European and move to Santorini or Nice, weeps, deep sobs which make her shoulders heave. You tell her not to worry. The word "love" is simply not in your lexicon.

Soon after they leave, an airport attendant announces your flight and asks all unaccompanied minors to please step forward. When she says this your body involuntarily jumps: you have not yet grasped that technically you are no longer a child. You remember flying alone at age ten, fifteen, to visit your grandmother in Florida or friends you met at summer camp. No one at home thought it odd that you were always off to strange places by yourself; no one noticed that all your friends, your "favorite people," lived in different cities, far away, and that no one ever came to visit you.

You think of this as you board the plane which is nearly full. You sit down and immediately drape your coat over your knees like a blanket, hiding your unhooked seatbelt. This is something you always do on planes: in part, it's an act of petulance and defiance, in part it's because you do not believe anything bad can happen to you *en route*. It's the arrival that scares you.

Out of the corner of your eye you examine the woman to your right. She has pearl-white hair and wears a monogrammed sweater; a twelve-inch cross dangles from a chain around her neck. The lines around her eyes are etched deeply into her skin, making her seem kindly and warm. The man next to her (her husband, you correctly presume) is skinny and bald; you soon learn that he has a tumor in his stomach the size of a peach. They are off to Lourdes, via Holland, to pray to the Virgin.

"Miracles happen," the woman says, gently fingering her cross. "A good friend of ours was diagnosed with tuberculosis. She went to Lourdes for a healing. By the time she returned to the States, the TB had disappeared."

You glance over at her husband, whose head is resting against his wife's shoulder. His mouth is open, his breathing labored; he looks as if he's in pain. The woman holds him to her, stroking his shoulder and occasionally kissing him on top of his head. You would like to rest against her, too. She asks where you're going; you tell her you're not sure, but that eventually you will end up in Israel. This comes as a surprise to you.

Before the plane lands, the woman straps her husband into his seatbelt and then fixes her own. She slips you a piece of paper with her name and address on it, and her husband's initials. She wonders aloud if you would please place it in the Wall in Jerusalem? After all, she says, you can never be too safe.

You take the piece of paper and stick it into your back pocket, telling her you will do your best. She says, "You know, we've known each other since we were 15. We have five children together." She looks away and then back, like a scared young girl.

This makes you more lonely than you could ever have imagined. And for some reason, you buckle your seatbelt.

* * *

In Holland, you grab the train from Schipol Airport to the center train station and head into the magnificent chaos that is Amsterdam. The city is cold for March, but you barely feel the chill, so exhilarated are you to be in a new place with only a backpack to weigh you down. It occurs to you that you crave traveling the way people crave caffeine, or nicotine; it is something you need physically, a drug, something you hunger for when you don't have it. The longing and emptiness which have always been with you are still there, gnawing at your insides, but they feel smaller, less insistent, and you find it easier to breathe air into your lungs.

You traipse up and down the canals with the light-footed freedom of a newly liberated prisoner. Soon, you lose yourself in the Red Light District. You push your nose up to the glass windows and peer inside, trying to get a response from leather-clad women, but they stare blankly ahead, too tired and worn to pretend to be alluring. Within minutes the entire city is enveloped in darkness: it grows colder and creepier and you feel around your bag for the pocketknife. When a toothless and unsavory-looking character offers "Something to eat, a drink, a fuck?" you slip into the nearest youth hostel. The walls are covered with rainbows and psychedelic mushrooms and a gigantic rendering of Rastas sharing a joint. You decide this would be a fine place to call home.

After paying for a mattress in one of the dorm-style rooms, you get into a hashish-inspired game of backgammon with a Birkenstocked and bespectacled Canadian named Les. Les is 28, a Cancer, and sprinkles his sentences with words like "transcend" and "karma." He has been in Amsterdam for six weeks and is slowly making his way to Manila.

"To buy an envelope?" you say, and break into uncontrollable laughter. You think this is the cleverest thing you've ever said. When Les takes your hand and says that you have a warm and beautiful aura, you raise an eyebrow and stifle a smirk. Long ago you decided that sensitive, skirt-wearing drum beaters were far more dangerous than skirt-chasing frat boys; you consider beating Les over the head with your aura. Still, when he places his palms on your cheeks and says "We are all free, eh?" you kiss him with the hazy passion of a woman who knows a temporary thing when she sees it. After all, it's not sex that you have problems with, but your expectations that often follow it.

Les proves to be an amusing and surprisingly creative lover, as determined and eager-to-please as a puppy dog, and even though you don't much like animals he wins you over. You tumble and fumble and grope in the room that is anything but private, but you don't care, and no one else seems to. Every so often Les stops what he is doing and says, "You're all right, aay?" And you smile because all right is clearly what you are.

After three days you have learned everything you needed to know but didn't learn in college: How to say "stoned" in seven different languages. How to create bongs out of apples and Evian bottles. How to quietly make love in a room filled with people. You have seen nothing cultural except the inside of the Van Gogh Museum, the Heineken brewery, and the infamous Grasshopper pub, where you sample space cakes and chocolate bon bons. You consider mailing your former lover an envelope filled with the sticky delights, scrawling the words HASHISH boldly across the front. You imagine his arrest, his doing time in jail, how right he would look in stripes and decide against it.

On the morning of your eighth day you are awakened by something wet against your forehead. It is Les, showered and dripping, coming to tell you he is leaving. You sit bolt upright and wipe the sleep from your eyes, your hands clenching into fists. The sunlight has finally broken through the clouds, he says, and that is a sign. "When?" you ask, your voice catching, the ache unfolding in your chest. Les plucks a train schedule from his back pocket and smoothes it across your stomach. "There's a two o'clock to Paris," he says. "Or a three-oh-six to Munich. One of those."

You lie back against the pillow and glance around the room. It is dirty and dank, and the man in the next cot farts loudly. Your brain is fuzzy from too much smoke and your mouth is thick with cotton and you realize that you do not want to be here anymore. Still, you don't want to be with Les, either, even though he has invited you to Manila to find "our envelope."

You smile sweetly and draw him close, running your fingers through his damp hair. You consider for a moment—after all, where else do you have to be?—but in the end you resist, feeling strong and powerful and independent. When he kisses you and says, "Thanks for sharing your energy with me," you know you have made the right decision.

Les has business to take care of, "loose ends to tie up," and you decide to meet at noon for a final good bye. From your bed you watch him walk downstairs, his sandals squeaking against the floor, his shaggy hair curling at the back of his neck. *Au revoir*, you mouth, while the man next to you farts again. You jump up and gather your belongings. You make it to the train station in time for the ten-twenty-two to Austria. You have thirteen minutes to spare.

\* \* \*

It is springtime in Vienna, the City of Music, and the hills are alive with the sound of it. You check in to a little hotel two kilometers outside of town and find your way to the Stephanshplatz. From a distance you hear singing, and as you wander closer into the square you make out such classics as "Country Roads," and "Let It Be." It only takes a minute before you see the perpetrators: the long-haired, leather-jacketed guitarist and the waif-like woman with a ring in her nose. You stop for a moment, watching the crowd sway *en masse*. It's not that the musicians are so good—they're not, she has no range and he can hardly pick a tune—but something about them strikes you. Maybe he reminds you of Les. Maybe they're so clearly enjoying themselves. Or maybe they're doing something you've always dreamed of—traveling, playing music—something you and your former lover discussed doing together just to prove you could, and the pain of lost opportunity hits you like a punch.

The duo's finale is an acapella rendition of "Amazing Grace," and it's obviously the one piece they have perfected. The crowd joins in, too, and the song sounds more beautiful and haunting than ever. Or maybe it's just the setting: the bells ringing in St. Stephen's Cathedral, the light breeze blowing, the promise of summer. All around you people are in pairs, the men wrapping large arms around their women's waists, the women resting their heads against their men. You notice the women—fat women, thin women, American, Asian, European women—whose hands flutter through their hair in such a way that the rings on their fourth fingers glitter triumphantly, and you want to hit them for their smugness and complacence. It is not the first time you think, The world is an ark, and as you watch the pairs your chest hurts so much you're afraid it will burst. You would

**256**

give anything for a reason to be somewhere, for a person to be somewhere with.

When the song ends the guitarist grabs the waif and plants a kiss on her mouth. Together, they take an exaggerated bow. While he greets fans, she weaves in and out of the crowd with an upside-down top hat in hand. When she passes it your way you drop in a ten-piece and smile. You want to talk to her, to ask if she's happy, or in love, or at least in a reasonable facsimile, but she doesn't even glance up at you and soon she is lost in the crowd.

You roam the city, which is clean and architecturally pleasing but could be Boston or San Francisco. There's a lesson in this, but you don't think you want to hear it. You find a card shop a notch above Hallmark and buy two post-cards: a caricature of Mozart, and one of Freud clutching a cucumber in his left hand. Your former lover thinks Mozart is the greatest thing since digitized sheet music; you decide to send the Freud postcard instead. You consider scribbling a hearty *Miss You!* across the left column, but you're not sure that he would care and you're not sure that you do. You think it interesting that the people you most want to leave behind always seem to follow you, but the truth is, you don't really "miss" him, you don't miss anyone. And if someone asked you to name the person you most want to see in the world, you would not be able to answer.

The next evening you sit in a cafe and watch couples promenade up and down the square. They are dressed for the opera; the night's performance is *Salome.* You order a pint of Guinness and a potato pancake and unfold your map when the leather-jacketed guitarist and his nose-ringed friend sit down at a nearby table. They dump out the contents of the top hat; he begins counting a wad of bills while she rolls coins into paper wrappers.

"Eighty-six!" she says a few minutes later, tapping the last roll against the table. Her accent is clipped and English. "Brilliant, Kirk!"

Kirk grins and lights a cigarette. "Yeah, I did pretty good today, huh?" Kirk is clearly American.

"We both did," she says, tapping a cigarette from the pack. "You couldn't have done it without me."

Kirk exhales a thin veil of smoke through his nose. "Jesus, Katie, of course not. I'm just saying—"

She waves her hands in his face. "Bloody hell! I'm sick of your 'just saying.' You think you're one step away from Carnegie Hall. Well," she says, dragging on her own cigarette. "You're not."

You rearrange crumbs on your plate and wait for Kirk's reply. You think she's probably right, that he's been taking advantage of her since they first met. You want to tell her to dump him and come with you.

Kirk doesn't say anything, and the two of them sit in angry silence. You remember similar dinners with your former lover, though they tended to be more explosive. The two of you argued about everything: the dishes in the sink; the GOP; why you were always so restless. You think it cruel and unfair that though no one seems to make anyone happy, they can certainly make them *un*happy. But as you glance at Katie and Kirk and then at the single place-setting at your own table, you wonder which is worse: to be with someone who makes you miserable, or to be miserable on your own.

Kirk finally mumbles something and kisses Katie on the mouth, cupping his hand beneath her chin and drawing her toward him. She hesitates for a moment, then leaps into his lap, knocking the top hat on the floor. You take this as your cue to leave.

\* \* \*

By the time you reach Israel you have been floating around Europe nine months. Along the way you have invented and reinvented yourself: you have been an anthropologist, an investment banker, the illegitimate daughter of Frank Sinatra. You have been a recovering Hare Krishna, a scientist from Biosphere 2. You have been in Madrid to act in an Almodovar film, in Prague to write a novel. Once, you were even a housewife.

You have seen Michelanglo's David, who, in his marble splendor, moved you more than any man you've ever known. You have posed naked for a beret-wearing sculptor. You searched all over Lourdes for the old woman and her cancer-stricken husband, and took a 22-hour boat ride with an Italian named Stefano. All night long you chain-smoked and discussed Carmen and Cicero ("Chi-chironi," in Italian) and the woman Stefano loved who loved everyone but Stefano. The next morning he brought you a steaming cup of tea and in his lilting, accented English said you were the most intelligent American he ever met. You smiled and thanked him, though you knew "American" was the operative word.

Since leaving the States you have spoken with your mother three times, your friend Lorraine twice, and your friend Jonathan once. It is he who tells you about your former lover, about his job with the symphony and his new woman, Simone.

"I thought you'd be interested," he says. "I didn't think you'd care."

You are at a pay phone in Santorini, not with the dashing European your mother worried about but with a Greek fisherman named Dimitri. As you talk to Jonathan, Dimitri smiles and waves from his motor scooter. You turn your back to him. "Who is she?" you demand, wondering if the word "replace" is in your former lover's lexicon.

"I don't know. Some oboist. But what does it matter?"

You feel the ache growing inside of you, gripping your lungs, suffocating you, as if a crowbar were lodged in your chest. It's not that you want to be with your former lover—you *don't*—you are just jealous that he has a reason to be. You remember someone saying there's no claim on happiness, that there's enough to go around, but so far you're still waiting for your allotment.

By the end of the conversation the connection is so bad you are both shouting. Finally, Jonathan sighs loudly into the receiver. "Why," he says, "don't you just come home?"

You think about this for a minute. "What's at home?"

"What's out there?" he shouts, and you hang up. You don't know how to respond.

That's when you decide to take the boat to Haifa.

*   *   *

At first glance, Israel disappoints you. In its barren state it resembles a less-populated, less-developed Fort Lauderdale. Tel Aviv has a certain energy to it, a certain bite, but the feeling that you could be anywhere still gnaws at you. Nonetheless, you discard your anti-tourist credo and do all the things you are supposed to in the Holy Land: You ask to play with a soldier's gun, commenting on how large it is. You visit the Diaspora Museum, the Holocaust Memorial, Masada. You see the ruins in Tiberias, the Wall in Jerusalem. You keep expecting and yearning to feel something here, anything, a tug at your soul, a pull, being in the land of your people and all, but the most religious experience you have is eating a falafel sandwich. You find the Israelis pushy and stubborn, and realize with a sad and unhappy flash that they are not your people, that you have little in common with them except you both celebrate Chanukah. They, after all, are Semites. And you, as you are constantly informed, are *American*.

After two weeks in Tel Aviv you drift southward to Eilat, a nomad-populated resort town by the Red Sea. You move to a tent community on the beach with travelers from all over the world, a veritable United Nations of wanderers. During the day you take odd jobs or bask in the sun; at night you build fires and drink. At dusk the mountains turn the color of burnt clay, and the sunsets are the most spectacular you've ever seen. But everything else is the same: the travelers' stories revolve around drugs, and scraping for money, and their unyielding search for a place that is "tranquilo." The stories are the same as always, the only difference is the language in which they are told.

A few kilometers down the beach there is a camp for wind surfers, who are in Eilat for some of the best sailing in the world. You consider moving close to them, but you don't. What do you have in common with people who smear fluorescent-colored cream on their noses and spend their days dodging waves? You remain on your end of the beach until an Australian named Rupert tells you about a mate who cut off his own hemorrhoids with rusty shears ("He just sat in the tub and went snip snip snip"); within an hour you pack up your bags and lug your tent to the opposite side of the beach.

The wind surfers' camp is filled with all the amenities of home—makeshift showers, refrigerators, bamboo huts—and you think how nice it is to be with people who have money and a little ingenuity. They welcome you without question; you figure they assume you're one of them. You pitch your tent next to a man named Mike, a refugee from the former Soviet Union who offers Gatorade and a shower in his hut. You accept; it has been weeks since you've bathed in anything other than the sea, and as you stand beneath the running water you realize just how much you have missed this.

Afterwards, you head back to your tent to change clothes; when you step outside again the sun is sinking and the mountains are glowing and for a moment you feel calmer and more peaceful—more "tranquilo"—than you can ever recall. Mike has made a fire from driftwood and dried seaweed; he invites you over and soon you are sitting with him and some of his sailor friends: Peter and Will, a forty-something couple from San Francisco; Lois and Karl, aging hippies from Nevada; and Matthew, their 20-year old, golden-haired nephew who does not say "dude" even once. They have been coming to Eilat for the past five years—for the sailing—and they treat each other with the respect and affection of old, important friends.

You huddle around the fire, sharing Maccabee beer, loaves of bread, and travel stories, and discussing the sport that is their life. They are amazed you know nothing about wind surfing, which is, you soon learn, an intricate and complex activity. The conditions need to be just so: a flat, calm, off-shore wind, decent-sized waves, and water that is both powerful and gentle. So far, they tell you, they have been at the beach three weeks; in that time, the weather has cooperated twice.

"I'm going crazy," Matthew says, and everyone laughs. Matthew has only been wind surfing for two years, and he treats the sport with the fever and passion of a new lover. He gestures toward the sea. "I hate sitting here when I could be out there."

Soon the conversation moves to the environment. Lois and Karl are nature consultants, former park rangers; they have traveled three times around the world on various ecological missions. People who carelessly drive their automobiles over the beach-shrubbery appall and enrage them. To you, the environment has always been a source of aesthetic pleasure, something important to maintain, but the status of shrubbery has never cost you a night's sleep. As Lois and Karl continue their tirade you contemplate the word "shrub," murmuring it over and over: *Shrub. Shruuub. Ssshhhruuub.* But as Lois and Karl rail further you realize that more than mere flora separate you from them. You envy people with passions strong enough to boil their blood.

As the evening rolls on the group grows larger then smaller and soon only you and Matthew remain. The night has turned cold—you are, after all, in a desert—and the two of you gather in close to the fire. Your stomach tingles with the possibility of sexual fulfillment; you ignore it and let your journalistic instincts take over, barraging Matthew with questions. Is he in school? Has he read any good books lately? How does he feel about the situation in the Middle East? And what do 20-year-olds think about these days? He tells you he is enrolled in a university, he only reads sailing magazines, Middle Eastern politics do not concern him and most of his energy is focused on the water. "That's all there is," he says, and again a pang of envy courses through you.

Matthew then plies you with questions, and you are glad to answer. You tell him about your work at the newspaper, about the irrelevant graduate degree you received, about the class you would like to teach called "Writing for Wind Surfers." Matthew laughs; he is impressed with you, the lone American woman. He wants to know if there's anything that scares you when you're on the road, something that makes you think twice before heading out, and in his wide-eyed sincerity you know he is genuinely curious. You hesitate a moment, wondering whether you should respond flippantly—*Diptheria? Salmonella?*—or if you should answer honestly. You say, "It's kind of embarrassing," and pop open a beer.

"So what?" he smiles, and you think how ironic it is that the most appealing male you have met on this trip is five years younger and swears by *The Weekly Wave*.

"Well, uh ..." You take a long swig. "Choking."

Matthew looks perplexed. "Choking?"

"Yeah," you nod, and before you know it the words are tumbling out and you're telling him all about it, about your fear of being stranded in the middle of nowhere and having something lodge in your throat—a chicken bone, an orange seed, a sip of water gone down wrong—and how terrified you are that your throat will tighten and your lungs will constrict and the ache in your chest will expand and explode and there will be no one to do the Heimlich Maneuver.

When you finish Matthew is quiet, and you polish off your beer in silence. But for once the silence doesn't make you uncomfortable; instead, you feel oddly relieved. Finally he looks up at you. "You know," he says. "You can do it to yourself."

"I know," you say, and your eyes fill.

The two of you fall asleep together, curled by the fire; when you wake the next morning he is gone. The day is cool and windy, perfect conditions, and you are not surprised to see the blue and yellow sails springing across the sea. You imagine the look on Matthew's face, his brows focused and determined, his hair matted beneath the wet suit; you know that if you believed in something as much as he did water, and wind, you would be okay. You think of all the places you've seen, of Les, of Dimitri, of the people you've been with on this trip, in your life, just to fill the emptiness. And you think how unimportant they are because none of them have penetrated you, really.

And that is when the decision to return to the States hits you. You are dirty, you are broke, you are sick of sand beneath your toenails. You are tired, but a different kind of tired from when you began. This tired cuts right to your bone, making you ache with something besides the need to roam. You remember your mother saying that you were always "saddled with wanderlust" (an interesting choice of words) but it's not the lust to wander that grips you now.

You return to your tent and stuff the junk you've accumulated into your backpack. You slip on jeans and a tee shirt and begin the arduous task of tearing down your digs. From the distance you think you can make out Matthew's sail, but how can you be sure? Still, you would like to say good bye, to give him your number in the States, to thank Mike for the shower and hospitality. You fumble around your pockets for something to write on, a scrap of paper, a matchbook cover, and feel a crumpled wad in the pit of your back pocket. It is the name and address of the woman from the airplane, the slip with her husband's initials. You forgot to put it into the Wall.

\* \* \*

The fact of your return has been inevitable, but only when you arrive at Ben Gurion Airport does the enormity of your decision strike you, stifling you with apprehension and dread. As you stand in the ticket line you wonder if a masked terrorist will suddenly toss a grenade into the crowd, transforming the airport into a fiery, bloody mess. Part of you hopes this happens, so the chaos around you matches the chaos inside you.

But the masked terrorist never shows up, and soon the El-Al people invite children traveling alone to step forward. There aren't any, though—they're all with their families—and you board a plane that is nearly empty. The fasten-seatbelt sign is illuminated, but you ignore it until a flight attendant wags a menacing finger. In heavily-accented English she says, "Don't you see the sign, ma'am?"

You peer up at her and think of the stewardesses from your childhood, the ones who handed out coloring books and sticks of chewing gum and plastic airplane wings. Those women were kind, gentle, checking on you throughout the flight and escorting you off when you landed. They were nothing like the person above you, who looks anything but friendly. "Ma'am?" she repeats, motioning to your lap.

"Don't call me ma'am," you say, and clasp the seatbelt ends together. Three minutes later the plane whirs into the sky and the airport becomes a mere freckle in the landscape. Your ears clog so much you can hardly make out the welcome-aboard message, but it doesn't matter. You know it by heart.

While the flight attendants roll out the drink and food cart you rearrange your bag on the seat to your left. You unpack the pocket knife, the remaining Trojans, the crumpled slip with the woman's name on it. You would like to send her a letter, but what if her husband is already dead?

You gaze out the window and survey the clouds, which remind you of ocean waves and lazy smoke tendrils of hashish. You drift into sleep and imagine Matthew in the seat next to you, his blue and yellow sail stored in the overhead bin. His hair is bleached white from the sun, his eyes big and sincere; he looks like an overgrown six-year-old. He is off to a wind surfing colony in Baja, California, and wants you to come along. You grin at him; you have waited twenty-seven years for an invitation like this, for someone to offer something resembling salvation. But just as your lips curl into a *Yes!* Matthew rubs a callused finger along your arm and says, "We'll sail all day and build fires at night," and with a heaviness you realize that you are dreaming his dream, that your salvation doesn't involve wind surfing and ocean waves. You are not sure what your salvation is, or where it is, or why, for that matter, you are returning to the States, but you know that herein lies the problem. And the lesson.

You awaken with a start, sweating, as a flight attendant asks everyone to please fasten the seatbelt. There are twenty minutes until landing. As the plane zooms toward Kennedy a surge of adrenaline and nausea overwhelms you, and the crowbar twists inside your chest. The lights below blink up at you, beckoning you, welcoming you, and suddenly you are very glad that you haven't told anyone about your return. You want to buy yourself a few days to adjust to your new old world, to figure out what you will do, to leave again should you need to. You think about this as the flight attendant walks by and points to your lap. You smile sweetly as she disappears down the aisle. Then you unhook your seatbelt.

# The Ravens of Arroyo Coyote

**Douglas Smith**

*A mad geologist discovers his arse.*

YOU WENT MAD, UTTERLY MAD! "We could see it in the letters you wrote; you went quite mad." My sister greeted me upon my return from six weeks of solitary geological field work on Cedros Island. This stint of field work was the final field season for my Geology dissertation. I had all the essentials for a Spartan life in the bush, including Joseph Conrad's short stories. "The sea eats young men. It devours the youth, and spits out the man. Pass the bottle." Conrad.

Cedros Island is a sparsely populated, rugged-beyond-rugged, island jutting one thousand meters straight out of the blue Pacific waters of central Baja California, Mexico. In prehistoric times a large spring on Cedros Island supported indigenous people who left great shell middens as witness to the bounty of the coastal waters. In historical times, the same spring supported seafaring adventurers and pirates who anchored Spanish galleons offshore in the era following Sebastiano Vizcaino's epic voyage. Now, the same spring (Aguaje Vargas) feeds a small-but-growing Mexican population and an indigenous ecosystem of deer, rattlers, mice, cactus, and ravens. Post-Ice-Age high sea level isolated Cedros Island from Peninsular California, leaving the ecosystem free to spawn new species of beast and plant. Unlike previous field seasons, I had no field assistant with whom to share the rugged camps and the passage of time. Like the isolation of the island biota in ages gone by, my own isolation wrought new forms of introspection—new strategies for survival. Perhaps I had gone mad.

In this brief account, I cannot share all the episodes: the fifteen kilometer paddle when the engine broke, the water spout, the night hikes, the feral dogs, the sleazy district in the pueblo, the gold mine, the acres of drifted treasures on the windward side of the island, the sea elephants, the porpoise, the fog, the salt, the heat, the cold ... the isolation.

A local fisherman, Francisco "Chito," would motor me in his small panga to trackless coastal arroyos far from the pueblo. It was customary for him to leave me with my tent, some canned goods, a fifty-gallon drum of water, twenty or

**264**

thirty hard rolls, a few beers (no ice), a liter of tequila, matches, and a fish, if there were a fresh catch. Chito left me alone in Arroyo Coyote on the morning of February 15, 1990.

Every Arroyo has its pair of ravens. The ravens are responsible for keeping their specific arroyo in order; ravens do not welcome change. By the time I had returned from one half day of mapping, the ravens had ravaged my camp. The tarps were torn, boxes were open, my hard rolls were missing, and paper towels were draped from yuccas 100 meters away. It would be days before I could restock camp with more bread. It seemed that they delighted in shredding everything shreddable; I feared for my tent, my backpack, my bedroll, my comfort.

Could I leave my camp unattended? I tried to trap them with the old string-activated, stick-under-the-box contraption. I tried to poison them with codeine-laced peanut butter. I tried to blindfold them with baited, sticky, duct-tape cones. Wily Coyote would have been proud, but the ravens were undeterred.

*   *   *

Once upon a campsite rugged, while I pondered, rather drugged, rocks, arroyos, sandstone, and whatnot; Suddenly there came a cackling, raised my nape as if in hackling, hackling with the eerie chill I fought; "Tis some visitor" I stuttered, encroaching on my camping spot—Quote the ravens, "Watcha' got?"

After a few days, I found the bits and pieces of hard rolls that the Ravens had scattered about. I ate them, despite the mold that had begun to form. I recalled my sister saying that peanut mold can kill you, but that bread and cheese molds will just taste bad. She was right about the taste. The sun beating down upon the fifty gallon drum transformed my water supply to a verdant algae swill. I drank at least a gallon per day.

My work along the steep, conglomerate cliffs was dangerous. My knee was recovering from arthroscopic surgery, so the long day hikes, and overnight sorties took their toll in pain. If I had fallen from the jutting outcrops of Cretaceous rock, Chito might have found me only several days later. I took my chances, but not without calculation and a measure of confidence. Living alone with danger day after day, like some poor soul trapped in a Conrad novel, led to a philosophical thread that yet serves me today, now many years hence. I digress below to introduce this guiding philosophy.

The flight from Ensenada, Mexico to Cedros Island is aboard a rickety DC-3. On occasion one sees cowling fly off, various loose rivets, and once, the back row of seats tumbled backward on take-off, leaving two old women screaming in panic. A mechanic came back to re-attach the seats by borrowing bolts from the remaining seats. On these flights the devout Catholic Mexicans cross themselves, then fashion a crucifix with the thumb and forefinger of one hand, and kiss the resultant cross. This they do upon roll-out for take-off, and approach for landing. This they do to relieve themselves of personal responsibility for their future. "I'm in your hands now, God." In essence they are kissing their asses good-bye. So defeatist! One day, following a particularly grueling hike, I felt especially strong and proud of my achievements—relieved to be in camp—warmed by the manzanita fire. My survival was undeniably my own responsibility, my own duty—the antithesis of kissing the crucifix. I was inspired to create a new hand symbol, an icon that gives credit where credit is due.

The next time you bring yourself back from the brink—when your long day is finally done, and you've made it to camp ... alive, close your eyes, take in a slow ... deep ... breath. Let the same breath slowly escape from your lips. Take a sip from that warm tequila bottle. Form a tight circle by curling the tip of your right forefinger into the base of your right thumb. This icon is the "sign of the sphincter." Now, pucker your lips and kiss that orifice with a light smacking sound. Kiss your ass hello, for a job well done!

# Under The Falling Sky

## Stephen Capen

*Seekers of a higher path are often met by humorous obstacles; one of which are wolves dressed in sheep's clothing.*

I WAS ON A PILGRIMAGE. Off to the Peruvian Andes in search of spiritual uplift via the mysteries of the Inca and the land, to seek the heights after a long road into hell fueled by the land's trademark drug: coca. What a way to begin, my host a playboy attorney who harrumphed with great disgust at anything *indigena*.

Ricardo Elias Iberrico was the heir to a lucrative family business: cement. His father had been an important man in the Peruvian government during the days of the *junta*. His grandfather was once the Minister of Security, the equivalent to the Director of the FBI or somesuch. All of this allowed him to lead the privileged life, stop by the plant in the morning and sift through his mail, snag the checks and head out to the coast south of Lima with his surfboard. He was a man of leisure, one of the landed gentry, sporting a beautiful wife of Swedish descent and two tiny children, a household looked after by his maid and nanny, and the groundskeeper, Genaro. A wily old *Lime–o* who looked Yacqui but was more likely Quechua, descendant of the ancient Inca I'd become so fascinated with, the reason I'd come to Peru.

They were supermen, harkening back to the most magnificent image of strength in my childhood, an Indian brave who was the symbol for a bank commercial on television, a bank named for a sachem in this part of New England, Shawmut. Every night before the six o'clock news the camera panned in on this semi-animated man of steel up among the clouds, who slowly turned and rose on his toes, raising his hand high to gesture peace and power.

There were the coincidences, omens prodding me on, confirming the trek was the right idea. A few days before my departure the *National Geographic* did a feature on Peru, with the emphasis on Cusco and environs, mentioning American expatriate and adventurer Leo Little, who ran a small restaurant and spent a good deal of his time digging for gold in the hills. I read de la Vega, Hiram Bingham. This was the culture that said Impatience is the sign of a mean, low heart. I'd been living in skyscrapers for years, longer than I cared to remember. Clawing it out in the media world, in the heart of the mean, low heart. It drove me to destruction, put me on all fours. Memories to look back upon like piling up furniture against the front door of a Manhattan apartment, to keep the wolves away.

My visit in Lima consisted of a tour—with a boring, perfunctory narrative by Ricardo—of Nazca, ancient mounds scattered across a sandblown coastal area in the Andean rainfall shadow south of the city. On a couple of days I wandered the city streets alone, drifted onto Plaza de Armas with the heavily guarded Pizarro House, the government palace. Slipped into a crowd attending a baptism in a small back street church. Found a community of artists selling their creations outdoors in the city's outskirts in more cushy, upscale San Ysidro. And watched a street comedian who promptly made the *norte americano* the butt of lowbrow ridicule to the extreme delight of the crowd. All the while itching to go higher to the old capital of Cusco, the omphalos, navel of the world to the ancient ones. Bad drug experiences had brought me to this pilgrimage. Up there, up there's where I had to go.

Ah, but for now it was coffee on the veranda, lots of bragging about Ricardo's wilder days, his own cocaine years, being hauled off in a paddy wagon ranting. Or wistful praises of surfing. And while the reason I had imagined I was there was to ascend into the shadow of the Christ of the Andes, it was apparent I had to go to hell if ever I was to get to heaven.

Ricardo's idea of a good time was to suddenly swerve his expensive American car toward the roadside to scare the hell out of an *indigeno* selling freshly caught fish, for the giddy pleasure of watching an old man fleeing for his life with a four-foot fish balanced on his head. Some people just don't know how to live, I'm certain he thought, exploding one night when I refused to indulge in his favorite roadside delicacy: calf liver on a spit. Why eat anything with a face, I preferred to think.

A train car mucked up with an overload of goats and chickens was an improvement over all this a week later en route into the mountains, to Cusco.

But even that was nothing compared to the sudden blast several miles ahead one afternoon, midway between the capital and the high plain, an explosion that rocked the train, catapulting huge boulders and showering scree down from the cliffs onto the tracks, burying them.

Greetings from the Sendero Luminosa.

The train came to a slow, grinding halt. The passengers emptied out onto the tracks chattering and muttering, quickly dispersing into the jungle to make their way to the nearest road and on to the closest settlement. A bus must pass through now and then, I thought, and it might be days before the tracks were cleared, so I joined in with several families who seemed to have an idea where they were going, and we trudged off into the undergrowth, bending under the brush for over an hour until we reached a dirt road. There was much smiling and relief as we collected ourselves and an older man, Bonifacio, produced a flask and passed it to me, motioning with a grin to have some of whatever was inside, and I did so reluctantly, squirting something bittersweet against the back of my throat that I could only imagine to be plum wine. None of the women would have any of it.

We set off on the uphill grade, for hours never saw a single car or truck, and not another human being. The jungle hillsides were placid and we walked in silence, one of the senoras holding rosary beads and reciting quietly to herself. Her chant was comforting, became the stuff of dreams, all the while the explosion on the mountainside echoing in my head. Bomb blasts in the hills. Peasants in Ayacucho taking machetes to journalists mistaken as rebels. Surfing Boy, down in the flatlands of smoky, sickly Lima, scoffing at the notion that these people who live on the altiplano, hard by the heavens in the Andean peaks, are worthless leftovers from another time, oblivious to anything outside his daily bread, scaring Indian peasants by the roadside, gobbling liver on a stick.

At one point we sat down to rest. The sounds from the hills meshed to form song, changing tone, wafting through the trees, one sound to the next taking solos. I was hauled back to the moment by a sound like that of whales, looking up through the leaves into the face of a bright red llama, munching. Bonifacio caught my surprise, smiled. "Llamas hum," he said.

A few hours after we made it to the village of Ollantaitambo, a bus turned up, and by nightfall we were in Cusco.

*  *  *

It is evening, and I am resting in a room by the cathedral in the main square. The church bells ring often, pealing away the tears. I miss my home and my family. I think of how I've done wrong. I am ripped to the gills with the blood in this soil. These heights probe one's depths, the bells chime mournfully, as if in pity for a civilization lost, a sad pastiche of humanity haunted by a grand past. Quechua women sit in the plaza selling products of multicolored fabric. An electrical storm moves in and the proximity of the city to the heavens leaves me awestruck by lightning, everywhere close. It's wild out there, the peaks go on forever, we seem in a land pushed tightly against the sky, nearer the tops of thunder heads.

The cathedral looms over the square, a Catholic monument built on the foundation laid by the Inca. Sacsahuayman, the great wall of automobile-sized stones, and yes, the Christ of the Andes at last. The last sounds I hear this night are from the great cathedral's tower.

# RV Damsel in Distress

## Marcia Reynolds

*When seeking enlightenment, don't forget the Samaritans who helped you along the way.*

WHEN I STARTED MY "VISION QUEST," I was hoping for peak experiences like those alleged by the 1960s spiritual pioneer and traveler to altered states, Carlos Castaneda. So I chose the wilderness of Southern Arizona for my journey, known for sightings of unexplainable phenomena. While hitching my Hi-Lo travel trailer to my Ford Explorer, I imagined talking animals and spirits of the night whispering secrets of the universe to me. In ten days, I would become enlightened and aware of my purpose on the planet.

I camped alone the first night in a grove of mesquite trees just inside the Madera Canyon State Park south of Tucson. As I cranked up the trailer jack, the wind hit hard. My lower door wasn't closed tightly. The force whipped it open, stripping the screws from the hinge. After retrieving the piece of door from the desert, I set it against the open doorway. The wind blew through the hole between the two portions of my door. I stuffed three towels into the hole. The wind still whistled through.

I looked around my trailer for something to do. Since hiking was not an option, reading and eating were my choices of entertainment. I sat on the couch and wished I had brought my battery-powered television set. A cool breeze brushed my ankles and arms. I grabbed a book and flipped on the furnace. The fan clicked on, then died out. I checked the battery gauge. The meter barely glowed at low. I stared at the gauge, hoping the battery would miraculously repair itself. Nothing happened. Facing a cold, dark night alone, I reconsidered the value of my quest.

I made it through the night huddled in my down sleeping bag, listening to meditation tapes and dreaming of talking to old friends in warm rooms. At dawn's first light, I jumped into my truck and turned on the heater. In my haste to leave, I didn't see the tree limb that smashed the window over my bed. I didn't see the damage until I set up in a campground that afternoon in the Chiricauha National Monument in the southeast corner of Arizona. I sat at a picnic table watching the Blue Jays eat cracker crumbs. My crippled trailer loomed behind me. I faced another evening with no heater and now holes in both my door and window. Looking up at the mountains, I tried to accept my predicament as prerequisite of my journey to enlightenment.

The second night was not as cold as the first. I hiked that evening and the next morning to rev my body heater. But a cold spell shot through the state the third night. Teeth-chattering and muscles locked, I decided to venture out on wheels in the morning. Unhitching the truck, I left my injured trailer behind.

I drove over the mountains and through the nearly-abandoned yet still charming mining towns of Paradise, Gayleville and Hilltop. The darkness of the rain clouds brought color to the desert below the hills. Looking out across a forest of yucca plants and saguaro cactus, I finally felt a moment of peace.

Next, I drove into Portal at the eastern base of the Chiricauha Mountains. Hovered over a steaming cup of hot chocolate, I wished for a warm bath and bed. The general store manager/innkeeper gave me a free map of the best places to spot trogons. She was so excited about sharing her secrets with me, I didn't have the heart to ask her what was a trogon. Later, I scanned my guide-books. In "Back Roads" by Arizona Highways, I found a picture of a trogon, a parrot-like bird found only in the US in the Chiricauha Mountains. No wonder she was proud of her secret. I was grateful for her gift.

From Portal, I traveled to Rodeo, New Mexico. I found a lantern at the RV park store. However, it was packaged with two flashlights. After explaining my dead battery predicament to the proprietor, she broke open the package and sold me the lantern. I thanked her for "enlightening" me. She laughed, but I knew the quip was really a punch line for myself.

The owner of the Laundromat was also helpful, sharing her living room and lap cat while my clothes were washing. When I returned to the machine, I found a park resident waiting to lead me to the most efficient dryer. We talked about trailers and heaters as we stared at the tumbling load. He suggested I drive into Lordsburg to buy a small propane heater. I could even stay in a cheap hotel for the night. A hot shower and warm bed might improve my perspective. Like a broken record, I repeated the words of gratitude that punctuated all my conversations that day.

I had to wait in Lordsburg for Manny, the gas man, to complete his rounds. Although he was sorry to make me wait, he wouldn't sell me a propane heater because he was afraid I'd suffocate or blow up my trailer. Suffocating didn't appeal to me, but I entertained the thought of blowing up the trailer. After begging him and promising to only use it outside, I convinced Manny to sell me his smallest heater.

I returned to my trailer in time to snuggle into my sleeping bag. The sun woke me the next morning. I shoveled down a bowl of cereal before riding the shuttle to the top of the mountain. I planned on hiking the nine-mile Heart of the Rocks trail with the intention of warming my body, feeding my soul, and uncovering one of life's universal truths before it was too late.

Two other women joined me on the shuttle. The three of us were lone hikers. Although I intended to journey by myself, Emaline gathered us together for safety. We wound up trekking the distance together, sharing conversations and our lunches. When we rested, I learned about making paper out of grass and the best places to hike in Nepal. Seven hours went by too quickly. Our goodbye was long and uncomfortable, ending with promises of pictures and Christmas cards.

Back at my trailer, I found a 30-foot RV parked next to mine. Up until then, my neighbors had been newlyweds who had set up their tent as far from my trailer as possible. I rued the loss of view and privacy, and hoped the owners were having such a terrible time that they would be gone by morning. Before I reached my door, I crossed paths with my neighbor. She invited me in for a glass of home-made wine with her husband, Jim. The three of us sipped and talked about trailers and heaters.

Feeling warm inside and out, I let Jim follow me back to my trailer to check on the battery. He found the battery, unscrewed the caps and shined his flashlight on six dry cells. I filled each with water then started my truck to see if the battery would hold a charge. Then Jim showed me how to pack the screws so I could fit my door back into place. Before he left, he taped a piece of thick plastic over my broken window. Jim seemed happier than I to find solutions to my problems. Again, I could only speak words of gratitude.

The next morning, I stayed in bed enjoying my heater in my air-tight trailer. When I heard my neighbors stir, I arranged a basket of oranges and grapefruit I had picked off my trees at home. They refused the gift profusely before I shoved it into Nan's arms. I'm a speaker by profession. I bask in the accolades of my audience. Jim and Nan allowed me to witness the grace in humility.

With four days remaining on my "vision quest," I looked forward to spending more time with my friends and to meeting new people. I'd been enlightened, but not by animal spirits and Indian ghosts. By being in need, I had opened myself to assistance from others. Letting them help me was my gift to them. In my obsession for demonstrating my independence, and in my quest to have a special experience of my own, I found the "secret" in connection. Wisdom came not from the trees but from the mouths and hearts of men and women. I will continue to journey, with others as well as alone. And I will find my adventures at home as well as on the road. I now go not to escape but to seek the greatest natural wonder on the planet: human beings.

# Ambassador of an Altered State

## Spencer Rumsey

*Ever had a rifle poked at your stomach because you joke too much?*

THE YEAR WAS 1975, a strange time to be a young American in Asia. Saigon was surrounded and evacuation was imminent. I was 22, a soldier's age, but an Antioch College student with a very high draft-lottery number and a three-month Nepalese visa. When I couldn't get another extension, I would travel overland through India, Pakistan, Afghanistan and Iran to Istanbul and fly home from Paris. While the war in Vietnam engaged many Americans, my battles would be strictly personal.

I'd wanted to go to a part of the world that hadn't been overrun by television. I had to go somewhere with just enough danger and a whiff of risk to test my suburban mettle. When you're a tourist, most times you can envelope yourself in a comforting illusion that you're protected from harm as if by right. If the bubble breaks, then you experience what a real traveler knows innately— any minute everything could change. Say your candle blows out after you've spotted a scorpion under your bed, you turn your ankle on a remote mountain trail, or your passport vanishes. What can you do? Strip open your senses, trust your destiny and hope for the best. And if you're lucky—that's cool, very cool. At least, that's what I believed then.

My adventures in Nepal I'll have to leave behind for now. Those Himalayas still exert their pull on my mind even now. And it was with a heavy heart that I had to turn my back on them when my visa finally ran out. The day I left India, Indira Gandhi had declared a state of emergency. There were power failures in New Delhi and the streets were full of protesters and police. I was glad to be on board the overnight train to Amritsar.

From there, I tried to cross into Pakistan. This border made me nervous, a far cry from what I experienced at Kodari, Nepal, gazing across the Friendship Bridge at Tibet. There I felt that time had stopped, as if an agreement had been struck by both countries. Here, outside Amritsar, I was fussed over by Indian bureaucrats in some kind of hurry themselves to get out of there, as if the state of war between India and Pakistan, which was then dormant, could get hot any minute.

I was brusquely shown to an open doorway. I hesitated at the threshold but there was no turning back. A dusty road lined with barbed wire and brown dried weeds took me to two young, clean-cut black-haired gentlemen. They were sitting in folding chairs under a large umbrella as if they were checking beach tags on the Jersey shore. Eagerly they scrutinized my passport as I stood uneasily in the hot sun.

"Your cholera shot has expired!" the man in the dark sunglasses smiled at me cobra-like. "You can't come into Pakistan without it, I'm afraid." With India consumed in a state of emergency I certainly didn't want to return there. History was hard on my heels and I was afraid to look back. I was headed west at all costs. I studied the barren no-man's-land defined by the lengthening shadows from the afternoon sun.

"If I send you back to India today, how much do you think you would spend, my friend?" I was dumbstruck. "You do something for him and he'll do something for you!" explained his sidekick. Fumblingly I reached into my leather money pouch and pulled out a wad of Pakistani rupees that I had obtained that afternoon.

"Well, I think I would spend this much," I said uncertainly. He plucked the bills from my hand and rifled them. He frowned.

"This money is no good," he said disdainfully. His friend scowled.

"What do you mean it's no good? I changed money today!"

"It's too old. It's worthless now." I'd been rooked by a slick souvenir merchant who had unloaded a hoard of Pakistani rupees printed before East Pakistan had become Bangladesh. During the war, Pakistan had printed entirely new currency. Here I thought he was doing me a favor and wasn't I a clever fellow! I should have suspected something when I noticed the gaping hole in his living room and he said he'd sold his doorjamb to a French couple. Fortunately, I did have some fresher Pakistani bills. "OK, I think this is how much I would spend."

He smiled. His friend grinned. Yes, the price was right. He stamped my passport and gave me 24 hours to get a new cholera vaccination. "America is a good friend to Pakistan!" he said with honeyed sarcasm. I cursed Richard Nixon to myself and angrily turned away.

I got vaccinated the next day at a small public health office in Lahore. The serum vial was on a window sill in the sunlight. "See," said the medical official reassuringly, "I use new needle for you!" It was small comfort.

I was eager to leave Pakistan, even if I had paid admission. Afghanistan was a much more exotic destination for me and I wanted to spend as much time there as I could. One day I was struck by a sandstorm just a block from my hotel that was so suffocating I wondered whether I'd make it back. Another day I was walking in a Westernized section of Kabul and saw on the sunny side of the street a laughing procession of young Afghani girls all decked out in their blue school uniforms, their dark hair shining and their eyes glistening while on the other side of the street two women clad head to toe in burqas seemed to glide through the shadows like a pair of ghosts.

But there was no arguing for an extension when my visa ran out. So, way before dawn, I was standing blearily in line for the Kabul bus to Herat, which was on the other side of the country. I'd swallowed enough Lomotil medicine to bring my peristaltic motion to a halt. That was a good thing because the towns, as they were, were far apart and, in between, that bus just stopped for prayers.

My New Zealand friend Mike and I were the only recognizable infidels on board. The other passengers were grizzled, bearded men all in white turbans. To my eye, they looked like they'd stepped right out of one of Scheherazade's tales. I don't know what they though of me, but they smiled at me whenever I turned around and their gums were green from whatever they'd been chewing and their teeth looked like yellow daggers. But then, at dusk, in the middle of the Dasht-e-Margo desert, they all dutifully trooped off the bus, unrolled their prayer mats on the sand and fervently kneeled down toward the sun setting over the desolate land. I had to marvel at such devotion, because at that point I believed in nothing more than total relaxation in a nice hot tub.

Twenty hours on the bus felt more like a thousand and one nights and we still hadn't reached our destination. Then we stopped and we all had to get off. It was pitch black. I couldn't understand what was going on. There was no tea shop. No police station. And no traffic. Nothing for miles but our bus's feeble headlights piercing the desert gloom. The passengers milled around beside the road. Long before dawn, it was much too early to pray.

I learned we were only a few miles from Herat, but there was a curfew in the city until morning. I wanted to sleep in a bed so badly it was driving me crazy. My whole body ached from being crammed into a bus seat that a lanky middle school kid on an Ohio football team would have found too small. The hell with the curfew. Why schedule a bus to depart at 4:30 a.m. if it has to kill time just before it reaches its final destination? It was simply torture and totally unfair.

On the spot I volunteered to teach them all a simple lesson in Western progress, starting with an immediate upgrade of their bus transportation system. I began by cajoling the driver to get us moving again and pointed to my watch. He shrugged and puffed his cigarette. I paraded back and forth. Surely, everyone was with me.

"Let's go!" I chanted. No takers. Then, for my piece de resistance, I lay down in front of the bus.

Mike looked at me quizzically. "I don't know what you're doing, mate." I don't think I did, either, but it was too late to retreat. The other passengers muttered among themselves. It felt wonderful to stretch my legs, even if I was lying on the dirty road in the middle of a desert.

An Afghani approached me and gestured at the darkness. I awkwardly stood up.

"See that man?" Suddenly a figure wearing what looked like a gray storm trooper's uniform stepped into the bus headlights. He had a rifle pointed at my stomach. My smile froze. "He think you joke too much. He want to kill you."

Where had he come from? I studied the soldier for a sign. He couldn't have been much older than I. At least, he seemed to be grinning but his aim was quite serious. The muzzle was level with my navel and his finger was on the trigger.

"Oh, I'm a funny man!" I exclaimed, trying to sound diplomatic. Still smiling, I actually stuck my forefinger in the gaping hole and gingerly pointed the rifle aside. I didn't want him to think I was going to grab it from his hands. "Salaam meleikum!" I said. He nodded. I felt the chill in the night air.

"Was he serious?" I asked Mike later. "You never know, mate," he replied.

I still wonder how I knew when to trust my impulses, and when to put a lid on them. I'd gone to Asia to get away from my suburban background and learn something about myself. But my identity was as clear as the nose on my face. ("Excuse me, Sahib, why all American presidents shot?" "Um, too many Westerns.") I wanted to blend in and become just a pair of roving eyes, but that, too, was impossible. Once, in a Kathmandu bazaar, a merchant grabbed my arm, held up a jar of what looked like tar and thrust a booklet in my hand, wherein I read (in barely literate English) that he was offering me a remedy for impotence, provided I applied the black goo to the critical area and left it there to harden for a month. That wasn't the cure I was looking for, I tried to explain. But he must have ascertained that I was certainly in need of some support. Too bad he didn't offer me a love potion.

After I'd been in Asia a while, I started to think of myself as some kind of ambassador from the 21st Century, a delegate from a future altered state. I naively embraced whatever happened to me; I just hoped that if I got in over my head I'd be granted diplomatic immunity.

# The Go-For-It Attitude

## Brad Olsen

*When you know deep down in your heart what you must do, no matter how difficult it may seem, don't hesitate, just do it.*

SO WHAT'S UP? "You guys coming with me, or you both gonna sit in this cafe all night and wimp out?"

I was charged with an adrenaline agenda. I knew precisely what I would do, step by step, all the way to my prophesied destination. I knew this night would be the ultimate manifestation of a three-year odyssey I call my World Tour, and with that dream so close to reality, nothing, not even these two spineless jellyfish, could possibly stop me. But actually I like these two. Yeah. The three of us have had some pretty good times together over the last two weeks. Sure, but by the look in their eyes I don't have to listen to their words to know that they'll both chicken out tonight.

"Dude," said Ray, half mockingly, half trying to be cool, "it's not that I don't like the plan, I mean it's wicked like you say, but there are a few things you gotta consider here."

When Pauly perked up and said "Yeah, there are a few things you must consider," I knew for sure that these two had conspired together to pull the tandem puss out. Actually, that would be okay. I had a feeling they would anyhow, especially this guy Ray calls 'Rolly Pauly' because of his paunchy waist-line. I just played along in order to gauge reaction.

Unflustered I asked, "Like what?"

Both began to speak at once and I thought, how pathetic, they can't even get their sequence down. Pauly conceded and Ray spoke while I leaned back in my chair with a faintly discernible smile.

"First off, this is an Arab country, man. They don't see things the same way you and I do. Things you say you have a 'right' to do, they say you can't. And since *it is* their country, they have a 'right' to throw you in jail and toss away the key."

I grunted a laugh and said "C'mon Ray, you know as well as I do, they're corrupt as hell."

"Okay then," he said "you'll have to pay heavy baksheesh if they catch you, and if they claim you did any damage up there, they could hold you until we bail you out, and you know we don't have that much money to bail you out ... *again*."

It's true, they loaned me money at the airport when I first met them. We were waiting in the customs line when I told them how I got burned the day before in Bombay. It was my fault really, trusting an Indian with my traveler's checks on a get rich quick attempt, but it was just a loan and I promptly paid them back when I recovered my stolen checks. So I know what they're thinking; "He's reckless. He's a loose cannon. He fucked up once and he'll do it again." And even I know the inherent risk in this venture. Sure, but this is all part of the go-for-it attitude I've been advocating for years to anyone who'd care to listen.

"There is the possibility we *won't* get caught," I suggested.

Pauly dismissed this, and himself, right away. "I'm not going, I mean I can't. You know how my asthma acted up from the dry desert heat on our horseback ride to Saqqara. See here, look at my hand, I've still got this nasty blister on my finger from those damn reins. And," he continued while shaking his head "my knees have always limited me from strenuous activities. Besides, I think there are way too many guards out there to pull it off, and also what Ray said. You really don't know what they'll do if they catch you. No shit man, these Muslims are hard core. I've heard that *even to this day,* they'll cut off a criminal's finger for something trivial, like stealing an apple. That's their culture, that's just the way it is."

Okay now, I don't know this guy very well, but I am sure I know him well enough. See, I've met dozens of Pauly-types on my World Tour. He knows and I know that the spew coming out of his mouth is nothing but a facade, a mask of his real fear. Sure he's overweight, lacks self-confidence, and would huff and puff on aching knees climbing up, but this is no ascent of Everest, and it's certainly no *major* crime. No crime at all. Inspired men all through the history of civilization have done it. No doubt in my mind. Moses climbed it, so did Herodotus, Alexander The Great, loads of Roman leaders, Napoleon, Mark Twain, Howard Carter, and quite possibly Jesus Christ. Here is a rare and very powerful energy spot, one of only a few acupuncture points on the physical planet, providing an ancient seat of humanity. Of course they climbed it, along with countless other travelers who've passed through this way over many millennia. Can't these two feel the aura surrounding it? I won't push. No. For Pauly's fear is not uncommon with most people, or Ray for that matter. For the fear they share is that of the unknown.

We hung out in the Giza cafe for another hour. I wanted to wait for the full moon to rise higher in the night sky for better illumination. I also wanted a few more guards to crash out. The cafe was nearly empty. Two Egyptians in their long robes and headscarves were playing some kind of domino game that they would both get real excited about from time to time. I hoped to see more action, but it never came. Their outbursts and facial expressions were quite humorous and far more interesting than Ray and Pauly's discussion of recent political events in their mutual countries. I ordered a shesha, which is a mono-stemmed hookah water pipe smoked with gummy Turkish tobacco. The tobacco stays lit from burning embers placed on top. These two knew immediately why I ordered it and began protesting. I knew they would, but I didn't care. After all, they were quitting on me tonight.

"Oh man, *don't*" Pauly lamented, "the waiter will smell it, or maybe those guys are cops." Even Ray knew this was absurd so he let up, and Pauly followed suit as usual. Besides, they knew me enough by now to know that I'd do whatever I damn well pleased, despite their objections. If Pauly continued his winging I would tell him no one was twisting his arm to stay. He stayed of course, just like the other nights I fired up.

I carefully positioned a few chunks of the primo Lebanese blonde hash I scored from our Saqqara horse guide into the bowl of embers and tobacco. The faint gurgling of the water as the smoke rose through the stem and into my lungs reminded me of collegiate bong-a-thons past. "Study high, test high, score high"—that was my motto back then. It didn't work too well for my G.P.A., but the subjects I got into, like my History of Egyptian Art class, I can now recall with vivid clarity and a new appreciation I never realized until I got out and traveled. My only regret today is that I didn't try hard enough. Pot makes me mentally lazy, yes, but it also helps me think abstractly and dream and plan and get me excited about adventures, just like the one I'm getting into tonight. Ahhhh yes, *adventures*. Now I'm feeling right.

Ray is getting stoned with me and we both chuckle at Pauly's apprehension. He senses this, mellows, and Ray offers him the stem. He declines.

After a few minutes of enjoying the buzz, I sit erect and grip the seat of my chair. They know what this means.

"Anyone change their mind?"

"No, not me." Pauly says.

"Ray?"

"Nah. This is your dream, man. Maybe you are meant to go about it alone. We'll read our magazines and wait for you here. If you're not back within two hours, we'll check the main guard station."

I took a deep breath, rose from the chair, and started across the cafe towards the door. Halfway across the long room I heard Ray call my name. "Good luck, my brother! Don't get vexed by the curse of the pharaohs!" I turned around and winked.

Out in the alley I turned a corner and there it was towering in all its majestic glory—The Great Pyramid of Cheops. History books call it 4,580 years old and the last remaining Wonder of the Ancient World. Mankind's mightiest wedge. As I started up the plateau towards it, I was clenching my fists and softly repeating "you're all mine tonight, you're all mine tonight, ..." over and over again, like a madman in some strange obsession.

\* \* \*

Approaching the Giza pyramid field I was expectantly cautious. Keen to my surroundings. Observing every movement. All senses honed. I showed my day ticket twice past two guard huts. Visitors are allowed up there at night, but climbing any one of them is prohibited.

I stopped at the base and looked up at the rows and rows of meter high blocks, so carefully placed so long ago. How proud Pharaoh Cheops must have been standing exactly where I am now, looking up and marveling at the tomb his architects and servants built for him. Awesome beyond belief.

I'm taken back to college and the re-creation diagram in Dr. Archer's office. It showed a dirt track wrapping up and around the pyramid allowing the servants to roll blocks along logs to their predestined locations. The road was dismantled as they worked their way down, fitting the polished casing stones into place without flaw. The casing stones were fitted so precisely that, even today, a razor blade can not fit between their seams. One can imagine how these pyramids must have shone resplendently under the hot desert sun!

The next pyramid over to the southwest is that of Pharaoh Chephren. It is nearly identical in size and shape, yet lacks most of the internal chambers held inside the Great Pyramid. Because it is on a higher level, most people think it is taller than Cheops' but actually it's a few meters shorter. The most interesting aspect of the Chephren pyramid is the top quarter, which retains a crown of the original casing stones. One can still get a feel for the eminently refined state all these pyramids once held.

The third one, Mycerinus, was the last built and just a fraction in size to the others. Although there are many other pyramids along the west side of the Nile River, it is these three that the world regards as 'The Great Pyramids' while Cheops' is simply 'The Great Pyramid.' It bothers me when people theorize the origins and construction to be aided by extraterrestrial beings. Why belittle human achievements? Or, if it takes an alien race to build a pyramid, why are there so many inferior ones down the Nile? Man reached perfection in pyramidal architecture largely through trial and error over hundreds of years. Give the Egyptians credit I'd say, they were building for God.

It's not time to climb yet. Yes, I see you mister guard over there by the road, and you must see me.

I should confront him before he can figure out what I'm up to. I approach him with an enthusiastic smile and say hello, something I reserve for special occasions after years of being battered as a tourist. We shake hands and he slips a small scarab charm into my palm. Now I know what he wants.

"Ahhh hello my friend. You like tour, yes? Come." He grabs my arm and turns me toward Chephren's pyramid, "I take you show you Funerary Temple. Yes? You come."

I break his grip and explain; "No mister. Look, I just want to walk alone, okay? I have no money." I must pull out my empty pockets to prove it. "See here, no money."

The smile is gone from his face and he takes the scarab charm back.

Walking away from the scarab guard, I hear him mention to another tourist that there is going to be a late night Sound and Light Show because of the full moon. So late, I thought the second show would be long over by now. I get to the northwest corner, the spot I surmised as being furthest from any guard hut, and now conveniently on the opposite side from the grandstands and lights. Just as I sit down beside the pyramid to ponder this new twist, the show begins. From the tombs and mastabas everywhere, banks of concealed floodlights begin illuminating the pyramids in slowly shifting hues. The Great Pyramid is glowing golden yellow on all four sides. They'll spot me for sure if I climb while it's lit, but if I wait until the lights go down, maybe their eyes won't adjust. This could be an opportunity and, ... the lights are coming down ...

*NOW!*

I press both hands on the first block and swing a leg up, step. Tricep press, swing the leg up, step. Up the third, up the fourth, this is easy! It's like climbing a mountain of stacked refrigerators. Up the fifth, up the ...

"Hey you! Hey, *get down!* Get down from there! No climbing the pyramid!"

Where did they come from? Oh, I wasn't careful enough. *Scheisse!* Think quick, no. Okay, the gig's up, climb down before they wake up the whole damn complex.

When I reach ground zero I walk by the guards and sheepishly shrug "I only wanted to watch the show." They say something to the effect of "read the signs, dumbass." So much for saving face. I quickly walk away until I round the third corner, where I slow down to catch my thoughts. Another guard passes me. The yellow lights come up again and are blazing on the eastern face, the side facing the grandstands. It doesn't look good now. No. Busted once, my confidence is in tatters. I have to sit down and think. Okay, what to do? Just the thought of returning defeated to Ray and Pauly really bums me out. What a buzzkill!

Something pushes me. I can't go down so easy. *No way, Ray.* I could crash out in the desert for a while and try again just before dawn.

Another guard passes and does not notice me in the shadows. That's a good sign. It looks as if he's the only one around and they all probably think, "who would be audacious enough to climb right in view of the grandstands?" Who indeed? The lights start to rise on Chephren, lower on Cheops. The guards are far away and the moon is high in the night sky. Do not think, TRY AGAIN!

The first ten blocks I'm sprinting up swift and sure-footed like a cat on a fence fleeing from a pack of dogs. My heart is racing and I am shaking all over with trepidation, but I am not slowing. No whistles, no shouts from below. I'm doing it and no one sees me. I gotta just keep moving, keep climbing while it's dark, the higher I get the safer I'll be, just ignore the pain ...

In a silent whoosh, the lights come up again and I dive for cover in the shadow of the blocks. I am about one-third of the way up, I estimate. Lying horizontally and perfectly still, my heart feels as if it's beating so loud it'll blow my cover. My experience now reminds me of what it would be like to be an escaped convict hiding from blasting prison lights. Exhilaration and fear mix a potent adrenaline rush. I haven't felt this stirred up since I snorkeled off the coast of Lanai with a mother and baby humpback whale a few years ago. Story for another anthology, but I was alone then too.

As I wait for the lights to go dark again I think about the day. Earlier, I took Ray and Pauly into this pyramid, through the entrance passage and up into the Grand Gallery to the King's Chamber. Just before entering it we passed through the antechamber, a phonebooth-sized foyer. I searched with my hands in the semi-darkness until I found what I was looking for. A protruding Boss Stone relief of the true inch, the Pyramid Inch, the only inscription to be found in this monument—unlike the bragging hieroglyphs in most other pharaoh's monuments. It's like those whoever built this thing were trying to transmit information important to everybody, for all time, because some of the computations you can make with the Pyramid Inch are absolutely mind-blowing. Here are a few, but first it's interesting to know that 1 Pyramid Inch = 1.001 British Inches.

5,449 is the height of the pyramid in Pyramid Inches, the weight of the pyramid in tons' times 100, and the number of letters and words added up from a pivotal quotation in the Bible, Isaia, chapter 19. Verses 19 and 20 of which are supposed to contain even more mysteries.

A convenient ten million Pyramid Inches equals our polar axis plus our circumference, our weight, the length not only of our solar year and our sidereal year, but also our catch-up or leap year ... not to mention the distance of our swing around the sun, or the error in our spin that produces the wobble at our polar point which calculates the 26,920-year Procession of the Equinoxes. This pyramid says, quite literally, that we really are entering the Age of Aquarius.

Also compressed within the scope and accuracy of the Great Pyramid's angles and proportions seem to be all the formulas and distances pertinent to our solar system, like the measure of the sun-distance with exceeding accuracy. Basically, computations continue ad infinitum, as far as you want to let your mind wander.

When the lights go off again I quickly begin climbing. The corner stones are well-cut and do not show the signs of age like the middle stones, which are fragmenting away from the elements. In order to minimize my impact I climb the corner stones, careful not to expose myself to the southern face where the scarab guard could see me. Higher and higher I ascend, and a nice breeze cools my sweaty face. Two-thirds of the way up the lights begin to brighten and I am relieved to take another break. Lying down in the shadows I dream some more about this amazing structure.

What a monument this is! Statistics flood my head: 2.3 million blocks, each weighing 16 tons. Enough blocks to build a one meter high wall around France, or thirty Empire State Buildings, or a one meter high wall from north to south across the US—take your pick.

I was reading in Ken Kesey's book *The Demon Box* about his experience and research up here. He writes, "And digging deeper in our stone safe we find deposited such blue-chip securities as the rudiments of plane geometry, solid geometry, the beginnings of trigonometry, and—probably more valuable than all these mundane directions and distances and weights put together—the three mightiest mathematical tricks of them all: the first of course being pi, that constant and apparently inconclusive key to the circle. Second, phi, the Golden Rectangle transmission box of our aesthetics enabling us to shift harmoniously and endlessly without stripping gears so long as 2 is to 3 as 3 is to 5 as 5 is to 8 as 8 is to 13. Get it? And, third, the Pythagorean theorem, which is really just an astute amalgam of the first two short cuts and about as attributable to Pythagoras as blues is to Eric Clapton.

"And all this is based on the admission that so far we have been able to comprehend and appreciate the pyramid's info in terms of and thus only up to *our own*, then how much must be contained in this five-sided box that we *cannot yet see*? Wouldn't a race of people who knew enough about the sun to utilize its rays and reflections be likely to have a suggestion or two for us on solar power? Chop-chop! Call the Department of Energy! And might not an astronomy so accurate as to aim the Entrance Passage tunnel in *pure parallel* with our axis at a starless space in space, or point a radius from the center of the earth through the summit of this stone pointer at the star Pleiades—that is indicated by drawings gleaned from centuries as the *center* star about which the *other six* of the constellation are orbiting and *perhaps our sun as well!*—have some helpful hints for NASA? Call them, I say, hurry-up! the Home Office, the UN, the Pentagon. What's a few billion in research to the Pentagon if they can get a ray so precise as to sink a whole damn continent from the face of the waters as to the mud and mire of mythology?" When I told Ray and Pauly about this they said I'd been smoking too much hooch and called me a 'pyramidiot.'

Darkness again and the final burst. The expectation is phenomenal as the corners begin to merge together and I can finally judge the distance to the top. Ten blocks, nine, eight, seven to go. The rocket is about ready for blastoff. Yes! Six, five, four, counting down the anticipation of an astronaut, three more to climb, two more, last block, SUMMIT! Instantly, as if planned, the lights rise on the Great Pyramid brighter than before, and I throw my arms to the moon and dance in wild gesticulation. Who cares if anybody sees me now, I made it and I'm celebrating. The world is at my feet and the power of the pyramid is surging through my entire being! Hoo-ha! This is life. This is what it means to be human.

Calming, I survey my surroundings. So very much of the actual top has been knocked away in medieval times as to leave a platform described by the Arabs as "large enough for eleven camels to lie down." There is a six-meter tall post in the center supported by three other posts to indicate precisely where the capstone once reached. I take some time to lay over each face and gaze downward, enthralled by the ant-sized guards moving about and the Sound and Light Show still in progress.

I feel akin to the enigmatic eye atop the pyramid on the back of a US dollar bill. The Latin text around it reads: "God has prospered our beginnings. New Order of Ages." Go figure!

The lights of Cairo blaze in stark contrast to the darkened void of the Sahara desert. A small mouse appears, makes a dash for another crack, and disappears. That's strange, I wonder how a mouse could possibly survive up here? Yes how, but I quickly remind myself that one should never underestimate the power of the pyramid.

There are all sorts of tales of mysterious manifestations taking place up here: compasses going crazy; wristwatches shedding their radium paint; people disappearing. Whatever my fate, I will soon find out. I position myself against the post, face the Chephren pyramid, and sit in the lotus position as rigid as the Buddha. I began to send loving prayers. Mom. Dad. Brother. Sister. Yes, it's been years since I have seen any of you, but the affection I transmit to you now has never been so intense. Aunts, uncles, cousins, in-laws, childhood friends, girlfriends, and new friends from my World Tour.

A solemn prayer goes out to all sentient beings on earth, especially the thousands of animal species that go extinct each year as they pack up the last of their evolutionary belongings and make ready to depart. Good luck in the void, I whisper. Please understand that not all humans are malicious and uncaring.

Alas, the longest prayer goes out to the greatest man I have ever known—this is for you Pa. My grandfather passed away while I was teaching English in Japan saving money for this trip, and I was not able to make his funeral. I felt I owed him that much and could not come to terms with it until this very moment. A heavy burden lifts and floats away. That was never an issue, he relates.

*   *   *

After some unknown time in deep meditation, my bliss changed abruptly. I started shaking uncontrollably, like a freezing shiver, yet it was rather warm outside. I became overwhelmed with an uneasy feeling that I was trespassing. Cheops was telling me to get down now.

I descended the same route I ascended, taking my time because a fall would be disastrous. Pausing once to scan for guards, I thought about my experience upon this sacred monument. What is happening here? The strong central control of manpower; all the friggin' resources to build it; that omnilingual, universal message suggested within—and that transcendental experience I just had? Jeez, *what is it?* Maybe there was help from aliens? I simply don't know. My entire reality is in question. One certainty is some kind of connection between the cosmos and a highly advanced race of humans that transcends what we presently comprehend. Something magnificent remains untold here.

The rest of the way down, it was so weird, I felt utterly protected, untouchable, *invisible.* Sure enough, I reached the bottom without guard interference and walked right out of the Giza complex a free man.

When I returned to the cafe, Ray and Pauly jumped up and laughed when they saw the wide grin on my face. "Did you do it? Were there many guards out? C'mon tell us!"

I didn't speak to them for a minute, and rightfully so. They had the opportunity and lost it. Yes I made it, fellas. And you were right Ray, I *was* meant to go alone.

# The Real World

## Ann Melville

*Out here, there are no perimeters. Out here, humans have no camouflage, security evaporates and nature rules.*

I'D BEEN WANDERING AROUND EAST AFRICA for two months—kind of going in whatever direction the wind blew, from Nairobi, to the Kenyan coast, the island of Zanzibar, and to the golden sandy shores of Lake Malawi. I was in the midst of enjoying a good week of road recuperation there, when I acquired a lift on a large overland truck heading southwest to Zimbabwe.

They were an organized tour from London, a conglomeration of crazies, (Brits, Aussies and Kiwis) who had already spent 4½ months bouncing around together over about 12,000 miles of Europe and the African continent. Some of the passengers had jumped ship (quarters had gotten a bit CLOSE) and there were some empty seats on the truck. Basically they were sick of each other and were seeking new blood—someone with some new stories to refresh the atmosphere. A new victim to tease. Normally group tourism is not my cup of tea, but for 2½ weeks of worry-free transport, food, and space in a tent, the $50.00 they were asking from me was a deal hard to resist! Besides, they were headed for the Okavango Delta in Botswana. Impossible to reach without a vehicle (no public transport to the area) it is a destination inaccessible to the solo budget traveler. Meeting them was an amazing stroke of luck. (The driver thought he was going to get lucky too—a gamble he lost! HA!)

The Okavango is the largest inland delta on earth—a sprawling expanse of wild bush and swamp where thousands of miles of vein-like rivers pour south, bringing abundant wildlife to a forbidding desert region.

We were camped outside a town called Maun at the edge of the delta, and heard about some local "guides" who were willing to take people up the delta in their dugout canoes for overnight walking safaris. Six of us from the campground met them at the designated starting point. They were a slick bunch, all in their mid to late teens, each sporting a pair of mirrored aviator sunglasses. They were not quite what we'd expected safari guides to look like, but they did not seem dangerous and the price was right.

The canoes were carved from whole tree trunks and propelled by large poles

**286**

which were dug into the stream bed to move us slowly along. Each canoe, which lay very low in the water, carried two passengers reclining against their bags, and one guide standing (with incredible balance) in the stern of the boat with his pole. We inched silently along over the calm water, observing the abundant bird life. Cooling breezes blew through the tall grass, which lined the edges of our liquid pathway.

The guides assured us that the water was safe to drink and from our low position in the canoe it was possible to lean over the edge, place our faces into the cool stream, and drink. The effect was complete magic. The water was like glass, absolutely crystal clear, and below in the aqua depths was a dream world of gracefully swaying plants and small fish swimming in the gentle current. The water was incredibly sweet and pure. It was an extremely calming sensation, floating there above that peaceful realm. The horrible stories I'd heard of hippo and crocodile attacks must happen in other parts of Africa, I thought to myself.

After two hours of blissful meandering, we pulled the canoes up onto a small island where we would camp that night, and unloaded our gear. One of the Aussie guys immediately started complaining about us not going "far enough up the delta." He said he had friends who had been there. They had gone "really far up," and saw elephants, and HE wanted to see elephants too.

From the looks on the guides' faces, it was obvious that they really didn't feel like pushing those canoes around in the hot sun any longer, but reluctantly they loaded us back into the boats, and leaving our gear behind, we continued upstream. After about 20 minutes one of them spotted something on the shore so we pulled up and had a look at what appeared to be a very large round footprint. "Elephant" declared one, in an ominous voice, and then leered at his fellows as if to say "this guy wants to see an elephant, OK, let's show him an elephant."

We left the canoes behind and began following the elephant tracks. With the whining Australian in the lead, the men bounded off into the bush ahead, leaving us women to lag behind at our own pace. One of the guides was walking along with us so we felt no danger. He was amazingly skilled at spotting hidden wildlife from great distances. We saw no point in rushing, preferring instead to soak up our surroundings, smell the flowers, appreciate the day. We soon caught up with the men, who were standing in a circle inspecting a rather huge pile of dung. Elephant dung to be exact, and it was so fresh, it was practically steaming! Onward we trudged, surely the elephant couldn't be far-off now.

In another half hour we saw the men begin running in the distance and disappear over a hill. They were continuing in the direction we'd been heading. "Oh," we exclaimed naively "the elephant must be running away! We'd better hurry if we want to catch a glimpse of it!" We began trotting in the same direction the others had gone. Almost to the top of the hill, and nearly out of breath, we suddenly heard a tremendous trumpeting sound. We looked at each other with mouths agape, and in a split second we knew ... the sound was headed in OUR direction.

There were no words spoken. A rush of adrenaline shot through our bodies, and the primal 'fight or flight' instinct had taken hold of us—we turned, and ran like hell. Bounding awkwardly through the thigh-deep grass, we scattered willy-nilly toward a line of trees at the bottom of the field. Behind us the angry trumpeting continued, and in the next instant, the sound of thrashing in the bush. I looked over my shoulder, and then I saw him, about 50 feet behind me: an enormous bull elephant crashing up over the crest of the hill, ears a-flapping, trunk in the air and blasting, and huge white tusks gleaming in the sun. He was charging straight for us, and he was pissed off! There was only one word going through my mind at that moment, "SHIIIIIIIIT!!!!"

Our "guide" was already a hundred feet ahead, hightailing it for the trees. He wasn't having any part of that elephant's wrath! Fat chance he was going to save us! My heart was pounding in my ears. I tried to ignore the vision of what would happen if I tripped and fell down. It seemed like miles to get to the trees, (like a dream when you're running in slow motion) and once we got there, THEN what would we do? The elephant would rip down those trees like toothpicks! "This is absolutely insane," I thought, "What the HELL are we doing out here?" Walking around like a bunch of idiots in the middle of Africa—wild animals everywhere, no vehicle, no weapon, with "guides" who are just a bunch of 18-year-old punks into the macho thrill of it all, and the few extra bucks to be made off stupid tourists!

By the time I made it to the trees the elephant was veering away from us. Apparently his charge had been a bluff. Soon the rest of our party appeared. The guides were falling all over each other with laughter. I'm sure they'd never seen white people scramble that fast! There were a few moments of tale telling, loud expletives, and wild gesturing before we realized that the elephant had veered off in the direction of our canoes!

Suddenly everything seemed so ridiculous. WE were so ridiculous; with all our senseless chatter, our Disneyland-like expectations, our spectator ignorance, our package tour approach to life, our insensitive, spoiled attitudes. We were NOT at the zoo. This was nature we were dealing with, and nature is serious business!

We spent the next two hours tip-toeing through the underbrush trying to avoid another elephant encounter. By the time we arrived back at the canoes, the sun had set. We prayed we could make it back to camp without another wild animal incident.

The sound of millions of insects surrounded us, and a silvery full moon rose up over the delta grasses to cast its reflection on the calm surface of that life-giving stream. I felt glad to be alive. I had never felt so alive as that day, when my life seemed on the verge of ending. I knew one thing for certain: If I lived to be an old woman of 100 years, I would never forget the specter of that huge animal, in all his fury, crashing toward me. It was a real wake up call; about the forces of nature, the nearness of death, the absurdity of human behavior, and a questioning of all the things that I considered *important*. The vision will remain forever imprinted in my brain, like a brand on a cow's rump.

# Gratitude

## Richard Bellamy

*The discomfort of an experience can oftentimes be its greatest reward.*

IT WAS A MOONLESS SUMMER NIGHT on top of a mountain near Taos, New Mexico. My friend Gene and I were waiting to enter a small Indian tent about four feet high. We were anxious about the unknown as we waited, but excited to be in a new challenge. Crawling into the ceremonial tent on my knees, I entered a very small area with a center pit about 12 inches in diameter. I sat on some animal skins facing the pit. Gene sat next to me.

Twelve of us seated inside: six women facing six men. Four large, hot rocks-glowing red in darkness faced east, west, north, and south. The Native American leading the ceremony gave his invocation as the temperature began to rise. His name was Hawk.

As I began to feel the heat from the glowing rocks, Gene leaned over and said he was feeling very nauseated. Hawk asked if he wanted to leave. Gene said no. The leader suggested that Gene lie down and stretch out between the rocks and people. Gene did so, and later told me that this allowed him to breathe slightly cooler air.

My lower-minded power below began to react to the discomfort. My brain noise justified and defended, exaggerated and minimized what I would, should, and could do to alleviate the discomfort. I considered grabbing Gene and dragging him out of the tent.

I knew that the Native American Indians had used this ceremony as a purification process and as part of an initiation into a spiritual experience, but at the moment I felt miserable and my friend was lying face down, gasping for air. It suddenly occurred to me that my power below had entrapped itself in a paradox between escaping discomfort or the embarrassment of leaving.

I felt Gene's posterior tibial pulse. It was weak and barely palpable. I asked him if he was all right, he answered, "Barely." I asked him if he wanted to leave, he said no.

After what seemed like an eternity, the leader opened the tent flap briefly and more glowing rocks were brought in and placed at the center of the pit.

Water was sprinkled on the rocks. The steam seemed to burn my lungs as I inhaled. The Indian threw some herbs on the rocks, which gave off a pleasant aroma.

It seemed to get more hellish. One person excused himself and left, gasping for air. I checked Gene's pulse again. I could not feel it. I asked if he was all right. He feebly answered yes.

I wondered again if I should take Gene out. It would have been a convenient reason for me to leave. The power within me—my true higher-minded nature—was like a non-judgmental observer watching my lower-mind. Suddenly I recalled that the only way to solve a paradox is to rise above it.

I began to mentally send love and gratitude to the Great Spirit and the people in my life. I touched Gene and imagined that I was receiving love from high and sending the healing power of love through me to him. I silently communicated love to each person in my life. I thanked each of them for how they had impacted my life.

I visualized myself in their presence, experiencing my gratitude and love for them. Suddenly, I realized the discomfort had eased considerably. I spent the rest of the time in the sweat lodge in a state of inspiration. More glowing red rocks were put in the pit. They passed a pipe with some herbs around as a ceremony for world peace. Three hours later we emerged, truly grateful! Gene and I noticed towers of heat shooting heavenward from each other upon exiting. As we began to dress we felt a peaceful calm, having persevered a trial by fire. A meaningful experience we would remember all our lives.

# A Perfect Gem

**Randal Thatcher**

*What profound wisdom may come.*

A FEW MONTHS AGO, my wife and I returned from a year long journey through developing countries around the world. I still can't say just what it was exactly that compelled us to quit our jobs, don backpacks and venture off like that. Impulsive, you could say, but at the time the call we both heard was unmistakable and irresistible.

Any of you who've heard a similar call and heeded it know that during the course of such travel, one simply cannot help but learn a few things about life along the way. And if you're lucky, one or two of these lessons may turn out to be a real nugget of wisdom. And if you're very lucky, one might even turn out to be a perfect gem. Sort of like finding a pretty rock by the side of the road, and upon taking it home and running it through your rock-tumbler, discovering that it's a pure Sapphire gemstone.

As we began the trip in China, it became rather difficult for me to be confronted almost daily with poverty and poor living conditions. And rather than get easier, it got harder as we went along. For how could I justify my comparative wealth and affluence? How to reconcile the huge disparity between the physical comforts and luxuries of my life compared with the poor, simple living conditions of the local villagers? I couldn't justify this inequality so I tried instead to rationalize it away, but this proved impossible. It became a daily struggle for me, as I wrestled with what I perceived to be something of an injustice.

Days turned into weeks, and weeks into months, as we traveled through China, Vietnam, Cambodia and Laos, and I was still no closer to a resolution of my internal conflict.

We traveled into Burma (Myanmar), and found it to be a magical country of mystical charms and wonders, and yet the poverty was here too, and my struggle continued. I would often borrow a large, heavy, Chinese-made bicycle from our guest-house and take long rides through the dusty streets of Pagan; Burma's ancient capital. And it was during one such late afternoon ride that I happened upon a small, make-shift village (more like a shanty-town, really) along the sandy shores of the Irrawaddy River. As I pushed my bicycle through the sand toward this cluster of shacks, my heart sank. For here I had found the poorest of the poor; the truly destitute, those clinging to the bottom rung on the ladder of life. Dirty, half-naked children running everywhere. I saw miserable, ramshackle huts dotting the riverbank, and anxious, bleak eyes staring warily out at me; the intruder. I hated to see such a scene so close up—impossible to ignore. My instinct was to turn my bike around and leave this pitiful sight behind me, but I couldn't do it. I pressed forward. An unwelcome intruder, walking uneasily through this poor settlement. And suddenly I was feeling *very* conspicuous in my top-of-the-line sport sandals; my high-tech, trekking pants and shirt; my Swiss-made, stainless-steel, water-resistant, quartz-crystal wrist-watch; and my wrap-around, anti-glare, polarized sun-glasses. A quick calculation in my head told me that the total value of the gear I wore on my body at that moment would easily feed any one of these families for the better part of a year. This was it. My internal conflict had just reached the crisis stage. I felt numb. I had everything, and these people had nothing! I felt desperate inside. I couldn't escape the reality that these people would never enjoy life's luxuries and pleasures as I did; would likely never own a watch of any kind, let alone Swiss-made! By their standards, I was magnificently rich, and by my standards, they were abjectly poor. It was hopeless.

As I stood there, staring helplessly back at the faces that were staring at me, I felt a strong impulse to leave this dismal place where I felt so uncomfortable and unwelcome. And just at that moment, as I turned my bike around to go, a most curious thing happened. This poor, bleak, pitiful village began to transform itself before my very eyes.

The sun was just setting, lighting the sky in a dazzling array of pink and orange hues. The river was ablaze with color. And in the soft, magical glow of twilight, I looked about me and beheld a decidedly altered scene from that which had appeared so dismal just moments before. Glancing toward the river, I saw a group of young men gathering; soap and towels in hand for their evening bathing ritual. A few of them were playfully turning cartwheels in the shallow water near the shore, as others ran straight and plunged in headlong. And fifty yards upstream, another group of bathers gathered (middle-aged women I thought), and they talked and laughed together while scrubbing each other's backs. And further up on the sandy banks, most of the younger children had started up an impromptu soccer game on a makeshift field in the sand, running back and forth, shouting and laughing all at once. And I noticed the orange glow of small fires springing up here and there among the huts as the families began to cook their evening meals (fresh fish, as you might expect from a village on a river). And in the doorway of one of the shacks nearest to where I stood, I saw a proud, young father cradling his infant child in his arms.

And suddenly these humble villagers no longer seemed destitute to me at all! They appeared perfectly content and happy. So much so, in fact, that I wondered how it was that I'd actually pitied them just moments before! And how is this then, that people with so very little can possibly be so genuinely happy? What was I missing here? This was a puzzlement to me. And I've often thought since, that I must have felt something of what the "Grinch" himself felt on that fateful Christmas morning; having stolen all of the Christmas goodies from "Whoville" the night before, only to have them all wake and *still* join together in singing songs of joy and love. *"And he puzzled and puzzled till his puzzler was sore."*

And while I stood there in hushed wonderment, I became aware of shouts and waves from the boys in the river, and finally realized that they were beckoning to me. I walked to the riverbank and one of them handed me a bar of soap and made scrubbing motions all over his body, then pointed to the water, and I gathered I was being invited to join them in their evening bath. Wanting their acceptance, I quickly stripped down, soaped up and plunged in, all to enthusiastic applause and squeals of laughter (most of the squeals coming from the middle-aged women bathers upstream!)

My new friends and I splashed and frolicked together in the river and spit water at each other. And I demonstrated for them the "Jellyfish float" that I'd learned as a child in swimming lessons and we all laughed and smiled genuine smiles.

Twilight started to give way to dusk, and I floated downstream a ways, reveling in a near-perfect moment. And as I floated on my back in the middle of the Irrawaddy River, gazing up at the deepening blue of the evening sky, and at the tiny sliver moon just beginning to appear, along with the first few twinkling stars, I had a profound thought. And later that night, back in my guest-house room, after having said good-bye to my new friends of the village, I wrote this thought down in my journal.

This is what I wrote:

*"The most beautiful, most precious, most valuable, and most important things in this world are all God given—and freely and liberally to all."*

After I'd written it, I read it aloud. And I read it over and over several times. And it sounded right to me, and yet I wasn't even sure that I entirely believed it. And I pondered on this thought, realizing that it was certainly not a new revelation, that I'd heard it said many times before in slightly different ways:

*"Life's simple pleasures are the best."*

*"The best things in life are free."*

And the more I thought about it, the more astounding this idea became. For, if it were true, then my friends from the village were not really as poor as they seemed. And by the same token, I was not necessarily as rich as I might appear. Why, this idea had the potential to turn my whole dilemma on its head!

I thought of little else for the next several days. And I decided to put this pretty rock I'd found into the ol' rock-tumbler to see just what I had here. And so I began to list out all those things in life that are of the greatest worth to the hearts and souls of we human beings; those things that truly nourish the spirit. Things like a miraculous physical body; capable of seeing, hearing, feeling, tasting and smelling all of the many wonders, large and small, that make up our world and surround us daily. A mind; capable of independent thought and reason, and of gaining knowledge, and hopefully, wisdom. A heart; capable of feeling love, gratitude, compassion and even sorrow. And finally, a spirit; capable of connecting and communing harmoniously with the spirit that exists all about us, every moment.

And there are personal talents and creativities which every human being possesses in some degree and variety, and all the resulting arts that inspire; whether music, literature, dance, theater, artworks or other.

And there is the love of family and close friends, and the pure joy that exudes from these sacred bonds.

And of course, the splendors of Nature, and the constant source of nourishment for body, mind and soul that it provides us continually.

I then began to consider and compare those things from the realm of man; the material things of the world, those things which are bought with and sold for money: House, car, clothes, microwave oven, big-screen television, Swiss-made wrist-watch, and et cetera. All sorts of tangible possessions that I'd always coveted and spent so much of my time amassing; the things that our society values and tells us to value every time we turn on the television or open any magazine or newspaper. I do not intend to suggest that these things are inherently bad. I *still* wear that same Swiss-made watch, while driving my car to my house to microwave something to eat while I watch occasional TV. However, I do suggest that when compared with our God-given gifts, these pre-fabricated, manufactured, mass-merchandised things of men tend to pale quite significantly. So much, in fact, that most of my material possessions, when compared with the edifying gifts from God begin to seem like superfluous clutter in my life; things to worry about and to suck up my time somewhat frivolously. And in the very worst scenario, this "flashy" clutter that society tells me I should own and amass will often become an insidious diversion—a 'smoke screen' distracting my focus away from those things that are of the greatest worth and value to my soul—those things that would lead me to true joy and happiness. And whenever this happens, the natural man takes over, and the spiritual man withers within me.

Okay, so what does all this actually mean? Well, to me it underscores the beautiful lesson that the simple, humble, hard working villagers of southeast Asia taught me: our lives can become truly rich, fulfilling and rewarding when stripped of much of the clutter and superfluities of our modern world ... stripped right down to its bare essence. And I'm grateful to them for showing me this truth. And I began to really try not to set my heart upon the things of our man-made world, but to constantly recognize, acknowledge and cherish the gifts from God—those gifts that are given freely, liberally, and equally to all. I now try to remember to partake gratefully of these glorious gifts, and to revel in them each day with a thankful heart. I began to recognize the enormous significance of what this newly learned lesson actually meant, and I knew that I would never see the world quite the same again. And this made me glad, for I finally understood that, in the grand scheme of things, and viewed from a more spiritual perspective, all the material wealth that I'd enjoyed was not necessarily the huge boon or blessing I'd initially thought it was. Sometimes less is more. And a simple life doesn't necessarily mean a "poor" life, for God grants wondrous, glorious blessings to all his children; freely, liberally, and equally. And with this realization, I reached into my mental rock-tumbler and pulled out a perfect Sapphire gem, and felt so very lucky to have found it. And I wrapped this gem carefully and kept it with me for the remainder of our travels. And passing through these same humble villages no longer caused me the anguished feelings of injustice or inequity that they had before, because I saw now with a new perspective, and with a better understanding.

I still treasure my little gemstone. I keep it in my pocket and take it out and polish it a little everyday to remind myself of the things in this world that are of true worth and value to my soul; the things that bring genuine happiness and joy; those generous gifts from a just and loving God. And I offer this gem to you now. To keep in your pocket, and to take out whenever you need a quick reminder that the best things in life really are free ...

May it serve you well, as it has served me.

# INTREPID ARCHETYPES

## They Broke the Mold . . .

*"The wise man travels to discover himself."*
James Russel Lowell

# The Man Who Would Be Chief

## Eric Seyfarth

*Deep in the Ecuadorian jungle, a white chief leads an indigenous village in their struggle to survive. Follow the persistence of an extraordinary man who lives in a world somewhere between the microchip and the blow gun.*

WITH THE UNDIVIDED ATTENTION OF 20 ONLOOKERS, Randy Borman is discussing the hunting technique of the king vulture, one of his favorite birds. He explains the keen vision and flying properties of the large Amazonian raptor. Then he begins the demonstration segment of the lecture. "I love to watch the wingtips. The wingtips are just fascinating. They go like this," he says, and spreads his arms shoulder height, splays his fingers, ducks his head and does a remarkably realistic imitation of a plummeting bird. "When they dive toward the forest floor after their prey, it is just the best thing to see." With his graying hair, trim moustache, slightly Midwestern accent, and powerful upper body, Borman could pass for a college biology instructor who spends a lot of time in the gym. But that impression is quickly dashed when one notices that Borman is shoeless, wearing a bright-blue house coat, accessorized with a necklace of red and white beads. All bets are off when one also notices that Borman has orange flower pedals lashed to his wrist, and his lecture is being delivered from the bow of a dugout canoe.

Borman commands the full attention of his audience, a group of California tourists. They don't have a choice. They are crammed into two dugouts like refugees on a lifeboat. A few of them even look like refugees, bug-eyed and edgy, drifting as they are down a blackwater river in the middle of the Ecuadorian rainforest, 150 miles from the nearest road. They have traveled by plane, bus and boat, about as far into the Ecuadorian Amazon as any tourist is likely to get, and a guy in women's clothing and a wrist corsage is leading them upriver into the shadowy depths of the jungle. Turns out, as Borman explains from the prow, gesticulating and rocking the boat, he is not wearing a dress. He is wearing a Cofan cushma. The flower pedals and necklace are traditional rainforest menswear. Relieved, I look to the edge of the river, where both banks grow dark with a tangle of vegetation. From the back of the canoe I squint into the forest and make a rough calculation—500 shades of Amazon green.

As Borman finishes his demonstration and the little boat is gratefully still, a guide next to me yanks in his jerking line to produce a six-inch piranha, its double rows of razor-sharp teeth snapping wildly. The fish is konked in the head with the butt of a paddle, the hook is wriggled out of its carnivorous mouth, and handed forward for the tourists to see. I take it first and quickly pass it along to my boatmates. The slippery, iridescent piranha is shuttled from hand to nervous hand, jaws still snapping reflexively.

"Watch your fingers with that guy," Borman says, "he can take a good-sized chunk out of you." Borman, the unchallenged expert in this neck of the woods, is pointing with his left hand. The forefinger is missing about an inch of the tip. I take his advice.

*   *   *

Welcome to Randy Borman's world. It is a rare, hard-to-find place of remarkable beauty, profound wilderness, and ecological diversity that is found nowhere else on the planet. It is also a place fighting for survival—for both the fragile rainforest and the people who live there. That fight, I learn over the course of the next few days, is being led by Borman, a white man and the son of American missionaries. Although the Cofan have survived in this unforgiving environment for generations, their world slides closer to the brink of extinction with each giant hardwood felled and each rainforest acre slashed and burned. They are being led to the brink by a sophisticated and relentless opponent—multinational corporations in a mad dash for what lies under the rainforest: oil. The great irony in this struggle is that their white chief is betting on the survival of a native culture by bringing in foreign tourists, primarily Americans and Europeans, and their money. In the process, Borman has become a sophisticated and relentless force of his own.

An hour after watching the king vulture impersonation, the group has climbed out of the dugouts for solid ground and the safety of Zabalo, the village where Borman and about one hundred Cofan live. The riverside community has five guest cottages, a small structure that serves as a meeting and dining room, as well as a number of huts in which the Cofan live set off from guests. All buildings are thatch roofed and rest on stilts. From the perspective of the Aguarico River, the traditional architecture blends with the looming jungle, making the Cofanes' existence indistinguishable from the rainforest, a harmony that extends into every aspect of their life. The only concessions to the 20th century are solar panels mounted amid the thatch roofs and outboard motors bolted to the long canoes.

"After spending my whole life out here, I am still amazed at the trees. I can hike five or six days and see nothing but forest after forest after forest. I feel this sensation of tinyness," says Borman. He is lecturing again. Instead of the bow of a dugout as his platform, he is standing in the front of a blackboard in the meeting room, chalk in hand, under the thin light of a solar-powered florescent bulb. Tonight he is wearing a purple cushma and a red handkerchief tied around his neck. "Then it occurs to me that we have the power to destroy something that is so much larger than us," he says. "The thought of that is obscene."

A stay in Zabalo features the nightly presentations by Borman. The subjects range from botany, to blow-gun hunting techniques, to Western education, to the cultural history of the Cofan. On this first night with the group, Borman is typically intense and direct. "What we are working for here in Zabalo is the survival of a people, survival of a culture, and the survival of an environment," he says, his two older sons, Federico and Felipe, play at his feet as he talks. This is one of the perks of his job. A thousand insects click and whir in the dark outside the room, while the Aguarico burbles from below the steep bank a few feet away.

Borman moves on to the evening's geography lesson. Zabalo lies at the heart of the Cuyabeno National Preserve. The Ecuadorian government appointed the Cofan stewards of 170,000-acres within the preserve. In exchange, the Cofan were allowed to fish and hunt, and operate their low-impact tourism business. The Aguarico flows east from its source in the soaring, snow-capped Andes Mountains on the way to the Amazon River in Peru. The eastern flank of Ecuador is part of the Amazon rainforest, and is known locally as the Oriente. In all, the greater Amazon rainforest accounts for one third of the planet's fresh water and one fifth of its known species. The habitat is a Noah's Arc of plants, animals and insects. The dense forest also produces a vast share of the world's oxygen. Together, the rivers and trees form the lungs and veins of the Earth.

Someone asks Borman how he came into this culture, why he chose to live his life in a small village in the middle of the jungle, where no one else speaks English. Borman is a reluctant extrovert. And when he explains his private life to a roomful of strangers, he insulates himself by making his experience the stuff of legend, and he is the central character. Borman recounts some of the legend for us.

When his father, Bub Borman, arrived by seaplane on the Aguarico River in 1954, all he had was a pack of provisions and his faith in his work as a missionary for the Summer Institute of Linguistics. His faith served him well. The Cofan brought him into their community, and Bobbie Borman joined her husband soon after. They raised three sons and a daughter in the riverside settlement of Dureno, where Randy, the eldest, learned to hunt howler monkeys with blow guns and walked barefoot on the forest. The Bormans taught the Cofan about their all-powerful god, and the Cofan taught the Bormans the ways of the rainforest, their spiritual home and source of everything.

Life in the Oriente was quiet until 1964, when the first oil exploration teams arrived, cutting forest to build roads and setting off explosions for seismic testing that scattered game and scarred the landscape. Texaco drilled its first oil well in the region in 1967, and overnight the oil-boom town of Lago Agrio (which translates, with no loss of irony, as Sour Lake) sprang from the cleared forest. The peace had been shattered. In 1972 a road was built to haul derricks, workers, and colonists deep into the forest, and a pipeline was constructed to siphon the oil out. Petroleros and colonos leveled the nearby forest, contaminated the rivers and streams, and Lago Agro became a seething scene of prostitutes, bars, ramshackle buildings, and oil-covered streets.

The Cofan society, which had already been trampled in the march of Western Civilization, began to disintegrate over the course of a few years. Roughly 20,000 Cofan lived in the rainforest at the time of Spanish conquest, but the deadly combination of European diseases, forest destruction, and finally, the ravages of the oil companies drove the population to 350. The Cofan were riding a tailspin into extinction. In the early 70s, when there seemed nothing left of the rainforest or its people, Borman left the Oriente to attend college—first in Illinois, his father's home state, then in Michigan. But the concrete jungles of the developed world proved to be confusing, disorienting, and chaotic. Convinced that he would always be a stranger in the United States, Borman returned to the rainforest for good.

When he arrived back in the Oriente, he was shocked by what he found: The destruction of the Cofan and their environment had accelerated while he was gone. Alcoholism, broken families, and the false promise of oilfield jobs had devastated what was left of the community. To pass the time and make money, Borman first worked as a guide for an American tour company that lead travelers into the forest. But he was haunted by the disintegration of the Cofan community, his people, as he helplessly watched. Finally, Borman had enough. He created a partnership with ten families, and the group moved as far as they could up the Aguarico, near the border with Peru. About 100 people transplanted to Zabalo, determined to maintain their traditional life. In 1987, at age 31, Borman married Amelia, a Cofan woman then 15 years old (the traditional age for marriage), and they now have three boys. Borman's commitment to the Cofan was sealed in blood. And Borman has committed to spill that blood if necessary to defend his cause.

"There has to be a willingness to spear people. We are living a life worth dying for and worth killing for," Borman says, pacing professor-like in the front of the room. A few tourists shift nervously in their seats. Maybe the solid ground of Zabalo isn't so safe after all.

That willingness has been put to test as oil companies move deeper into the rainforest to support the petroleum habit upon which the Ecuadorian economy fully depends. Oil is the leading industry in the nation. When a seismic-testing team was discovered inside the Cuyabeno National Preserve in 1991, Borman took the crew hostage for a day and escorted them out. Shortly after that, a drilling platform was discovered and Borman had it burned down. The most critical test came in 1993 when an operating well was discovered deep in the forest, a clear violation of the Cuyabeno preserve agreement. The Cofan traveled to the isolated well—accessible to the rest of the world only by helicopter—with shotguns and spears, surrounded the site, and the foreman was told to stop the drilling. He did, and he also radioed the military who arrived by helicopter, sporting battle fatigues and automatic weapons. The future of Borman's bold experiment had come down to a single moment.

"If the oil companies are willing to push us, we have to be willing to match their aggressiveness," Borman says, still pacing in the thin light. "When we went to the oil well, they knew we were serious." The military and the national oil company, Petro-Ecuador, backed down. Government and company officials were flown to the site, and an agreement was signed. Drilling resumed, but fate delivered a dry hole. Borman proved that he was serious, and the Cofan have survived, ready for the next inevitable challenge to their way of life.

*  *  *

Toward the end of my stay, I meet with Borman on the front porch of his house. His childhood friend, Lorenzo Crilollo joins us. Borman's sons and a few other kids from the village play with toy cars on the porch floor. As we talk, a thunderstorm of Amazonian proportions blows in, and buckets of rain are unleashed from dark clouds. The downpour bounces off a metal roof just above our heads, sounding like a jet engine. Crilollo settles in across from us. A large man, Crilollo sits straight backed in a chair with his hands on his knees. He has classic Cofan features, red-brown skin, high and wide cheekbones; his black hair frames his face with straight bangs across his forehead. He wears a traditional red feather in his nose, placed sideways through a pierce in his septum.

With the roof roaring overhead, I ask Borman the question that has been with me since I arrived in Zabalo: What is it like to be the white chief of an indigenous village, a man who lives in a world somewhere between the microchip and the blow gun. "I am me. I'm not something of one culture and something of another culture. I am myself. I am living in the forest with a group of people who are my friends," he says. Those friends accept him for who he is, Borman adds, because being Cofan is an issue of culture, not race.

The rain is bending tree limbs and forming miniature whitewater rivers on

**304**

the ground. Crilollo sits motionless, with his eyes fixed on Borman. "The Cofan culture is the people's response," Borman says, his voice rising above the din, "to the social and physical environment around them, and it has changed dramatically, so the culture obviously changes. That doesn't mean that it's not Cofan culture anymore."

The battles with the oil companies have been won for the time being, but inevitably, Big Oil will be back. Although Ecuador has enjoyed a period of relative stability, it is still a Latin American country, and one can never be sure when a political or military storm will open the floodgates of development in the rainforest. Despite the change and uncertainty, Borman keeps the faith of a missionary's son.

"When we were fighting the oil company, it was not just the Cofanes' fight; the whole population of Ecuador was behind us," he says. "Don't get me wrong, I'm sounding like there is all the hope in the world. It's not quite that way. I am saying that there is quite a bit of hope; it's not a totally lost situation." What would happen if your hope is dashed, and the oil companies drill with impunity, and the colonos stream in to level the rainforest?, I ask. "We would just go gorilla. And we would make life absolutely hell for those people."

The roof quiets, and the rain stops as quickly as it started. Rays of light shoot through the clouds and hit a thousand leaves glistening with water. In the new light I see a dazzling mosaic of green. Two chickens scare up the courage to sprint from under the house, across the red-clay yard, and into the thick brush fifty feet away. All is quiet and still after the storm, and I imagine that I can hear the trees drinking the rainwater. The place has a way of giving you thoughts like this. I realize that this raw and profound landscape is the most beautiful that I have ever seen. I understand now what Borman meant about the obscenity of destroying this place. Here in the clarity of the rainforest after a storm, the veneer of progress and development are washed away to reveal ignorance and destruction at their core.

Later that day, Borman shows me several books written by his father. They are arranged on a rough-hewn table in the bright sun. The mission of the Summer Institute of Linguistics is to translate the bible into indigenous languages, and spread the word of a new religion to ancient cultures. The Cofan, as with many indigenous communities, never had a written language, so while Bub Borman introduced a new belief system, he also has preserved a culture that otherwise might have gone extinct. This is another of the many paradoxes that emerge in Randy Borman's world.

The books on the table document the crafts, hunting techniques, dress and architecture, and legends of the Cofan. Borman gives me a book of legends.

One story catches my attention, and I read it several times in my hut on my final night in Zabalo, amid the roar of insects and the other sounds of a living Amazon night. The legend predates the Spanish conquest and is called, "The Cofan Hero Raised by the Savages." The story is briefly this:

A Cofan woman and her son went across the river to gather plantains. Savages captured them. The mother and son were held captive by the savages, and the boy was raised by them to be a shaman. Because of his powers, he could not be hurt by spears. When the boy was a young man, the savages decided to kill the Cofans. The boy snuck off in the night to the Cofan village and warned them that the savages would invade the next day. The next morning the boy arrived in the Cofan village just before the savages, went into his father's house, changed into a cushma and beads, and ran out to defend the village alone. The savages tried viciously to kill the boy, but their spears would not injure him. After they threw all of their spears, he gathered them up, ran after the savages and slaughtered them as they yelled, "It is our shaman-trained Cofan who is killing us." He went to the savages' village, killed all the women and children, and brought his mother back to his father. He went out for several nights after and killed the savages in the other villages, four in all. In the last village a man and a girl escaped, crossed a great river and multiplied in the forest, always to be a threat to the Cofan. The Cofan shaman lived to be a very old man and died.

The next morning, I loaded into a dugout with the group of tourists. A steady drizzle fell, and we settled in for the eight-hour ride back to the developed world where I would spend an uneasy night in Lago Agro, the shanty town built by the petroleros, followed by a fuel-guzzling flight to the capital city of Quito, and then back to California, where cars buzzed everywhere, concrete filled the land, and I could turn on the television anytime I wanted. As soon as we had tucked our packs under tarps and taken our seats on the boats, the entire village came out in the early morning rain to see us off. It was a perfect Cofan gesture, showing their hospitality and compassion for us most fully when we were at a respectful distance on the river. They were a rainbow of bright colors, waving as we buzzed off. Borman stood with one arm around Amelia and the other holding his three-month old son.

I thought about the legend recorded by Bub Borman that I had read the night before. So far the spears of the savages had glanced off Randy Borman. For now, he stood protected on the bank on the safe side of the river. But the savages are multiplying on the other side. I wondered if Borman would die an old man, by the river with his community around him. Or whether the charm would wear off all too soon, and Borman would become one more victim of the long spears hurled viciously by the civilized world.

# John Muir: A Man Unafraid

**Basil Northam, Sr.**

*"Throw some tea and bread in an old sack and jump over the back fence."*
*—Muir on expedition planning.*

IF *IN SEARCH OF ADVENTURE* HAS A COURAGEOUS THEME, well, John Muir is the synonym. Muir was born in Dunbar, Scotland in 1838. By the age of five he was a relegated naturalist. Unfortunately, young Muir and his father, a religious zealot, had an ongoing battle over the years—Muir often cried himself to sleep. The Muir family moved to Wisconsin when he was eleven. They were pioneers.

Muir attended the University of Wisconsin and later became a supervisor in an Indianapolis factory. Multi-talented, he invented things like an "early rising bed" that would dump the sleeper onto the floor at an appointed time! He built his own clock and could handle and repair large machinery. A genius for things mechanical and a talented administrator, he could have become a millionaire. Nature writer E.W. Teale noted, "Muir was rescued from the threat of financial success."

While supervising a broom handle factory, he was working on a lathe belt when a file flew up and hit him in one eye, blinding it. In immediate sympathetic reaction the other eye also went blind. He laid in bed for three days taking no food or water and spent a total of four weeks lying in a darkened room thinking he would never see again. When his sight returned he took a walk through the woods, seeing trees, wildflowers and all that nature had to offer. Muir made a decision on the spot; he would never again make a living related to tools or machinery.

What to do? An easy choice for Muir—take a three-year sabbatical, including a 1,000 mile walk—from Indianapolis to Cedar Key, Florida, steering by compass, avoiding the cities, through forests, over mountains, swimming streams and rivers. At one point in the journey he came upon a solitary flower which brought tears to his eyes.

After the trek he went to San Francisco seeking "anywhere that is wild." He became a shepherd of 1,800 sheep who ate their way eastward to Yosemite. Muir cared well for his herd, but despised them for eating everything in their path including delicate flowers. He nicknamed them "hoofed locusts."

Knowing early on that, "the mountains are calling me and I must go," beholding the mountains and canyon views at Yosemite made him shout and gesticulate wildly with approval. He explored range after range, studying glaciers. Upon witnessing windswept snow blowing off the mountain summits and leaving a mile-long trail across the sky, he declared them "snow banners." Walking hundreds and hundreds of miles, he never tired of the wilderness, his relentless energy soaring up and into the High Sierras.

On one trek, risking his life on a nearly vertical cliff on Mt. Ritter, he could not retreat without great peril and was "suddenly brought to a dead stop with arms outspread, clinging close to the face of a rock wall unable to move hand or foot either up or down." Seemingly doomed to fall to his death, he panicked for the first in his *career*. A "stifling smoke" momentarily invaded his mind. When his alertness returned he "seemed suddenly to become possessed of a new sense." His "other sense" took control, firming his trembling limbs and allowing a gradual ascent to safety.

On these trips he never took a coat nor blanket. Luggage was not his style. On flat land he had a peculiar, shuffling gait, but in the mountains he was all ballet, bounding from boulder to boulder. He carried a sack with him, filled with bread, tea, oats, and water. If he stumbled, he quickly pitched the sack in front of him for protection. At bedtime it became his pillow. When Muir gained new summits he would almost take on another personality; exalted, he'd *found* another peak. The lowlands had nothing to offer him. He would have stayed up there forever, emotionally, if he could.

Upon the summit he would locate a spot to keep warm during the night, for he often "slept over." On a few occasions his campfire barely kept him alive in the face of freezing winds. To stay warm he danced for hours around the fire until exhaustion necessitated a brief nap. Before freezing to death he awoke to dance again around the fire until dawn. In the early light of morning he would descend only to discover another range to call home and continue dreaming.

On another jaunt, Muir was compelled to hike in the forest while a violent gale was blowing down trees, "at the rate of one every two or three minutes." Suddenly seized with an urge to climb a wind-whipped tree, he chose the tallest Douglas Fir in his range and had no trouble scaling the 100-ft. giant. Reaching his perch near the top, he clung like "a bobolink on a reed." Pitching forward and backward in an arc of twenty to thirty degrees, he reveled with the waves of wind bending vast regions of forested mountainsides, illuminated by a rainbow of shimmering light. He closed his eyes, listening to the rushing wind chaffing tree branches and savored the piney fragrance streaming past. He clung to his perch for hours, exhilarated, climbing down when the gale passed. Author Loren

Eisley said of Muir, "Something utterly wild had crept into his nature."

Muir's early efforts in conservation were inspired by the depredations being committed by sheepmen and loggers in and around Yosemite Valley, which was at that time a state preserve. Century Magazine began publishing a series of Muir's articles describing both the magnificent beauty of Yosemite and the Sierra region and the desecrating sheepmen and loggers. Those articles aroused crucial public interest. Ralph Waldo Emerson came to visit Muir at Yosemite. Emerson, finding "the right man in the right place," asked Muir to come east to become a professor. Muir declined.

Muir had another visitor at Yosemite, a kindred spirit and US president, Teddy Roosevelt. Muir took Teddy under his wing for three days of walking, riding, and camping. Here were two well-known nonstop talkers; Roosevelt instinctively knew to hear Muir out when on his turf. Muir explained how privateers were destroying wild places for their own profits. There were even blueprints to commercialize Yosemite (imagine that?). Long into the night Muir presented a case for the ecological benefits of unblemished wildness and the need for people to find inspiration and healing within its grandeur. Two visionaries sitting around a campfire beneath huge sequoias were creating the national park service.

Roosevelt didn't just listen. Upon returning to Washington, D.C. he enacted legislation protecting 148 million acres of national forest and established 14 national monuments. Later, he pushed through legislation creating four more national parks. Parts of two of the monuments he established, Lassen Volcanic and the Grand Canyon, were later elevated to National Park status. Muir gained international fame as the spokesperson for the cause of conservation, known today as preservation. He founded the Sierra Club, becoming its first president.

Writing did not come easy to Muir, though he persevered for the sake of saving the wilderness. He christened the snowy Yosemite and Sierra the "Range of Light," and his descriptions seem to flow effortlessly: "... and after 10 years spent in the heart of it, rejoicing and wondering, bathing in its glorious floods of light, seeing the sun bursts of morning among the icy peaks, the noonday radiance on the trees and rocks and snow, the flush of the afterglow, and a thousand dashing waterfalls with their marvelous abundance of irised spray, it still seems to me above all other the Range of Light, the most divinely beautiful of all the mountain chains I have ever seen."

Within this Range of Light Muir also proclaimed, "Thousands of tired, nerve-shaken, over-civilized people are beginning to find out that going to the mountains is going home, that wildness is necessity, and that mountain parks and reservations are useful not only as fountains of timber and irrigating rivers, but as fountains of life."

"In this world," eulogized Teale, "where men are afraid they will catch a cold, afraid they will lose their way, afraid they will be eaten by bears or bitten by snakes, or touch poison ivy or fall over a log, John Muir, faring forth into the wilderness unarmed and alone, was the man unafraid. He was unafraid of danger, of hardships, of wildness, of being alone, of facing death. He was unafraid of public opinion. He was unafraid of work and poverty and hunger. He knew them all and he remained unafraid."

The man who once dodged the frozen fate of a blizzard that socked in the summit of Mount Shasta by shadowing a steam vent, died in 1914.

"I am hopelessly and forever a mountaineer."

# Pledge Allegiance to the Future

## Johanna O'Sullivan

*The author stared at a commemorative stela of a Roman family—a mother, Kyrilla, huddling with her children. The marble ruin spoke these verses.*

IMPRESSION OF AN EARNEST, somber, Roman nuclear family

beholds the empires fall from grace

and is gradually buried by soil.

Unearthed, catapulted to another epoch

the trio remains transfixed with foreboding stares

into the looming apocalypse of another civilization.

Kyrilla's family steps from the exotic bathhouse

onto an unemployment line.

Strolling from the amphitheater into the hostile metropolitan night

only robes shielding the urban blight.

United they stand, still, stone-faced, bleak.

Woman for all seasons, mother of time. Hold on.

Grasp those implements of creation and Faith, for our sons also bypass childhood.

Serfdom's squalor feeds a black hole of random violence

... our husbands die in wars for the empire too.

We need your hopeful eyes, your eternal pledge of strength.

We learn from your imperceptible smile and the shielding of your genitals.

Simple pleasure must be heavenly.

*Still* on guard, slender hand on your heart ... Pledge allegiance to the future.

Hedonistic humanity, evolving, devolving.

Hold on, Kyrilla.

# Amelia Earhart

## Swami Dyhan Santosh

*Some of us push extreme adventure to the limit—no matter what the cost.*

A T A TIME WHEN WOMEN WERE FIRST RISING as 'masters' of their own destiny, one amazing dynamo emerged to lead the way. Amelia Earhart became a role model as a tousle-haired, trouser-clad daredevil, a person who would prove beyond all measure of doubt that women were equal to men. Although soft-spoken and camera shy, she was rarely at a loss for words when it came to flying. Perhaps best known is her impassioned remark that in aviation, "it is ability, not sex, which counts."

Following the remarkable success of Charles Lindbergh's cross-Atlantic flight only one-year prior, Amelia Earhart became the first woman to cross the Atlantic by air—and became equally famous. Aviation fervor swept America, and Lindbergh and Earhart emerged as national heroes overnight. But Earhart was not satisfied with fame alone. She had something else to prove to the world. "I flew the Atlantic because I wanted to," she remarked casually. "To want in one's heart to do a thing, for its own sake; to enjoy doing it; to concentrate all one's energies upon it—that is not only the surest guarantee of success, it is also being true to oneself."

Record setting became her passion. She became the first woman to fly solo across the Atlantic in May, 1932. The first solo aviator to fly from Hawaii to California in January, 1935. The first soloist to fly from Burbank, CA to Mexico City in April, 1935. And the first person to fly nonstop from Mexico City to Newark, NJ in May, 1935. The media adored her, admirers sent her fan mail from around the world and she became the most famous female aviator in America, if not the world.

The ultimate quest for Amelia Earhart was to do what no person had ever done before—fly a plane around the world at its widest area, the equator. A US Army Air Service team had already circled the globe in 1924 and an aviator named Wiley Post had done it twice, yet the entire 29,000-mile global circumnavigation victory was still up for grabs. Amelia Earhart courageously rose to the challenge. Flying only with her navigator Fred Noonan, the round-the-world flight began in the early hours of May 21, 1937, from Oakland California.

They flew nearly every day, keeping to their well-developed schedule. The flight plan went from North America across the Caribbean to the northeastern coast of South America, spanning the Atlantic at its shortest part, transversing Africa along the fringes of the Sahara, bypassing the Middle East, then heading across India and down the Southeast Asian archipelago into the vast Pacific. Returning to North America was the ultimate challenge of their journey.

The longest leg was 2,556 miles from Lae in eastern New Guinea to tiny Howland Island in the South Pacific. However, this leg was never to be completed. Earhart and Noonan disappeared some 21 hours after takeoff on July 2, 1937 without a trace ever to be found. Based on her final radio messages, the logical assumption is that she failed to locate the island, went into a search pattern and ditched into the ocean after running out of gas. The best estimates place the sunken craft 17,000 feet underwater, somewhere in a 2,000-square-mile area west of Howland Island.

In search of adventure, Amelia Earhart set off on a journey from which she would never return. Ironically, just before leaving on the history-making trip, she told a reporter that this would be her last record attempt, her last "stunt" before opting to live a quiet life. Venturing into the unknown may have cost her her life but it opened up a whole new realm of possibilities for women worldwide. Since then, multitudes of women began to emulate her courage and explore the world on their own terms. Flying made Amelia Earhart famous, vanishing made her legendary.

# Naked Native Frisbee

## Bruce Northam

*"It is an interesting question how far men would retain their relative rank if they were divested of their clothes."*—Thoreau, Walden 1854

WHAT IS IT ABOUT MODERN CULTURE that feels the need to impose a foreign language, way of life and religion on a people that sit seminude and smiling, living in communion deep in an impenetrable forest? The well-intended but genocidal policies of outsiders continue as western New Guinea's highland tribes succumb to alien coercion. One force driving this aborigine extermination is the frontiersman psychology. Sledding to the Poles, summiting Everest, rowing across the Atlantic? It's *all* been done. However, in an age when earthbound pioneer glory is virtually unattainable, I partook in a premiere—playing naked Frisbee with Stone Age, New Guinea natives. It was only a matter of time.

*West Papua* is the western half of equatorial New Guinea, a huge Melanesian island that is "Indonesia's" least populated territory. The awe-inspiring mountain ranges in the heart of the isle are permanently covered in snow and ice, while low-lying areas preserve tropical jungles. Torrential rivers plunge from the peaks into gorges and lush lowland rainforests, then out to coastal plains. Palm tree-lined beaches rim the island. Accessible only by air or a month of hacking through steamy jungle with a machete, the highlands are a spellbinding holdout for some of our last primeval rainforests, mountainscapes and undiscovered humankind. Even today, representatives of tribes unknown to the outside world periodically emerge from the forests. In 1990, a previously unidentified group surfaced. Ambassadors of the tribe, evidently shocked by what they saw, immediately disappeared again.

I spent a month trekking in these highlands, a zone overlooked by pop media. The rugged terrain secludes intimate *Dani* tribe villages, apportioned by stone fences, surrounded by neat sweet potato vine gardens, canals, and steep, terraced mountainsides. The dark-skinned, Afro-resembling, Melanesian aborigines still wear only penis gourds, an early model jock strap made from petrified yellow squash shells that are fitted over the genitalia and fastened skyward by thin strings tied around the waist. They are akin to wearing only a small, curved wiffleball bat sheath. The women wear only skimpy grass skirts.

My adventure was a blend of valley walking, high endurance climbing and harrowing cliff scaling. The walking routes are the natives' prolific trade trail system. Occasionally I *pulled over* to allow trios of bow-and-arrow toting hunters to pass. Mud abounds. You haven't officially trekked until you've had a boot sucked off by a foot of mud—never a concern for the barefoot *Dani*.

Rafts of trailblazer types have filtered in and out of these valleys since the Second World War. Few others had the fortune of befriending Ruuf, my *Dani* guide for the first leg of my trek. He led me, calm, wise and barefoot, leaping nimbly from slippery log to log. When I lost him, I tracked his mud prints. A long grass, mesh-like *billum* bag, slung around his forehead and draped across his back, contained sweet potatoes, a palm-leaf mat that doubled as a rain poncho (resembling a flight-worthy nun's habit), compressed tobacco, leaves for rolling cigarettes and a small bag of salt. His primordial briefcase.

Unsuspected downpours are common. One monsoon shower was especially enlightening. Betrayed by flooded boots and soaked by sweat inside my rain gear, I caught Ruuf smiling under his temporal teepee, not even a drop of water on his petrified squash. Pausing there in the downpour, I contemplated my departure from the essential laws of human survival. Darwinian perfection and a mail order misfit; a defeated poster child of Western survival gear. I was seduced into surrendering to my innermost nomadic calling—the contents of my backpack later transformed to gifts. Luxuries are often not only dispensable, but hindrances.

En route, we encountered twenty local men who were resting on a protruding bluff overlooking a terraced valley and the thundering Baliem River, which exits the uplands through an extensive and spectacular gorge system emerging in the south coast lowlands. The barefoot party was hauling supplies to their village thirty miles away. Suddenly, they broke into three-part harmony acappella, an ancestral call to unite and energize the group. Their simple, spirit-lifting chant reminded me of the feeling you get when a bird hops over and sits by you in the forest—date and time momentarily evaporate. Sublime.

Ruuf and I shared many bowls of rice. We nibbled small fingerfulls, caveman like, and peered about the forest. I heard birdcalls, Ruuf heard food. I showed him a photo of my girlfriend. Mixing pantomime with intonation, I inquired:

Have you ever seen the sea? "No," he answered.

What is your favorite food? "... Sweet Potatoes."

What do you dream about? He glanced down at the photo of my blonde girlfriend and grinned wide.

Archetypal humor.

I imagined a rhyme he might sing: One potato, two potato, three potato, four, leave the blonde here and continue your tour.

People usually are more complex than an initial impression may convey. Frequently, one of the first questions upon meeting someone is "What do you do?" for "what you do" is often misconstrued as who you are. How would Ruuf answer this question? We may never know. The man for all seasons and I parted with a final exemplar prehistoric handshake, lasting a minute, graduating to a bicepshake and adjourning with a condoning nod. I headed for a nap in a village dwelling and he ran off, barefoot and naked, into the jungle.

* * *

Historical documents suggest that a Greek scholar in the second century BC created the first earth globe. Over the next millennium the blank areas of the globe shrank as explorers charted the seas and made their way into the interior of continents. Today, there are few unmapped patches left—interior expanses of the world's second largest island, New Guinea's highlands, remain unmapped at the dawn of the 21st century. This dominion of startling contrasts was initially claimed by the Dutch in the mid-1800s as part of their Spice Island empire, but by 1940 they had not explored further inland than the coastal plains—the uplands were considered wilderness too harsh for habitation. In 1605, south coast lowland tribesman ate the first "out-of-towner," Dutch ship captain William Janz.

These upland tropic natives got their first glimpse of an outsider in 1938 when an American pilot, searching for possible World War II airfield sites, flew over the 5,000-foot high Grand Baliem Valley. The pilot was astonished to "discover" a densely populated area inhabited by agrarian tribes. Further examination found that these virtually nude people were engaged in constant tribal fighting. Many tribes' people were fierce headhunters and cannibals. Time remained irrelevant there, however, until a Dutch missionary settled in the valley in 1953.

In 1961, the Harvard Peabody Museum sponsored a major expedition to the Baliem Valley to document this Neolithic culture in its pristine state. Michael Rockefeller, who was part of the expedition, mysteriously disappeared after he chose to stay an extra season. Rumors spread quickly that Rockefeller had either drowned or was gobbled up by alligators or worse, by cannibals. His disappearance remains a mystery.

The 1970s and 80s saw a resurgence of missionary and foreign government activity; the vaporization of aboriginal hideouts, and consequently their innocence, accelerated. Today, uncontaminated indigenous culture hangs on in the remote valleys that are far removed from the rapidly westernizing Baliem Valley town of Wamena.

Indonesian officials, who view the wearing of clothes as measure of progress, have failed in getting all of the inhabitants of the *wild east* to support "Operation Penis Gourd," designed to get them out of their traditional getup and into Western clothing. Gourds and grass skirts have not yet given way to clothes for natives older than fifty years. The life expectancy in the region is 60 years. When these seniors pass on, this sartorial tradition and much of their old way of living will be history. In and around Wamena most native youngsters wear clothes.

Many men and women—especially converts to Christianity—have abandoned the traditional clothing for shorts and skirts, which are expensive to buy. The Indonesian Rupee has devalued their homespun currency, the cowrie shell, into oblivion. One consequence is that communities don torn, soiled clothing. Once "clean" in traditional garb, they now resemble other impoverished, "Third World" environs.

It's difficult to process the rugged, amazing beauty of these Neolithic Melanesians who discarded stone axes for steel in the mid-1900s. They remain primitive, hunting and gathering like our early ancestors, spending their days as deliberately as nature. They live communally in small isolated valleys. Radiant and clever, they do wonders with cooked sweet potatoes and spinach, which becomes the staple of trekkers who don't carry in enough dried or canned foods. When was the last time *you* speared dinner?

Traditionally, men fought battles and guarded the women while they worked. The small, wiry women still do most of the chores: raising the children, pigs and sweet potatoes—often lugging up to 80 lbs. of potatoes, and a baby, for miles up and down steep mountain trails. Women bear the brunt of the fieldwork while the men generally walk around, chat, pose for photos and smoke cigarettes. Intrepid archetypes indeed! The men also tend the squash-to-be-gourds, which they train to grow according to the shape of the manhood sheath they fancy.

They live in tidy, wood-thatched, grass-domed huts called honays. Men and women sleep and pass time in separate two-story huts. I was permitted to sleep, and reflect, in honays after receiving consent from a village chief. A whole, empty eggshell atop the roof indicates that there is a sick person inside. Certain bungalows are the privilege of men who've established themselves as warriors. A tad rustic, if you focus on the fleas and mice, these alpha-male sanctuaries are fertile pastures for the imagination—all around hang superstitiously invested shrunken animal heads, spears, weaponry, and charms.

*Dani* converse in very soft tones, if they speak at all. There we sat in a circle, puffing clove cigarettes and noshing on soft, warm sweet potatoes enveloped in dimly lit smoke, illuminated only by a well-tended fire. A serene, Cannabis euphoria was obtained by inhaling tobacco as deeply as the boys. Knee-deep in nomadic cache, I accepted the silence as meditation, in a corner of the world where safety pins were once fair trade for a shrunken human head. Reigning thought in my mind during the interlude: Einstein prophesied that he wasn't sure about the outcome of a third world war, but asserted that the fourth world war would be fought with sticks and stones. Surely, these vanguards would

**317**

endure, in spite of New World insistence on their obligatory umbilical attachment to the international moneyline.

Pigs are central to a man's economic and social status. Their other primary concern, wives, can be purchased with pigs (hog size matters, the bigger the better). One semi-functional contribution of the Indonesian government to the West Papuan people is the construction of bleak, corrugated tin roof residences. These structures are unlike anything you'd find in a traditional village. I met a few countrymen who awarded these clime-inefficient buildings to their pigs and built traditional huts nearby for themselves.

Safety pins remain a prevailing souvenir trade item. They have become their all-in-one toolbox: surgical implement, fishhook, necklace ornament, wood etcher, earring and so on. Velcro is also making a splash. A visitor probably won't be able to haul home a pig as a souvenir and bows and arrows aren't yet for sale beyond the tourist zones. Purchasing six-foot-long arrows was one task, getting them through airport security and onto eight different connecting US-bound planes was another—made smuggling home a custom-fit gourd seem simple.

I had a day in church. A racquetball-court sized wooden cabin with a corrugated tin roof, packed with quasi-clad *worshipers*. My view from the rear of the cabin: women and young girls on the left, men and boys on the right. A lonely, dead-battery clock loomed above a makeshift wood box altar—behind it the rambling missionary preacher, the only other person wearing clothes. Seated beside me was a man wearing only his beige gourd, a band of greasy chicken feathers on his head, and a clove cigarette stored in his large earlobe pierce. Patiently waiting to interact with the preacher, he inserted a quarter-moon-shaped pig bone into his pierced nasal septum. When their discussion began, everyone else listened intently, the women sitting with their net-like *billum* bags slung around their heads, bulging with provisions and babies. An unsympathetic gatekeeper declined to let people leave before the service concluded.

During prayer, all eyes are closed and heads lowered. They cover both eyes with one hand during prayers in fear of going blind. First came the peek-a-boo glances at the peculiar white man, then the restrained library chuckling. When the service ended the women rushed past me nervously to exit the church, their handshakes missing digits. The little girls were absolutely shocked by my presence. Then, someone broke out a guitar and another ceremony emanated from the rear of the shrine.

I learned that the older women cut off one or several finger joints as part of cremation ceremony when someone in their immediate family passes on, usually a male relative. Some women I met were missing most of their fingers. Severing a corner of the earlobe is the corresponding practice for men. Once common, this fading custom lingers despite the reproach of outsiders.

**318**

In *Walden*, Thoreau speaks of a "realometer," a raw, instinctive gauge to detect our individual certainty. Regularly, my realometer was pinned to the maximum. Likewise, foreign visitors can beguile and astonish the natives. Icebreakers range from charitable food and medicine donation to my contribution: a Frisbee. They were riveted by this exciting, simple aircraft that employs the basic principles of physics—dandy pie-tin cum UFO.

The flying saucer captured their imagination and made them bellylaugh. Initially, I was concerned that by introducing this game, I was further adding to the ruination of a traditional way of life that deserved to be preserved. But, Western influence is on the rise and no doubt there to stay. A Frisbee is harmless, and they really enjoyed hurling it. Though my first instinct went against introducing a non-neutral item into their culture, unanimous child happiness cemented the verdict. And it isn't difficult for them to replicate a disc using preexisting items—their rattan "place mats," we discovered, also flew.

A neon-blue flying disc landed in the primeval frontier and they rejoiced wildly over it. While other tradition-defying forces impose religion and outlander value, I tossed in my Sputnik. Upon entering a small village, I'd stroll into an open area, usually the courtyard in the midst of the honay complex, and spin the disc so it hovered and descended gradually into the waiting huddle. Some ran to it, some ran from it and kept on running. Perhaps the biggest single event to hit these villages since the first explorer donated matches. Now that's *ultimate* Frisbee. The New Guinea natives, having developed for millennia in isolation, have many unique traits including a hunting talent for throwing and launching spears. Straightaway, many of the younger flying disc converts advanced from having never seen a disc to being able to wing it 50 yards—using unconventional hand techniques.

I played sort of nude, too. At first my gourd was a discomfiture; some of us wage a continuing struggle against fashion. The string tied around my waist failed to hold up the hardened vegetable case that kept fumbling downward, and it itched. I didn't like sprinting barefoot across rocky fields and I was paranoid about injuring my scrotum. I concluded that some of them intentionally tossed the Frisbee astray so I'd have to run for it. They laughed at that too.

\* \* \*

Although Indonesia annexed the area in 1963, the take-over has not been universally accepted by native Papuans and discontent prevails in certain areas. Indonesians call their former Dutch territory by a different name, Irian Jaya. Indonesia "owns" West Papua, though the highlanders have little in common with western Indonesians and the rest of the world—except that they love their families and savor tobacco smoke.

The *Dani*, former cannibals, must now be the most gentle and hospitable people on earth. Their perpetual smiles are an unheard ripple. Modern sorcery and witchcraft, such as mining, deforestation, government intrusion, and insensitive tourism threaten one of the richest *civilizations* and biomasses on the planet. The Baliem Valley, one of the few places on earth where the human agrarian and architectural touch enhanced nature, is now importing satellite dishes. Fortunately, some tribes continue to resist contact with the outside world, maintaining a way of life where so-called "literacy" is non-existent and unnecessary.

Furthermore, the Indonesian government judges that the indigenous people don't have a right to lay claim to land that's not being "used." Evidently, farming, hunting and gathering doesn't rank. While Irian Jaya's mineral and oil resources are exploited, the bleaching of native tradition is compounded. Many villages can now be accessed by road or prop plane. These evils are exacerbated by an imposing influx of Indonesians coming from other islands as part of the massive transmigration project, similar to China's resolve to water down Tibetan culture.

Let the final refuge be. Thoreau suggested that a man is rich in proportion to the number of things he can afford to let alone. May the mountain people give one more rallying cry for their indigenous, environmentally gracious and wondrous ways. Our *real* crown jewel is fading. Stuck in between two worlds, lacking economic resources, they can neither advance nor go back. The original inhabitants of New Guinea don't need petrochemicals, the hammering corruption of an alien government, religious missions or environmental exploitation. Though, in a surge of serendipity, they adopted one exegesis of the times—flying plastic. All this for a culture that doesn't bother to keep track of their age.

\* \* \*

It will be some time before Frisbees rival the importance of pigs in this quiet corner of the world. Near the end of my sojourn back in time, I entered a village and tossed the flying disc into another curious horde. The village chief had difficulty catching, throwing and comprehending it, as did some of the other elders. His discontent with the game grew when the disobedient aircraft drifted into the pigpen, spooking the priceless swine. The chief abruptly disappeared into the men's honay.

The sun was settling and the Frisbee fanfare winding down when the chief reappeared. Strutting erect, bows and arrows slung across his back, he paused in the center of the village and drew an arrow. Focusing, he aimed skyward at the hovering disc. A second later the Frisbee's heart was punctured. Crippled, it wobbled to earth. Justice. My realometer flared. Game over—the chief retrieved the impaled UFO and retired into his hut.

A valley wind whistled through my gourd.

# Interview With a Wanderer

## Basil Franklin

*From a perpetual traveler's point of view, answers come easy.*

THIS ENDURING WORLD TRAVELER supports his crusades by piloting a horse-drawn carriage around Manhattan's Central Park. Twenty-five years living out of backpacks, he rarely parks for longer than a season. When you put Basil on paper, color drains like a dying trout. To steal a few excerpts from a single act is to seduce Michelle Pfieffer with your pants on. Roaming is his life. —interview by Michael Pinkus

**Q.** Do you miss being young?

A child can turn an empty lot into a jungle, a droopy tree into a forest or a bed sheet into a Sunday morning fort. If snow fell you packed it, when leaves fell you picked colored ones. I remember an attraction to mud, avoiding concrete unless at school and balancing on anything that looked like it needed it. Climbing along the length of a rusty golf course fence became a Himalayan knife-ridge. I still think and live this way.

**Q.** Reflect on a surreal experience.

Warm organs hauled from a deer's chest diced with coriander and garlic. It's bad manners to refuse wedding food from a Lisu hilltribe family in Northern Thailand.

**Q.** How is one seized by wanderlust?

What you're experiencing is basically a genetic echo—if you recline in cool moss early on, you want to lie down again. Curiosity and the attention span of a common house fly led me onto America's highways hitching in the 1970's when trust prevailed. A cardboard PLEASE sign helped, and hiking 1,500 miles on the Appalachian Trail really flipped back my blinders.

Defined: A strong or irresistible impulse to travel.

**Q.** Are you in touch with nature?

Humans are part of nature. I'm a street anthropologist who believes that we all fit into different tribes, but drifting is tolerated. There you are in Burma's outback ... you feel heat on your neck, the tribe sends a scout to check out the backpacker—it's raining and they know it.

Nature touched me once ... hopping freight trains, I ended up in Jasper, Canada. Slept on the edge of town with a beer buzz, forgot to hang my pack. Rustling in high grass, an oncoming black bear ignored my territorial yelps. Lying frozen, he sniffed my sleeping bag and then nudged me from head to toe. He tore apart my pack, wolfed my Kool-Aid and ½ a loaf of French bread, then wobbled on.

**Q.** How do "politics" affect world travel?

Lightning bug sparks have caused prairie fires, bad breath has killed cactus and politicians really do care.

Currencies, like moods, inflate and deflate.

**Q.** How does a carriage driver hold someone's attention?

Remember you're competing with TV. A pond without an inlet or an outlet dies. Cut to the chase.

**Q.** Why is TV so popular?

You can't have sex all the time.

**Q.** If you could be anybody, who?

A crossbreed of John Muir, Jack Kerouac and Wilt Chamberlain.

**Q.** What does adventure mean to you?

Getting lost and following it ... My Dad instilled a keen sense of escapading. A teacher with a romantic imagination and plenty of vacation time, he loved setting out on aimless quests. Long ago, he coined a term: Booming—Intuitive, blind adventure—commonly on dirt roads that disappear into deer trails. Whimsical walking.

**Q.** And your Mom?

Mother Theresa in plain clothes.

**Q.** What was your wildest time warp?

Living (here) in a civilized society that impounds their elders into nursing homes?

**Q.** What do you do to overcome language barriers and break the ice in distant lands?

Pantomime. Forsake some of your ingrained reality and be open to people who aren't racing on a hamster wheel. Get creative. Occasionally, I imitate animals. Trumpet like an elephant, caw like a raven, clap feet and bark like a seal and you've got a connection (with the kids at least). Humor lubricates the universe.

**Q.** What's the downside of a nomadic lifestyle?

A stimulus junkie always wants more. Higher peaks, more primitive tribes and one more off-limits, spooky nightspot. *That's* when its time for another ten-day silent meditation retreat, *or* a drive down to Central America.

My Peter Pan never left, and we still hang out.

**Q.** What else?

Check out this world before the next. This isn't a rehearsal.

(Suddenly, Basil was distracted by something else.)

# Inquiring Emperors Want to Know

## Brad Olsen

*Alexander the Great was the youngest and most successful military leader in the ancient world. Some exploits were more challenging than others—such as his dialogue with the Brahmins of India.*

HISTORICALLY, TRAVELING ABROAD WAS NECESSITATED BY WAR. During the centuries of "kill or be killed," travel was a most dangerous undertaking. While most who participated did not choose their fate, some young men eagerly enlisted and found their adventure in danger and conquest. Conversely, a select few took the opportunity to seek the wisdom of great masters en route. Those who overcame their fear of strangers were left seeking the highest enlightenment this world had to offer. For them, travel was a wisdom quest. One such quest defines 'epic.'

Alexander the Great (356-323 B.C.), the young general from Macedonia, intensely sought the wisdom of enlightened masters during one of the most extraordinary military careers in history. By the time he was 25, he had conquered Greece, Turkey, Syria and Egypt. In control of the eastern Mediterranean coast, Alexander next renewed his assault on Persia, crushing Darius' army in a series of impressive victories. With his old foe finally eliminated, Alexander again turned his attention east and crossed the Indus River into India. There his army met fierce opposition—intimidated by the bizarre spectacle of defenders riding upon armored elephants. The army refused to proceed any further east against India's highly advanced civilization. Moreover, the Greek army resented Alexander's attitude toward the conquered Asians—for he insisted on treating them as equals, not subjects.

Tutored in childhood by Aristotle, Alexander developed a keen interest in philosophy, literature and the natural sciences. His uncommon intelligence and astuteness led him to seek out all the great minds in his newly acquired empire. While encamped in Taxila (present-day Pakistan), Alexander called on a number of Brahmin ascetics noted for their adept skill in answering philosophical questions with pithy wisdom. Alexander asked all the questions, which, along with the replies, were recorded at the time by the historian Plutarch:

"Which be more numerous, the living or the dead?"

"The living, for the dead are not."

"Which breeds the larger animals, the sea or the land?"

"The land, for the sea is only a part of the land."

"Which is the cleverest of beasts?"

"That one with which man is not yet acquainted." (Man fears the unknown.)

"Which existed first, the day or the night?"

"The day was first by one day." Upon this reply, Alexander feigned surprise. The Brahmin added: "Impossible questions require impossible answers."

"How best may a man make himself beloved?"

"A man will be beloved if, possessed with great power, he still does not make himself feared."

"How may a man become a god?" (From this question, it is apparent that the "Son of Zeus" had an occasional doubt that he had already attained perfection.)

"By doing that which it is impossible for a man to do."

"Which is stronger, life or death?"

"Life, because it bears so many evils."

So impressed with the wisdom of the Brahmins, Alexander succeeded in finding a mentor in India, a yogi named "Kalanos" by the Greeks. The sage accompanied Alexander to Persia, where on a stated day, Kalanos gave up his body by entering a funeral pyre in full view of the entire Macedonian army. Historians record the astonishment of the soldiers who observed the elderly man never once showing fear of pain or death, nor moving from his position as he was consumed by the inferno. Before his cremation, Kalanos lovingly embraced many of his close companions, but had refrained from bidding farewell to Alexander. The Hindu Brahmin merely remarked to his pupil:

"I shall see you later in Babylon."

Alexander left Persia and a year later, died in Babylon a week short of his 33rd birthday. The prophecy had been the Indian guru's way of saying he would be with Alexander in this life, and in death.

# Bush Tucker

## Larry Habegger

*Deep in the Australian outback, nutriment abounds.*

WHEN WE GOT TO THE AIRBOAT clouds darkened the sky. Max Davidson, ex-farmer, longtime bushman, buffalo hunter, and now our guide, surprised us all by firing up the engine and blasting us with water, leaves, and a wide grin. We laughed at his impish delight, then helped get the boat into the water to explore the billibong in this isolated region in northern Australia known as Arnhemland.

Rain started to fall. By the time we headed up the channel it was pouring. We pulled rain jackets around us and tied on hats. Already we could see the water was rising; since yesterday it had come up a couple of feet and we had little trouble getting through the stretch that had clutched at us the day before. We hadn't been on the water more than a few minutes when the storm broke, the rain falling in sheets, lashing the water, the boat, all of us exposed on that silver sheet of billibong. Rain jackets were worthless. We were soaked to the skin. And then Max pulled up under a dense canopy of mangroves and shouted above the roar of the engine, "Do you want to hold up for a while?"

"Why?" I laughed. "Makes no difference to me."

"Can't get wetter than we are," he yelled, and off we went, Max's poncho blowing in the wind like a shroud.

It was like flying through a thunderstorm in an open plane. The air was water and we could hardly see. Forward, faster. Birds scattered, the boat raced over the water, across vegetation. I expected to hit something that would give us a jolt and send us flying into the jaws of hungry crocodiles, and once we almost did, sliding on soil and about to stop when the boat shook free to deeper water. Again we were off, running out from beneath the storm.

Gradually the rain let up and eventually stopped. Now we had a chance to look at the land, illuminated in soft, heavenly light. Max edged the boat aground so we could get out and rest awhile. Soaked as we were, boggy as it was, it was nice to be on land.

Max began digging in the earth with his bare hands to collect some "bush tucker," food the locals have been eating for millennia. Earlier he'd shown us many edible things, plants the Aboriginals and hunters like himself could survive on for weeks at a stretch.

A billygoat plum, a native tree with small fruit, has 50 percent more vitamin C than an orange. Green ants are lemon flavored (I know, because Max offered me some to sample and I could hardly say no), and Aboriginals take the whole nest, scrunch it up, mix it in water, and drink to treat colds. They eat the bloodwood nut, and use the flaky bark from the paperbark tree to build ground ovens for cooking almost anything. They start with hot rocks in a hole, add a layer of paperbark leaves, some water, more layers of leaves, then fish, wallaby, buffalo, whatever is the day's meal, and cover with paperbark layers. Termite mounds (conical eruptions of the red earth that sometimes reach over six feet tall) are used for medicinal purposes. The pitaradia acts as a decongestant; there's a grasshopper here that eats this plant and nothing else.

Paperbark is a mellelucca, the family that provides tea tree oil, and the bark grows in dozens of thin layers to become several inches thick. Early whites who came to Australia did paintings on paperbark, but the Aboriginals didn't. They used stringybark trees instead. Max was on his knees, digging with his huge hands. I was amazed at the breadth of his back, the taut muscles of his shoulders, the girth of his arms. He was as broad as he was tall, with a big belly that must have taken years of effort to acquire, a blondish-white beard trimmed close. I couldn't tell if he was 55 or 75, but clearly he was a strong fellow who was completely at home in this environment.

He was digging for legumes from the roots of grass, busting up the knotted earth. Clumps of grass flew this way, clots of soil flew that way. He dug, and dug, fingering the roots, rejecting them as too scrawny. He kept at it, oblivious of my calls to stop. "It's OK, Max, we don't need to taste them."

He seemed obsessed, as if starved, and I began to think he deposited us here just so he could get some of this bush food. He was up to his elbows now, hunched over the Earth as if reaching into the depths of its soul, reaching down as if to touch his own soul deep in the bowels of the land. He was grinning, glowing, completely consumed by this communion with the Earth.

And then he found them. He pulled up some skinny bulbs, knocked the dust off, put them in his mouth and chewed. He smiled, then looked at me, eyes bright.

"This one'll be sweet," he said, handing me a dusty clod. It wasn't. It was dry and starchy, something I wouldn't choose to eat but could live on if I had to. But to Max it was pure heaven, God's own repast, and he waited only an instant to make sure I approved before he dug for more.

Suddenly a wave of melancholy swept over me. Looking around at this extraordinary land of billibong and flood plain, I felt a deep emptiness, a loneliness rooted in my sense of having no connection to the land. Where was I from? What did I know of ancestry and Earth? Was this just a malady of my own, or symbolic of a malaise shared by all First Worlders? The kind of connection I lacked you can only get from working the earth, coming from it, knowing it as part of your spirit. The Aboriginals had it. Max had it. But looking at that amazing green land carved in squiggly patterns by rivers and streams and buffalo channels, I knew it was something I would never have, unless I changed my life completely. And maybe even that wouldn't be enough.

On the way back we took it slowly, enjoying the flight of magpie geese, the purple reflections of clouds on the water, the calm after the storm. Suddenly a huge splash erupted to our left and Max stopped the boat immediately. Waves two feet high coursed toward us from the single flick of a crocodile's tail, and the boat rocked as if crossing a wake. There wasn't a sound on the billibong until Max uttered, "Now that was a big crocodile."

The image of that crocodile we didn't see stayed with me. The power of that creature, so ominous, so primeval, so bent on satisfying its hunger and nothing more, reflected the frightening beauty of these wild places. There are things here we cannot fathom, powers that make a mockery of our civilized concerns, hidden creatures with clear meanings. We are at the top of the food chain, yes, but only by a thread.

# TRAMPLED UNDERFOOT

The elusion of boredom isn't
always a vacation.

*"You are never given a wish without also being given the power to
make it true. You may have to work for it, however."*

Richard Bach

# Curses! It's That Sinking Feeling

**Robert Ragaini**

*Never take a local curse lightly.*

THEY SAID THE CURSE HAD EXPIRED, but they lied. I should have guessed when I saw the boat. It was tied to a concrete dock with no fenders to protect it, a scratched, dented, and dirty mockery of the spanking new Gib Sea 92 pictured in the Pelangi Cruises brochure. When I opened the aft cabin the smell of diesel fuel was overpowering. "Normal," the charter company rep claimed since there was no blower to disperse the fumes.

At that moment I should have walked, but my experience with cruising sailboats was limited to a couple of week-long courses. He said it, I believed it. The final tip-off, though, was the name. One of the letters in Mahsuri Dua had fallen away. And Mahsuri was the woman who had cast the curse.

The story goes that in the not too distant Malaysian past a lady of royal pedigree was falsely accused of adultery. Justice being what it was in those days on the island of Langkawi, she was put to death. But as Mahsuri lay dying, she vented her wrath on everything and everybody on the island for seven generations to come, a sort of total coverage curse. I set foot on Langkawi at the beginning of the eighth generation.

My partner and I sailed off in the 31-foot yacht past dramatic monoliths of limestone jutting from the Andaman Sea, trailing a rubber dinghy that was visibly losing air. Our destination was a narrow channel between two cliffs recommended as a mooring by the same company faithful we shouldn't have listened to in the first place. Arriving at dusk, I went forward to drop anchor. What I found in the locker was a ridiculously oversize hunk of plow-shaped metal connected to yards of heavy chain covered in thick, slippery muck.

I let it out. And out—into what appeared to be a bottomless pit. "Wait a minute," I thought when the chain finally gave way to line, and put on the brakes just before the loose end slipped through my fingers. I cleated it fast, but now we were anchored with far too little scope in a place where we clearly should not have been. So I sat on the deck and began to haul. The slime formed a puddle around my haunches as the chain slipped through my hands and nothing, but nothing came up.

**332**

After futile attempts to improvise a winch, I found some rags for gripping the chain, sat on deck, braced my feet, and with much fervent cursing of my own, lugged the monster aboard. As I bent and strained, my wrath increased with each muscle-wrenching pull. This was meant to be fun, and fun it most definitely was not.

Around us, black velvet hills melted into a pitch black, starless sky. Motoring slowly, we felt our way along the coast, reading a depth finder that seemed to think all depths were .7 meters, and finally moored in the center of a small cove.

Exhausted but relieved to be safe, we were downing the last of our canned tuna when we heard a rumble of distant thunder. Soon the wind was whistling through the rigging and the Mahsuri Dua was tugging and tossing at the mooring like an angry dog on a leash.

On deck, clutching the mast and pelted with warm, heavy rain, we marveled at a sea alive with phosphorus. Crests of thousands of inky waves glowed in the dark, a violent procession of tumbling bands of light. Sheets of lightning strobe-lit the bay and until the storm passed we were transported to another galaxy, a fabulous other world.

Next morning all was serene. Except for my mood when I discovered the dinghy was deflated and the pump was broken. Back we sailed to Kua, Langkawi's main town, where we were promised a new dinghy "tomorrow."

Pelangi Cruises did indeed provide us with a "new" dinghy, one with a slower leak, and a pump that worked, so off we ventured once more. The aforementioned rep had taken our provisions to the boat and when I returned, said there was a great deal of oil below decks. This puzzled us. We'd used no cooking oil and the engine gauge read full. He meant, of course, the diesel fuel, but that didn't occur to us.

Mahsuri was speaking, but we weren't listening.

We sailed some, motored more—the winds were fickle at best—and in late afternoon ducked into a channel between two islands. As the lowering sun turned the hillsides to emerald and the sea to cobalt blue, we drifted into the midst of a dozen or more fishing skiffs containing families of men and straw-hatted women and tawny naked babies. It was as if an entire fishing village had gone out for a watery evening stroll.

We sailed through this magic assemblage trading smiles and waves, and turned the corner into another enchanted bay. Dropping anchor in the shallows we dove into the soothing warm sea and as the cares of the world washed away I thought, "This may not be heaven, but it's close enough."

Next morning we set off early, hoping to reach our lunch spot before the brutal sun fried us to a crisp. In a fresh breeze we turned west and beam

**333**

reached along Langkawi's northern coast.

All across the horizon fishing boats were strung like beads on a string, their bows upswept and delicate, unlike the thick prows of Western work boats. Close above us was Ko Ta Ru Tao, Thailand's southern-most island, and far ahead, enveloped in mist, the dim outline of mainland Malaysia.

The wind had been steadily dropping. I was in the bow in the shade of the Jenny when my friend decided to put on the motor. I heard it kick over, then catch with a strange racing sound. I was about to ask if something was wrong when I heard a bang and a shout: "My God, we're on fire!"

I turned and saw smoke rising from the cabin. Running aft I jumped below and grabbed the fire extinguisher, but not before seeing that the entire engine compartment and aft cabin were enveloped in flame. Now the smoke turned thick and black and in seconds the cabin was filled with the greasy, palpable and suffocating stuff. Jumping on deck, I discharged the fire extinguisher into the inferno to absolutely no effect and screamed, "Get into the dinghy!"

Moments later we were bobbing in a partially inflated raft without a paddle, watching the white, fiberglass sloop belching smoke and flame, already half consumed and turning a stomach-wrenching, bubbling black. We watched, dumb with shock, as the sails were eaten away, the mast toppled into the water, the hull burned like a floating funeral pyre.

After what seemed like an eternity, two fishing boats converged on us. The crew of one helped us aboard and hoisted our raft and as we looked on from a deck strewn with nets and little silver fish, played hoses on the flaming hulk.

Soon other boats arrived, each boat packed with excited humanity craning to take in the spectacle. At one point our rescuing skipper took out a passport and showed me that he was from Thailand. Then he brought us close to shore, set us adrift in our dinghy with a plank for a paddle and we made our way to land.

The rest is anticlimax—the tedium of police reports, the kindness of Malaysian officials and passing strangers, replacement of passports, credit cards, clothing, cameras, airplane tickets, the hundred and one items taken for granted until they are suddenly reduced to ashes. At long last, subdued and weary, we were more than ready to leave.

But as we stepped aboard our flight to Kuala Lumpur at the Langkawi airport I could swear I heard a low female chuckle rising from the jungle by the landing strip. "Goodbye, Mahsuri," I said under my breath. "I hope we were the final beneficiaries of your terrible curse." The plane banked as we flew over the island and I tried to see where the boat had gone down. "Or perhaps they got it wrong," I thought. "Not seven generations, but seven times seven."

# A or B

**Andrew Bill**

*The departure of health can create lucid revelations.*

SURELY I AM MORE THAN THIS? A winter shelter for the mules I can hear braying and scraping in the yard outside. This window, a crude lattice of sticks through which the mountain light knifes, alive with straw dust. These flies that drop to drink my sweat, then lift in a swirling veil, their hum steady like the engine of a boat at night. This body, pathetic and yellow on a makeshift bed.

To make the minutes go by, I let the poem wash through my mind, the words trickling by in a steady stream. I don't need to read them anymore. Just shaping the first line lets all the rest pour into place as if there is nowhere else for them to go.

> *In Xanadu did Kubla Khan*
>
> *His stately pleasure dome decree*
>
> *Where Alm the sacred river ran*
>
> *Down caverns measureless to man*
>
> *Down to a sunless sea.*

And I wait for Pemba to come, to tell me whether I will live or die. A or B?

\* \* \*

Eighteen months ago I was someone so different from the body on the bed. So changed that, even if he came into the room right now at the height of my loneliness, I would have nothing to say. Thousands of miles of road and lifetimes of experience have created an impassable gulf between me and the 25-year-old that left home—a Londoner with a family, a solid job at *Reader's Digest*, seven business suits and one future.

Even five days ago, I was someone else. Filled with beauty, I was strength. After traveling all those miles, I had reached a plateau where movement was stillness, where the present was all that mattered. If it was not for a sweat-stained passport bearing the stamps of Australia, Indonesia, Malaysia, Thailand, Burma and Nepal, my near past might easily have belonged to another man.

In moments of lucidity, that come in the slack between tides of fever, I replay the details of the previous weeks. Leaving Katmandu on the six-hour bus ride to Pokhara in Central Nepal. Hiking out of town along a white chalky road, then up into the foothills, climbing switch backs and skirting valleys a mile deep. Each day had brought the big peaks closer until they crowded the foreground and scale dissolved. Lying on my back in the darkness of the stable, I can see the black mass of Machhapuchhare looming within arms length, its fish-tail summit cutting out the afternoon sun with the finality of an eclipse.

Each night, exhausted as much by the beauty as the climb, I had stopped at a *bhatti*, a basic Nepalese inn of mud-bricks and staves. Over a dinner of *dal bhat* (lentil soup over rice) and *chiyaa* (tea) I had talked with fellow hikers, sat outside exploring the wide-open spaces of meditation, or watched the waves of dusk melt away the mountains. I remember how invincible I felt, leaving the smoky interiors in the mornings, shrugging the pack on to my back and walking off through a world divided equally into sunlight and shadows. My legs were rock, my mind as clear and cool as one of the mountain streams where I bathed and filled my bottles.

And I remember reaching the end of the trail: Deuthali, the Sanctuary. Leaving Machhapuchhare Base Camp two hours before first light, trudging upwards in the thin air to reach the top in time for sunrise and return to 12,000 feet before the snows melted in the morning sun. In my mind I see clearly the first rays making sense of the darkness, outlining the rim, then giving definition and depth to a vast amphitheater of mountains serrated with the peaks of Tharpu, Singu, Hiunchuli and, in the north-west, the sheer face of Annapurna climbing into the clouds.

*It was a miracle of rare device*
*A sunny pleasure-dome with caves of ice*

As the morning grew, this great world of rock and snow, the snow cones silhouetted against a now blazing sky, had become more unworldly, more divine with each increment of light. Looking back now through the blurry lens of fever, I am sure it was the sheer weight of beauty that did me in. During those 30 minutes in the Sanctuary, it had filled my body; displacing strength.

From that point onward, I had felt the shadow gaining ground, jostling to overtake. Three days later, half way back to Pokhara, I had walked on through dusk, long passed the usual stopping hour, anxious not to be caught in the open of the ranges. Giddy, I had somehow lost the main path and stumbled down the wrong side of a hill as the first blanket of fever fell on. Before long it had dragged me to the earth, my skin on fire, a pulse throbbing in every finger. And there I had stayed unable to move for long desperate hours, straining into consciousness, falling into darkness.

*... And from this chasm, with ceaseless turmoil seethin,*
*As if this earth in fast thick pants were breathing ...*

Pemba had found me and carried me back to his stable draped over the back of a mule. He had laid a blanket on the straw, and tried repeatedly to give me food. But in the five days since then I have been unable to hold even a mouthful of rice. A sip of tea sends my body heaving. The fever comes to smother me every night, searing the skin, cracking the lips and throat. When the chills come; I burrow deep.

One day, thinking perhaps by the way the words sit on the page that it's a prayer, he left a page ripped from a book of poetry dropped no doubt by some other trekker. Without anyone to talk to or anything else to read, I have spent hours forcing sense from the tangle of images in Coleridge's poem.

Another day a local doctor dropped by on his weekly round of the hill villages, and told me what I already knew. I have Hepatitis. Even by his callous appraisal, it's a bad case. Temperature of 105; urine the color of cola; skin, yellow and translucent; hair wispy and lifeless; eyes aglow like yellow suns. My liver protrudes under clearly defined ribs. Standing on his portable scale I find I have lost 30 lbs. Talking is an effort. Walking is out of the question.

The only question is A or B? Hepatitis A is a miserable disease, but passes sooner or later without any ill effects. B is totally different, viral and much worse, leading to chronic liver disease, cirrhosis and death. The liver simply refuses either to work or regenerate and the body ceases its effectiveness until ... until ... nothing.

The thought of what my present had become—dying alone, here in this shelter, on this bed, by this window—made me sob uncontrollably. Tears as hot as molten beads. The doctor looked on impassively; he had seen too much misery to be swayed by one more case. He will test my blood back in the clinic in Pokhara and, in a few days, send word.

I hear Pemba approaching long before the plank door creaks open and releases its wave of blinding light. I watch his face as he walks over to where I lie, sits down on the ground near my head and, with his hands pressed together in greeting, whispers *namaste*.

I hoist myself up on to one arm. "The doctor?"

He nods. The flies buzz more loudly overhead and a mule rubs against a wall, its collar of bells jingling. "I'm sorry," is all he says.

> *And all should cry, Beware! Beware!*
> *His flashing eyes, his floating hair!*
> *Weave a circle round him thrice,*
> *And close thine eyes with holy dread,*
> *For he on honey-dew hath fed*
> *And drunk the milk of Paradise.*

# Transcontinental

## Lynn Cothern

*Robert Louis Stevenson once said, "I travel for travel's sake. The great affair is to move." Sometimes the rest is a blur.*

A COWGIRL ESCAPES EAST USING DEADMAN'S CORNER CUT-OFF. A woman drives out of Tremonton, Brigham City, Devil's Slide, Utah; into Green River, Rock Springs, Bitter Creek, Wyoming; and Kearney, Nebraska. Years or miles ago a whitewater tower proclaimed Buhl—THE TROUT CAPITAL OF THE WORLD. Now a rear view of Idaho trails behind the car.

Tonight in the Buffalo Motel she cuts her hair with fingernail scissors, drinks gin from a plastic cup. The TV screen hums blue in the darkness while a celluloid cowboy on a bucking bronc tames the cringing wilderness with a gun, a knife, a whip, plunges down a river of no return on a raft, red-painted whiteskins on the warpath, the cavalry in hot pursuit. A strapping blonde swoons and the hero lays his hands on her breasts, mouths her with a savage kiss. She is limp.

There are no children left behind.

*   *   *

AT&T marks their words, four wheels their miles. She says *I love you* from Nedra's Chevron in Tremonton, Utah; *I love you* from the Rodeo Pit Stops 20 miles west of Laramie. He will say the words *when are you coming back* in Coralville, Iowa, one more bit of flesh the emigrant leaves on the barbwire prongs behind her.

This woman lies on the bed and remembers the child she left behind, listens to another woman moan on the other side of the world. Water runs, the toothbrush tapping the sink from behind the wallboard is the sound of a child's tennis shoes, snow-sodden, in the drive outside the house, is the smell of the spring rain through the open hospital window the February night he was born. A motherless child dreamed of place loosened and let go.

Tomorrow she'll cross the Mississippi, stash the .22 in the glove compartment and see Spring Valley, Illinois—A GREAT ALL-AMERICAN CITY; Chicago—20 ACRES FULLY PAVED; and the car ahead—There Aren't Enough Homes for Them All—stared at by a dog. She's crossing frontiers. Monroe, Indiana's silos spike a darkening sky. Washington, Richmond, Baltimore—eastern cities lie unsuspecting like red-eyed jack-rabbits in the headlights.

**338**

# The Bus Plunge Highway

**Tom Miller**

*Rules of the road in Ecuador's high country.*

To REACH THE TOWN OF FEBRES CORDERO I took a bus to Guayaquil—at 1.6 million, the country's most populous city. The 150-mile ride started smoothly despite my apprehension. Bus rides through Latin America have always induced fear in me, brought on by years of reading one-paragraph bus-plunge stories used by newspapers in the States as fillers on the foreign-news page. The datelines change, but the headlines always include the words bus plunge, as in 12 DIE IN SRI LANKA BUS PLUNGE, or CHILEAN BUS PLUNGE KILLS 31. "We can count on one every couple of days or so," an editor at *The New York Times* once told me. "They're always ready when we need them." Never more than two sentences long, a standard bus-plunge piece will usually include the number feared dead, the identity of any group on board—a soccer team, church choir, or school bus—and the distance of the plunge from the capital city. The words ravine and gorge pop up often. Most of the stories come from Third World countries, the victims comprising just a fraction of the faceless brown-skinned masses. "A hundred Pakistanis going off a mountain in a bus make less of a story than three Englishmen drowning in the Thames," noted foreign correspondent Mort Rosenblum in *Coups & Earthquakes.* Is there a news service that does nothing but supply daily papers with bus-plunge stories? Peru and India seem to generate the most coverage; perhaps the wire services have more stringers in the Andes and Himalayas than anywhere else.

If an Ecuadorian bus driver survives a plunge fatal to others, according to Moritz Thomsen in *Living Poor*, "he immediately goes into hiding in some distant part of the country so that the bereaved can't even up the score. There are rumors of whole villages down in the far reaches of the Amazon basin populated almost entirely by bus drivers. This is probably apocryphal ..."

If you anticipate a bus trip in Latin America, go through the following check-list prior to boarding:

* Look at the tires. If three or more of the six tires (most buses include two rear sets of two each) are totally bald, the probability of a bus plunge increases. Visible threads on the tires mean a blowout is imminent.

**339**

* Does the bus have at least one windshield wiper? Good. If it's on the driver's side, so much the better. Try to avoid buses whose windshields are so crowded with decals, statues, and pictures that the driver has only a postcard-sized hole through which to see the future. Shrines to saints, pious homilies, boastful bumper stickers, and religious trinkets do not reflect the safety of a bus. Jesus Christ and Ché Guevara are often worshiped on the same decal. This should give neither high hopes nor nagging suspicion.

* The driver's sobriety isn't a factor. The presence of his wife or girlfriend is. If she's along, she will usually sit immediately behind him, next to him, or on his lap. He will want to impress her with his daring at the wheel, but he will also go to great lengths not to injure her. If he has no girlfriend or wife, the chance of a gorge-dive increases.

* You can't check the bus for breaks. Once I asked a driver in Guatemala about the brakes on his bus. "Look," he said, "the bus is stopped, isn't it? Then the brakes must work."

* On intercity buses, seats are often assigned before boarding. Refuse the seat directly behind the driver or in the front right. If your ride takes place during the day, you'll be subjected to at least one heart-skip a minute as your bus casually passes a truck on an uphill blind curve or goes head-to-head with an oncoming bus. At night, the constant glare of approaching headlights will shine in your eyes. At any hour, the driver's makeshift radio speaker will dangle closer to your ears than you'd like.

* Always have your passport ready. Random military inspections take place when you least expect them. I once delayed a bus full of cross-country travelers for ten minutes a couple of miles outside Esmeraldas, on the Pacific Coast south of Colombia, while frantically searching first for my bag atop the bus, then my passport within the bag.

In defense of Latin-American buses: They go everywhere. *Everywhere.* No road is so dusty, bumpy, unpopulated, narrow, or obscure that a bus doesn't rumble down it at least once every twenty-four hours. The fare is very little—Cuenca to Guayaquil cost less than three dollars—and, barring plunges, they almost always reach their destination. If your window opens, you'll get a view of the countryside unmatched in painting or postcard. Your seatmate may be an aging *campesina* on her way home or a youthful Indian on his first trip to the big city. Dialects of Spanish and Quichua unknown to linguists float past you. Chickens, piglets, and children crowd the aisles or ride on top.

At Cuenca's *terminal terrestre*, the bus station, I had a choice of taking a regular bus or an *aerotaxi* to Guayaquil. The former travels slower, hence theoretically safer. The latter, a small twenty-four-seater, whizzes along far faster, has less leg room, and is more plunge-prone. I resisted the odds and took an *aerotaxi*.

The trip, five and a half hours long, begins at eighty-four hundred feet above sea level, climbs somewhat higher, and descends to a sea level straightaway for the final ninety minutes or so. The advantage of the drive toward Guayaquil is that the precipitous ravine usually falls off on the left side of the two-lane road; the disadvantage is that you're headed downhill most of the way. Guard railings, few and far between, relieved a bit of my fear, except when the downhill section was bent outward or was simply broken off. For the better part of the first hour we followed a cattle truck, which moved only slightly faster than its cargo could have managed on its own.

The cattle turned of at Azogues, and we pushed on deep into the province of Cañar. The temperature dropped. I looked out the left side onto the clouds surrounding peaks nearby and distant. The thin air above the clouds in the Andes gave the sunlight colors unknown below. Only occasionally did our driver attempt a suicide squeeze—overtaking someone around a blind curve—and we settled into a quiet passage. Crude signs advertised local cheeses. Small piles of *toquilla* straw lay on the ground near doorless houses where women sat in the entrances weaving Panama hats. Julio, the driver, knew all the potholes and bumps on that road and managed to hit every one. Pepe, his helper—the driver's assistant is almost always a younger brother, son, or nephew—fidgeted with the radio until he found a distant station whose static muffled a brass band. We passed Cañari Indians heading home; in front the father, directly behind him his wife, behind her a passel of kids, and bringing up the rear a burro and a goat. Each party in the procession was connected to the one behind by a rope tied around the midsection. A dog yipped alongside.

We descended into the thick of the clouds and Julio downshifted. The white line down the center of the curving two-lane road was his only guide; even the hood ornament had disappeared into the clouds. After five minutes he slowed further and then stopped. Pepe walked through the *aerotaxi* collecting money. I nudged Horacio next to me. "What's this for?"

"We're at the shrine," he replied. "Each driver stops at this shrine along the way and leaves some money. It's their way of asking God's blessings for a safe journey." Often the saints are next to a police checkpoint so that the driver can make two payoffs at once. Offering insurance money to some saint required a gargantuan leap of faith, but if it would assure us a trip free of bus plunge, I wanted in. I coughed up a few *sucres*.

Pepe trotted across the road to leave our money at the shrine when suddenly a half-dozen Indian faces appeared out of the clouds pressing against the windows. "*¡Choclos! ¡Choclos! ¡Diez cada uno!*" they were selling sweet corn cooked with onion, cheese, and egg for slightly more than ten cents each. Two barefoot Indian women in felt hats and thick mud-stained ponchos slipped onto the bus and walked up and down the aisle. "*¡Choclos! ¡Choclos! ¡Nueve cada uno!*"

**341**

The price had gone down some. Another vendor with a glazed look in her eyes and a baby in her arms rapped desperately on a window trying to get a passenger to open it. Her shrill voice seemed as distant as her eyes. Pepe returned, and the Indians withdrew into the Andean mist.

Bus drivers' assistants throughout Latin America display keen skills at hopping on and off moving buses, keeping track of which passenger is due how much change for his fare, pumping gas, climbing through a window to the roof to retrieve some freight before the bus stops, and changing blowouts. Pepe performed all these feats in the course of the run to Guayaquil, and excelled at hopping on the bus when it was already in second gear. Trotting apace of the bus, he first took a short skip on the ground to get the spring in his feet, then a short jump at a forty-five-degree angle calculated to land him on the first step while he grasped a metal bar next to the doorway. His motion appeared so fluid and effortless, he seemed to be simply stepping onto a bus in repose.

The right rear tire blew out on the southern edge of the town of Cañar. Julio pulled into an abandoned service station and Pepe had us back on the road within ten minutes. In more restful moments he sat on a makeshift seat between Julio and the door. The only job forbidden him was highway driving, and even then he was allowed to maneuver the bus around the terminals.

The ride down the western face of the Andes settled into a relatively peaceful journey once the tire was changed and the saint paid off. We went through long stretches where the only hint of life was an occasional *choza*, a straw thatched hut, set back from the road. Valleys with streams and rivers flowing toward the Pacific held small towns. Our descent to sea level was practically complete and we entered a different climate, province, and culture. Bribing the saint had worked; we had passes the bus-plunge zone safely.

The air hung heavier, more humid, and warmer. Roadside vegetation grew more lush. Thick grass grew right up to the roadside. Towns suddenly burst upon the highway—healthy, lively towns, active, jumping, noisy, uncaring. A church was just another building near the plaza, nothing more. Men and boys wore shorts, thongs, and torn tee shirts. Women and girls wore slacks or short, loose cotton dresses. Card tables were surrounded by men who looked like they'd sat there months on end encircled by a floating crowd of onlookers. Shot glasses of *puro* were constantly drained and refilled. Every structure was made of bamboo—split, dry, and aged. There was loud laughter, backslapping, gold-toothed grins, ass-pinching, life with few worries, and less money. We had encountered our first *costeños*—people who live in the coastal region. Julio raced to Guayaquil on a road studded with potholes bigger than our *aerotaxi*. The tropics had begun.

# Slides from a Greyhound Bus

## Christa Kirby

*... as the world turns from the perspective of a l o n g bus ride ...*

THE MORNING'S FIRST SUN
Jolts me out of slumber
Reminding me once again that
My eyes are aflame
My throat is parched
My back is convulsed
You are not with me
And I am still
      On a bus.

Through tinted windows
the landscape approaches
      and recedes
In here
the Parade is end
less

Curt Curtis who
Stud stutters—a
Me mechanic and
brag Braggart whose machismo
is 3 times
big bigger biggest
than his
actions.

    HOPE
a ripe grape in her purple coat
(and beacon of her namesake)
makes painstaking efforts to surround her flesh with her hands

and confine it to one seat
as she tells of a Ft. Bragg
boyfriend—her destination—
who may or may not be
in Saudi Arabia now.
Betsy
from the Midwest
whose rattling drone weaves
in        and        out
with my consciousness—
her beaded barrette
sweeps limp hair into a clump
            revealing
electric blue eyelids and
2 pink slabs of blush in
front of her ears.


Bert, the world's first pregnant man
Who embarked and then
Embarked: on a monomaniacal eating
Binge            His stop. (was Boise)


Cora
The lusty senior citizen
with her chameleon eyes
surveying at once above and
                        beside me;
seemingly harmless and mild-mannered
in waking life,
she becomes
Fiendishly flatulent during
(too, too frequent)
naps.


Vincent B. with his battered black briefcase &
unironed pants who will tell you his story
if you glance his way
through a mouthful of Chiclet teeth.

The nameless Shinto priest
(I would call him Yasuichi)
sports orange monk's garb and a
Patagonia stocking cap
—replete with tassel and strikingly incongruous—
Except for his penchant of
"Please pass,"
he clings tenuously to his rite of
Silence.

3 days and T H R E E   N I G H T S
have now passed
(or is it 40)
I am Noah
     On a bus.
The scenery shifts gears
(unlike the driver)
pastoral-urban:
Colorado-New York.
If I personally
never slept much
on This Journey,
My arms
    legs
     and ass
         certainly did.

The City greets me
with Jaws Agape
I step into the Night
  a-
  lone;
You are there where I was
I am here
where you're not.
where you're not
coming back
Again

# Fridge Over Troubled Waters

## Claudia Martin

*The fine line between death and the valor of strangers.*

I HAD LIVED ALONG THE DELAWARE RIVER ALL MY LIFE and thought I knew it well. But all of this changed on the night of July 3rd, some twenty-five years ago.

That summer I had taken a job as an arts and crafts counselor at a children's camp in the Catskill Mountains so I could be near my boyfriend who was then living on a farm outside of Syracuse, New York, less than a two-hour drive away. I got one day off every other week and I planned to spend them all with him.

My first day off started the evening before July 4th. I caught a ride with the handyman from the camp to the northbound on-ramp of Route 17, a meandering highway that parallels the Delaware River through the Catskills, then dog-legs due west towards Lake Erie.

I stood on the roadway's edge with my thumb prominently pointing northward, a study in calculated indifference to the passing traffic. In those days it was not unusual to see a girl hitchhiking alone, so I thought nothing of throwing my knapsack over my shoulder and hitting the highway. With no car and little money, I had become an old hand at traveling according to the rule of thumb: anyone in a VW van or Bug was probably okay, and even an adult was a good ride if you were willing to sit through a lecture on the dangers of hitchhiking.

Within a few minutes I was picked-up by someone I knew driving a red Bug. John was a teaching assistant at my university, and we had a nodding acquaintance. Someone I knew and a Bug: the omens were good. The first hour we spent chatting about this and that. He was going within five miles of my boyfriend's house and could give me a ride to the door. "Wow, good karma," I chanted.

As we approached the town of Hancock the sky became dense and black. There had been flashes of heat lightning for the previous twenty miles, but now great luminous veins of electricity were bulging in the sky around us followed instantly by booms of thunder that made the Bug shudder. Traffic had been light when we started, but now we were the only car on the road.

**346**

Within moments hail-filled raindrops began pelting the car, making it seem as if we had wandered into a war zone. Bullets of heavy liquid sprayed us from every direction. We rolled-up the windows and the windshield fogged-up. John continued driving while I wiped the glass. But the VW's puny windshield wipers, inadequate in the gentlest of showers, were bowing under the weight of this cloudburst.

John pulled off to the berm. The suddenness and intensity of the rain made us each certain it would end in a few minutes; it didn't. A half hour later and great sheets of windbourne rain were rocking the car ferociously. The gullies along the road's edge were over pouring onto the driving surface. Huge branches flew about battering the car, whipping through the air like crazed witches on broomsticks.

"I think the next exit is Deposit," John said. " I think we better get into a town and out of this car." I nodded vigorously, wondering where all that good karma had gone.

Driving slowly, warning lights flashing, John held the steering wheel tightly while I made little circles of visibility on the windshield with my hand. As we moved towards the exit the storm intensified. Power lines flailed about, loosened from their supports by the twisting winds. The thunder was non-stop. Its roaring entered my heart causing it to beat wildly.

"I know a little hotel and restaurant a few streets up, " John said. "Maybe we can get rooms there and leave early in the morning."

"I don't have money for a hotel," I cried.

"Don't worry," he responded, "let's just get there and get out of the car."

Deposit was an old logging town built into the steep slopes of wooded hills above the Delaware. The town was laced with tributaries and small canals that had been used a century before to send felled trees down to the river for transport. As we slowly drove through intersections water rushed down at us from these small channels which were now overflowing their banks.

We made it to one intersection that was filling with water, and then could go no further. Until that moment we had each forgotten the one ineluctable truth about VW Bugs: they float! Suddenly we were no longer in a car but in a seaworthy vessel, rising and sinking with the gray torrents that rushed down what had once been a street. Huge chunks of debris banged into the passenger door: pieces of fencing, metal trash cans, boxes, bricks, and bicycles. Anything not deeply rooted in the earth crashed into us.

Ahead of us some figures were waving flashlights. John rolled down the window just as a great wave smacked into us, drenching the interior of the car.

"Get out," a man's voice said. "Get out of that car now!"

**347**

John turned to me. "We'd better get out on my side." I nodded, hanging onto my small sack.

"The Canonsville Dam's been breached," the voice shouted. "Get out of the car."

There were four or five men leaning into the Volkswagen to prevent it from floating down the street. John got out without any problem, but I had to climb over the stick shift and with the car being rocked about I lost my balance and fell out head first.

I was sucked under the car, sucked into the water turned demon. I couldn't breathe. I was taking in water. My eyes were blinded with mud. My mouth filled with silt. I struggled to get my head out of the water. I was being banged into by pieces of backyard sheds and mailboxes, by front porches and chunks of trees. I heard people shouting, but couldn't tell what they were saying or where the voices were coming from. I was choking, sputtering with mud, drowning.

The noise of the water was deafening: a chorus of terror augmented by howls of thunder. I was being carried along in the rapid current towards the dead end of the street where I could just make out the shape of a low guardrail. It was my only hope of preventing myself from dropping hundreds of feet over the cliff to the rampaging river below. I would need to grab that railing.

A sudden undertow pulled me below the surface of the water. The Volkswagen sailed over me, rushed towards the street's end, and then over the guardrail. I bobbed to the surface. I was near enough now to reach out and try to grab the barrier. "Try and grab the guardrail," I told myself. I tried. I heard the awful smashing of metal and glass. I tried. I tried but couldn't reach the rail.

Something hit me. Hit me hard in the head. Did I lose consciousness? I lost all orientation; I was sputtering, gasping, taking in water, unable to catch my breath. I was pressed against something. The water rushed at me. I kicked myself upwards. I wiped my eyes and looked. It was white, this thing I was being pushed against was white and boxy. It was an old refrigerator that had become wedged against the guardrail. It was all that was preventing me from the same fate as John's car.

The refrigerator shifted. There was a moaning of metal. The guardrail was giving way. The faces of people I knew came to mind all at once: my parents and sister, my boyfriend, my friends. These images rushed faster than the water through my brain.

"I will never see them again," I thought.

Then I thought, "God, my mother would kill me if she knew where I was," and even as I thought this the ridiculousness of it made me laugh, and for some reason I raised my right hand straight into the air and someone grabbed it.

"Hold tight," a voice shouted. "Just hold tight." And I held onto the hand of this faceless man as I have never held onto anything before or since.

Another man's voice followed and I felt myself being carried in arms now, saved from the angry rage of muck and river water.

I must have blacked out because the next thing I remember is lying on the floor in a corner of the bar at the Deposit Hotel, raincoats and sweaters piled on top of me. I was caked in rank-smelling mud and shivering uncontrollably.

Someone with a warped sense of humor had pumped a bunch of quarters into the jukebox, for over and over again it played Simon and Garfunkel singing "Bridge Over Troubled Waters." Across the bar an old man was standing in the doorway shouting to the heavens, "Where's Noah when we need him? Where's Noah?" I laughed. I laughed for hours.

# Committed to Kalalau

## Sue Lebrecht

*Determination to reach a destination sometimes leads to a pot of gold.*

S O WE'RE SITTING IN THE TROPICAL FOREST IN THE NIGHT, buck naked under a canopy with rain streaming heavily on all sides and we hear this anxious holler of "Hello." We're upstream a half-hour hike from the ocean, three hours from the trailhead parking lot, and here in the pitch black is some guy on a trail slippery enough to create a new sport.

Andreas goes to investigate, putting on his shorts and taking the flashlight, leaving me with two last beers and the light of a flaming candle. Ahead in a clearing shines a full moon through the rain. Behind me clumps of long, thick bamboo shoots squeak against each other although there is no apparent wind. I lean to smell the fresh white ginger flower upright in an old wine bottle, a thoughtful welcoming to this site by who knows who.

I'm on the Kalalau Trail in Kauai, Hawaii at the first campsite area near Hanakapi'ai Beach. I met Andreas at the State Parks Office in Lihue while obtaining a camping permit for the trail and gave him a ride in my rented cherry-red Sunbird Convertible, roof down, tunes cranked.

We've got no clothes on because we just finished dipping in the stream; there's a great swimming hole at the end of an overgrown path leading downhill from the campsite. And because it's hot, and because he's German, my parents are German and nudity is quite natural among Europeans, and because, well, he didn't put his clothes back on and it seemed neat to sit naked and try and act natural.

I first read about the Kalalau Trail in Ray Riegert's Hidden Hawaii, "Kauai's premier hike, one of the finest treks in all the islands ..." It is an ancient footpath through dense tropical forest along the rugged Na Pali Coast. Beginning where the sole northwest road stops abruptly at Ke'e Beach, it spans 11 miles to Kalalau Beach, a sand patch bordered by sheer cliffs and the sea. It traverses up and down the flank of 3,000-foot ridges—a succession of them that jab into the ocean and form valleys in the mountain side. There are three stream crossings and three campsite areas—at Hanakapi'ai after two miles, at Hanakoa after six miles, and at the trail's end, Kalalau—each sporting an unmaintained trail leading up the valley.

**350**

"Purists will claim you've got to `do Kalalau' to see the Na Pali Coast ..." Riegert writes, and enticed, that's what I wanted to do. I read that it could be reached in a day—but I hadn't alloted time for inevitable sidetracking and the unexpected. I've traveled; I should have known better.

We began the hike late, having stretched the required two hour ride from Lihue into four hours, exploring road side caves and shooting tourist photos at lookouts. Our pace was relaxed. We stopped to lean into the fierce wind on outcrops with dropoffs that poised in the horizon of ocean and sky. We stopped to taste guavas, picking them from trees, prying them in half and sucking out the seeds and juice of their middle.

The trail was well-trodden, and for the most part it tunneled through tangles of tropical growth, warped and woven. In places you couldn't see the trees through the vines; in this jungle they hug, hide, protect, perhaps even love trees to death. Flowers were a splash of color here and there in the greenness.

At the first stream crossing, at Hanakapi'ai, I stopped to feed a whole can of turkey to a little black pregnant cat. Feral cats were left by squatters years ago. She hit my soft spot; my cat died recently. At the base of the stream is a gorgeous blond beach fringed by black cliffs. It is a popular destination for day hikers. On the other side of the stream are campsites—terraced sandpatches underneath palm trees with an ocean view. Though they looked inviting, we averted to the upstream trail leading to a waterfall for a site enroute recommended to us at the permit office.

Andreas returns and says he walked the guy to the coast. He had started late for the falls and got stuck in the dark. His parents were waiting at the parking lot—probably quite worried. I dab on mosquito repellent and start a fire. We decide to hike to the falls tomorrow since we're part way there anyway. This is when I knew I wouldn't make it to Kalalau Beach, but I didn't know then I'd later be obsessed with the idea of returning.

The early bird gets the spiderweb, wrapped around the head, leg, arm, whatever touches it first. After two veils I ask Andreas to lead. The trail is slick. Trees have fallen across it and the ups and downs are increasingly steep. There are protruding roots and loose mossy rocks; we seem to cross the stream an unnecessary number of times. I love the groves of bamboo and wish I knew more about the fruits and foliage of the island. We find a fruit that looks like strawberries and plucks off like raspberries and tastes like their combination. We try bites and nibbles of all sorts of unknowns, though we know this is risky. We smell this red blossom and that blue cluster. We find stones wrapped in broad leaves placed on rocks and I remember reading about them: offerings to a local God to ensure a safe journey. We follow suit and sandwich a rock. It's a perfect temperature; I'm walking in my bathing suit, not sweating.

The falls are a 400-foot towering shoot of water with a deep turquoise bowl at its base which overflows into a network of basins. Again, we take off our clothes and swim. The falls fall hard and spray stings our flesh as we approach. It's apparently impossible to swim behind it.

On the way back we bypass a river crossing in lieu of a noticeable secondary trail. Before not long, its obviousness peters into the perhaps as the trail narrows, disappears, then reappears sporadically. We're in a swamp, in a brash of bamboo at the base of a delicate fern-covered cliff, absently being led away from the river. Out of reach overhead against a cliff hangs a decaying rope ladder leading up into the unknown. We pass by.

Next we're standing under the dark shade of a massive tree under which nothing grows; only leaves decompose in its dampness. This is a dead end; no path leads from its circumference so we wing it into the thick of things, not without apprehension.

I've never had the urge to go where no man has gone before. I'm a path follower and this is the first time I've lost trust in a trail. I'm getting anxious. I see hoof marks in the ground and my imagination takes over. I can visualize a wild boar charging out from under a ledge, his tusk boring into my leg, his muzzle of spiny teeth crunching the bones of my ankles. Enough. I keep watch for climbable trees and decide these hoof marks are sheep. Yeah. That's it. Sheep.

We're going nowhere fast, in fact, my feet are stuck. No, they're sinking. I lie face first, Andreas pulls, my feet pop and he reaches back into the black muck holes and recovers my running shoes. We stare at one another; it's my lead. I'm thirsty.

We bushwack to a cliff edge, follow along its brim and finally hit a stream which has worn the side into a slope. We immerse and help each other down, hand over hand, level after level, shivering in the cool wetness until we reach sunshine and the main stream below. Continuing downstream, we leap from one boulder to another where possible; wade shallow edges and swim across deep troughs avoiding channels of current which plunge. Ultimately Andreas plows through the growth on the other side and finds "the" path.

We drink lots of water, wash up in our swim hole and while Andreas cleans his clothes I return to the campsite, just in time to meet Don.

Don must be one of the purists Riegert refers to. "Are you planning to hike to the end?" he asks. "Kalalau is a must." I tell him I have a flight to Maui and must be off tomorrow, unfortunately. He says he could use a ride into town and asks to join me on my hike out.

Don is a "New Age" person into spirits and energy fields and such. "Energy is the highest in the islands and no where is it greater than at Kalalau," he says. "Some people can't handle it. They have to complain."

Don says he's lived in this valley for seven months; he originally comes from Connecticut. "Rangers will fine you $50 if they catch you staying, but, well $50 for seven months—I could manage that. It's easy to get work and most jobs start at $6 an hour." He survives on food stamps. "You can get guavas anytime but to live off the land you need a garden."

As he speaks I notice for the first time an old garden bed around the campsite—an overgrown flat patch upheld with fine stone work. Whole communities lived here until the 1920s and it is one of many markers of the past.

Hawaiians first settled at Ke'e Beach in 1200 AD and as their population grew they dispersed into Na Pali's valleys. They cleared forests and built terraces for growing taro, the stable crop. The peak of production was in the 1600s when up to 200 acres were cultivated and each of the large valleys supported several hundred people. Families finally moved to more easily accessible villages lured by running water and regular schooling.

In the bush off the trail lies a hunk of rusting machinery once used in a coffee mill. Further upstream is an old stone fireplace—a site in which four people recently lived for two months, according to Don.

Trails apparently lace the forest, but unmaintained, they are disguised with growth. I tell Don of our day's escapade and he says he's aware of the trail that led us astray. About 12 years ago it was the trail to the falls but now is used only by wild pigs. "Ornery things," he says. "They've got tusks, can bore right through—" I interrupt. I know already.

A sudden breeze washes over the leaves above us and has the bamboo squeaking in circles. Don is on his way to visit a friend on the other side of the stream. We say good-bye until tomorrow, and in parting he says I should consider flying back after Maui. "You need just three days: one day in, one day out and one day to hang out."

We're fast asleep when at about 3:30 a.m. there's a thunk near our tent. Startled, I shine my flashlight at a flashlight shinning on me. "Oh sorry," says a voice, "something, mumble"—can't make it out—"but the mosquitos are so bad."

"WHAT?" Andreas booms, just waking up. "Who's there?" The voice asks, "Is this the half way point to the river?" Half way to the river? You're beside the river, er, stream. What are you doing so close to the tent? Is this Don? I'm glad I'm not alone. The voice says he is going to sleep here if we don't mind.

Two hours later there's heavy panting and sniffing outside the tent. I prop up on my elbows, straining my eyes to see. Suddenly a four-legged silhouette stops and growls. I see teeth shinning in the moonlight, then not four, but 12 legs.

"Eh!" says a voice. The growling stops. Someone is visiting our visitor and

**353**

that someone has three dogs who are having a heyday around the campsite. Is this a local? A hunter? Don's friend from across the river?

There is no sign of the dogs or strangers of the night in the morning; Don has not shown up to hike out with me. I bid Andreas farewell, place a fresh flower in the old wine bottle and march back to my convertible feeling discontented.

I was going the wrong way. I yearned to hike the trail's end—Kalalau—with a hunger I had only felt once before seven years ago in Nepal. There I had flown out of the Annapurna Mountain Range with my friend, having hiked in, only to feel I was missing something terribly important. Knowing I'd kick myself if I didn't give in to the compulsion I flew back the next morning hoping to fill the void.

I hiked over Throng La Pass at 17,600 feet, along the other side and days later found myself on a peak in sudden sheer fulfillment. This is what I had returned for—a sensation with the power of a milestone. There, standing with a little dog at my side, I was floored with an uncanny revelation: I knew then that it was my destiny to be a writer. Fairytale-type stuff. It was a career decision out of the blue, never entertained before and never looked back on since. So, what, if anything, do the mountains here have to tell me now?

\* \* \*

Five days later I'm back in Kauai. My knapsack packed, I'm leaving the Sheraton Coconut Beach Hotel in Kapaa and the Bell Captain says, "Doing the hike? Hope the hurricane doesn't hit." Say what?

She's racing northwest towards the islands at 115 m.p.h. and could hit the Big Island tomorrow afternoon and Kauai the day after. She'll likely cause high waves and heavy wind and rain within a 100-mile radius.

I'm on the road with no change of plan. I pick up a hitchhiker, the fifth person I've met from mainland U.S.A. who came to visit and stayed to call Hawaii home. Couldn't even give his return ticket away, he said, there were no takers. We reach his stop and he wishes me luck.

I skirt the tunes and key into local 570 AM for the latest report. "Cloudy, windy with a good chance of showers," said the broadcaster, "stay tuned for an update on Marie." I'm in the final stretch, the rolling windy road to the trailhead and reception peters out to the sound of ripping paper. I entertain the idea of backtracking to hear the report, but I'm too committed to stop the wheels from rolling onward.

Police are cruising the parking lot. Go ahead, they say, but don't try and cross any streams if she hits. Go to high ground, find a cave and stay put. Mountains with a twist; I like it, I like it.

Set and determined I'm off at a steroid pace. The trail is muddier than before. I pass a couple. She's in beach whites and pink running shoes carrying a plastic bag with lotion and a towel; he's carrying a big styrofoam cooler with both hands. Hey, what do you think this is—a picnic? The Sierra Club rates this hike a nine on a difficulty scale that reaches 10. I don't ruin their date with adventure, I smile, say hi.

Hanakap'ia comes fast and then I'm into new territory. That was either thunder I heard or the grumblings of a hungry mountain. Dark clouds are hiding mountain-tops and rain is taunting with sprinkles. It brings a sense of urgency. Rain, rain go away, come back when I've pitched my tent. A huge centipede crosses my path—it's at least the length of my foot. I remember Don said he was once bit by one and was in bed two days with wild hallucinations.

The trail leads up steep switchbacks then into thick foliage. I'm Alice in Wonderland looking at plants that seem familiar but out-of-proportion big. Then I'm back to reality, exposed along a precipitous cliff face. No one is around and I want to take a picture of myself here. I wedge my camera sideways in a crag, set the timer, heave my knapsack back on, release the timer, run back down the trail, turn, and walk nonchalantly back. So cool. Actually I'm hot. I've sweat so much my backpack feels soggy. I peel off my shorts to be clad in my bathing suit only.

I'm at the stream crossing at Hanakoa and I don't like the look of it. There are huge boulders standing like upright eggs that you're supposed to hop along with the help of a strung rope overhead for balance. The boulders are too far apart for my legs, there's no way I can hop, bounce or jump with this knapsack and the rope is sagging in the middle.

My attempt is an award winning photo were anyone there to take it. I wrap my arms around the rope, thoughtlessly dependent, step wide and get stuck. I can't move and suddenly I'm off balance leaning backwards, doing the splits. I get out of it somehow, but not before—of all times—I am passed by a hiker who flits over the rocks farther upstream, smiles kindly and suppresses a bowl of laughter, I'm sure. The lesson of the day is to assess possibilities beyond the given route.

This is Hanakoa Valley. Campsites are on terraced fields; rock-bundled plateaus of soft grass. I'm hiking through ghost villages. A path leads up the valley to a waterfall and while it is only half a mile long, I don't stray to push my luck. A sign warns hikers to boil water before drinking it. I meet a guy who's returning from a week-long stay at Kalalau Beach. He looks as relaxed as melted butter.

I round the mountain range that bisects the wet and dry sides of Kauai. Change is noticeable. Land is dry and open, I can see for miles the fluted cliffs of Kalalau Valley. As I round a ridge—forever blasted with the trade wind—I try to spot the trail on the next one. This is more than a diversion, it draws me on. A blister has formed on my right big toe. I'm tired, my pace is slower. Looming clouds are darker. Recent landslides are obvious and they are unnerving to cross on a path all too fresh. Then I'm on a long narrow ledge, a two-foot wide fringe from a 1,000 foot plummet. There is no room to play. I do not stop, I do not take a photo, I step directly onto the trail.

Later, with my feet on more secure ground I meet bow hunters on the track of goats. They are friendly but I don't wish them luck. I know their story: helping to control goat population so they don't ravage the land then starve—but I can't bear to imagine an animal in pain. Mountains up the valley have knife-point peaks and vertical walls forming a giant fortress.

I see quite a few Jet and Zodiac boats running tours along the coast and hear helicopters doing the same in the air above. It's an unnatural sound but they are not close enough to be obnoxious. Then again, I'm biased. I took a ride with Papillion Helicopters when I first arrived on Kauai for a bird's eye view of the playground. What a wild experience: to skirt tree tops through a narrow canyon, rush up a cliff and suddenly poise in front of a three-pool waterfall so close that spray hits the window, spoiling a photograph.

I hear braying and discover a small goat herd on a ridge crest below me. The trail narrows, becomes more rugged and even precarious in spots. It slithers down loose red rock and suddenly I see the beach beyond; a glistening half moon of white, sun rays upon it.

Finally Kalalau Beach is before me, and I take off my runners, almost in reverence. The first step has silver powder sifting through my toes. There are a number of tents well ahead and I take my time arriving among them. I look no more to the dark billowing clouds behind me, only to the deep ball of orange ahead. I mark my spot with my tent and when the pegs don't hold in the sand I gather rocks to secure them. From the grass plateau above the beach a naked man stands and tells me to make sure they're big—the rocks. A tent blew away the night before, he said. I heed his advice and after hefting some damn big rocks, get applause from my naked neighbors.

I ask if anyone has heard wind of Marie. They've heard, but haven't felt her presence. Then I'm standing naked, turning around, being cleansed under a waterfall in a small alcove. I return to the beach just in time to witness the lightshow of sunset with others spaced here and there near the ocean's edge. We are not many; perhaps 10. There are no mosquitoes. After sunset really big frogs hopped past my tent towards the sea.

The stars are bright. There are loud crickets droning like electric shavers in high pitch. The waterfall sounds larger than I remember it and the ocean sounds like an airport with jet planes taking off every 10 seconds. I'm not complaining. Not at all.

In the morning I awake with my tent alternately puffing out then sucking in with the regularity of the ocean's breath. I've had bizarre dreams but they are lost as I regain my bearings: lying in my tent on a secluded beach in Hawaii.

I meet Kim and Cathy from Calgary—the first fellow Canadians—and we decide to hike the valley trail. They came to Kalalau campsite by campsite, in three days.

It's a glorious, sun-filled, cloudless morning. We pass a landslide area where karins have been placed in homage to the mountains and peaks beyond. Kathy has a hiking guide that says this was a pre-Christian worship ground.

We get lost following a chute into an open field where bananas grow, then backtrack; get lost alongside a small stream that curves from one bowl to another, then backtrack. We agree we are on the wrong trail when we have to move branches and step with effort. I am learning.

From out of the jungle we enter an unexpected open field in the Kalalau Valley. We stand on rocks and gaze. Then re-entering the jungle we find extensive agricultural terraces that have plum, guava and large mango trees on them. The trail ends at a large deep pool which slides into another pool. We swim, slide, pick and eat guavas.

Back on the beach, we explore caves, huge surf carved pockets. One cave is occupied with a tent; another has a huge sand dune forming in front of its entrance. I wish I had brought a flashlight to see into the deep recesses. It's amazing how these real lava rocks look like the fake thing. They are globs with an edge here and there, patches of gray and black, some streaked with limestone sediment.

In the afternoon I lie alone on the beach. As I soak in the sun the most amazing rainbow appears. It arches over the peaks and ridges and the path that lead me here. Another rainbow archs over the first and then I see its elusive end. This beach is the pot of gold, and I'm lying in it.

# Final Night

## Marilyn Hope Smulyan

*When a volcano blows, even the best laid plans can change in an instant.*

STAY INDOORS! the radio announcer commands. "Yeah ... right," I mumble, and then begin to laugh, as I look at my singular option—a small, light-weight and very thin-walled backpacker's tent. Standing in a secluded camp site at Alaska's Portage Glacier, I cannot imagine that my child-size tent is the kind of "indoors" that he has in mind. Nevertheless, I know he is right; I have to get inside. The tent is my only protection.

What a change from just a few minutes earlier. I was beginning my evening ritual—trying to write thoughtful prose and poetic descriptions in a tattered trip journal. It was my last night out after a summer of wilderness travel, and I had a lot to consider. Ten weeks ago, I had secured the panniers on my bike in Whitefish, Montana and started to pedal to Alaska. Yes, it was a solo, soul-searching adventure.

First I rode up through the Canadian Rockies and then across British Columbia. I island-hopped in southeast Alaska, enjoying the relaxation of the Alaska Marine Ferry. In Haines, again I loaded the bike and rode up the backbone of the St. Elias Mountains. Then it was on to Fairbanks, Denali, Valdez, and another ferry ride—this time to Seward—and finally, to the Portage Glacier.

I had just started to write. It was my plan not to stop until I had, at least, one life-changing revelation.

*"Final night. Camped in the shadow of a glacier; blue ice staring down. Glacial waterfalls rumbling in the distance, but—how unusual—tonight from the birds there is not a sound. Grey clouds. Early darkness. It's darker now than it has been all summer. Hey, what's going on? It's really getting dark out here!"*

The journal entry abruptly ends, I slowly rise from my camp chair and look around. I walk in a circle and search for a clue. Something feels eerie, but I am having trouble finding an appropriate explanation. "Dark," I repeat over and over. "It's getting dark out here." In most situations this would not seem so odd, but after a summer of almost perpetual light, the sudden change in the night is disconcerting.

**358**

A silence hangs in the air. The air feels heavy—like when covered with a blanket of dense, coastal fog—but there is no fog and nothing is wet. Then I realize, that I am mistaken. The silence is an illusion. My ears are clearly sensing a sound. It is soft and consistent, but its name continues to elude me. That is until my eyes spot its source on the ground. Slowly, I begin to make sense of the situation.

"Dust!" I yell, although not a soul is around. A light rain of dust ever so gently is falling down. I look up to the sky and discover a huge black cloud. I watch for maybe a minute. Yes, it is moving in my direction. I do not know how I know what it is, but I do. I have never had a similar experience. Maybe I know because it just seems so fitting that out here in the Alaskan wilderness I can become a spectator to one of the earth's most basic land-forming operations. This is nature at work; it is the remains of a volcanic eruption. This dry rain contains billions of pulverized grains of pure volcanic ash.

I dig into the pannier that is still secured on the back of my bike and finally find the small radio stored deep inside. The announcer's tone is urgent, "Mt. Spurr erupted between 4 and 5 p.m. It blew a plume of ash 11 miles high, and, over the next few hours, the winds are expected to blow the ash across Anchorage and Turnagain Arm. Go inside and stay indoors. It is not healthy to breathe in the ash."

Quickly, I try to settle in for the night. Inside the tent, everything is so silent that my adrenaline begins to rush. I am startled by the sound of the beat of my heart. After a frantic search, I finally find the flashlight that, sitting idle for the past two and a half months, has worked its way into the sideseam of my pack. I try to write but my mind has lost its focus. I am completely distracted.

I force myself to read, and, after a while, my mind begins to drift. I remember learning about Pompeii, and the instant burial of more than 2,000 of its citizens when Mt. Vesuvius unexpectedly erupted. Seventeen centuries passed before their remains were discovered. Eventually, I slip into a dream filled state, but at some point in the night, I awaken with a start. I am totally disoriented. My eyes are open, but everything is black. I cannot even see my hand held directly in front of my face.

In the morning, I am awakened by the light. The tent feels strange, like its walls have thickened overnight. The air in my throat is unusually dry. Carefully, I open the tent. I have no idea of what to expect. As the fly falls to its side, a pile of ash drops to the ground. Baby powder soft, with a pinkish cast, everywhere I look, it clings to the surface. Leaves, trees, ground, glaciers, my bike, my tent and my hanging bag of food, everything is touched.

I have absolutely no idea about what I should do next. Just a day's bike ride away from Anchorage, where good friends await my arrival, I know that I must find another means of transportation. The radio announcer continues to implore, "If you can, stay inside. Whatever you do, do not go outdoors to exercise! The airport is closed and remember, drivers, ash can clog your engine and stop your car in its tracks."

A young couple appears in a daze. "Do you know what's going on?" the young man, named John, slowly asks. "We fell asleep in our tent quite early last night and," looking around with puzzled eyes, "we awoke to this."

"Yes," I explain, "the Mt. Spurr volcano erupted. Everything is covered with a thin layer of ash."

They have a rental car and are not concerned about the effects of the ash on its engine. John offers to drive me and my bike into Anchorage. I dampen a bandana, place it around my mouth, and tie it in the back of my neck. In slow motion, I disassemble the tent and lower the food bag from a neighboring tree. I try to pack up, breathing in a minimal amount of ash. Before we head out, John drives to the headwaters of the Portage Glacier. All of the ice is covered. No longer white, no longer blue, now it almost resembles a jumble of large, dirty rocks.

When we arrive in Anchorage I am surrounded by friends and three nights pass before I have the time to sit down and write. Again, I try to sum up the past two and a half months of my life. I want to describe my love of adventure but every time I start to write, I keep coming back to the Mt. Spurr volcano, *"Final night. Camped in the shadow of a glacier ..."*

# BEGINNINGS

## Setting Out

*"And bold and hard adventures t' undertake,*
*Leaving his country for his county's sake."*
Sir Francis Drake

# The Discreet Leak

## Annalisa Layton Valentine

*Many people become Scuba certified before setting off on an exotic adventure.*
*Classes are strict, and the fun is a long way from beginning.*

Ten Scuba diving students huddled around a gouged workbench in the small back room of the Berkeley Dive Shop. Besides Walter, the instructor, I was the only person over thirty years old—or over forty or even fifty.

On Thanksgiving, only five days earlier, my son David and I had decided that we would go trekking in Nepal for his college graduation present the following spring. Our flight home would stop in Thailand, and we agreed that it might be fun to go Scuba diving on the southern beaches. David said he would learn to dive in San Diego where he went to school, and I was to get certified in Berkeley. The spring trip meant that I would have to postpone shoulder surgery. I had severed 30% of my rotator cuff tendon during a rock climbing competition a few weeks earlier and I was still in a lot of pain and unable to lift my left arm above my head. "Diving will be good exercise," I told myself. "After all, you're weightless in the water."

As Walter lectured that first night, his gaze never left the bosom of a thirty-year-old woman named Donna. "I'll lecture from seven to ten each Tuesday night, and we'll spend those three hours in the pool each Thursday," he told her left breast. Donna was basking in the attention. She looped one arm over the back of her chair and her chest inflated about four inches.

"For the first hour tonight, I will describe the equipment you'll need for diving," he said to her other breast, "and during the break, you can try on fins, masks and snorkels. You'll need to have all of the equipment by Thursday."

By the end of class, I had learned the effect of water pressure on the body's air spaces, understood that your lungs can explode if you hold your breath while ascending, purchased $200 worth of dive gear, and witnessed an amazing seduction. Donna had a quiet orgasm as Walter described the tingling sensation one feels, prior to having the bends.

En route to the pool session the next Thursday, I bought a large slice of eggplant-garlic Chicago Pizza and a giant Coke. Walter gathered us into a circle on the concrete floor of the changing room. He looked different. On Tuesday he had had a fringe of gray hair surrounding a bald spot. Tonight he had a shaved head and the light from the lone hanging bulb created an eerie halo.

"Before we begin instruction," he said, "you have to demonstrate your water skills. I want you to swim 16 lengths of the pool, then one length under water, then tread water for ten minutes. For the last two minutes of treading, you have to hold your hands out of the water."

He told us that the women could change into bathing suits in the pool house; the men outside. "As you see," he added, "there are no toilets here, so you'll just need to control your bladders until you get home. I want absolutely no peeing in the pool. I have a marker dye in there that will turn bright orange on contact with urine." With a lingering anticipatory glance at Donna's chest, Walter left with the four men in the class.

I was first to exit the pool house. The night-air was so cold that I could see my breath. "Better dive in before you freeze," Walter said, awaiting Donna's impending emergence.

I ran the four steps to the end of the pool and entered with a racing dive. I surfaced and used the momentum to kick and stroke furiously. But as soon as I brought my left arm out of the water, sharp pain radiated across my shoulder and down my arm. I turned onto my right side and nestled my poor left arm against my chest. What had made me think I could swim with such a severe rotator cuff injury? I labored to the deep end of the pool, doing a right-armed sidestroke. "If I can pass this swimming test," I told myself. "The rest should be do-able." I turned to begin a second lap and was hit with a dreadful nausea as the garlic and green peppers from my pizza began refluxing into my throat. Swimmers were splashing past me. By the time I had managed five laps, every one else was at sixteen and beginning ten minutes of treading water. I completed my sixth and called it sixteen. But now Walter was watching more closely, I wouldn't be able to cheat on the underwater length. With all my strength, I pushed off the shallow end wall. I stroked furiously with my right arm. The imbalance caused me to swim a left-curving arc of the pool and I surfaced through a forest of suspended legs. During the 10-minute water tread, my stomach was too upset for me to move. I took an occasional deep breath and floated just below the surface.

"Annalisa, you're supposed to be treading water" Walter reminded me as I bobbed for a breath.

"This is how I tread," I retorted, then slid back under the water.

Now, two minutes with arms out of the water. Everyone else was finished with this drill and getting into their wet suits. Walter was feasting upon Donna, so I meandered to a dark corner of the pool and just floated around on my

**365**

back, the very tip of one index finger peeking out of the water. When I finally emerged from the pool, I was certain that the worst was over.

But now I had to coerce a dry wet suit onto my wet body. This three-eighths inch thick rubber suit was about as pliable as a new cowboy boot. I tugged and twisted and pulled, but in ten minutes, I had only managed to get it lodged just above my knees. Clearly the suit had no intention of accommodating my womanly thighs, and now my injured shoulder was in agony. The rest of the class was lined up to enter the pool when Walter realized that I wasn't even suited up. "I'm sorry," he said. "I thought a men's medium would fit you." The entire class watched me struggle for a few more minutes, until finally Walter and the assistant instructor took pity. One on each side, they lifted me off the ground by the sides of my wet suit and shook, as if they were working a feather pillow into a damp pillowcase. The rest of the class watched in smug amusement as my breasts bobbed with the jostling. The wet suit moved about a quarter inch with each shake. Even the instructors were giggling by the time my thighs gave up the fight. I had won the battle, but not the war. Combat continued, getting my arms into the long, rubber sleeves. Nobody came over to help me with that step. Nobody knew how injured my shoulder was. After another five-minute struggle, I felt like the Michelin man after a train wreck. The arms had gone on twisted, killing my shoulder, and I had no strength to make adjustments.

"Put this on." Walter said as he handed me a wide belt, woven through three ten-pound lead weights. I took the belt, but immediately dropped it, unable to hold the thirty pounds. By now, everyone understood that I would be that one student who wasn't quite as sharp as the rest, struggling and fumbling at each activity. The contrast already made all of them look good. Walter picked up the belt and held it to my waist while I secured the latch.

"Put on your hood, booties, gloves and fins, then your dive buddy can help with your buoyancy vest and air tank," he said.

The dive hood was also made of thick neoprene. It fit tightly over my head and neck, up to my chin and most of the way down my forehead. A small oval of eyes, nose and mouth was my only exposed skin. I sat on the concrete deck to put on my neoprene booties, which had to be zipped over the ankles of the wet suit and about four inches up my leg. The wet suit jacket fit so tightly around my chest and stomach that I could barely breathe when I bent to reach my feet. By the time I had managed the bootie zipper, I was close to passing out. I had to rotate onto my hands and knees in order to stand up again. Lastly, I pulled on the neoprene gloves. My body temperature shot up as sweat poured from my exposed facial area.

Chrissy Rotolo was my assigned dive buddy. All of 98 pounds, she was too small for the smallest wet suit. I was sweating with exhaustion, and her lips were already purple with the cold.

I used my right arm to lift Chrissy's buoyancy vest (with the 30-pound air tank secured at the back). She latched it closed, and we made sure the air was turned on, and the mouthpiece was in easy reach. She did the same for me. We inflated our vests and put on our dive masks. Chrissy looked like a housefly, with large multi-faceted eyes protruding from its head.

Walter treaded water, as one-by-one we stepped to the edge of the deep end, took a giant stride into the pool, then came up and gave the OK sign, (fingers tapping on the center of the head). Planted for my turn, I felt like Dustin Hoffman in "The Graduate." A complete fool, wearing sixty pounds of awkward equipment. I was sweating so profusely that my mask had completely fogged up on the inside.

"You're last," Walter said. Reluctantly, I took my giant stride into the pool with a splash that would win any cannon-ball contest. I bobbed to the surface, gave the OK sign and swam to meet the rest of the group at the shallow end. Now I was sure the worst was over.

The first skill was merely to kneel down. We gathered in a circle and the rest of the students dropped to their knees. The bubbles of their breathing surrounded me. I took this moment to consider whether I was really meant to be a diver. I don't know what happened next. Perhaps I leaned back a little, but suddenly my tank and lead weights were tugging me from behind. I threw my arms out for balance, and hopped backwards trying to get underneath the weight. The more I jumped, the more the weight pulled me. Like a gymnast gone awry, I bounded back and back and back until I bashed into the pool wall. Slowly then, and with no control over events, I slid down the wall and found myself lying on my back, arms and legs flailing like a beached turtle, and facing the possibility of drowning in four feet of water amidst ten people. Luckily I had my regulator (source of air) in my mouth. Walter's face appeared above as he pulled me up by the shoulders and positioned me on my knees.

For the next two hours, as the rest of the class learned how to clear their masks and recover their regulators, I sweated profusely and focused on nothing but severe shoulder pain, suppressing an overpowering urge to throw up and an increasingly pressing need to relieve my bladder. The others stayed under water, watching and waiting their turn to perform. I stood and sweated. When it was my turn to perform a skill, Walter would motion me down. He would demonstrate what I was to do; I would attempt the skill, then immediately stand and try to keep from vomiting. My dive buddy, Chrissy, became hypothermic, and between each skill, Walter had her at the side of the pool, hanging onto the edge and kicking her legs to generate heat. I worried that I would flunk out of class on this first lesson. I hated every moment of learning, but I was determined to complete the course. After all, there were five other women in the class and they were doing fine. If they could learn to dive, so could I, dammit.

By 9 p.m., my Giant Coke was not to be ignored, and by 10 o'clock I could no longer control my bladder. Walter had warned us about this. I prayed that he was joking about the orange dye. I was still standing and sweating and the rest of the class was still under water when I decided to go ahead and take a discreet leak in my wet suit. It wasn't easy to get started, but the flow finally set forth. I could feel the wet heat surrounding my upper leg and trickling down my wet suit. At mid-thigh level, the heat movement stopped, changed direction and began creeping up my abdomen. I felt as if I was slowly slipping into a luxurious hot tub. As it continued its seepage, it enclosed my waist, then my ribs, one at a time. It enveloped my breasts, and then began a slow trickle into my armpits. That's when I began to worry. My arms were floating high in the water, and once my armpits were full, the pee level began enclosing my neck. I had no way to stop what I had started. God, what if yellow fluid started bubbling out at neck level? What if an orange ring formed?

The rest of the class suddenly rose from underwater. "That'll be it for tonight," Walter announced as I surreptitiously bobbed my neck in and out of the water. The class headed for the ladder, and I loitered in the water a few more minutes, waiting for this painfully slow function to finish, relieved to see no discoloration around me and believing that perhaps there is a God. Once I got out of the pool and after an agonizing debacle of trying to remove my wet suit-turned pampers, I asked Walter where to wash it.

"You don't wash it," he said. "You can use the same one next week. Just hang it in the pool house, near the heater to dry."

It was not without trepidation that I arrived the next Thursday, sniffing for rancid urine, and quietly grabbed Donna's wet suit.

# Mushing 101

## Brian Patrick O'Donoghue

*Alaska's annual Iditarod dogsled race is a big league event.
So is training the dogs.*

AFTERNOONS IN MID-AUGUST the temperature in Interior Alaska cracked 70 degrees more often than not, but evening's cool relief had the dogs strutting with pent-up energy; the time had arrived to begin training.

I bought two carts for $75 each: a three-wheeled all terrain vehicle and a low slung, Honda Odyssey. Neither vehicle had an engine. Pushing them was a chore. It seemed like overkill when Tim "The Mowth" Mowry, a sportswriter at my newspaper and self-appointed coach of my Iditarod campaign, insisted that we install new brakes. It was a stretch to imagine our untested recruits could even pull the heavy things.

The closest trail ran through a birch and willow forest on the far side of Chena Hot Springs Road. Traffic on the two-lane road was light. But we lived along one of the few sections of pavement unblemished by permafrost and drivers tended to highball it past our cabin. That made it too risky to run teams out our driveway. Stringing scrap chains between trees over on the far side of the road, we created a staging area for up to a dozen dogs, safely spaced apart.

The temperature was about 55 degrees and falling the evening Mowry and I brought the dogs over, two by two, for this would-be racer's inaugural training run.

We used the old Odyssey, which had a hand break and room for a second person to ride on back. Tying the cart to a tree, Mowry played out the gangline from the front chassis.

We put Chad and White Rat, two experienced leaders, at the head of the line, leaving space on the gangline for three more pairs of dogs pulling the cart.

"You're hopeless O'Donoghue," Mowry said, watching me harness a squirming husky.

After nearly a month chained to trees, the dogs were insane with delight. They were going someplace new! They egged each other on, baying, leaping in place and grinning like wolves in a old Betty Boop cartoon.

Mowry climbed into the driver's seat. I loosened the knot on the anchor rope. The rope coils slipped on the tree, slowly gathering speed like a rocket lifting off the pad until the last loop fell away, instantly catapulting dogs and cart into motion. I chuckled at my skepticism. OK, they can pull this thing. The better question is—can I hang on!

The ride was a blur of leaves, slapping branches and the whirling squeal of the Odyssey's brake. We made a short circuit through woods and dirt residential roads, less than two miles total, pausing several times at puddles to let the dogs slurp a drink. They were panting hard by the time we finished.

Building stamina is important, of course, but instilling confidence is the main objective of early-season dog training. A musher aims for short, fun runs, building the dogs' faith in themselves and in their all-knowing driver.

That's the theory.

Mission complete, we shifted the dogs to the picket line and spread out pans of water, which they lapped greedily, another bit of conditioning. Dogs too tired to care might still drink from habit during the race.

Mowry was moving down the line with a water jug when Chad, our golden-haired main leader began digging.

We paid no attention until yellow jackets streamed from the hole in the forest floor. They first landed on Chad's back and began tunneling into his thick fur. The assault rapidly spread to the other dogs, all of whom were still chained in place. They whimpered and thrashed. Some mashed their heads in the ground, whining and flailing like spastic squirrels. Others quietly pawed the bees crawling on their snouts.

Mowry and I plucked off bees barehanded and turned dogs loose fast as we could. The bunch of us retreated across the road in a rout.

Chad got the worst of it. Back at the cabin, Mowry was still flinging bees from his thick coat. Our main leader was a trembling wreck, probably traumatized. So much for creating a positive training environment.

That night we doused the hive's mound with a gallon of bug killer. Vengeance!

* * *

Our training route followed a dirt trail shared by horses and whizzing ATVs, then looped home along a rough power-line path. The dogs began each run like tigers, whipping the cart like a car hauling a tin can on a string. That energy surge lasted about 100 yards. By the time we hit the power line, the slightest hill slowed the dogs to a crawl. I'd jump off the cart and push from behind.

Strong as they at times appeared, I had trouble imaging these critters would ever pull me 1,000 miles.

In September I began taking the dogs out alone. We were running three to five miles now. The weather had turned cold and rainy. That was a plus because anything above freezing is on the warm side for sled dogs. Planning our runs around strategic puddles, we never took the same route two days in a row. That was another of Coach Mowry's training principles; variations teach dogs to follow orders.

They gained strength daily. After a few weeks, the brake barely served to signal a pause. I learned to halt, quickly straighten out tangles, then leap for the cart as it skidded forward.

One afternoon traveling parallel to Chena Hot Springs Road, I stopped to untangle Spook, a nervous blond male who'd been running on three legs with a paw caught in his harness. He was about 10 feet ahead of the cart, running in the second pair of dogs. As I reached for his collar, Spook shied, tangling himself even worse. I was straddling the gangline, wrestling with the shy guy, when the other dogs bolted.

My leg snagged in the lines and I found myself hurtling backwards on my stomach, eyeball to eyeball with Bo, a very surprised wheel dog. We traveled a good 30 yards before the dogs paused to celebrate. I lay on the ground, recovering my wits, feeling pissed, embarrassed, and praying to God that our neighbor Rick Swenson, Iditarod's all-time champ, hadn't seen my predicament. I was about to jump up and show the dogs who was boss, when Bo gave me a big wet lick across my face.

He and the other dogs were staring at me somewhat fondly: Look at the poor retard.

The things I worried about—cars, horses, and maniacal ATV drivers—never caused problems. The near disasters always started with my own mistakes.

One afternoon I tested Chad responsiveness by ordering a sudden, surprise turn. Golden Dog responded on cue. I was admiring his brilliance when the middle section of the team slammed against a power pole.

Chad, Rat, Raven and Root, were already by the pole, straining forward. Pig and Digger, the next pair in line, were rearing backwards, fighting the pressure dragging them toward collision with the looming barrier. It was my fault; the turn I'd chosen was impossibly sharp for a dog team.

Pulling the gangline away from the pole, I worked the dogs around it, pair by pair. Freeing the cart proved more difficult. First the front wheel caught on the pole, then the cart's side, and then the rear wheel. The moment it finally cleared the team took off, knocking me down. I clung to the Odyssey's side, plowing through clumps of bushes and ferns until Chad finally stopped to piss.

"At least I hung on," I muttered, tasting dirt on my lips. That was the bottom line: A musher can't ever let go of the dogs.

\* \* \*

Operating a kennel offered a host of unexpected responsibilities and pleasures.

We bought dog food a half ton at a time, 25 sacks worth, $423 a load. Merely stacking it all was mind boggling.

We mixed food for Deadline Dog Farm's 27-howling athletes three buckets at a time, serving it out in huge soupy portions. A 40-pound bag of high-quality kibble lasted two and a half days.

The biggest surprises for this novice were the distinct personalities within the kennel.

Sibyl, a small wiry brown female, was our resident escape artist. Whenever a dog broke loose, the lot exploded with frenzied barks and joyful excitement. The escapee nearly always stayed nearby, darting around the yard, visiting friends or sniffing the food buckets. The cause behind a breakout was generally obvious. Most often, a dog had simply slipped its collar. Chad was particularly good at that. He'd back up and pop the neck ring over his ears. The empty collar would be lying there, still hitched to the chain. Broken snaps were another common cause for escapes. Or a snap jammed with ice or dirt.

Not with Sibyl.

She always took off wearing her collar and left no clues. There was never anything wrong with her snap. Her empty would be left discarded in the dirt.

She never strayed far. But that didn't mean she was easy to find. She liked crawling into other houses. I learned to track Sybil down through the reactions of her kennel mates.

One afternoon I heard crying from the lot. Truly woeful whimpering. It was Sibyl's neighbor, Daisy, a shy black dog hardly bigger than a pup. Sibyl had again vanished, leaving her young friend immobilized between two chains, each clipped to her collar. Houdini would have appreciated it.

Like I say, the individual personalities were something to behold: Rat prancing in delight as I got down on my hands and knees to retrieve her meal pan from the deepest rear corner of her dog house; Skidder's playfully snapping his teeth whenever I passed close by; Digger's daily progress, limited only by his chain's reach, as he tunneled for China.

My favorite of all: Listening to the many voices meld together into one howling chorus after feeding.

Mowry handled even the endless poop scooping without a thought, such chores being second nature to someone raised on a 180-cow dairy farm.

It all required more effort for this transplanted Washingtonian.

As training intensified, we added Kobuk Formula Fat to the regular dry food.

The white glop was supposed to toughen the dogs feet and thicken their coats. Nutritional I'm sure, but I hated touching it.

Carrying a gummy bucket of food to Marcie, our manic white pup, I stumbled, bumping the heavy pail on the ground. The contents exploded upward, drenching my hair, face and glasses.

"Aaargh!" I cried. The stuff was unbelievably greasy. Attempts to wipe it off my glasses left the lenses smeared even worse.

Marcie, meanwhile, looked bloated and content. She lazily wagged her tail as I resumed feeding and no wonder: the overturned bucket was empty.

It was an election year, but dogs called the shots on this reporter's calendar.

I ducked covering a gubernatorial debate to take care of more pressing business at the Fairbanks North Star Borough landfill. The woman working the scale looked appalled when I shared the contents of the dozens of recycled feed bags, 1,220 pungent pounds of poop, heaped on back of the pickup.

The dogs' most private habits became my obsession.

I could describe individual dining preferences, whether they licked bowls clean, or, like Screech, enjoyed the seasoning provided by tipping her bowl and mixing in dirt. I knew which dogs lived to be scratched and which ones, like Chad, were more likely to hump my leg when it came within reach. We also had skittish dogs, Spook being most notable of these, who were happiest when left alone.

Screech and Digger loved to kick their shit away. Pig took his dumps in the roots of a nearby tree, a lovely place to try and keep clean. Skidders pissed inside his doghouse by the gallon, creating a growing yellow glacier after it turned cold. A single day's load from Jethro, our biggest dog, more than filled a full-sized shovel. At least, it did in the beginning.

We put off running Jethro. He was so big we worried he might overheat. And then, well, he just didn't seem healthy. The big dog's turds changed from fat sausages to little squiggly things.

This fascination with bowel movements may sound bizarre, but there's always a reason for such changes. By the second week of September, Jethro's appetite fell off and the big dog's rear began to swell. After watching a couple days to make sure Mowry and I weren't imagining things, I took Jethro to see our veterinarian, Mark May.

Doc May first thought Jethro might be suffering from a gland infection. Then he found a fluid-filled pocket containing chunks of white tissue. Eighty bucks and a prescription of antibiotics later, Jethro was back home sporting a drain tube. And we had instructions to "milk" his swelling each day.

Easier said than done.

The drain kept plugging up, allowing the pocket to refill. And Jethro was not keen on people fingering his butt.

"I'd try softening the tissue with warm water," May said over the phone, stressing the need to keep draining that fluid.

Mowry and I teamed up for the disgusting duty. We spread newspapers on the floor of the kitchen each night and brought Jethro inside. One of us, usually me, held the big galoot, while the other worked him over with a wash cloth and a pan of warm water.

Over time Jethro came to appreciate our kitchen clinic sessions. The volume of extracted fluid—thick yellow stuff with traces of blood—was amazing. When we got a gusher flowing, his relief was unmistakable. The big dog seemed to be aware that something was wrong. His aggression was gone and he looked worried.

I took Jethro in for a follow up visit. Fifty dollars bought no new answers; his swollen butt wasn't getting any better.

A few days later, May paid us a house call to start the team on a series of vaccinations. He gave each dog two shots. It cost me $125 for the bunch, a fair deal when you consider the cost of clinic visits.

The vet frowned examining Jethro, whose butt bubble was again expanding. May made me a proposition. Rather than keep the meter running at the clinic, he offered to take Jethro home for a week where he could monitor the big dog's progress.

"Sometimes this way I can salvage them."

Several nights later, we found a grim message on the answering machine. Jethro's odd symptoms stemmed from a rapidly advancing cancer.

"I suggest we put him down without delay," May concluded.

The final clinic bill spelled out Jethro's fate: "sedation," $10.50; "examination," $23.00; "final arrangements," $32.50.

"This was a very 'hot' prosthetic cancer," May wrote on the bill. "Hence the initial symptoms and the rapid hard swelling and abscessation. Sorry to lose one like Jethro."

The whole episode cost $190. I didn't begrudge the money, but it underscored the unpredictability of kennel expenses.

Early on, Coach Mowry had recommended allowing $250 for veterinary bills. Thinking I was being conservative, I budgeted $400. A good chunk of that was gone and snow wasn't even on the ground yet. And I had 26 of Jethro's friends to worry about.

# Beginnings

## Michael Cervieri

*We all know that every trip has a beginning, a middle, and an end.*
*But where does it REALLY begin?*

IT BEGAN IN KANSAS, somewhere between a rickety sign posting a turn-off to see the world's largest prairie dog and another for a five-legged cow. Or maybe it began before that, in a dusty eastern Colorado parking lot clustered with pick-ups and shotgun racks. In a little diner Gregory and I were taught that white folks don't really like being around black folks. It was assumed that black folks don't like being around white folks either but, being eastern Colorado, there wasn't really anyone to confirm this with.

Mark swears it all began at the Mayan ruins of Tikal when we ate mushrooms and sat on pyramids and yabbled with the monkeys. He puts it sometime between 2:30 and sunrise, northeastern Guatemala.

Scott thinks Colombia. Somewhere around the time that Danny tried to ride a horse from San Augustin in the southwest to Cartegena in the northeast. The horse died about forty miles into his trip. It seems Danny didn't know anything about horses except that he liked *Don Quixote* and had done his best to memorize 16th and 17th century cowboy expressions that no one understood. He'd laugh and shake and then look bewildered when no one laughed and shook with him. He'd try explaining what he'd said but he didn't know enough Spanish outside his solipsisms so got nowhere with that. Jenny, who was with Danny until he rode off on the horse, says that the farmer who gave it to him told him that it would die in a matter of days. *Mover, Morir* it was all the same.

So while Jenny and Danny differ on what was actually said (*the horse will move in a few days*, or, *the horse will die in a few days*) she also disagrees with Danny about where it all began. Back in Ecuador, she says, where she was fucking a man named Rodolfo who had a gay brother so in love he was heading to San Francisco to learn how to fly helicopters. Let me backtrack. Rodolfo's brother's lover killed his aunt and uncle. One excuse was that they didn't like having a fag for a nephew. The other excuse was that they and their bank account were just out of reach of their nephew's greedy palms. Better put: they, and only they, stood between the nephew and a bank account. This, as the Ecuadorian prosecutors pointed out, was the real deal. He was written into their

**375**

will. He was the recipient of everything in it save for a farm that was to go to the Church. Now, fast forward. Rodolfo's brother hatched an escape plan. If he learned how to fly a helicopter, he could hover over the prison yard, drop some rope, and fly into a rainbow-colored never never land.

Rodolfo has no opinion about where it all started because he generally never had any idea what we were talking about. His brother had ideas about what we talked about but wasn't with us later so claims he just can't tell. "*No se*," he says. Or something like that. The nephew? Well, he was in jail at the time. We assume he still is since Rodolfo's brother, after arriving in San Francisco, suddenly had this crazy revelation that what he was doing was absurd. He learned to fly though. He also fell in love with Eric. Eric was his teacher. Still is in certain ways. Eric has no opinion on any of this.

Noah does though. Noah has an opinion on everything. Listen, he explains, arms all flapping by his sides, bouncing up and down in his seat. Listen. So this is what we listen to: Noah was in the Chilean desert in a town called San Pedro. There are cacti in San Pedro that go by the same name. If you peal back the bark, take the inner pulp, have someone spit in it, and let it brew overnight, you can drink it the next day. When you do drink it, you slowly lose the functioning of your gross motor skills. Then you vomit. After crawling on the ground for a little bit you slowly figure out how to stand again. Then you trip like a madman for 10 to 20 hours.

So that's San Pedro.

That's what Noah was on when he hit an eclipse party out in the desert. That's what he was tripping on as hippies banged their drums and a rumble filled the air. It was still what he was tripping on when he thought that walking across a bed of coals was a good idea. All in all, he was still tripping hard when various people loaded him on their backs because he had third degree burns up and down his legs.

He scratches these when he tells us about where it all began.

Maybe it didn't really happen in Kansas or Colombia or Guatemala or Ecuador or Chile. Maybe it didn't really happen until later because it wasn't until later happened that I could put Kansas into perspective. Maybe that does mean that Kansas is where it started? But, let me get to that later.

Later (which happened after New York where I sliced open my hand late in the night before heading to Guatemala and had to sleep in an emergency room) we were in the Venezuelan jungle. Danny and Noah came to blows here. The campesinos we stayed with laughed at them for being so stupid. Then Danny and Noah laughed at themselves. I missed the whole episode. I heard about it when I came back from a scouting mission. I saw a tarantula the size of a large frisbee. A real tank of a spider with legs as thick as my middle finger. I also watched giant ants march up and down a footpath. They carried big chunks of leaves, forming a bobbing, weaving canopy train. One ant ran up and down the ranks telling everyone where to go. I called him Señor Comunicador.

Jenny sometimes thinks it didn't happen in Ecuador with Rodolfo at all. She sometimes points to the Darien Gap between Panama and Colombia as the spot where it all began. She hiked there with an Australian doctor named Hustle. Hustle's real name was Robert. No one's very sure how he got his new name and he hadn't practiced medicine for a few years. Instead, he roamed Latin America looking for something he left in Australia. Namely, a sense of home.

So Jenny was with Hustle in the heat of the Darien Gap when their guide cut his leg open pretty bad. Hustle stitched it up and somehow the three managed to hike something like 17 miles to the guide's village. On the first evening, a villager busts into the hut where Jenny was straddling Hustle, their bodies all sweaty and heaving, and throws Hustle a spear. Come on, he says, we're going hunting. Hustle says he doesn't know how to hunt which is the equivalent of lobbing a big fuck you at his hosts. So he goes hunting. Two days later he's delirious. Three days later he's vomiting convulsively. Four days later the villagers place him on a canoe and send him downstream. One village sends him, another receives and feeds him and sends him on to the next. He recovers in Panama City. Jenny, who accompanies him on this little trip, hitches a ride on a sailboat from the Panama Canal. She ends up in Ecuador and meets Rodolfo.

Mark, who we'd last seen in Tikal, shows up in Peru. We were in Cusco planning to hike past Macchu Pichu down into the jungle where they've been uncovering some crazy ruins. Noah and Danny and Jenny and Scott and I were all there and we'd been drinking pisco. Around 2 a.m. we stumbled about town looking for our place. None of us quite remember what happened, only that while looking for our place we lay down to rest in the central square. Noah opened his eyes first. My head slipped off his stomach and hit the ground when he jumped up to greet Mark. When I steadied my drunken head, a lot of hugging was going on.

Mark had his arms around two Peruvian women. They'd driven him from Lima. He was smiling.

Lima?

Yeah, Lima.

It turns out they'd surfed down the coast. Their boards were stolen near Moquegua. When we asked what they were doing so far south, they laughed. Following waves, man, following waves. But Moquegua is inland and what a group of bandits wanted with surfboards is anyone's guess. Mark shrugged, they'd been trying to figure out how to get rid of them anyway. Which is also why he had a big lump on his head. Mark being Mark, thought it funny to ask for money. Bandits being bandits missed out on the humor and hit Mark above his eye with the heal of a machete. Even here Mark said sometime between 2:30 and sunrise, eastern Colorado.

But let me backtrack.

When I was younger, no more than five or six, I sat face pressed against the window in the back seat of the family wagon. We'd go on these seemingly endless drives from

Massachusetts to New Hampshire. I stared at stars. My sister stared with me. We imagined what it was like up there and created planets and life and the goings-on of life up there among the planets. We pawed away at the fogged glass so we could get a better look. Time passed very well this way as we traveled from one world to the next.

Actually, that gets me nowhere.

Neither does the fact that I later stood before endless fields of snow nestled between ragged mountains. I was in Argentina then having left Gregory and Mark and Jenny and Danny and Noah and Scott and everyone else behind. Something inspired me to walk. Across the fields, into the mountains. Snow. White. There weren't any aliens. Just me and the frostbitten winds. I set camp. I listened. It's where I first wondered when in the world it all began that I should end up here.

September 1998, Harlem

# A Bug in My Ear

## Lori Szczepanik Makabe

*Before entering the jungle, extracting a bug from your own ear
can be a real odyssey.*

FUNGAL CREAM, INSECT REPELLENT, bed bug spray, Larium. In four hours, I was leaving for a one month adventure to the Baliem Valley, located in the interior of the island of Irian Jaya. I felt ready for anything I might encounter in exotic Indonesia.

My first destination that morning, however, was the spa, where I could warm my muscles and stretch, in preparation for the long flight. When I grabbed my baseball cap to hold my hair up, like I always did, I felt a slight tickle across my cheek. I swiped at it and the critter accelerated. I swatted again and the next thing I knew, it crawled into my right ear.

I knew exactly what it was. It was an earwig. They love my house and my yard, and they really like my hat. I store my hat on top of my thongs just inside the sliding glass door that leads to the spa. The day before, I had seen an earwig fall out of my hat when I raised it toward my head to put it on. I meant to do something about it then, but I forgot.

So now I found myself in a predicament. It was six o'clock in the morning on the Fourth of July, I was standing naked in my kitchen, with an earwig on it's own little journey to the interior of my ear. This was not in my plans. As the bug penetrated my ear canal, I could hear the annoying voice of my grade school nurse; "You should never put anything smaller than your fist into your ear."

Then, it began to wiggle. I think it was trying to turn around. It was very unsettling—this living thing in my ear, with its six legs, two antennae and a pair of nasty pinchers. I thought for sure that it would just crawl right back out. When it didn't, I got scared. I could hear and feel every move it made.

At first I didn't feel any pain. I turned my head to the side and jumped vigorously, like I used to after swim practice, to clear the water out of my ears. It squirmed. I cringed. I worried about my eardrum. As soon as I thought about my eardrum, I felt pain. It almost seemed like the bug had discovered that thin membrane, and was drumming it's way through it. Or was that my heart pounding? Pain shot through my inner ear. I could not even think straight.

\* \* \*

Was it affecting my mind? Had the earwig gone all the way through to my brain, like the one in that Twilight Zone episode?

My knees became weak and I began to tremble. I dialed the local clinic, but it was a holiday; they weren't open, at least not at six in the morning. Looking out into the quiet neighborhood, I hoped to see someone, anyone, out walking a dog, getting the paper, or watering. No one was out.

My next panicked thoughts flew to surgery, a broken eardrum and worst of all, a canceled trip, all because of this stupid insect. I didn't know what to do. I knew that the earwig was big enough to cause some damage and make my twenty-three-hour, pressurized flight miserable. Follow-up care would be difficult to come by in Irian Jaya.

I wondered if I should go into the spa to try to flush it out, but what if it goes the other way to avoid the water? I definitely needed to do the right thing. I decided to try to grab the earwig with tweezers, and when I finally found some, I realized that extracting something from your own ear is very difficult, if not impossible.

Then I thought of my friend, Boo. She is a Pediatrician and since kids are always getting objects stuck in their ears and other orifices, I figured she could help me. Boo lives about fifteen minutes away, on the river. I made the call.

"Sorry to wake you Cliff, is Boo awake?" I impatiently asked her husband, also a doctor, who answered the phone.

"No, she's sleeping," he whispered.

"Will you please wake her up?" I squeaked, my voice quivering.

"What's wrong?" he asked.

I explained my problem and Cliff seemed insensitive, like he hated to wake his wife for such a ridiculous situation. The earwig squirmed again and I felt the pain. This time, Cliff heard my plea for help. He decided to wake Boo, and I could hear him as he spoke to her, "Boo, talk to Lori, she's got a bug in her ear."

Boo, who has a tremendous sense of humor, came to the phone sounding sleepy, yet giggling and asked, "You've got what?"

Then, being the doctor that she is, she asked me some questions.

"Has it perforated your eardrum?" she asked.

"I don't know."

"Do you have drainage?"

"No"

"OK—come on over." I hung up without saying goodbye.

I felt relieved to have some direction, and as I moved quickly to get dressed and into my car, the earwig wiggled sporadically. I bent over with my hand on my ear to try and handle the pain. I wondered if I would be able to drive the narrow levee roads without going berserk and driving into the river.

On the drive over, the earwig settled down a little bit, twitching only a few times. I began to feel a dull and constant pain. I raced from the car to the house, and was greeted by both doctors. They laughed and teased and I laughed and cried. It relieved some of the tension to laugh, even if I did still have this insect in my ear.

Cliff had two dictionaries out and began reading the definitions of earwig:

"Websters says: 'Earwig; beetle worm. Any of a family of harmless insects having slender many-jointed antennae, and a pair of large forceps like appendages at the end of the body;—so called from the mistaken belief that they crept into the human ear.' "

We all laughed.

"Funk and Wagnalls says: 'Earwig; An insect with horny short fore wings and a caudal pair of forceps: erroneously believed to enter the human ear.' "

Erroneous my ass, I thought, as Boo sat me on the couch. She took her medical light and looked into my ear. The earwig did not like the light and tried to avoid it by going deeper. This hurt and I joined in the squirming. I could tell that this was not going to be fun.

"I'm gonna have to do this quick—sit still," Boo demanded. I bit my lip and sat as still as I could. It was nerve-racking to have this bug in my ear. It wiggled and Boo's first attempt was unsuccessful. "Here, lie down," she said, agitated. I laid on my side with the earwig ear up.

I felt her probe, heard a crunch, felt a tickle, and there she stood with the writhing earwig held delicately between her forceps. Relieved, I reluctantly took a good look at it. It was a pretty good sized one, measuring almost an inch in length. Boo decided that I should keep it, so she put it in a baby food jar and we watched as it limped around and around.

They both examined my ear, and although I still had a bit of pain, it was nothing like it was before the extraction. Boo explained that the pain was probably the pressure of the earwig pushing against my eardrum and that it didn't look like I had anything to worry about. Unburdened, I thanked Boo and her husband, took the jar, and drove home.

Arriving at my house, I took another good look at the earwig, walked out into the back yard, and let the crippled insect go. Back to my last minute packing, I included an extra set of ear plugs. I was ready for Indonesia.

# New Freedom for Adventure

## Brad Olsen

*Welcome to the golden age of touring Planet Earth. The explorers of yesteryear would be green with envy at how easily we roam about.*

IMAGINE THE VAST POSSIBILITIES OF WORLD TRAVEL. For a moment, consider yourself part of a great traveling collective with an amazing opportunity. Contemplate how no other generation in history has had the luxury to travel as freely and safely as we can today. When before could someone just get on an airplane and go virtually anywhere on the planet within twenty-four hours? We live at a time when nearly every nation welcomes us with open arms, and allows us the freedom to explore virtually anywhere. Modern transport is accessible, easy and cheap. The English language is emerging as a universal tongue, which simplifies communication for Western travelers. Virgin turf opens up regularly and there is nothing to inhibit solo backpackers from roving wherever their imagination rides.

Extensive travel is a good thing, on par with a good education. Life abroad stimulates an educated worldview—seeing how "the other half" lives allows us an empowered outlook into our own lives, and a renewed compassion for our own culture. By traveling, we witness the environmental destruction of the planet and fathom how we can repair it. Empathy bonds people from other walks of life. Travel can be the most enjoyable and transformative experience of our lives, yet there is an inherent risk in the journey. We must account for ourselves with a combination of street smarts and a patient ability to deal with a variety of situations.

Independent travel is an acquired taste. Not just anyone can hoist on a backpack and "leave" for months or years at a time. For example, not everybody has the courage to venture far into the unknown, and certainly not everybody wants to travel so extensively. But for the few that do, be certain there are other wanderers out there just like you. Come join the world party, there is no dress code. Cash in on your new freedom for adventure.

# Campfire Wanderlust

## David Hatcher Childress

*Those who travel far and wide rarely lose their enthusiasm to share an adventure story with a stranger.*

WE CAMPED THAT NIGHT BY AN OLD SHACK on the Bay of Fundy—Tom and Carey, the two hitchhikers, made a fire while I gathered some driftwood. Later we ate a road-kill guinea hen that Tom suddenly produced and roasted slowly over the fire, basting it with butter.

They were off on a summer adventure, taking a few weeks to explore eastern Canada, maybe going up to Prince Edward Island. They inquired about my adventures, and were amazed that I'd traveled for many years across Asia, Africa and South America.

"How did you do it?" Tom asked. "Were you born a millionaire or something?"

Hell no, I laughed. You don't have to be a millionaire to travel around the world. I used to live on a few dollars a day. I hitchhiked quite a bit as well, especially in Africa and the Middle East. If I had a few thousand dollars on me, I could go for a year, depending on where I was. I would stop and look for work from time to time as well. It wasn't tough once I got going. It's getting started that is the hard part. Cutting yourself off from your job, friends, family and responsibilities is the most difficult part, as the great Chinese philosopher Lao Tzu once said, "The journey of a thousand miles begins with a single step."

We sat quiet for a while, and then I told them about the time I was dozing in my seat on an overnight bus through the Andes to Cuenca—packed with Ecuadorian *campesinos*—as it wound its way through the high mountain passes. Suddenly, at about 1:30 in the morning, I was awoken by a commotion. We were just coming to the police station of a small town where the bus was slowing down for a routine police check. A tall man sitting behind the driver jumped up and pulled a pistol out of his pocket. He held it to the driver's head and shouted in Spanish, "Don't stop! Don't stop!"

The bandit, intent on robbing the bus but not having the time because of the unexpected police check, was desperately trying to stop the police from discovering that he had a gun, a serious offense in Ecuador. He pressed it to the driver's head and yelled again, "Don't stop!" Meanwhile, the police continued to motion for the bus to pull over. I realized that the robber was probably after me, the rich *gringo* with the backpack. I fingered for the tear gas canister in my pocket, when suddenly the mechanic who sat on the steps of the bus beside the driver grabbed the gun and struggled with the bandit. At the same time the driver attracted the attention of the police by driving the bus into the police station. The corner of the bus sheared the edge off the red tile roof.

As I emptied my canister of tear gas in the bandit's face, his gun discharged, and the passengers screamed. The bandit quickly bolted out the open bus door and ran off into the night. A cloud of tear gas filled the bus. A police officer looked in the door and asked the terrified, choking passengers, "What's going on?" We stumbled out of the bus and stood by the road. The bandit had escaped into the night, but had left his gun behind. The bus was banged up but driveable, and we reboarded and continued on our way, guided by the stars of the Andean night.

Tom and Carey gazed silently into the campfire. In their minds, despite the danger, they were resolving to travel the world, or so I guessed. Canadians, like Australians and New Zealanders, seem to have a greater sense of wanderlust than many Americans. They appeared ready to begin a world-wide adventure. I tried to encourage them as much as I could. I firmly believe that travel is the best education one can get, though I must admit that having traveled around the world and seen many sites doesn't impress many employers. Unless you want to be a travel writer.

# Travel Canons

## Bruce Northam

*42 time-honored inklings and incentives to facilitate an epic adventure.*

AFTER CIRCLING THE GLOBE A FEW TIMES I wrote *The Frugal Globetrotter* and began presenting a lecture/slide show on the university circuit about what I'd observed and learned *out there*. These aren't rules, just random road-tested musings—globetrotter lore endeavoring to enrich your journey and simply remind you to hit the road. Go set your gypsy blood on fire. Dismiss common sense, leave the herd for a while.

**CANON 1:** You'll never know what's on the other side until you land there.

"New earths, new themes expect us."—Thoreau

**CANON 2:** Concoct a mission. The "I was really off the beaten path, they'd never seen white people before" rap is getting rather tired. Super, we're all Marco Polo. A means of comprehending a culture and candidly harmonizing with the locals is devising a hobby-inspired crusade—birding, animal-powered transport riding, attending religious services, festival-hopping, learning massage techniques from the local healer, watching musical instrument craftspeople at work. Invent a quest and find out where the local guru works or hangs out.

This strategy moves you past the other skulking, bumbling tourists who wait to be fleeced by the gratuity-incensed layer of con artists that plague many destinations. You'll save money by discovering the heart of the region's honest people.

**CANON 3:** Choose guidebooks that will support your "mission." Whatever it may be. Experiment by comparing what several different guidebooks detail about a locale with which you are already familiar.

**CANON 4:** "I see more of what is going on around me because I am not concerned with finding a parking place."—Taxi Driver Wisdom

Take advantage of your foot power. Lose the main road, walk, you don't always need a plan. When driving, stay off the interstates when you can, they hide the landscapes and the people. Life doesn't happen on the asphalt pipeline. It's against the law.

Go up to the roof of the place you're staying. Look around and pick an interesting direction to go for an all-day walk. Bring a daypack with your camera, a note pad and some water. Then just smile and be open to meeting new people. If you pass an interesting factory, school or business, go in and check it out. In many places, particularly in underdeveloped countries, people are happy to let you watch their daily work, whether it's making hats, drying fish or teaching math to a roomful of 8-year-olds. This is where fun hides.

**CANON 5:** Do we spend the first half of our lives figuring out what we want to do with the second half of our lives, or do we spend the second half of our lives wondering what the heck happened in the first half? Tough call. Traveling helps us figure it out. Go see for yourself.

"Everything must end; meanwhile we must amuse ourselves."—Voltaire

**CANON 6:** Take a media sabbatical. If you haven't circled the globe yet, maybe there's an umbilical cord attached to your TV convincing you that the world is an unfriendly place. IT'S NOT. The media "news" is 95% bad. You *CAN* do it.

Close your eyes and imagine that you are eighty-five years old, rocking away, contemplating your life. How would you feel if you'd never had a genuinely wild journey? Globetrotting isn't for everyone, but here you are—questioning what lies beyond this prodigious land of mountain ranges, shopping malls, plains, baseball stadiums, coastlines, drive-thru restaurants, forests, lakes, and 33% taxation. If you can't stand the thought of not taking a big trip, start packing.

**CANON 7:** Exercise Halloween-at-age-twelve style caution. Be prudent. Monitor your partying—many misadventures occur when we're *under* the influence.

"The major causes of problems are created by a drug interaction between alcohol and testosterone."—Philosophical Venezuelan Policeman

Women roving solo; There's safety in numbers: band with a pack of locals or fellow travelers before roaming into the unknown. Heed no advice first-hand, get a second or third opinion.

"Better an honest loincloth than a fancy cloak."—Swahili Proverb

**CANON 8:** Go where the locals go. Cops and Bartenders know their terrain better than the local chamber of commerce—and they work nights. Inquire about the best meal deal, zones of peril, reasonable accommodation, safe strolling, camping, worthwhile attractions and hangouts. Cordially *interview* them when you roll into town.

**CANON 9:** Get back in the kitchen, it's the most fun room in the house in other countries too ... Deep in the heart of Morocco's Riff Mountains, I hiked a rocky hillside that was shadowed by olive trees. I befriended a thirty-year-old shepherd, wearing a ski cap crowned by a pom-pom. He was the commander of fifty goats and twenty sheep. After a lesson on flock-control fundamentals (tree branch coaxing, throwing pebbles, grunting and hissing), we exchanged butter rum Lifesavers and cashews. I helped bring home the herd to his dwelling, lost somewhere in the narrow, winding byways of Chefchaouen. We settled in the dirt-floor kitchen, drank Moroccan whiskey (mint tea) and smoked kayffe, employing a 60-inch pipe (pipa). The peace pipe ceremony gained momentum when his mother, brother and sister arrived and we all played the Arabic/English name that kitchen utensil game. Meanwhile in the next room, the livestock *bhaaahd, grunted and moood*. The grass is greener down at the roots ... Moroccan sunsets forever on my mind.

**CANON 10:** In many parts of the world, latrine flushing and personal cleansing is done with the left hand using a few splashes of rainwater held in a nearby vessel. Don't shake hands lefty in these places.

Squatting low within a Goa, India restroom (an *outhouse* accommodating a porcelain crater at floor level), I was frightened by a sudden slosh and clatter—odd, since traditional Asian style toilets don't "flush" Western-style. The commotion below, identified by peering between my legs, was a spasmodic pink apparatus flapping about wildly. I exited, darted to the rear of the structure and barreled into a humongous pig that was voraciously groveling its snout deep into the outflow pipe of the outhouse. These "pig-toilets" are clever spin-offs of traditional Asian toilets, wherein you hunker down, resting your buttocks upon your ankles, hovering above an opening in the floor.

What distinguishes a pig-toilet from traditional undeveloped country latrines is the ravenous pig that consumes your poop, without delay. The sound of flushing, common in Western bathrooms, is replaced by a hog slurping on the other side of a wall. Indeed, there's a sensation of a closed-loop ecosystem when your waste is recycled back into the food chain before you've even pulled up your pants. (New perspective on pork too.)

**CANON 11:** Avoid the Unsavory Tourist Syndrome.

*Six Americana impulses that obviate your tourist classification while bumbling abroad:*

1. High-fiveing everyone.

2. Wearing high-top sneakers and baseball caps backwards.

3. Talking incessantly (volume set on loud). Observation: There are *two* North

**387**

American languages: English and louder.

4. Defending America's defense policy.

5. Giving 'em the enthusiastic thumbs-up sign, accompanied by a lightheaded grin.

6. Prefix your sentences with "yo" and "like"—respond with "totally" and "definitely!" *Then*, high-five again.

**CANON 12a:** Bypass neurotic travel partners, which usually means roving solo, since spending 24 hours a day, 7 days a week with anyone breeds dementia. Nine-to-fivers don't comprehend *"24/7"* until they cross India on a bus together. One advantage of traveling with someone you're not in a relationship with is being allowed to separate for a few days.

**CANON 12b:** When traveling with friends or family, undertake an exhausting itinerary. My Dad and I walked 200 miles, coast-to-coast across Northern England. Meandering 20 miles a day along towering shoreline cliffs, through dense forests and over forbidding mountain ranges left us no energy to recycle any debates about my tenth-grade car crashing spree.

**CANON 13:** Keep a journal.

"... I think about all the different ways we leave people in this world. Cheerily waving goodbye to some at airports, knowing we'll never see each other again. Leaving others on the side of the road, hoping that we will."—Amy Tan

"... be careful in traffic. Mopeds are often the family car in many Asian cities. Taipei, Taiwan has wide, busy streets where there seem to be no rules. Lawlessness, such as ignoring signals, is aggravated by leaning on the horn. Low grade fuel emissions cloud the air. It's common to see up to four people crammed onto one moped. Mopeds move freight as well. Today I saw a fellow weaving through traffic on a small scooter while hauling a king-size mattress and box spring upon his back."—journal entry

**CANON 14a:** Avoid money hernias. Don't haggle people to extinction. The same shoppers who beat down an impoverished Javanese innkeeper fifty cents probably shop back home at The Sharper Image. The test of adventure greatness depends on the depth of the traveler's vision, secondary is their amount of time, and last is their bank account.

Don't become a sporting-goods hero. Do you really need a personalized odometer/altimeter for that day hike? Although K-Mart and Wal-Marts have crushed small-town intimacy, these retail coliseums sell tents and walking shorts priced way below the mall-rat outfitters.

**CANON 14b:** Dancing is a great, inexpensive form of entertainment.

Economic prudence once led me to a gut-level, Caracas dance hall where the landscape relaxed with a continuous warm-climate, mañana attitude. Usually, the higher up on the socioeconomic ladder one travels, the likelihood of meeting an English-speaking acquaintance increases. In local, easy-going joints on the "wrong side of town" your chances of encountering an amigo capable of speaking English are slim. No worry, lacking Spanish skills makes your search for a dance partner a bona fide challenge. One option is to persuade one of the more senior *senoritas* to familiarize you with the hand and foot placements. Even a language-impaired visitor soon realizes that dancing, like eating, is routine here, a national sport, where everyone's clued in. Albeit exciting, dancing faces remain expressionless, as dreamy eyes hover calmly aloft dimly-lit, slyly meshing torsos. Somewhat like a thriving high school gymnasium dance, minus the US-style cotillion theatrics.

Once you understand the dance partner search strategy (approaching a table of people and extending your open hand with a smile), finding a partner is easy. Four out of five women accept these *extended hand*, dance floor invitations, not bad compared to North America's woesome one for six average. On the dance floor, your gringo status goes undetected, unless you open your mouth—a habit for many States folk. So hush, treasure the sundry, close-up dances and the immediate, innocent intimacy. A majority of the combinations seem to inspire either entranced, locked-at-the-mid-section gyrating, or, earnest, pelvic collisions. In any case, you'll be in close quarters. Try watching other couple's hands and feet out of the corner of your eye until you get the hang of it.

Dancing endures as a hedonistic life force that's not deadly or illegal. Wherever you roam, discover the local music scene by hanging around the "tape market." Translation: locate an outdoor cassette market, when you hear something that moves you, find out where they are playing or DJ-ing. Dance zones remain indifferent to status. Infectious music lets UBU.

**CANON 15:** The first thing you pack is yourself. And *that* should be an open, positive thinking, compassionate person. Buy things there, it helps you blend. With the exception of Frisbees, feminine products and antibiotic ointments (for ferociously itchy insect bites, jock itch and stinging bungs) you can often buy basic items en route cheaper—Japan and Scandinavia are exceptions to this decree. Unless you're scheming to ice climb to do naked Yoga above the tree line, hold off on buying boot crampons.

Bring earplugs. Aside from safeguarding snore-stressed marriages, they're protection against blaring buses, trains and bracing humans.

**389**

Backpack. The most important feature is the zippers, when they fail, the backpack *isn't*. Darker colors hide dirt, and thieves, like bugs, seem lured to bright colors. And, before stuffing your pack, recognize that the real essentials are what's in a globetrotter's head—background knowledge, resourcefulness, a considerate perspective and a smile.

Pack to give away. Clothes, footwear, Bungee cords, safety pins, etc. They need them more than you do. Bring balloons for the kids. People who've never seen an ocean love sea shells. Photos of friends and family also create smiles. Pack a cassette mix fave or two—lost Brazilian villages sometimes have generators that make a few hours of juice per day. Many people learn English via music.

Airline giveaway paraphernalia (slippers, eye patches, toothbrushes) make great gifts in undeveloped countries. Business Class travelers always leave these gifts behind, collect them as you deplane.

Gifts purchased on the road? Follow your impulse. An $8 Balinese wood-carving turns more heads than another tee shirt. Occupational tools such as bamboo fish traps, spears and handmade backpacks can be purchased (though they may not be for sale) at a fair price.

**CANON 16a:** Europe? Please hold out. Visit the distant lands of undrinkable water and witch-doctoring while your immune system is hearty. Delay western Europe for when negotiating stairs is a bitch.

**CANON 16b:** And jeez, believe me, when you do visit Europe don't attempt to photograph the Amsterdam red-light district prostitutes unless you're wearing running shoes. After relentless rejection, I offered one *pro* the fee for her usual services to snap one photo. Nope. I snapped it anyway. Suddenly, an army of heel-clacking harlots were sprinting my warpath, intent on destroying more than my camera.

**CANON 17:** The trip starts before you leave. Befriend a fellow globetrotter at the airport before the plane boards; the alert travelers wearing sensible footwear (and the sense they wouldn't be crushed by a rainstorm) are easy to spot. En route, learn from the existing traveler's subculture. How do I get started on the SE Asia trail? Partner with a European or Australian road warrior who dropped by three years ago, and hasn't left.

**CANON 18:** Inoculations. Seems to be two schools of thought: absolutely and forget it. Many unvaccinated veteran travelers escape without incident, but some rookies get cerebral malaria. You decide. Your local or county health department should be cheaper than the tropical disease specialist and after they both send your itinerary to the Center for Disease Control they'll probably urge the same thing—a bucket load of pills and shots. Avoiding many diseases, like malaria, is 90% prevention. Better safe than sorry. Try acupuncture and homeopathy for what ails you before you go as a preventative measure and if you get sick on the road. Many over-the-counter, unnatural Western medicine panaceas eventually backfire.

**CANON 19:** You only stumble when you're moving. Expect setbacks. The Chinese symbol for crisis represents both breakdown and opportunity. Have a book, a conversation, or a drink handy for waiting out avalanche-blocked roads or for when the trekking permit office in Katmandu invents another holiday. Every now and then, you might have to grin-and-bear a tourist trap that's in bloom. Keep moving boredom-fighting soldiers!

BOOKS: Pack a masterpiece, complicity often sneaks in. I read this apropos inquiry in Thoreau's *Walden* while trekking amongst naked New Guinea aboriginals: "It is an interesting question how far men would retain their relative rank if they were divested of their clothes."

**CANON 20:** Romance on the road. Pack a coffin. Nah, when you and honey quarrel, chant the Chinese idiom, "Even a typhoon doesn't last a day." (Review Canon 12a). Quarrels often ensue on departure and arrival days under the duress of laboring through airports and getting ripped-off by unscrupulous cab drivers.

"Of all the things I've lost, I miss my mind the most."—Anonymous

I piloted a horse-drawn carriage around midtown Manhattan for a year. Most riders were couples. The most useful missive I beheld from blissful older couples was that a sense of humor breeds timeless compatibility.

**CANON 21a:** Resist complaining. Period. It may be a symptom of your *cubicle-infested office allergy*. If you must whimper, break out your translation dictionary or phrase book and transcribe your conundrum to a local. You may realize that your dilemma is a tad pathetic, and you might even learn the language.

Lacking a translation dictionary, my fuse was tested on a 3rd class train ride across China. "No room" in the sleeper car, third sleepless day, scores of snoozing Chinese families on the floor and in the spaces between cars, nowhere to stretch out. Flocks of live chickens stowed in the bathrooms and huge sides of butchered meat hanging from the overhead luggage racks. Mothers periodically posing their babies outside of the moving train windows so they could poop. Black diesel engine smoke blowing into the car, never traveling faster than 40 miles per hour, all the while, odd vendors pacing back and forth, endlessly peddling peculiar dried crustacean snacks. One group, snacking on a greasy chicken carcass, amused themselves by drooling profusely and randomly expelling any undesirable foodstuffs about the car. Not a napkin in sight. Coughing up and spitting phlegm onto any nearby floor is also part of the drill. On day three, I finally comprehended that an eighty-cent payoff was required and the conductor led me into a totally empty sleeper car for my nap.

"When a man has something to say he must try to say it as clearly as possible, and when he has nothing to say it is better for him to keep quiet." —Tolstoy

**CANON 21b:** You may not *have it your way* ... I winced when I caught my first glimpse of freshly lacquered, skinned, beheaded beagles and other dog torsos. More than one of my China dining affairs was botched when shallow buckets of dog and cat heads came into view. You soon realize that anything moving on the mainland is edible. There seem to be colonies, or at least entire streets dedicated to slaughtering and selling anything not human. You may find yourself sprinting to the end of one of these streets of carnage, deep in the throes of nausea. China is wonderfully bizarre and beautiful too. Go.

**CANON 22:** Consider thumb-touring. Japanese are trusting people, and hitching is not a problem. A truck driver gave me a lift from Tokyo to Osaka, bought me lunch midway and continuously tried to illustrate the immensity of Mount Fuji. The only word we had in common was "Madonna." Arriving in Osaka after midnight, I had difficulty explaining that I needed to find a very cheap place to sleep. The confusion continued until he drove me to the police station in search of an interpreter. After a momentary exchange with the police, he waved goodbye. A policeman then set folded blankets and a pillow on a cot that was inside one of the jail cells. He motioned me into the cell, returning with biscuits and a glass of juice. Smiling, he said, "Morning," exited and closed the door.

Hitchhiking can be very dangerous. If you must do it, try creating a sign for a destination that's in the opposite direction of your actual destination and display it while thumbing in the direction of your *desired* destination. When a concerned driver pulls over to correct your blooper, explain the tactic and request a lift. Other sign options: Please, Harmless, Free Beer, Mountains, Hello, Mom, Trees.

People are proud of their homeland and hitching is a dandy way to identify with a region. Thumb-tour anonymity breeds honesty and free therapy. Enter a different mind on the hour! (Don't be afraid to refuse a ride from suspicious drivers.)

PS: If driving in Mexico and you are pulled over for an "offense," have a few collateral Playboy or Penthouse handy—fork one over and they'll usually call it even.

**CANON 23:** Don't defend the USA, unless you are very good at it. For example, you're gathered beneath a thatched palm-leaf roof Thai restaurant pontificating with two Germans, an Aussie and a Swede when the state-of-world politics controversy surfaces and they all pick on the American. Take the fifth or try this one: "Smaller countries have bigger outlooks."

**CANON 24:** Unsettling things happen. Move on. Life ain't fair? Well, the *fair* comes to town once a year and it's not reality.

"Fall down seven times get up eight"—Buddhist quote.

Bumming-out over a Philippine flight delay, my brother had a change of heart by chancing upon an impoverished, seven-year-old boy who was joyously flying a kite that he constructed by tying a long string to a billowing plastic trash bag. Why worry? The well-to-do tend to dwell on luxury problems.

**CANON 25:** Assume an identity. Fabricate an I.D. Shush. Bogus journalist and student cards, or anything you aspire to be, are easily procured in Bangkok, Hong Kong, Amsterdam and New York. I've wielded my "Journalist ID" to slip into untold concerts, Knick games and MTV parties. Keep it off my record.

**CANON 26a:** "If you come to a fork in the road, take it."—Yogi Berra

And when you choose a fork, remember John Muir, naturalist extraordinaire, the definitive lone wolf. A brilliant, intense, cantankerous man, his handsome features obscured by a beard suited for nesting. His passion was Yosemite Valley, with which he was locked in a lifelong metaphysical embrace that made his human associations secondary at best. He was famous for climbing a Douglas Spruce high in the mountains in the midst of a riotous lightning storm, where he swayed back and forth in the topmost branches, yowling with crazy delight.

**CANON 26b:** Get Wild. On India's Anjuna Beach I attended a full-moon dance party thrown by the nomadic, Western hippies who are still busy elbowing the edge of the psychedelic frontier. These untamed, clothing optional *cotillions* last all night, the campfire amplifying the day-glo face paint. Undulating to the techno music sensurround, expatriate mothers grooved lavishly to the rhythms while simultaneously breast-feeding their babies. Lactose tolerance.

**CANON 27:** "Be a good date."—Kurt Vonnegut, Jr., lecturing on writing.

So you want to write? Aspiring travel writers might dare sending editors nifty postcards from the road. Scribe theirs only after you've practiced penning the panorama to your pals. The pencil is mightier than the pen—some mistakes are erasable.

"I put a piece of paper under my pillow and when I could not sleep I wrote in the dark."—Thoreau

**CANON 28:** Respect their culture. We haven't strip-malled the entire planet yet.

Tell me, was this a bonehead move? While trekking high in Nepal's Himalaya, ten days walk from electricity and presidential sex scandal, I happened upon a medicine-chest-sized mirror hanging on a teahouse wall. Reminiscent of my juvenile epoch, I removed the mirror from the wall, walked outside and used it to transmit the immensely powerful sun reflection around the village. Fifty Nepalese villagers soon gathered to witness the miracle of this invention that had graduated to transmitting the godlike solar laser beam to villages across the valley. For the remainder of the day, as I gradually hiked up and away from the village, an elderly woman sun-beamed *me* every twenty minutes. Though they had the means, things may never be the same.

**CANON 29:** Apply the Travelers' Safety Code of Conduct. It's OK not to trust anyone right away. Experienced travelers are not offended by cordial "distrust" between new acquaintances, even if they share a room. It is accepted that life on the road makes an easier target. If a friendship is being built to last, neither individual will take offense to precautionary wisdom—like toting your valuables with you every time you hit the toilet and storing valuables in your pillow case while you sleep. Unlike the hit-and-run thief, con artists have all week.

**CANON 30:** "Remember what you have seen, because everything forgotten returns to the circling winds."—lines from a Navajo wind chant.

Wherever you wander, behold sunsets whenever possible. It's therapeutic to gaze into the sun as it sails into the horizon, allowing the availing lithium rays to nourish your genius. Sunsets are, involuntarily, the most pensive minutes of the day.

"Things do not change; we change."—Thoreau

**CANON 31:** Follow the surfers. If you are bargain hunting for *tranquilo* fun in the sun, trust that the career surfers have touched down where Valhalla has no service charge.

But don't follow me into the subway. One night at 3a.m., when I was twenty-one and living in Queens, N.Y., I was returning home from a indulgent Manhattan debutante ball. Waiting on the station platform, sporting a tuxedo, overwhelmed with impatience and inspired by a robust champagne buzz—I jumped onto the subway tracks and ran beneath the East River all the way to

Queens. I eluded passing trains by pinning myself against the tunnel wall. Upon arriving at my station, I climbed up onto the platform, straightened my collar, and winked at the crowd waiting there for the next train.

**CANON 32:** The good old days are now. "It" is not ruined. Ignore traveler's snobbery. Bali, Thailand and other supposedly overrun paradises are still great places to visit, even though it may have been more *real* fifteen years ago. Your first time is your first time, virgin turf simply is. The moment you commit to a trip, there begins the search for adventure. Excitement finds you.

**CANON 33:** "People don't take trips—trips take people."—John Steinbeck

While on a long bicycle journey to wherever, I happened upon a sole Chinese woman tending to a crop. Mutually surprised by the encounter, I dismounted my bike as she leaned her chin on the handle of her shovel. For a moment we scrutinized each another. The two of us couldn't have come from farther corners of the world. I wondered how she kept her white dress spotless in the fields while she puzzled over why I might be riding a bicycle across her quarter. After a silent, timeless minute, we simultaneously burst into smiles. Feeling self-conscious yet light-hearted, we continued smiling at one another without words for what seemed like eternity. I waved a good bye and rode away. Before coasting out of view behind a hilltop, I glanced back at her. There she stood, still leaning on her shovel, beaming, waving. With her, I shared one of those inestimable, aesthetic flashes. Her benign image echoes within my mind long after the vaunt of many museum portraits diminish.

**CANON 34:** Go ahead and cry. One lonely night in Malaysia (in the midst of a year abroad), I saw *Harry and the Hendersons*, a PG movie about a family who adopt a cuddly Big-Foot. I sobbed and felt better.

**CANON 35:** Practice People-Watching. Yes, doing anything is sometimes a problem. But you can always watch people. A spare part of somebody else's conversation can make or break a dull day. Even if your life feels like an incurable, sexually transmitted disease, look over there at *them*. Eavesdropping isn't as risky as those ridiculous attempts at forced dialogue that backfire. I remember riding a Berlin train when a chipper American said hello, without warrant, to the dour German passenger seated across from him. The German dryly inquired, "Do I know you?"

People-Watching Decoys:

a. Walking the dog

b. Sunglasses

c. One-way mirrors

d. Toting a baby

**CANON 36:** Don't rush home, not much has changed. The mist hovering over home life clears when you leave for a while. Somewhere in the journey, make a checklist of things you want to accomplish and eliminate from the home front. Brain-dump everything and cross off items when they're either actualized or hurled into orbit. Warning: your Buddhist tranquility may diminish three weeks after returning home, when you find your worldly self once again yelping at traffic jams.

Take everything in moderation, including moderation itself.

**CANON 37:** Hop the fence. If you are budgeting (sleeping in dumps), enjoy the bathroom and pool side chase lounge at the fancy hotel across town. Do a quick-change stash into your day pack. Act familiar.

**CANON 38:** You can be *wild* anywhere. The defining highlight of a New York Yankees baseball game I attended occurred when a thrill seeking fan *escaped* from the outfield bleachers and ran onto the field, disrupting the game. The *new* game became applauding the nimble, sprinting fan as he eluded three stocky security guards for five minutes. Tag extraordinaire. An adult version of elementary schoolyard keep-away brought the packed stadium to its feet. With each failed security guard attempt to dive and capture the fugitive the fans redoubled their grand-slam style uproar. Upon apprehension the security guards were emphatically booed. Just before the hero was hauled out of sight into the stadium penitentiary, he managed to wrestle free one arm and wave his cap to the crowd—a victory gesture that earned him a final, frenzied ovation. People just don't have to be grown up all the time.

**CANON 39:** Guarantee: THE RAT-RACE WILL STILL BE ON WHEN YOU RETURN. Besides, the problem with the rat-race is that even if you win, you're *still* a rat.

Ponder this: get in touch with the urgent starscape by sleeping outside—one time, exist outdoors for a week. Attempting au naturel puts you in touch with our celestial dome and inadvertently your own dome.

**CANON 40:** The grass is always greener on the other side, especially when you first arrive. Check out this world before the next.

"Most people have that fantasy of catching the train that whistles in the night."—Willie Nelson

**CANON 41:** Have your mid-life crisis now. Don't postpone travel happiness indefinitely. A life of WORK can be dreadful. Escape while you can. Listen to your heart and ignore the boss' grimace upon your forthcoming sabbatical.

"Do your thing and I will know you."—Emerson

**CANON 42:** Give something back to the people whose lives you pass through. Day after day, villagers see travelers tramp through their space, pay them for food, ogle their lives and then move on. Enrich *their* lives with a song, painting, sport lesson, recipe, poem, smile, hug? ... the possibilities are endless.

*Live Loving*

*Die Dreaming*

—epitaph in Guayaquil, Ecuador's Cemetery General

# THRIFTY TRAVEL SAVVY

## Cheap Tricks

*"I think that to get under the surface and really appreciate the beauty of any country one has to go there poor."*

Grace Moore

# A Stunned, Heavily Perfumed Bunny

**Anthony Grant**

*Charm, guts, and guile go a long way for pretty girls on a low budget.
Except on German trains.*

SHE CAN SEE I'M CONTENT gazing into the blackness out there, so, having awakened, adjusts her pink blouse, rubs her eyes with delicate Park Avenue knuckles and proceeds to distract me with the sort of benign interrogation one comes to expect from fellow passengers in faraway places.

"Were you in Prague on business or pleasure?" she asks.

"Is there a difference anymore?"

"Well I came to take in a little culture, but ended up meeting Günter here"— she identifies a dormant Teuton, flat on stomach, legs stretched over her lap, mouth almost kissing the little ash tray beneath the thickly-paned window— "and, well, the old *histoire d'amour* kind of thing, you know."

"Well, I'm not really coming from Prague."

"Oh. From where then?"

"Olomouc."

"Olomook? Isn't that like the new Buzios of Bohemia or something?"

"Actually, Olomoats" I start, re-pronouncing it to my Czech phrasebook's specifications, "is—" but I am interrupted by the locomotive equivalent of a telephone ringing—the sliding open of the door that seals our compartment off from the narrow corridor outside. Enter a mustached conductor with signature cap on head and ticket puncher in hand. Ready to punch. The customary, ever-charming salutation: "Tickets."

I go first. My Czech ticket took me as far as Domazlice, but this conductor's Terminator-esque accent and Aryan-Sears Roebuck model looks tell me we must already be in zee Fatherland. So I proffer my Eurail Flexipass for inspection. He punches his little hole next to where I've written in the date, manages a "thank you" and turns to the girl who turned out to be Melissa, grinning that "I am Lord and Master of the Railways" grin.

**400**

"Ticket, please. And his."

"Günter has both. Hold on one minute," she says, drawing out the "one" as she jostles her swain's hind quarters.

"Get up Güntie, it's ticket time. C'mon hon, roll over."

But he is, for the purposes of this situation, dead. The repetitious lurching of the train has carried Günter up and away, I imagine, to a fair green land where chocolate milk comes from horses and American women do the farm chores topless. The conductor inhales, flares his nostrils.

"Wake him," he demands. Only he says "Vake."

"He's out like buffalo mozzarella and tomato salad," Melissa says, and with that pushes his legs away from her and reaches for his side, shaking it with as much gentle violence as she can muster. But Günter is now rowing down the crystalline Rhine under the mild Bavarian sun, so the touch of foreign hands wrestling him from unconsciousness must feel like some invisible force yanking him from his dinghy. He tumbles onto the floor.

"There! There they are!" Melissa yelps, pointing to a standard issue EurailPass and some other kind of ticket now visibly protruding from Günter's shirt pocket. She lunges for the goods, hands them over to the conductor.

He examines the EurailPass ticket first, index finger plying the bristly upper lip. I can sense what's coming next.

"Erasable ink."

"What?" asks Melissa in that mock-incredulous way people talk when they know they've done something wrong but still think they have a chance of getting away with it. Not that I, also budget-conscious, didn't sympathize with her.

"You have used erasable ink up and down this ticket. And you do not erase very well." Conductor-as-Satan syndrome strikes again.

Yes, leave it to Melissa to resort to the oldest trick in the book in the worst possible place. I can see there are 15 blank spaces on her ticket. That means 15 days of unlimited train travel in Europe as defined by dates the ticket holder is obliged to record, in permanent ink, each day before she hops aboard a train. But as anyone who has ever spent a summer or college semester abroad knows, a quality erasable pen will do wonders to stretch two weeks out by, oh, another week or so. You have to know, however, where you can pull this scribbled stunt off without a hitch so you don't end up thumbs up alongside a rainsoaked foreign highway. In Italy no one bothers to look at your ticket. In France you can generally dodge a conductor's ticket check by camping out in the bathroom. Same for Switzerland. But you never, ever mess around on the German railways.

"You must pay the maximum allowable fine right now or leave the train at the next stop. The fine is, roughly, 250 American dollars."

**401**

"But!"

"No buts. And now his." He eyeballs Günther's ticket. "OK," he says, handing it back to the smiling sloth. "But not you."

"But I spent all my money on folk puppets! Günter, do you have any—" but his head is already shaking.

Now she looks at me with wide eyes and fully flexed cheek muscles, not unlike a stunned, heavily perfumed bunny.

"Sorry—only six korunas to my name."

"Come with me please," the conductor said.

"No, no! Just let me send a fax! Or could you send a fax, please!?," she implores me. "To the Hotel Mirador in Montreux. My ex-fiancé's playing accordion at the jazz festival. He could wire ..."

Too late. The conductor shuffles her, followed by Günter, to the vestibule from which she will be summarily expelled at the next stop. Judging from the sudden deceleration of the train, it's only moments away.

Alone again.

# The First Ascent of Mighty Trashmore

## Paul McHugh

*Forget expensive mountain climbing excursions—some of the most remarkable summits can be found right out back.*

TRASHMORE REVERSES THAT OLD ROMAN POET'S DICTUM. Here, mice have labored to give birth to a mountain.

That was to be one of my last lucid observations as I struggled upward through a methane-laden miasma. Up here, at elevations several yards beyond 100 feet, my very consciousness could easily become mighty Trashmore's chew toy.

Coarse grasses coiled like snakes about my legs. Rough pebbles slipped into my sandals. Despite these difficulties, an awful wonder grew steadily in my mind. I was, after all, in the throes of my life's most epic quest: the first solo ascent of the tallest peak in the continental US—south of Miami. For more than two days, I'd been forced to wait out the capricious South Florida monsoon. I'd grown fidgety, even a little cranky, as I watched my jalousie of opportunity slowly open, only to swiftly slam shut before I could even swing out of my lawn hammock. But now, all those besotted hours of waiting were over, and the supreme physical challenge had begun.

It is worth emphasizing that the mountain I trod upon was none of the Almighty's handiwork. Men themselves had reared this peak against the heavens! Begun only in the 1980's, within a decade Trashmore already held some eight million tons of festering garbage. Never let it be said that South Floridians shrank from the daunting task of erecting a monument that stands as emblematic of our time as the pyramid of Cheops is of the antique empire of the pharaohs.

The rearing of Trashmore against the skies has its roots in some remarkable statistics. In the United States, the average amount of solid trash generated by each person per day totals about 3.5 pounds. With a clear sense of mission, heroic South Floridians more than double this figure: they generate waste to the tune of eight pounds per person each day. Most of that gets stacked on Trashmore—or other vertical landfill behemoths—that are rapidly bringing some relief to boring levelness of the South Florida horizon line.

Sadly, not all of the Florida waste gets devoted to this geologic function. Much of it gets, well, wasted—by being burned in giant incinerators. These merely fumigate the landscape with insubstantial toxic plumes, instead of being invested in more lasting monuments, like this fine vertical dump.

Trashmore and his brother peaks got an unexpected windfall, so to speak, from Hurricane Andrew's largesse in late 1992. You've undoubtedly recall the still photos or video footage. Hundreds of thousands of poorly designed, inadequately inspected and shoddily constructed homes went whiff! under the hammer of an event any meteorology student could have predicted would occur sooner or later. Be that as it may, this gargantuan mound named Trashmore is South Florida's premier landfill and is also—quite probably—the most remarkable artificial mountain to erupt since hanging gardens bloomed on Nebuchadenazzer's ziggurats. Culturally, it has more significance than the gambling chip midden outside the Vatican's rear windows.

Such musings, fueled by my panting inhalations of methane and ammonia (spiked by the odd passing zephyr of oxygen) heaved through my feverish brain as I stumbled up Trashmore's slopes. I was just beginning to fantasize that the slopes of Trashmore would probably be a good place for astronauts to train for manned missions to the moons of Uranus, when my attention was riveted by a rustling in the headwall formed by rank vegetation just before me.

Could it be ...? Yes! I burst through a grove of deformed shrubbery to see scores of the legendary garuda birds hopping and flapping on an exposed seam of that unique Trashmore formation, "ordurite." The huge birds dramatically stretched long, naked necks, clacked their beaks, waddled gracelessly, and launched themselves into the air. Some of the low might refer to garudas as mere buzzards, but such folk have never seen these glorious fowl at the noisome epicenter of their habitat. For a moment, one blotted out the sun. He was almost heraldic, with a maggot-riddled mullet clenched in his right talon, a crumpled tract of abandoned political promises in his left.

In days of yore, these garudas had been overshadowed aloft by teeming flights of roseate spoonbills, egrets, wood storks, and other feathered waterlovers winging in and out of the Everglades. But the wetlands, freshwater flows, and clean natural foods needed by these wading birds had dwindled, while fresh supplies of roadkill and garbage continued a spectacular rise. So eventually the songbirds, waterbirds and woodpeckers moved on, and now the mighty garudas ruled the skies.

I spun around to share this moment of grand discovery with my support crew down at our Base Winnebago, parked far below at the barrier fence. However, even over the immense distance of more than a quarter-mile, it was apparent that no one stood down there at our tripod-mounted spotting scope. I felt abandoned, bereft, marooned on the sharp end of an unraveling rope. Then, I suddenly remembered that my base camp crew had promised me a fresh fish dinner upon my return after the probable triumph of this summit bid. Perhaps they had just strolled off to bob baits in the torpid stream we called Miasma Creek—which gurgled right past the ingrown toenails of mighty Trashmore.

An unsung attribute of Trashmore is that this manmade mountain concocts springs and freshets of type never seen in nature. Juices in this gargantuan heap, by methods arcane, steep and slowly blend together into a noxious brew deep in its massive interior. This cocktail of ammonia-laden leachate is cleverly collected in a system of interior drains by the mountain's builders, then mixed with sewage donated by generous local communities. The resultant brew is deep-well injected into salt caverns 3,200 feet below Florida's limestone layer. It is not known if these caverns have any outlets to the sea, or up into the freshwater aquifer. In any case, the potent broth offers a rich legacy to future generations.

What might be achieved with this magical potion staggers the imagination. Some leachate escapes into Miasma Creek from the unlined portion of the landfill—and already locals have affectionately nicknamed this stream the River of The Three-Eyed Fish! A farmhand, Geraldine Riviera, ate a small portion of her day's catch, and two weeks later gave birth to triplets with magenta hair. What made this especially remarkable was that Ms. Riviera was 76 at the time. Knowing that my loyal support crew was even now probing the dank Miasma waters for my victory dinner, I cheerfully plodded onward, ever upward. Distant though it still was, I could say in certain terms that I smelled the summit.

I experienced no small difficulty at the final terrace, where Mallomar and Irving had last been glimpsed by basecamp observers before they vanished forever into the Trashmore fastness, leaving not a trace of their ultimate fate. While making my ascent of this sloping feature, I stubbed my toe against some old oxygen tanks, had to sweep crusty cameras out of my way with the Batso Mallet, and then got it tangled up in a windbreaker wrapped around a heap of bones and notebooks. But eventually, I was free to ascend.

One step. Two steps. Skip once, hop on both feet, skip and stop. I repeated this rhythm over and over. Over and over. Over and over again. Over and over, some more. The true mountaineer must always be on his toes, responding to each fresh challenge with some creative movement. It is only because of our innate superiority that we are able to tread sacred places in which the coagulated mass of lesser humanity remains totally uninterested.

Then, mirabile dictu, I was there. On the very peak of Trashmore! Tears of ersatz ecstasy leaped from the corners of my eyes. They'd all sneered, calling me a sportclimbing gym rat. They'd be laughing out of the other side of their snouts now, with a climb like this to my credit! A solo first ascent of Trashmore by its direttissima would 'scribe my name in glory, far above peak baggers with mere bagatelles like taking K-2, Makalu and Desilu in a weekend, the Himalaya's infamous Triple Crown. Let others brag about their skills on verglass-sheeted rock, jumbled glacier seracs and overhanging ice. My abilities on crushed plastic, crumpled cans and wet newspaper had just been proven supreme.

Through a murky smaze to the north, I could now discern the fabulous Miami skyline, only slightly eroded by impacts from small arms fire and rocket grenades since the martyrdom of Mayor Sonny Crockett. In the panorama that spread to the south, Turkey Point Nuclear Power Plant reared up the swollen phalli of its smokestacks and cooling towers. My heart beat with pride as I thought of generations unborn. "Someday," I murmured, "Someday, all of this will be yours."

A kind of panegyric rumbled up from my very bowels.

"O Trashmore, thou art the art of man, supreme! How magnificent that we have caused a peak to lurch up where none stood before! In other regions, people may blindly seek to minimize trash, to remove and conceal it. Only here is its true potential discovered and unleashed! In benighted areas like Everest, climbers organize expeditions to remove litter from basecamps. Fools! Don't they see how Everest's paltry tectonic upthrust of a few centimeters per year could be wonderfully enhanced? All they have to do is pack all that refuse up to the summit and stack it there!

"Today's waste is the treasure of Tomorrowland. Eco-freaks and other feckless nabobs of nattering negativism would prefer seeing Trashmore shackled to a height of no more than 250 feet. I say, set Trashmore free. Bring in lorries of refuse from neighboring states. Import it by barge from around the world! Get this peak and many others up above 12,000, even 14,000 feet!

"The Appalachians for example—poor stunted hills—could be the foundation for a new crest more mighty than any that stood here in geologic history, a towering escarpment of garbage stretching all the way from mighty Trashmore to the front stoop of the US Bells Shop in Prospect Harbor, Maine.

"Future generations will reel in astonishment at our achievement. We may feel quite certain, with grandiose monuments like Trashmore to contemplate that they shall—at the very least—never forget us."

# Confession of Nagoya Fats

## Robert W. Bone

*Some men spend much of their lives trying to come out ahead at pachinko,
the traditional slot machine of Japan. These noisy, vertical pinballish
facades have been installed in colorfully lit pachinko parlors throughout the
country.*

RICK CARROLL, A REPORTER FRIEND OF MINE, and an old hand in Japan,
taught me pachinko, during a 1991 visit to Nagoya. He sat down at a
machine and deftly began shooting some little steelies around the board for
several minutes, using 100-yen coins (then worth about 75 cents each) each
time for the privilege.

"Here, let me try that," I said, and Rick obliged by giving up his seat to me
while he moved on to potentially more fertile mechanisms. For the first time in
my life, then, I played pachinko, inserting just one 100-yen coin in the slot and
then twisting some kind of a doorknob-like handle.

Suddenly all kinds of whistles and bells seemed to break loose. Lights began
to flash. An attendant ran over with a colored flag to place on my machine,
gushing something I couldn't understand. With a steady roar, steel balls began
to spit and pour from the mouth of the mechanical monster in front of me,
and the man had to hook on a special plastic tray to catch them all.

It seemed like it took five minutes for the tray to fill up with everything the
machine had to disgorge. With sign language, the attendant motioned that I
should carry it—a heavy task—over to a counting machine. In a few seconds,
it toted up, I believe, some 3000 pachinko balls.

For these, I was given a group of mysterious small boxes gathered together in
a larger cigar box, together with a chocolate bar. Some prizes were displayed
on a nearby wall, but instinctively the attendant knew I was not going to be satisfied with a new toaster.

"Come," he said. "Get money."

Now he was speaking my language.

He led me outdoors and on a long walk down the street and through a narrow, dark alley to what appeared to be some kind of a small shop. I might have

been worried, except that I was followed by Rick and a few friends who were witnessing these awesome events. At the store, the woman behind the counter ignored the candy but counted and stashed the boxes, and then handed over 5000 yen in cash (about $40). I calculated later that she might have taken around 1000 yen in commission.

Later, back at the hotel, I used my new wealth to buy us all a round of drinks. We should have gone to a neighborhood bar. It didn't go quite far enough at the Hilton. Rick helped subsidize my generosity and then asked me when I was going to try pachinko again.

"Never," I told him. "I have retired as a totally undefeated champion."

Eight years later, I can still claim that title.

# Rules of the Inn

## Unknown Author

*The weight of history, intensified by a Welsh pub placard ...*

NO THIEVES, FAKIRS, ROGUES OR TINKERS.

No skulking loafers or flea-bitten tramps.

No 'slap an tickle o' the wenches.

No banging o' tankards on the tables.

No dogs allowed in the kitchen.

No cockfighting.

Flintlocks, cudgels, daggers & swords to be handed to the innkeepers for safekeeping.

Bed for the night 1 Shilling.

Stabling for horse 4 pence.

1786

# Balanced on a Thumb

## Brendan Lake

*A callous blow to the state of US hitchhiking occurred when truck drivers'
insurance policies cut hitchers out of the picture. The sensation-hungry
media also makes today's drivers and riders mutually suspicious. But the
tradition lives on, and you can still thumb a ride into the 21st century.*

L ET ME TELL YOU A STORY.

I'm 18. Stuff my bag and take eighty-five dollars on the road. Wearing a
fifty-pound pack, I pace DC's streets, trepidating. Georgetown students leer as
I roam campus and then play late night piano in their chapel. Ride a suburban
afternoon train to the end. Hitch down the mall-stripped asphalt in the evening
rain. Van slows to a stop, a Religioso who drives around for an hour, preaching.
Buys dinner and then leaves me, lost. A drowning rat splashing in the gutter,
tears flowing in the rain. A city bus slows to a stop, door opens, driver looks
down, asks, "Where ya' headed?"

"Out West."

"Oh boy ... get on." No charge. The people I sit near relocate. The driver
drops off the last passengers, parks in the city terminal and offers me a ride in
his car to a truck stop. Tide turns.

Strange looks as I sip coffee. Distrust. Outside, I sit on a picnic table, trying
to make eye contact with passing truckers. Hard to miss the three-hundred
pound man walking straight toward me, looking mean. Stop breathing as he
passes, then follow him with an eye that finds his glance.

"You're a damn fool" he barks. "Your first problem is you don't have any
boobs. Ain't one trucker out here who's gonna' look at ya' twice."

"You did" I remind him, preparing for turbulence.

Walk into a motel and convince the desk to let me nap on the lobby couch.
Rise before the sun and find the exit ramp. Need a shower. A monstrous, black
18-wheeler rumbles the earth as it works down through a galaxy of gears.
Climb up to the door.

"Goin' to Albuquerque, no further. And I ain't buyin' ya a damn thing to eat so don't even ask," the oddly familiar voice rumbles. A couple of states later, conversing at 90 miles-per-hour, he samples my dehydrated chili mix.

Sit on the curb in front of a skanky restaurant, gnawing a chunk of cheddar. A mangy little mutt trots around the corner, greets me with old-timer nuzzles. We sit together looking out over the dreary city. A motherly waitress' voice turns our heads, a plate of leftover food in her hand. She looks at the homeless mutt, "He can have the burger." She leaves; we split it.

Crawl under a fence, make my way across a disturbed meadow, enter the realm of the homeless. Interstate traffic buzzes overhead. On the median strip in a strange city, stranded like an animal. Set up camp there and sleep lightly through the night, an empty malt liquor bottle nearby, just in case. Woken rudely by a crow, cawing from a looming tree. Peek out from under my tarp.

The crow returns my look and hushes. The homeless hideout population doubles by dawn. I pack, my crow spying.

Resting on another truck stop curb, I eat an apple, keeping an eye out for rides. An annoyed manager insists I leave the property. Walking slowly across the lot, another crow looks at me invitingly from his perch on a truck's rear-view mirror. Don't think twice about knocking on the door. On my way to Colorado.

Walk on, not hitching, feel radiator heat on the back of my legs. No sketchy challenges up to this point, wonder if luck will hold. The Shoshone medicine man sees my congestion and passes me a small root suggesting minute nibbles. The bitter root clears my passages and heats up my ears.

Back to back van rides. I wrestle my pack through a sliding door and introduce myself as I make my way to the front seat. No response. He returns the look, states that he's deaf, a lip reader. Chills up and down my spine. I repeat my name and homeland clearly. Without looking at me he responds that he's a lead guitarist. Confused, it doesn't seem possible for this man to be deaf. I ask him how far he's headed. He seems to be looking in his rear-view mirror rather than at my lips. As he answers, I realize that he's adjusted the mirror to read my lips.

Another high-speed ride into Aspen. Five days later, I'm swinging ski-lift chairs under over-privileged butts, living downtown. In the small park looking at Mt. Sopris, sit on a bench among burbling pigeons. My mind is centered by the alpenglow. I stand when the moon rises over a mountain. The sun sets behind another peak. In the center of the park, I gaze between the moon and sun.

"Yo Bro', you balancing?" a voice calls from a group of dread-locked rovers. I send a smile.

# A Clean, Affordable Buzz

## Mark Schwartz

*Can a haircut change all that much? There must be a reason for everything.*

INTO MY LAP SHE DROPS what must be the standard men's styling book for Latin America. "Which one do you want?" the professor asks, and I leaf through the book. Each yellowed page is arrayed with ink drawings of *pompadours*, DAs thinly tapering sideburns. Leering grins topped with pencil-thin mustaches; muttonchops extended to the chin. "Tell you what," I say smiling. "Do whatever you want, but in the end, I want to be soup."

I was looking to lose myself. Working and traveling around southern Mexico for six months seemed a good way to do it. No doubt a pretty common reason for travel, especially after schooling; nothing unique there. Most find the distance, the immersion in another land a broadening experience. But for me, it was specifically a shortening one.

After a stint in the highlands of Chiapas and a run round the Yucatan peninsula, I arrived in Oaxaca looking every bit the itinerant gringo: bearded, with long brown ringlets of hair falling halfway down my back, my shirt sleeveless and stained with mango juice. How this qualified me for a job as restaurant cook remains a mystery. Yet within a week I was sweating over a grill, turning out tacos and tortas, shunning the hairnet I was given unless the patrona herself showed up in the kitchen.

"If you want to look like a girl, you have to wear the hairnet like a girl." This was the order from my immediate superior, a terse, sclerotic woman named Guillermina, skinny as the cigarettes she smoked into the ventilator fan before the dinner rush. The other, fuller-figured ladies of the kitchen agreed with Guille. "You would be so much more handsome with a man's haircut," advised Laura, who did the dishes. "You could get a Mexican girl like that," opined Marta the day cook, with a snap of her fingers.

They didn't know that I had already tried to cut it once before. In Juchitán, a dusty town on Mexico's narrow girdle, I sat before a mirror in a roach-infested hotel room, determined to go to the nearest barbershop and remove the mane, that vestige of another me. My hands quivered as I plucked four locks as keepsakes, each over fifteen inches long. The sky immediately darkened, rain spat-

**412**

tered the corrugated roof and I rolled up in a ball on the bed, rocking in a fit of anxiety until I passed out.

I would take it slower this time. I spent a few weeks in Oaxaca, pacing around the colonial plaza called the *zócalo*. From my seat under a palm tree or up against the Baroque limestone facade of the cathedral, I overheard muted conversations in Spanish bumping up against Zapotec and other Indian languages. I became familiar with the mantra of the longhaired local scammers—smoke? pot? mushrooms?, with the town lunatic toting a toy machinegun to "rob" passersby of pesos, with the endless stream of campesinos come to the big city to air their grievances.

The job was ten-hour shifts six days a week, with one day of rest. The pay was miserable by Mexican standards; it took three weeks to scrounge rent for a room. The first day off with money in my pocket, I got violently drunk on mezcal. The next I decided to cut off all my hair.

This was the clean break I had waited for, thousands of miles from home. But there was another reason I wanted the haircut, and it was a delicate one. My months of wandering through the republic had made me a lonely man. The kitchen ladies, all middle-aged mothers left abandoned by death, divorce, or misadventure, were little consolation. While each desired the gringo curiosity in her own way—Laura wanted a young lover, Guille a father for her three kids—I yearned for a woman less crushed by the weight of the world, in whom lingered still the perfume of youth.

Smelling of onions, taco grease and poverty, I was out of my mind. Women my age in Oaxaca were married. If not, they shunned drifters. The girl from the language school was an exception, but her dad wouldn't let her leave the house. If what Marta said was true, and I could get a girl by looking like a man, I'd do it.

I gathered the vocabulary surreptitiously. No one could know what I was up to; I wanted no input—the decision had to be mine or I'd chicken out. "Hey Guille," I asked, "How do you say this?" I mimed taking the cleaver to my cheeks and chin. She told me the word for shaving a beard. "Is that the same as shaving a sheep?" She wanted to know if I was making lamb chops, and told me a different word for that. This was tricky. "If you saw a guy with no hair," I asked finally, "how would you describe him?" She told me a word that I had previously thought meant "soup."

One bright morning as I made my usual circuit around the cobblestoned Avenida Independencia, there was unusual commotion in the *zócalo*. I could see the white crests of tents pitched the length of the square. Indian women in red ponchos and long braids darted in and out of the stalls, as did aproned housewives, men in cowboy hats and boots, and young girls in black Quiet Riot tee

**413**

shirts. Each cradled in their arms pink bricks of lava soap, drums of evaporated milk, burlap sacks of rice and beans, and long ribbons of some kind of scrip. Radios blared jerky cumbia music A loudspeaker crackled. A man trumpeted the bounty of Mexico, the beneficence of the government and the sale-a-bration that was this, the National Health Fair.

Following the crowd from booth to booth, I saw children lined up for inoculation. Cartoons warned against lice, diarrhea and AIDS. I got a free toothbrush with instructions, and my own discount brick of laundry soap. All around me, white-coated doctors peered into the eyes of Indian babies with flashlights, nurses discreetly dispensed condoms, and social workers lectured on alcoholism and the finer points of boiling water for safety. Then I saw the haircutters.

In a long row of chairs, happy Oaxacans were getting free haircuts. Yes, *compañeros*, haircuts *gratis*, thanks to the Institutional Revolutionary Party. Young girls, their lustrous black hair tied back sensibly with butterfly barrettes, bent over their customers with shears. The head of the government beauty academy strode behind them, flashing a mirror for their clients to admire.

Free haircuts! This was my hour. But would the Party be so generous as to grant a free haircut to a foreigner? I didn't want to risk it. Guille had told me before that I could pass as a Mexican from DF, the capital—where they weren't as Indian-looking as Oaxacans, and they even have Jews. Approaching the professor, I asked, in my best impersonation of the sing-songy Mexico City accent, if I could get a free haircut. Of course, she said, and smiled. "I want you to shave it for me—bald," I said. She looked at me like I'd asked for a lobster.

Very slowly, the professor explained that they had no electricity outdoors for the clippers. But I could come by the beauty school that week, and they would shave my head. She repeated this a couple of times, throwing in some English words to make sure I got it.

I told the ladies in the kitchen that I would be a little late for work on Wednesday—personal business. At four o'clock, I mounted the stairs that led to the beauty school.

Bathed in soft afternoon light, one empty barber's chair faced a long mirror. The counter was studded with shiny jars of shaving tonics, long oiled shears, and heavy electric hairclippers. Seated in folding chairs arranged haphazardly around the room were 25 young Mexican women who dreamt of being beauticians. Each was habited smartly in budget fashions and costume jewelry, all sporting shiny black flats. To the accompaniment of harps, they applied makeup, plaited each other's long black hair, fussed with nails. Knots of them poured over pop magazines.

I seated myself in the back of the room. Twenty-five pairs of dark eyes widened with gossip, discharging whispers and giggles until the professor made her entrance. I was introduced as today's model. The gringo boy-girl who wanted to be bald.

The professor's firm brown hand gathered up the long curls and held them above my head, in a motion assured and regular, as if she were uprooting carrots or bunching spinach for cutting. Fingers manicured pink and appliquéed with care tickled the back of my neck, rounding up loose locks. Seven years of my hair in her grip, she produced a cartoonish pair of shears. In a single stroke, she lopped off a rabbit-sized bundle of curls, and let the shocked remainder fall just below my ears in a startled pageboy.

The trimming, the tapering, letting each of the students try out the clippers—it took hours. I didn't want it to end. I had entered the salon as Grizzly Adams—midway through I was Erik Estrada. "You're done now?" the professor asked me. "No, shorter!" I demanded, over and over again as the girls squealed in excitement. This reckless gringo! Finally, the class's combined efforts achieved a fair approximation of a fade.

I ran my fingers through the stiff, short hair that remained atop my head. I tickled the fine stubble on the sides. The nape of my neck and the skin surrounding my ears was white verging on blue, baby's skin. It hadn't seen sunshine north or south of the Rio Grande in a while. In the mirror, looking back at me, was a stranger—haloed in the brown faces of the beauty school class, floating saint-like in a cloud of talcum powder. "Now," the professor said, "who are you taking back *al norte*?" I stood up from the chair, inhaled deeply. Was it Barbasol or possibility that tickled my lungs?

**415**

# GOING HOME

## The Final Hurdle

*"There are only two emotions in a plane: boredom and terror."*
Orson Welles

# The Fez

## Stephen Fine

*The person sitting beside you can leave a stronger impression than your vacation.*

ICAN'T REMEMBER WHICH AIRLINE IT WAS, or, for that matter, anything else about the vacation; all I can remember is that my wife and I were stuck in the back of a packed jumbo with our infant son, penned in by at least one hundred Vesuviuses serenely puffing away for eleven hours straight. It was a return flight from Paris to Los Angeles in the days when smoking sections were still the norm so if you were late to check-in at the airport that's where you wound up. Why were we late? No, it was not because of the baby coming down with a high fever at the last minute. I did that. It was the flu. Or was it bronchitis? Or just simply the worst head and chest cold of my life? Whatever it was, back in the hotel my wife said it was suspiciously well-timed, and the symbolism clear: "You don't want to go home."

Not a bad diagnosis. One thought of the job awaiting me the next morning was enough to spike my fever to 104. My wife turned down a plea for another week in Paris. (I had hoped to make myself whole again with a steady diet of brie and good Burgundy wine.) And being more frightened of losing my job than my life, I crawled out of bed and into some clothes and even managed to drag a suitcase after me down to the airport shuttle. Take off didn't bother me, since the plane waited on the ground for so long I was able to drift off into a fluish stupor and forget my apprehension. Then:

Ding!

Warily, I cracked an eyelid. The 'Fasten Seat Belts' sign was off. But wait, I was in luck: the 'No Smoking' light was still on. So far so good. Even my son was cooperating, sleeping beautifully in his mother's lap. As a bonus, there was actually room enough to stretch out a little, and my immediate neighbor to the left was a happy find as well: a little man of olive brown complexion wearing a rumpled suit that looked as ancient as he was. He radiated simplicity and an aura of quiet dignity I found reassuring in a way that I couldn't quite put my finger on. Best of all, he did not appear to have the slightest inclination to bend my ear in conversation. I lied. That wasn't the best thing about him. The

**418**

best thing about him was that he did not contest the armrest, which I seized the moment he lifted his arm so he could scratch his nose. What an agreeable neighbor! North African, probably. Is he Tunisian? Moroccan? Maybe an Algerian. And is that really a fez on his head, or a trick yarmulka, a pop-up? (For the record, it was a fez. Remember, I was quite feverish at the time.)

"What are you smiling at," my wife asked. I said it was a private joke, then I coughed up the last of the phlegm to plague me as dehydration set in. I stuffed the soggy *Kleenex* into an ashtray at the end of the armrest. There! That should discourage "The Fez" from using it. Stuffed ashtrays make good neighbors. I settled back and tried to get some sleep.

Ding!

The instant the 'No Smoking' sign went off people stirred to life all around us, shifting this way and that searching for cigarettes. A crinkling of plastic wrap behind our seat; it sounded like an advancing prairie fire. To the left, flaring matchheads; to the right, cigarette lighters clicking open. Within five minutes the smoke was so thick that when I gasped for air it was like swallowing a bucketful of hot paving asphalt. My lungs, seared black, contracted like a punctured balloon. I had a pounding anvil of a headache. I couldn't see. I couldn't think. I was lost, suffocating, in a lethal vale of swirling ash.

I do not exaggerate. Half the passengers on that flight were French, and all the French smoked. *Donc*, except for the odd *Marlboro* in their midst, all the cigarettes were *Gauloises*, which to the American olfactory system registers the same as cigar smoke. It was like being stuck in an all night poker game played inside of a spinning laundromat dryer.

Somehow I staggered into the aisle and made it up to the first class cabin, slipped into one of the bathrooms and splashed some water on my face, then I sat on the toilet seat and tried to get some sleep, but I was chased out by a flight attendant because a line of people were waiting. By the way, was I a First Class passenger? Ah, hah, she thought not. Please return to your designated area if you need to use the lavatory.

I did, but all the stalls were occupied, so I killed time hanging out by an exit door, gazing through the window at an endless sea of white clouds. I was shooed back to my seat because of air turbulence, which I kind of enjoyed; the panic triggered off by each abrupt pitch and roll of the jumbo was a welcome distraction. Unfortunately, ten minutes later all was smooth sailing again and by this time I was too exhausted to move. Anyway, the aisles were blocked by flight attendants serving drinks and appetizers. "No thanks, I'll pass." I checked my wristwatch. *Merde!* Another nine hours to LA! I should live so long as to breath its sparkling atmosphere. My wife, who I held personally responsible for my misery, suggested I stop complaining and get some sleep. What an original idea! "Now, don't be nasty," she said, "just because you're a little under the weather. Oh, and remember to drink plenty of fluids. Ask the stewardess for some juice."

"Chain smoker."

"Excuse me?"

I jerked my thumb to the left, indicating my neighbor. "Watch." Unlike most of the other people around us, who at least took a breather every so often, *The Fez* never stopped: he blew on the nub of his cigarette until it glowed red and used it to light up a new one. "See that? Does it every damn time. I know his game—do the whole flight on one match!" She cautioned me against raising my voice, but I was on a roll: "It's probably a national sport. He's trying to set a new world record in cigarettes smoked consecutively on one flight!"

Feeling the heat, my quiet little neighbor turned his head and our eyes met. What large pupils he had, deep and black like two matching tar pits. Taking in my pale face, sunken feverish eyes and hostile glare, he calmly turned away to consult with his neighbor, a burly young man sitting to his left, probably a relative, possibly his son. Who knows? The important thing, the incredibly annoying thing, was he was chain-smoking, too. But without a fez.

"Excuse me, sir?" He leaned half way across the old man to blow smoke my way. "There is a problem?"

"Yes. I am very sick. And highly contagious. For your own safety you should move."

Either he didn't understand or he pretended not to. I was about to repeat this friendly piece of advice when I felt my wife's fingernails digging through my shirt at the shoulder. "Number one," she whispered urgently in my ear, "they have a right to smoke as much as they like back here, and number two, threatening people with disease is not very bright. If they alert the crew, then we'll be quarantined in the airport."

"You want smoke?" Now the '*Son of Fez*' was offering me a *Gauloise*. "Very good smoke."

Before I could bat it away, my wife took it and thanked him kindly for his generosity.

"What is the explanation for this betrayal?"

"Just being polite," she replied, "to avoid an international incident." Which wasn't over as far as I was concerned, because now '*The Fez*' was playing the gallant by offering the glowing end of his cigarette. Passing the torch, so to speak. I was on the verge of threatening divorce if she dared to light up, when she waved her hand lightly, declining the offer with the excuse that she had to nurse the baby. Frankly, I was amazed our son was still breathing, let alone thirsty. In any case, her timely diplomatic intervention had defused the situation: my adversaries looked the other way when she undid the top three buttons of her blouse and shifted junior in her lap so he could suck. Ah, but I caught them peeking from the corners of their eyes a minute or two later. Unfazed, 'The Fez' smiled and nodded his head approvingly, whether in admiration of my wife's natural breast feeding technique or simply of her breasts, he didn't say, and I couldn't complain since she had insisted upon asserting her rights. They looked away again, talked a little, chuckling once or twice, and then resumed smoking in parallel isolation.

I couldn't touch dinner. After the food carts were rolled away and the cabin darkened for the in-flight movie, I drifted off into a series of fever dreams that at one point were so disturbing they seemed to merge with the flickering images on the movie screens. Not quite awake, I gave up trying to make sense of the multiple fireballs and self-detonating aliens dancing around the cabin to focus as best I could on the most peculiar image of all: a fez lying right in my lap. My best guess was that it had slid off my neighbor's head when he nodded out. His forearm lay across the armrest, his gnarled fist curled around the butt end of a cigarette. It was still glowing. The ash made an unbroken line ending at a sprig of black tassel. "Um ... Excuse me, sir, but I believe this is yours." Gingerly, I lifted the fez by one edge and transferred it to his lap, where it suddenly ignited.

I have a vague recollection of turning onto my side and trying to get back to sleep while pandemonium reigned all around me. I don't know how trustworthy that is, because after the plane had landed in LA and I had a chance to pop my ears and gulp my first mouthful of fresh air (relatively speaking), I asked my wife about the incident: Was there a fez fire? But rather than confirm or deny it, she just became irritated and told me to keep quiet until we passed through customs. Could I do her that small favor, please?

*　*　*

That was a long time ago. I don't have the flu anymore, nor, come to think of it, that job I hated. I am still married and to the same woman; she is just as wise and far kinder than I made out. And my son is a teenager. As for 'The Fez,' well, if he didn't catch my bug and die shortly thereafter, then I suppose he can survive anything, even another twenty years of smoking. He must be past one hundred by now. Why not? He doesn't worry about lung cancer and emphysema, so why should they worry him? One day, he will inhale, cough up a little gob of black blood, be mildly surprised, lower his chin and die. Until then, he shall remain unmolested, free to pursue his chief occupation, which I imagine is to sit all day in the doorway of a small house made of cinder blocks on a bluff overlooking the Mediterranean Sea, observing the shadows crawl across the pebbled lawn. A serene figure content to pollute the local environment in quiet contemplation of a life well lived.

# Blood is Thicker Than Lager

## Mary Roach

*Stopping for a pint in an English village unearths a long-lost family*

IN 1913, MY FATHER TOOK A BUZZ SAW to the family tree. At the age of 19, he left England and never looked back. He'd tell you how he left, on the S.S. Lusitania with $25 in his pocket, but he wouldn't tell you who or what he'd left, or why. You could get him talking in that direction, back through the years, all the way to the steerage class bunks of the Lusitania, but he'd always stop dead at the Liverpool docks.

No amount of wheedling could get him to step off that boat and back into his childhood. All my mother and I ever got from him was that he was born in Widnes and that he "had a lot of sisters." Case closed.

And so it would have stayed if my father hadn't, at the late age of 65, sired a bullheaded daughter with a late-blooming curiosity. After he died, I began to wonder who this man had been before he was my Pop. Why had he left England? Who were these people he left behind? Were any of them still there?

I was in London on business and found myself with a couple of free days. Widnes is only five hours from London by train, so I bought a ticket and planned to spend the day. I didn't expect to discover much. My father would be 100 now, and it was unlikely he'd have brothers and sisters still alive. I figured I'd lift a pint or two at the local pub, check the phone book, call some Roaches, get nowhere, lift another pint, and return to London.

The train to Widnes was nearly empty. I passed the time chatting with a sprightly old woman in a lavender coat. The conversation ended abruptly when I asked her if she lived in Widnes. She looked at me as though I'd just leaned over and spat in the aisle.

"I live in Hough Green. Widnes ..." she shuddered. Until this moment I had believed the shudder to be a purely literary invention. Like the swoon or the eyelash flutter, it didn't actually exist outside of historical romance novels. Yet here it was. The woman literally shuddered.

She spoke of the pall of yellow smoke from the chemical works, how it hung above the town on hot summer days. My father's departure suddenly began to seem less of a mystery. "Horrible place," she said. "They say the grass hardly grows. Spend an hour in Widnes and you've been too long."

"I have family there."

"Oh I see." She smiled very sweetly. "I understand they've redone some of the shop fronts of late."

It was a rude surprise. For twenty years, I'd let myself believe that Widnes was one of those quaint, rural English hamlets, all thatch and trellis and lowing Guernseys. The sort of place where the pub sells homemade Shepherd's pie and groceries are still delivered, by local boys in tweed caps, eager to earn a few pence for a bottle of pop and a Saturday matinee. There was no place in this Widnes of mine for a chemical processing plant.

I arrived at noon. The Widnes train station was quiet, but not in a quaint, rural way. More of a deserted, derelict way. A group of teenagers was standing around in the parking lot. They were holding brown paper bags, but not the kind that contain grocery deliveries. The teenagers pointed me in the direction of the one hotel in downtown Widnes, which is upstairs from a pub, which does not serve shepherd's pie.

I disappeared to my room with a pint of something dark and succoring and the hotel's phone book. There were twelve Roaches in Widnes, not counting the two by my sink. The last one on the list reached out and grabbed me by the aorta: "W. Roach, 3 Sandringham Road." This was the name and address of the witness who'd signed my grandfather's death certificate in 1949. (I'd tracked it down at London's General Register Office.) The witness was identified as my grandfather's son. My uncle. Here he was, 46 years later, still alive, still at the same address. I dialed the number.

"Hello? Is this the W. Roach who had a brother named Walter who went to America in 1913 and never came back?" There was a long pause, as if I'd asked him if he had Prince Albert in a Can.

"This is William Roach, yes." He sounded like my father.

"Well, I'm your niece. I'm here in Widnes."

In guarded tones, my uncle asked if my father was still alive. It was only then that I began to consider what my father's disappearance had meant for his family. What was to me a lively little mystery, was for them, more likely than not, a source of frustration and hurt. For fifty years, my father had ignored his family. He couldn't be bothered to send a wedding announcement or a photograph of his children. They probably hated him.

Whatever he may have felt, my uncle did the English thing. He invited me over.

In the car, Uncle Bill filled me in on my father's departure. It was no more dramatic than this. My father was a dreamer, and there were no dreams in

Widnes. There was manual labor at the chemical works. There was church, there was family, there was the pub. He'd wanted something more. He had an uncle in Chicago. Of course he left.

My uncle Bill is 83 now. He'd been an infant when my father left. Of my father's five brothers and sisters, the only one old enough to have known him was Carrie, a 97-year-old spinster, toward whose nursing home we were now headed.

Unfortunately, Auntie Carrie harbored no fond memories of my father. "Why didn't he write?" She grabbed at my sleeve. "All those years. We thought he was dead. Why didn't he write?"

It seemed I could tell her everything about her brother's life except what she wanted to know. Why had he cut himself off from them? I'd hoped she'd be able to explain it to me. I'd assumed there was some elaborate feud, some festering bitterness that led him to sever the ties. In fact, I learned, he had kept in touch for fifteen years. Whereupon he joined a traveling theatre troupe and was never heard from again. As far as anyone could surmise, he had no compelling reason for not getting back in touch. No doubt the same reason I lost touch with my best friend from high school. Laziness begets sheepishness begets guilt. The guilt gets bigger and uglier until one day you can't stand to have it around anymore. You dig a hole in the back of your mind and throw it in and forget about it.

Hoping to mine some long-buried vein of sisterly love, I asked Carrie what my father had been like as a boy. "I never thought he was friendly. He spent all his time with the Rooney boys." She stared at me crossly, as though I too had spent all my time with the Rooney boys. "I can't remember ever talking to him."

"Is there anything you can remember that ..."

"He was very aloof."

"But did he ..."

"Very superior."

I began to understand why my father's memories were of "a lot of sisters." In reality there were only two, but Carrie by herself was a lot of sister.

Word of my arrival had been spreading. By the time we got back to Uncle Bill's house, cousins were pouring in. I liked them all instantly. They were warm and welcoming and smart and funny. I was lucky. Unearthing family is a risky proposition. It's like opening the phonebook and pointing to a dozen names at random and forever-after owing them Christmas cards. I'd been warned about this by the proprietress at my hotel. "A lot of folks come 'round doing what you're doing," she'd said darkly. "And they don't always like what they find."

**424**

Phooey on her. My relatives are grand. They came bearing photo albums and letters from my father. For the first time in my life, I saw photographs of my grandmother, the Irish rose from Wexford, and of her father, circa 1890, in the doorway of his thatch-roof cottage. I heard stories about my grandfather, the "biggest shovel in Widnes," with his quart bottles of stout and his strongman's chest ("48 inches, unexpanded," as he liked to say). My Uncle John had brought a picture of my father aged 21, fishing on the banks of the Mississippi, and another of him in his World War I uniform. I never knew my father liked fishing. I never even knew he'd enlisted. In three hours in Widnes I learned more about my father's past than I had in thirty years of being his daughter.

Then a strange thing began to happen. My father began to fade from the conversation. It was as though, having brought us together, he could step away now, like some reluctant, ghostly matchmaker. All along, I'd been thinking of these people as my father's family. Suddenly they were my family.

And just as suddenly, I was leaving them. Early the next morning, my cousin Clare drove me to the station. She hugged me twice and waved until the train disappeared.

For all the things I learned about my father's life, in some ways, it's more puzzling to me now. I can imagine wanting to leave Widnes. But I can't imagine not wanting to come back.

# Home Under the Range

**Ron Gluckman**

*Coober Pedy looks down in the dumps for good reason; film makers have long used the place to portray a nuclear strike zone. Still there is a certain zany charm to the desolate underground desert mining town, and you don't need to dig too deep to find it.*

WAY OUT IN AUSTRALIA'S OUTBACK, where the lakes are salty and the beer is warm, men with big arms and funny hats cook thick slabs of kangaroo and crocodile over open fires. River races are run in bottomless boats by louts scurrying Flintstone-style over dry bedrock.

One can easily grow jaded on the outback oddities, until arriving with a jolt in Coober Pedy, the underground town.

Marlon Hodges, of Alice Springs, recalls passing through a decade ago. "It was right after they filmed the second Mad Max there. We stepped off the bus, and everyone in town had a huge mohawk. It was bizarre, all these ten feet tall, mean-looking guys covered in tattoos."

The hair has grown back, but Coober Pedy remains weird as ever. The town of tunnels, where reclusive residents live in caves, has been seen in many movies. Besides "Mad Max Beyond Thunderdome," Coober Pedy's credits include Wim Wenders' "Until the End of the World." Perhaps most noteworthy is "Priscilla, Queen of the Desert," not for winning an Oscar, but because it's the first film to portray Coober Pedy as anything other than a nuclear strike zone.

There is an eerie apocalyptic resemblance. Set in sun-scorched desert, Coober Pedy's best feature is a field of conical hills. Tourists visit at sunset, when the golden glow frames small, pyramid-shaped silhouettes. It's scenic until you remember you're standing in a gravel pit, gazing at piles of dirt kicked up by the world's largest opal mines.

Aesthetic concerns are pretty much on par with ecological considerations in this rough and tumble town of miners and drifters. Resident Trevor McLeod recalls a controversial proposal to level the hills to fill in the mining holes, partly because a few tourists tumbled down the 90-foot shafts and died. The idea got about as much support as suggestions to halt strip mining, which, like most things in this frontier town, remains legal.

"Anyway, those piles are nice to see on the horizon," Mr. McLeod says. "If we pulled them down, what would we look at?"

* * *

Dirt walls, mainly. About 70 percent of Coober Pedy's 3,500 residents live underground. It's simple survival, since summer temperatures soar above 55 degree Celsius. The boroughs remain cool in summer, and warm in winter.

Many are former mines, but some are underground mansions. "This is the kind of place where, if the wife wants another room, you dig her one," jokes Mr. McLeod. Some underground homes even have swimming pools.

Yet, the oddest thing about Coober Pedy is that the underground dwellings are by no measure the oddest thing here.

Coober Pedy's golf course has no trees or greenery to mark what is essentially an enormous sand trap. Nine dreary holes are dug in dirt mounds of sand, diesel and oil. The fairway is marked by a grove in the moonscape. Once inside, players can tee off a tiny piece of Astroturf they carry.

At first, it was a local laugh, but every Easter, more than two dozen professional duffers play in a Pro-Am tournament. Dennis Ingram, who retired from the links to Coober Pedy, was pressed into service as resident pro. "My first impression was disbelief," he says. "This place gives a whole new meaning to golf."

While cinemas elsewhere may worry about customers toting alcohol, the local drive-in had to ban dynamite. In this town, tempers run thin and everyone packs a blasting cap or two. The *Coober Pedy Times* rubbed someone the wrong way and found its office fire bombed. That case was never solved. Likewise the bombing of the local court magistrate's office a few years before.

Yet neither incident irritated the community, certainly not as much as the fire bombing of Acropolis. "That was the best Greek restaurant in town," sighs one old-timer. "Now, that was a REAL crime. Who could have done such a thing?"

Such questions are seldom asked. Coober Pedy is a mind-your-own business place. It's always been that way, ever since opals were found at Big Flat in 1915. Within seven years, hundreds of prospectors were tearing up the turf.

Depression drove them away, but a new find in shallow depths at Eight Mile in 1946 combined with massive immigration from Europe after World War II to set off a boom that has never completely subsided. Civilization started creeping into Coober Pedy in the 1960s, with the opening of a school and the Opal Motel.

The major finds are remembered mainly in museums nowadays, although flashes of color can still be found in the fields. Increasingly though, the town has turned to the motherlode of tourism. The signs are everywhere, literally: Opal Mine, Opal Cave, Backpackers Cave, Opal Factory and Opal Centre. The Red Sands Restaurant and Nightclub sits above a Mobile gas station-road-house-opal shop. The Desert Cave, opened in 1989, offers luxury underground rooms.

Still, the offerings rarely keep visitors beyond an overnight stop between Adelaide and Alice Springs. A short distance outside town is Australia's own Great Wall, the "dingo fence," a 9,600-kilometer barrier that runs the length of the country, from sea to sea.

Another attraction featured in all the brochures, is the Big Winch, which, upon even a cursory inspection, turns out to be just that, a really big winch.

Coober Pedy's cave homes are far more engaging. Boring machines can dig a four-bedroom abode in a day. The cost is 20-30 percent less than conventional housing, but the real saving comes in energy. While several air conditioners struggle to cool a normal house to under 30 degrees in summer, Coober Pedy's caves remain a comfortable 25 degrees, year-round, free of charge.

In many ways, housing construction is a cracker-jack trade here. Mr. McLeod tells of a friend who built a 17-room house. "He found enough opals during excavations to pay for the entire place."

Indeed, luck—good and bad—is what brings most people to Coober Pedy. For gamblers and gits, it's a second-chance city, the last exit on the road to nowhere.

# The Plague

**Jay Golden**

*You get what you pay for ...*

Ηow could I pass up saving a hundred bucks? The Heathrow-JFK Air
India flight would be just as smooth, and take just as long, right? I did-
n't need the extra pillows, the police movies, the snooty stewards that come
with international air travel: I needed the hundred bucks.

I pulled my worn rucksack from the back of the closet, sifting though remnants of my Indian voyage. From a hidden cell of my past leapt visions of
Indian transport: rickshaws, ox-carts and Ganges River barges sent me reeling
into an incense mist. Among various indecipherables, I dug from my pack san-
dalwood beads, some chapati crusts, and a bag of Rajastani sand. Too many
months had passed since I had felt the inexplicably erratic pulse of Indian life,
and I figured an authentic curry would do me just right. Oh, the great triumph
in reaching point A from point B. Oh, the excitement of planning to lose one's
luggage.

The airline requested four hours advanced check-in. Upon arriving at the Air
India desk, I was sent back in time. The lack of personal space was reminiscent
of the Varanasi train station. People were spread all over the floors, chickens
pecking beaks out of baskets, women in saris bobbing their heads adamantly.
And nowhere was my flight listed. "I'm flying to New York!" I said, pointing
west. Only when I produced a Statue of Liberty key chain did the attendants
have an idea where to send my bags. I wondered if they'd let me ride up top of
the plane.

The plane sat motionless for two hours without any explanation for our
delay: I was being held captive in a portable nation. I remembered the indifference of Indian customer service representatives. At least we finally got a curry,
passed hand over head from the isle. I kept trying to find out what was going
on, but the flight attendants avoided me as if I had the plague.

Because I do. I have the plague.

Upon purchase, Ourways Airways Booking Service neglected to disclose the
cute epidemic sweeping across India. And just before the curry was served, Bill
from Stratfordshiretown chose the opportune time:

"Every morning I wake up without the plague is a good one," he chuckled, cauliflower jiggling in his chops.

Plague, what plague? Why did I think he wasn't kidding? Of course! The plague, a modern bubonic burning through the subcontinent! I had seen it on CNN International, the traveler's source of all tragedies. A wheezing cough emanated from the dozing Sikh on my left flank.

Words fell slowly from my lips, "How ... is ... the ... plague ... passed?" Blood, right? Rat bites. Eating elephant shit. Swimming in the Ganges, right?

"It's airborne," Bill sneaked between now bellowing fits of laughter. But Simon from Manchester would not hear of it. The nervous copier salesman couldn't accept that Air India service wasn't up to Air Spiffy standards. He twisted his stiff torso around in his under-sized chair to face us. "Plague? Plague? I haven't time for the plague. I've got a meeting in three hours with the Director of TNA International!" He gazed out the window at the ground workers playing catch with what looked like a piece of the wing. Then he looked back at me and shook a meaty finger, "You, son, may have nothing better to do than sit around in Heathrow all day, but I've got business to attend to."

I took great offense to his accusation of my indolence because it was accurate. I really had nothing at all better to do. But if I was to not do anything better, I'd rather have done it without the plague. Simon wasn't bothered by the plague; he was bothered by the poor meal service. Where, he asked, were the warm towelettes? Where the small packets of over-salted nuts? The international finance magazines?

"I will not accept a meal until I've been brought a beverage! Where is my beverage? Beverage!"

Then Bill, myself, and the plague-man were given our food. With each spicy bite, the cabin began to shrink. I wasn't so concerned with the lack of communication from the captain—we still had not moved one inch from the point of origin, coming on three hours—as much as I was with the lack of circulation provided by the now-defunct air ventilation system. Certainly, the resemblance to an Indian train—hot, crowded, and immobile—was only to make the passengers from Bombay feel more at home?

Simon was missing his meeting. I was missing a good slice of New York pizza. Bill was missing a few marbles, but we were all missing the point: that at any minute, as a result of the plague, our joints would begin to crumble, our tongues turn black, and our belly buttons would fall to the floor. I had seen it all on CNN, just as deadly as the flesh-eating streptococcal virus. What good is a beverage to one without lips?

The hours ticked by slowly. With each hacking cough from the pajama man on my left I became more certain of my fate. Destined to die a traveler's death,

I'd always hoped it would be at least in baiting a lion or dangling from a cliff, or at least from too many poppy seeds on my bagel. But no. Instead, any minute now, I'd collapse into the remnants of my uncollected curry plate, having sucked in not only the plague but also emphysema, and probably cholera. And indigestion.

Three hours and still no word. The lights kept flashing on and off, and the minor appeasement caused by the food service was now erupting into hysteria and intestinal gas. The utter chaos among passengers and crew alike definitely brought back fond memories of days on Indian roads—an allusion I would have undoubtedly enjoyed more without the plague. The plague wasn't something one worried about once contracted; death was imminent, so I ate a ½ lb. bag of M & M's. The only thing missing was a letter of explanation from the Department of Health.

A few moments later, just after the crew finally got the bright idea to open the main deck doors to circulate some fresh air—then closed them right up again—we each received a letter of explanation from the Department of Health. Of course, I had not traveled from India, but I may as well have swapped bodily fluids with a dobey wallah for all the cellar air I'd sucked down over these three hours. The note discussed the minuscule chances of infection and recommended this:

*If during the next week you become unwell with any of the following:*

*1. A fever*

*2. Coughing or breathing problems*

*3. Tender swellings in the neck, armpits, or groin*

*Please seek medical advice from a doctor immediately.*

Now, as we finally make our wobbly approach to JFK, my question is this: even in ideal health—after nearly three hours before boarding, four hours locked in an air-tight airplane cell, the ensuing three hours of wandering through the airport awaiting instructions, a bus ride to a shitty hotel, a 5:30 am wake-up call, three more hours of lines, and a seven hour curry and high-powered air-conditioning flight at 35,000 feet—who will NOT show these symptoms?

Who has time for the plague nowadays, what with instantaneous worldwide communication, and traffic tie-ups as they are? Certainly nobody on this flight has time for the plague after sacrificing a whole weekend to the God of Budget Travel. I, for one, look forward to a tender swelling in the groin, if it means I'm off this flight. But I certainly cannot afford to rush off to the doctor and spend all the money I saved catching the plague just to cure it.

# Signs of Inner Peace

## Swami Dyhan Santosh

*Let's face it, traveling can sometimes be very stressful. Those who survive and thrive away from home for extended periods have a common denominator—they harbor inner peace. In search of adventure, a calm and peaceful demeanor can transform a hazardous situation into an agreeable one.*

FINAL JOURNEY: ATTENTION TRAVELERS. Be on the special lookout for signs of inner peace, a condition spreading from person to person in epidemic proportions. This could pose a serious threat to fear-mongers, commiters of hate crimes and the fairly regular state of a globe in conflict. Top Ten Signs:

**10.** A tendency to think and act spontaneously rather than on fears rooted in the past.

**9.** An unwavering ability to enjoy each moment.

**8.** No interest in judging other people, nor interpreting their actions.

**7.** A loss of interest in conflict.

**6.** Depleted ability to worry (a sure symptom).

**5.** Frequent, overwhelming episodes of appreciation.

**4.** Content, connected alliance with people and nature.

**3.** Frequent smile attacks.

**2.** A tendency to let things happen rather than to make them happen.

**1.** An increased susceptibility to the love extended by others, mirrored by an uncontrollable urge to return that love.

On this rollercoaster ride called modern life, we are increasingly confronted by choices of right and wrong. It has become all too easy to slip into poor habits, i.e. absorbing the negative messages created by mass media. Consequently, people bearing these signs seek their own truth, identifying with the doctrines of non-violence promulgated by Mahatma Gandhi, Martin Luther King Jr. and William Penn. This non-violent, forgiving voice engages our highest conscience. By correct action, those with inner peace collectively open the planet's heart chakra and subvert the dominant paradigm of fear and paranoia. This option settles disputes without war, spreads equality to all, and renders militaries of the world obsolete. "One Love" never meant so much to so many people at such a crucial time. Individual random acts of kindness can and do make a big difference. Again, be on special lookout for these signs, they have a tendency to change people's lives, and thus, the world we all share.

**432**

# Road Rage, Hope, and Daddy

## Ken Chaya

*Sometimes, as trying as the trip may be, it is good to remember Robert Pirsig's advice to his son in 'Zen and the Art of Motorcycle Maintenance,' "To travel is better than to arrive."*

THE IDAHO SUN WAS SETTING angry and unwilling—the only way it knows how—in this rugged country. Orange Flames of color blazed across the plains reaching further and further toward the mighty Tetons in the distance like the outstretched fingers of a doomed prophet. "And so another day comes to an end," I declared to my son, Lukas, sitting contentedly for the moment, pondering the collective wisdom of all his two-and-a-half years, in his car seat in the back of the 4-door rental. "You know, we only get a certain amount of them, it's best to use each one wisely" I counseled him in my 'Father Knows Best' voice. Four days earlier, my wife Joan and I arrived in Idaho, from New York City, where we live, love, share, and argue over who's more tired after work. We had been making daytrips, enjoying the natural splendor of the area for the last two days. An amount of time sufficient for enough food to feed a small country to somehow accumulate beneath Lukas' car seat.

I was on assignment to photograph a convention of sober young people some 700 miles away in Estes Park, Colorado. Recalling my teen years somewhat dimly, I was curious to see how the other half lived. I decided to expand our itinerary however, by flying out to Jackson Hole, Wyoming, to spend some time at a friend's rustic camp located just over the pass from Jackson. A beautiful area dubbed with the unappealing name of Driggs, Idaho. I love Idaho. Rugged country, nice folks who like people to visit—and then go home—not move there.

We were about fifteen miles this side of the pass, and the rose-purple thistle flowers on the east side of the road pulsated with color from the sun's final flurry of brilliance. A small, deserted, pioneer-style log cabin appeared up ahead of us. Backlit by the finale of the solar light show, it glowed like a lone coal in a field of fire. I slowed down and considered the shot. Ansel Adams radiant, or corn-cheesy calendar-kitsch? Sometimes you just can't tell until you get the film back. Let the pictures speak for themselves is usually the best policy. I've pulled off the road—often in fierce traffic—sometimes to get a shot that was well worth the effort, and sometimes to find myself sadly disap-

**433**

pointed. But I've also passed up just as many uncertain opportunities, and always felt uncomfortable with myself for the next mile or two. "Do it," I thought. I had just stocked up on a dozen rolls of fresh chrome in the only photo store in Jackson that stocked more than the common tourist's choices of color print film. The car crunched gravel as I eased it off the side of the rural road. I stepped out into the lonesome quiet vermilion and knew right away that I had chosen wisely. I opened the door to the back seat where the precious cargo—my son and my camera bag—rides. Lukas looked up and smiled as if he hadn't seen me in a week, ready and willing for whatever life has in store next, in the way only two-year-olds know how. I smiled back at the unreadable mischief in his dimples as I reached for my camera bag ... no bag. No bag! AND THEN I REMEMBERED: Lukas was his typical two-year-old self in the photo store. Meaning I had about two minutes to get in, make my purchase—while keeping him in grabbing distance—and get out. REMEMBERED: He was tired from the full day at Yellowstone, and the hours in the car, and appeared to be beginning his no-nap, pre-bedtime meltdown early in the store. He didn't understand why he couldn't be allowed to knock tripods down like bowling pins and then use them to bang on plate glass display cases. A worthy demonstration of both his physical prowess and acoustic appreciation. REMEMBERED: Carrying Lukas, fussing, out of the store with one hand, film and camera bag in the other, and I had to put the bag down to unlock the car. I buckled him in securely, despite his protests, closed the door, and walked around to the opposite side of the car, got in, and drove off. Leaving my favorite (now out of production) camera, with its three lenses, ten irreplaceable exposed rolls of Yellowstone film, plus my new film purchases there in my veteran camera travel bag on the sidewalk in downtown Jackson Hole. The nausea hit my stomach at the same time the rage hit my brain. I closed the door so my son wouldn't be exposed to a scene that would surely have him curled up on some therapist's couch for years. I quickly walked away from the car out into the mad glowing fields like Lon Chaney Jr., beginning to transform, trying to spare innocent blood by putting as much distance as possible between myself and the human race. And then I howled at the sun, screamed at the sky, hissed at the ground, pulled my tee shirt collar out until the neck tore, clawed at the air, cursed at God and Satan in the same sentence, body punched unseen demons, kicked at invisible phantoms, screamed every profanity I had ever heard—and then invented some new ones, stomped the ground, rolled and spat, shook my fist at the heavens, and threw rocks at God's windows. For the safety of my family and others traveling on that road, I worked it all out, all the way. Finally, having pushed all the acid and rage out of my emotional system, I collapsed to my knees, panting and shaking. It was too late now to turn around and drive back over the pass. My special New Yorker's blend of cynicism and contempt told me to kiss it all good-bye. So I collected what was left of myself, centered it, put it in a safe place, took a deep breath, and stood up and walked back to the car. The setting sun projected a monstrously long shadow of myself out in front of me for me to study as I made my way back. I got in and sat down. My wife was wearing the "I want to be supportive, but you really have me worried," look. Lukas, unable to control his amusement, broke the silence. "Daddy, you're *funny!*" he blurted. "Lukas, please leave Daddy alone now" Joan quietly cautioned him. I glanced at her to let her know I was human again. We drove all the way back to the cabin with me silently battling the demons of acceptance, while using the same club on myself. The sun sank below the Idaho horizon leaving the sky turning the colors of a fresh bruise.

That night, I put Lukas to bed with tenderness, and many favorite stories. One thing I have learned in these many years is the best way out of my bad times is to focus good energy on another. And my son is my favorite recipient. Two-year-olds burn with the pure unrestricted energy of life. Try to outlast them at this and you will lose every time. I have budget-traveled through Asia, bluffed my way past road blocks of automatic-toting, teenage military members in deep Venezuela, slept in canoes on Ecuadorian jungle rivers because of the rats and snakes on shore, sidestepped trouble while stranded for three days in Turkey, motorbiked to the Thai border where I slipped across the river into Burma only to be picked up by a student rebel army whom I (luckily) managed to convince that I was not a spy or sent there by anyone for information. They let me stay with them, and more importantly, leave when I wanted to. But none of it exceeds the constant challenge of a toddler, or traveling with one. Indeed, parenthood changes everything you thought you knew about life, and traveling through it.

If it use to take fifteen minutes—make it an hour. If you've been carrying all you need in a backpack—get ready to step into adult shoes and buy your first set of luggage. Diapers, wipes, non-spill drink containers, strollers, toys, food, and a change of clothes are now minimum essentials for even simple daytrips. And yet somehow despite all the new chaos and upheaval, we still manage to travel together beyond the scope of the "family vacation" circuit. I recall in a pinch, having to change my son's diaper in public, on a street in a small coastal village in Mexico. It drew a crowd of curious women and children who perhaps never before witnessed this act performed by a man. Upon completing the task, I held him up high to the cheerful approval of all. Since his birth, he has been the most exciting real-life adventure of my life.

Hope is an alternating current, running hot and strong one split second, and gone the next. But always returning to haunt and provoke you into accepting it's hand in an offer you know is probably too good to be true. I truly believed my equipment and photos were now a part of my past, but the fact that I always had kept some business cards stuffed into my bag needled me. What if a Mormon passing through town noticed it, or a member of the clergy on vacation.

*   *   *

When I checked the next day there was a message on my office phone in New York from a couple from Hellertown, Pennsylvania. They were on vacation and had traveled recently through Jackson Hole, where they claimed they had found something that belonged to me. Since they were now on the road, they left me their home number, and the date when they would return home. Hellertown sits on the west side of the Delaware river, about 100 miles from New York City. It's a nice drive along Interstate 78 in the fall. I took Lukas along with me for the ride.

# Watch the North Wind Rise

## Jorma Kaukonen

*Every ending is a new beginning.*

UP IN THE MORNING WATCH the north wind rise
Bringing fire down from the skies.
Hey we've got a long way to go
So keep on loving and make it slow.

Nighttime falls like a crack of doom
Fills the sky with the shining moon.
Silver siren just got please
Feeling your loving down in my knees.

We're going home
Won't be long
Hear in my song
That loving you ain't never done no wrong.

Well baby mine
One more time
Run your hands, down my spine
If you say you've got to go
Take some time for just one more.

# Author Bios and Quotes

**Richard Bangs** is founding partner of Mountain Travel Sobek, the largest adventure travel company in the world. He led expeditions that made first descents of over 30 rivers around the world, from the Zambezi to the Yangtze, the Bio-Bio, Indus, Tekeze, Euphrates, and on. He has authored 12 books and over 500 articles on adventure and international travel, produced 20 documentaries, several pioneering CD ROMs and websites, and has lectured extensively at venues such as the Smithsonian Institute, The National Geographic Society, The Explorers Club, museums, universities and such. He has won seven Lowell Thomas awards. He was editor-in-chief on Microsoft's pioneering adventure magazine, Mungo Park (www.mungopark.com), and now serves as Editor-at-Large at Expedia.com.

*"Men go out into the void spaces of the world for various reasons. Some are actuated simply by a love of adventure, some have the keen thirst for scientific knowledge, and others again are drawn away from the trodden path by the 'lure of little voices,' the mysterious fascination of the unknown."*
—Sir Ernest Shackleton.

**Dr. D. Richard Bellamy** is a dynamic speaker, author of *12 Secrets for Manifesting Your Vision, Inspiration & Purpose*, consultant, training instructor and successful Chiropractor in Houston, Texas. In addition to natural healing, his true meaningful passion is in helping others discover their uniqueness and purpose through personal and professional development workshops. Dr. Bellamy is an in-demand speaker around the world and is available for consultations, keynotes and workshops.

*"I believe we all have a calling within us to experience all the wonders on the planet."*

**Andrew Bill** has been driven to work many times in the course of maintaining his life-long travel habit. Under 'career experience' his resume lists stints as a river guide, road sweeper, commercial fisherman, painter, farm hand, and construction laborer. He has also worked (briefly) in an Australian strip-joint (as a waiter), an English sewer, a French greenhouse factory and a Scottish Outward Bound camp. Failing to find his vocation in any of these professions, he turned to travel journalism nine years ago. To date he has visited over 75 countries and contributed to many of the leading magazines, guide books and anthologies. One day he will finish his novel.

*"The spirit of a country is like a wild animal. The more you chase it, the more it moves away. But sometimes—if you're lucky, if you sit quietly in one place and wait—it will come to you."*

**Robert W. Bone** learned the fine points of syntax at the elbow of a major in the Training Literature Department at Fort Knox, and of travel reportage while failing to mix perfect martinis for Temple Fielding, the late guidebook guru. Stints as a foreign correspondent (England, Belgium, Puerto Rico, Brazil, and Spain) didn't help a heck of a lot, but marrying a New Zealander did. He now lives and writes in Honolulu. "Editors, flacks, hacks and other masochists" are invited to check out Bob's one-man show web site at http://members.aol.com/robertbone. One admirer dubbed it: 'More links than a sausage factory.'

*"For me, travel is a natural high, produced by placing myself in an unfamiliar situation where unusual things happen. Yet I manage to find my way through this new environment and to learn a thing or two in the process. The experience is enhanced by a penchant for telling thousands of others about it."*

**Marybeth Bond**'s books include *Gutsy Women, Gutsy Mamas, Travelers' Tales: A Mother's World* and *A Woman's World,* which won the Lowell Thomas Gold Award for best travel book. Marybeth traveled alone around the world for two years at age 29. She has been seen on CNN, NBC, ABC, and the Travel Channel and is a regular adventure travel reporter for Outside Radio Network and a columnist and "Travel Expert" for ivillage.com: The Women's Network. Her latest book, *A Woman's World II* (Traveler's Tales) was published in spring 1999. "The End of the Road" was first published in *Traveler's Tales: A Woman's World.*

*"The only trips I regret are the trips I didn't take."*

**Tim Cahill** has been writing about (rough) travel for over twenty years now. He is the author of six books, including *Pass the Butterworms; Remote Journeys Oddly Rendered* and *Jaguars Ripped my Flesh*. He is also Editor at Large for *Outside* magazine, and co-writer of two IMAX documentary screenplays, *Everest*, and *The Living Sea*, which was nominated for an Academy Award. He travels approximately six months out of the year. The question he is most frequently asked is: "yeah, but what do you do for a living?"

His least modest reply: *"I create great literature that will live in the minds and hearts of men and women for time immemorial, god damn it."*

**Stephen Capen** is a New Englander living in California. Whenever he feels himself shrinking from the rigors of travel, he takes out a Vonnegut book to remember from whence he comes, and recall Zorba's maxim: 'Life is trouble. Only Death is not. To be alive is to undo your belt and look for trouble."

*"May you journey with the words."*

**Michael Cervieri** returned to the United States after spending a year in Latin America and worked as Senior Editor for *Blue* magazine. When asked why he went abroad he says he doesn't really know. Ditto for returning to the States except that he'd run out of money. He lives in New York City but is considering making a triumphant return to Peru as an Alpaca rancher. He is currently writing a novel and playing in a band. He is the producer and editor-in-chief of interlingo.com.

*"China is a big country, inhabited by many Chinese."*— Charles de Gaulle

**Ken Chaya** is an artist, designer, and photographer who, over the past twenty years, has produced numerous best-selling nonfiction books for *Reader's Digest*. He recently left the nine-to-five corporate grind to pursue a healthier lifestyle, which includes painting, writing, traveling, birdwatching, "and spending time with my wife and son while I still have some snap left in my garters."

*"When everyone thinks the same—nobody thinks."* —unknown

**David Hatcher Childress**, considered 'the Real-Life Indiana Jones,' is best know as the Founder of the World Explorers Club and Editor of the magazine *World Explorer: Far-Out Adventures in Far-Away Places*. His fascinating *Lost Cities* series covers most of the 'known' world in six books. Childress also developed another series of six books on what he calls the "lost sciences," the scientific wisdom of those technologically advanced civilizations that existed over 15,000 years ago. His new series of books focus on the Lost Cities of the South Pacific.

*"Every mystery solved brings us a step closer to the big mystery."*

**441**

**Bryan Clayton** was spawned on *Isla de Long* (Long Island euphemism). He left horse-drawn carriage driving to pursue storytelling. When his attempt at exporting goat-drawn carts to Japan failed, he became a Bellevue addictions counselor, and later a flight attendant.

*"Ladies and Gentleman, this is your dining car attendant. I had the baked chicken and it changed my life"* —Amtrak waiter

**Tom Clynes** is a freelance writer, brewer and hack musician whose passion for music and travel has taken him around the world. Tom writes about travel, music, and beer for such publications as *Outside, Escape, Men's Journal* and the *Washington Post*, and is the author of *Wild Planet!* (Visible Ink Press), a critically acclaimed guide to the world's extraordinary festivals and celebrations. Tom is based in New York City, but he continues to wander the world, trying to satisfy "a thirst for spectacle and a fascination for the planet's cultural nooks and crannies."

*"When you hit the road, make friends with uncertainty and expect something extraordinary to happen."*

**Lynn Cothern** grew up in the west but her home base is now Takoma Park, Maryland. At this writing, she just returned from Australia. You'll find her if you can find her on a world trek the latter half of 1999 and studying yoga in Pune, India. She has a Ph.D. in American studies and has been published in *Caliban, Blue Mesa, The Redneck Review,* and *Louisiana Literature.*

*"You don't have to travel far to travel far."*

**Anne Cushman** is the author of *From Here to Nirvana: The Yoga Journal Guide to Spiritual India.* She is editor-at-large of *Yoga Journal* and has written for the *New York Times,* the *San Francisco Chronicle, Salon* magazine, and the *Utne Reader.* She is currently a writer-in-residence at the Kripalu Center for Yoga and Health in Lenox, MA.

*"You have already arrived."* —Thich Nhat Hanh

**Carolyn Durkalski** is a freelance writer living high off the land in San Francisco, enjoying the great outdoors. In between travels, she writes ad copy and is working on her first book. Her adventures on living in New Orleans have appeared in *Trips* magazine.

*"I travel. It's more fun than therapy."*

**442**

**Abby Ellin** has gone on a camel safari in India, danced with Massai Warriors in Kenya, been scuba diving in the Red Sea, jumped out of an airplane just to prove she could, scoured the Grand Canyon for Bobby and Cindy, and got manicured and massaged at the Golden Door Spa, in California. 'Geographical Cures,' she swears, is fiction. Ellin writes the "Preludes" column in the Sunday Money and Business section of the *New York Times,* is a contributing writer for *Travel Your Way,* and has written for *Spy, New Woman, Cosmopolitan, Mademoiselle, POV, Maxim,* and *The Boston Phoenix.* She has her MFA in Creative Writing from Emerson College, in Boston, and lives in New York City.

*"Moments—that's all we're allowed. The true traveler knows this"*

**John Ferguson** is an eternal surfer, pool shark, aircraft mechanic and humanitarian. He ventures nowhere without Lucky (Yellow Nape Amazon Parrot), Zeus (black Labrador) or Apollo (purebred mutt).

*"Now I've got what he's got"* —J. Ferguson (after kissing his parrot, Lucky)

**Doug Fine** spends a fair amount of time engaged in 'concerted efforts not to be confrontational.' Despite this, the 28-year-old Fine is annually adding to the list of countries in which he is officially banned. He tends to report from places such as Tajikistan, Laos, Rwanda and Suriname before fleeing amidst gunfire and filing. Pending sufficient investors magically materializing, Fine is filming *Migration,* a feature film he wrote, on location in Alaska in late Spring, 1999. A Web site of his work is at www.well.com/user/fine.

*"Terrified on a strange road is the only time I can be sure I feel like me."*

**Stephen Fine** is the author of the science fiction satire, *Molly Dear, The Autobiography of An Android,* published by St. Martins Press. He is also the founder/publisher of *Amazing WebTales!* (http://www.webtales.com), a popular stop on the web for putting up free writers' display pages and contributing to open online serials.

*"Hello, I must be going."* —Groucho Marx

**Basil Franklin's** voyage was baptized with a cross-country hitch at 16. He continues to drift across the continents ... Apalachicola oyster shucker, Wyoming animal-hand for Wild Kingdom, Mississippi tree planter, slapdash hitchhiker, edible seaweed picker (Canadian dulce), mountaineer, river runner, Burma gem smuggler and Central Park horse-drawn carriage pilot. Summering in Idaho's Teton Valley, he is still looking for a new twist, new smiles. "If bored, maneuver the heart from toe to head."

*"Go not as a missionary or developer, but rather a modern Marco Polo whose strongest desire is to sit around the evening fire and chuckle with your hosts."*

**Kathryn Gardner** is a freelance writer and photographer living in British Columbia, Canada. When she is not writing about human issues, the outdoors or her adventures, Kathryn leads groups on active travel vacations for Backroads, Inc., Berkeley, California.

*"Travel for me is discovery. Writing is my way of sharing discoveries with others in hopes that we can learn from each other, and work towards making the world a better place."*

**Don George** roamed the world and wrote a weekly column as Travel Editor at the *San Francisco Examiner* from 1987-1995. His adventures continue in cyberspace, where he founded and continues to edit Wanderlust, the award-winning travel site of *Salon* magazine (http://www.salonmagazine.com/wanderlust). When last seen, he was assiduously researching a book on outdoor cafes.

*"Travel seems like the opposite of staying home, but if you travel with a sure sense of your roots, your family, your place, in your head and in your heart, then home is wherever you are."*

**Ron Gluckman** was born by the beach in San Francisco, squandered his youth with rock rags, then paid his dues with newspapers in northern California and Alaska. For the past eight years, he has been roaming widely around Asia from his base in Hong Kong. His travel stories appear in the *Wall Street Journal, Time, Newsweek, Discovery,* the *Toronto Globe and Mail, Sydney Morning Herald, San Francisco Examiner, Los Angeles Weekly, South China Morning Post* and numerous airline magazines.

*"Life has always been about motion. Survival started it all off, but, those of us who have moved beyond food and shelter, feed on observations and images. For us, stability is static. Motion is life."*

**Jay Golden** was introduced to travel at age 4, when his family picked up and moved to Idaho in search of the perfect basketball team. His first memories of intrigue entailed shooting underhand freethrows in front of half-time crowds and scoring free cokes from foreign snack bars. Today he passes his days executing the 'pick and roll' for Guatemalan bus seats and diving for behind-the-back chapati tosses. He's currently working on a travel-themed children's book.

**444**

*"I see a vision of a great rucksack revolution, thousands or even millions of young Americans wandering around with rucksacks, going up to mountains to pray, making children laugh and old men glad, making young girls happy and old girls happier, all of 'em Zen Lunatics who go about writing poems that happen to appear in their heads for no reason and also by being kind and also by strange unexpected acts keep giving visions of eternal freedom to everybody and to all living creatures ..."* —Japhy Rider, "Dharma Bums"

**Margie Goldsmith**'s first novel, *Screw-Up* is about a young college graduate who travels through Europe to learn what it means to be a woman. Goldsmith is presently working on her second novel *Fragments*, while exploring the world. She is the Adventure Travel and Sports Editor of *MetroSports Magazine* and has written about her trek in Bhutan for *Marco Polo*, her summit of Mount Rainier for *SpaFinders,* and for other publications. She is president and founder of MG Productions, a NYC award-winning video production company.

*"What I have learned about adventure travel is that the greatest thrill of all is not having to accomplish anything."*

**Anthony Grant** has written for *The Independent, The Moscow Times, The Malibu Times, Men's Fitness* and *France-Soir* (Paris) and reported for AP. Recently he co-authored the first edition of the *Rough Guide to Boston.* He also produces S p l i t (www.splitnews.com), which he describes somewhat seriously as "an anti-tourism travel review." His contribution to *In Search of Adventure* appears in slightly different form in "Degrees of Departure," available exclusively via S p l i t. "Travel displaces the body and realigns the soul."

*"The true traveler knows that home is where the suitcase is."*

**Jeff Greenwald** is the author of four books, including *Shopping for Buddhas, The Size of the World,* and *Future Perfect: How Star Trek Conquered Planet Earth.* He is a regular contributor to *Wired,* and writes science and travel articles for various print and online magazines. A resident of Oakland, Jeff divides his time between California and Kathmandu. You can contact him via his website: www.jeffgreenwald.com

*"If you look like your passport photo, you're too ill to travel."*
—Will Kommen

**445**

**Larry Habegger** started writing about travel in the late 1970s when he discovered that his nonfiction sold better than his fiction. With co-author James O'Reilly, he wrote serialized mysteries for the *San Francisco Examiner* in the early 1980s, and since 1985 their syndicated column, *World Travel Watch*, has appeared in newspapers in five countries and on Internet-based information centers. Currently he is co-editor of the *Travelers' Tales* book series. His story originally appeared in *Travelers' Tales Food: A Taste of the Road.*

*"The best way to find a true sense of yourself is when you're in motion. Travel gets you moving, loosens the bonds of obligations and cleans out the clutter in your head, opening windows onto your soul."*

**Ruth Halpern** is a storyteller who performs in North America, Europe, Central and South America. She tells tales of adventurous heroines from around the world and stories of communication and miscommunication from her own experience and the folk tradition. Whether she's telling tales beside a jungle waterfall, on top of an Alp, in storm or drought, she conveys the terror and humor of her story as if it's happening at that very moment. Contact her at rhalpern@halpernandholt.com

*"The story is the fire and we are the marshmallows, drawn up close to melt in its warmth."*

**Bridget Henry** lives in Chicago and is never truly happy unless she is planning her next trip to some exotic land where she doesn't speak the language and doesn't want to know what the ingredients are in the local stew.

*"I have yet to find a foreign beer I didn't like."*

**Gail Howerton**, MA, CLP (Certified Leisure Professional—an authentic credential!) is the CEO (Chief Energizing Officer) at Fun*cilitators promoting peak performance through playful professionalism by facilitating fun and effectiveness in keynote speaking, and training sessions. Author of *Hit Any Key To Energize ... A Caffeine-Free Guide To Perk Up Your Spirits,* and creator of *Zip Kits* (fun*aid kits for stress rescue); she takes her fun seriously and strives to play as hard as she works. Contact Gail at www.funcilitators.com or (800) 930-6096 for presentations or products.

*"You won't know if you don't go ... go big or go home. It is not necessarily where we go geographically in our travels, but where we go in our heads that really matters."*

**Jorma Kaukonen** was inducted into the Rock and Roll Hall of Fame in mid-career. Lead guitarist and vocalist for bands such as *Jefferson Airplane* and *Hot Tuna*, his thirty-five year recording and touring legacy, including dozens of solo projects, has inspired nearly fifty records/CD's. 'Watch The North Wind Rise' originally appeared on *Hoppkorv* (The live version on *Double Dose* is equally epic). Renowned for his unique finger-style picking technique, Jorma keeps the tradition going with his Fur Peace Ranch Guitar Camp project in Athens, Ohio. The Fur Peace Ranch is a residential retreat style facility with 17 two-person cabins and one handicap cabin. There are guest instructors who will vary from year to year. In 1998 they had Rory Block, Jack Casady, GE Smith, Chris Smithers, Robert Jones, Jeff Acheson, Roy Book Binder, Michael Falzarano and Jorma to name a few. For the Ranch try (www.furpeaceranch.com) and for Hot Tuna try (www.hottuna.com).

*"Try to keep your mind as open as the road and good things are sure to follow."*

**Carla King** rode a Russian sidecar motorcycle around the United States in 1995, sending dispatches to the Internet about getting stuck in small towns all over America. In 1998 she did the same thing, only in China on a Chinese sidecar motorcycle, illegally, and with a lot more breakdowns. A slow learner, she is presently planning a similar trip to yet another continent. All dispatches are published at http://www.verbum.com/jaunt

*"When more women travel, more women will travel."*

**Christa Kirby** is a writer and actress who lives in New York City. A native North Carolinian, she is a graduate of Duke University. Highlights of her travels include: hanggliding in the Pyrenees, scuba diving in Thailand, biking across Shikoku (Japan) and camping in the Australian outback. She is currently starring in the long-running, serialized hit *Burning Habits. The New York Times* described her performance as 'a knockout' in this eight-episode play, in which there are 'kidnappings, institutionalizations, hunchbacks, backstabbing and special appearances by three dead lesbian nuns.'

*"We're thinking your luggage might be in Nebraska."* —Greyhound baggage attendant, New York City

**Michael Kirkpatrick** is an explorer of inner space who occasionally musters the courage to travel the outer terrain. His illustrious pursuits have included teaching kindergarten, electrical work, Psychopharmacology (no, really), Sinology, kickboxing, firefighting, Monastic Buddhism, and creative writing. He is currently hiding out in a small liberal arts college, where he teaches Psychology.

*"When the going gets weird, the weird turn pro."* —Raoul Duke

**Sam Khedr** co-authored *Let's Party! Europe, Let's Party! San Francisco* and contributed to the *Chicago Party Guide* (Globe Pequot Press). In-between mapping-out the world's nightlife and updating the Party Guides to Europe and San Francisco, he founded a web-site focused on travel networking found at www.VagabondNetwork.com

*"Traveling the world offers a wide, colorful palate of scenes within which you can dip your brush."*

**Brendan Lake** is a 23-year-old boat builder who resides on a 24 foot Sharpie Schooner he made with his father. Lake Watercraft, 26 Barrett's Way, Woolwich, ME 04579—boat building/plans inquiries only please.

*"Occasionally they'll jump off the hamster wheel to eat."*
—Basil Northam, Jr's. rat-race reflection.

**Sue Lebrecht**, a Toronto-based freelancer, writes a weekly column in the *Toronto Star* newspaper and is the author of *Mountain Bike Here: A Trail Guide to Southern Ontario and Western and Central New York, Toronto Parks, Adventuring Around Vancouver Island, 52 Weekend Activities Around Vancouver,* and *52 Weekend Activities for the Toronto Adventurer.* Email:energie@idirect.com Homepage: http://webhome.idirect.com/~energie

*"Writing is my mission, my official business that allows me to play."*

**Antonio López** cracked his head open four times before the age of six, the most serious injury caused by his grandfather's painting flying off the wall and splitting his forehead. Fate has it that López now covers art for a Santa Fe, New Mexico daily. López is a self-educated DIY journalist who learned the ropes editing and writing for an early-'80s punk fanzine, *Ink Disease.* A mix-blood coyote and aspiring flamenco dancer, López travels the Americas and Spain as a chakaruna (quechua for "bridger") with the goal of healing the wounds of the Spanish conquest. email: eltiki@chakaruna.com or web: http://www.chakaruna.com/eltiki

*Arriba, abajo, el centro, para dentro."* ("Above, below, the center, down the hatch") —drinking toast

**Randall Lyman** is a journalist and travel writer with the *San Francisco Bay Guardian,* as well as a poet and the author of *America's New Left Bank: The Birth of Prague's (mostly) American Expatriate Subculture.* He lived in Prague from 1991 to 1996, working as a reporter for the English-language newspaper *Prognosis* and as a translator of Czech fiction and poetry.

**448**

*"Sometimes in life it's necessary to go a long distance out of your way in order to come back a short distance correctly."*

**Katya Macklovich** grew up in Montreal where she was stolen by gypsies when she was a little girl. Although she was eventually recovered, she has always wondered whether this incident stimulated her penchant for the nomadic life. Her travel stories have appeared in *Travelers' Tales Paris* and in *Salon* magazine.

*"I think, therefore I go."*

**Lori Szczepanik Makabe** is a freelancer, adventure travel enthusiast, windsurfer and physical education specialist. She has written numerous articles for windsurfing publications. With a passion for the outlandish, Lori has circled the globe several times. When she is not traveling, Lori divides her time between windsurfing communities in Northern California and Southern Baja, Mexico.

*"That which does not kill us, not only makes us stronger, but makes for the best storytelling."*

**Claudia Martin** was dropped on her head as an infant, which, according to her mother, explains just about everything you'd ever want to know about her. She has been a trial attorney, law instructor, worm picker, go-go dancer, cocktail waitress, pastry chef, editor and writer. Her travel stories have been featured in the *San Francisco Examiner,* and in *Delta Sky, Salon* magazine and in other travel anthologies.

*"I don't travel. I'm just trying to find my way home. Damn those birds for eating the bread crumbs I dropped on the way out!"*

**Michael McColl**'s passion for travel was first sparked during a year spent (nominally) studying at the University of Barcelona. Soon thereafter, an impoverished attempt to get back to Europe inspired McColl's first book, *The Worldwide Guide to Cheap Airfares.* McColl was one of the founding writers of the Fodor's budget travel series *The Berkeley Guides.* His current project is a web site that teaches travelers how to get the best bargain for their money. If you hate paying too much when you travel, check out www.travelinsider.com

*"Wisdom is never gained in school so much as on the road. So what are you waiting for?"*

**449**

**Linda Watanabe McFerrin** is a poet, travel writer and fashion merchandiser. She has been a contributor to over 60 literary journals, newspapers, magazines and anthologies including the *San Francisco Examiner*, the *Washington Post*, *Modern Bride* and *Travelers' Tales*. She is the author of two poetry collections: *Chisel, Rice Paper, Stone* and *The Impossibility of Redemption Is Something We Hadn't Figured On*, 1990, Berkeley Poets Workshop and Press. The winner of the 1997 Katherine Anne Porter Prize for Fiction, her work has also appeared in *Wild Places* and *American Fiction*. Her novel *Namako: Sea Cucumber* is new from Coffee House Press.

*"Don't plan too hard. You have to leave room for the serendipitous and the disastrous, either of which makes for adventure."*

**Paul McHugh** was born amid Hurricane King in 1950 in a rural Florida hospital. After getting his feet wet in the Everglades, he stomped off into other wild zones around the globe. Among his preferred claims to infamy: he was aboard the US Surf kayaking team which took a world championship in Ireland in 1988; and he now frequently places among top finishers at Northern California sea kayak races. He published a novel, *The Search for Goodbye-to-Rains* in 1980 (still available from Amazon.com); edited a book of outdoor travel essays, *Wild Places*, in 1996; and has produced documentaries on environmental themes for PBS. Currently, McHugh is outdoor writer/editor for the *San Francisco Chronicle*, a post he has held since 1985.

*"The edge is where you put it."*

**Ann Melville** is a Cultural Anthropologist by degree, she's dabbled in such occupations as gas-station attendant, nanny, waitress, museum lab assistant (paleontology/archaeology), sailing crewmember, house painter, English teacher, and election supervisor. She has lived and worked in over 60 countries, assisted scientists collecting bats and rats in Indonesia, bicycled Southeast Asia, spent 2 summers exploring rural Greece by horse drawn cart, hitched through Zimbabwe and South Africa with her 69-year-old mother, braved the toilets of NW China, and everywhere enjoys sampling local moonshine.

*"If anyone's dumb enough to give my mother their address, they really don't know what they're in for!"*

**Pamela Michael**'s books include *A Mother's World: Journeys of the Heart, A Woman's World II*, and *The Gift of Rivers*. In her youth, she crossed the US several times, by thumb, rail, bus and car, sometimes with her infant son in tow (and often her Irish wolfhound as well). She didn't leave the continent until she was over forty, but has made up for lost time, visiting dozens of countries in the last decade. Also a radio producer, Michael hosts a travel show on

KPFA-fm in the San Francisco Bay Area, and wrote and produced a critically-acclaimed radio series on Buddhism in the United States, narrated by Richard Gere, which was broadcast nationally. She is director and co-founder of *River of Words*, an international children's environmental poetry and art project. 'The Khan Men of Agra,' her first-ever travel piece, won the 1994 Book Passage/British Airways Travel Writers' Conference Grand Prize and was also published in *Travelers' Tales: A Woman's World.*

*"And which part of the world is suffering in your absence, Madam?"*
—Question from a New Delhi rickshaw driver.

**Tom Miller**'s books include *The Panama Hat Trail, On the Border,* and, most recently, *Trading with the Enemy: A Yankee Travels through Castro's Cuba* (Basic Books). He has written for *LIFE, Smithsonian, The New York Times, Natural History,* and a slew of other publications. Miller, who lives in Arizona, has been widely anthologized, and his commentaries have appeared on National Public Radio. His collection of nearly one-hundred versions of the song "La Bamba" led to his Rhino Records release, *The Best of La Bamba.*

*"Never pack for your next trip before you've unpacked from your last."*

**Mur** was born in San Francisco in 1947—raised in Michigan—dropped out of Syracuse University in 1967—when his Higher Spirit called him "TO WALK TO INDIA" during an intense visionary experience. Thereafter, Mur scored a cheap one-way flight to Luxembourg and hitchhiked overland along the Hashish Trail from Istanbul to India at 20 years old. Mur currently lives near San Francisco, where he owns Earthpeople Press, printing hippie fiction and non-fiction. He welcomes e-mail at earthfun@ix.netcom.com

*"After living in more than 50 countries during the last 30 years, I profoundly understand—WE DO NOT NEED NATIONS ANYMORE!— we one-world EARTHPEOPLE can manage our Planet Earth magnificently for ourselves."*

**Steve Millward** is a 20-year friend of author and wanderluster Bruce Northam. Steve finally succumbed to his persistent advice and took off for adventures unknown in Asia. To hole-up and write his first book, Bruce literally moved into Steve deserted house. But before he could say "home sweet home" Steve had been robbed blind and was calling for help from Istanbul. Bruce's crucial words of encouragement urged Steve to pull up his bootstraps and get on with the fun! Six weeks later, the odyssey's finale was an emotional pilgrimage to the very room of his birth in the Philippines. Steve is an avid disc golfer who recently competed in his fifth Professional Disc Golf World Championships. He and his lovely wife Pam reside in Raleigh, North Carolina.

*"Now I know the difference between a trip and a journey ..."*

**451**

**Basil Northam, Sr.** presents lecture/slide shows on the art and history of Long Island and New York's Adirondack mountains. His favorites include Thoreau, Muir, Emily Dickinson, Will Rogers, Mark Twain, Teddy Roosevelt and Adirondack 'characters.' "Libraries will get you through times of no money better than money will get you through times of no libraries." —American Library Association

*"We all travel the milky way together. When we try to pick out anything by itself, we find it hitched to everything else in the universe."* —John Muir

**Bruce Northam** is an animated world travel lecturer. His lecture/slide show, 'In Search of Adventure,' captures the essence of circling the globe five times and is presented throughout the US. His first book, *The Frugal Globetrotter*, provides rat-race exit blueprints and counsel for people on academic and workaholic binges. He's written for Details, Swing, and Blue and is a frequent guest on CNN and radio nationwide. His resume includes piloting a Manhattan horse-drawn carriage, acting as a stunt man in Chinese action movies, shepherding in Morocco, moonlit beach dancing in Goa, India, walking coast-to-coast across both Northern England and Wales with his father, and playing naked Frisbee with New Guinea natives. He compiled and edited this anthology. For lecture/slide shows, public appearances or additional information call Bill Paquin, Greater Talent Network, Inc. (212) 647-6316 (email: northamlecture@hotmail.com) To order *The Frugal Globetrotter* call Fulcrum Publishing (800) 992-2908 or amazon.com

*"The first thing you pack is yourself."*

**Brad Olsen**'s *World Stompers: A Guide to Travel Manifesto*, now in its fourth edition, was lauded by film director Oliver Stone as a 'subversive masterpiece' and *Publishers Weekly* as a 'Quirky Chain Pleaser.' He is an editor for *Trips* magazine and the author/illustrator of *Extreme Adventures Hawaii* and *Extreme Adventures Northern California* (Hunter Publishing). His travel web site (www.stompers.com) was Microsoft Network's 'Site of the Week.' Brad is the President of CCC Publishing in San Francisco and publisher & editor of *In Search of Adventure: A Wild Travel Anthology*. His forthcoming book is *Sacred Places: 101 Spiritual Sites Around the World* (CCC Publishing). Brad's commentaries have appeared on National Public Radio, and he enjoys giving lectures on low-budget global excursions, adventure travel, and journeys to sacred places. For travel book or lecture inquiries, please e-mail Brad at: cccpublishing@juno.com

*"There is no such thing as fear. Embrace this truism and suddenly there are no limitations."*

**Eileen O'Connor**, originally from upstate New York, is an actress and writer living in New York City. She is currently starring in the serialized cult hit *Burning Habits*. *The New York Times* calls her portrayal of a suicidal debutante, a delusional barfly and the oldest living nun in captivity 'Fabulous.' (As well they should, she cannot even begin to go into the emotional turmoil and suffering such rigorous roles demand ...) She is presently at work on a screenplay.

*"When the going gets tough, get out of town."*

**Brian Patrick O'Donoghue** is a long-time Alaska journalist best known for his newspaper and television coverage of Big Oil, politics and sled-dog racing. In 1996 and 1997 he broke new trails on the web with Starfish Software's *idog* (Iditarod Daily Online Guide). O'Donoghue's perilous last place finish in the stormy 1991 Iditarod, mushing Chad and 16 other sled dogs, is recounted in *My Lead Dog Was a Lesbian* (Random House 1996). Now 43 and married, but evidently no wiser, last winter O'Donoghue took his dogs on the more mountainous, every bit as nasty, 1,000-mile Yukon Quest International Sled Dog Race. Another book is in the works. He can be contacted at brikate@polarnet.com

*"An old pitch from the Maryland State Lottery struck a chord I've never forgotten; 'To win, you've gotta play.'"*

**L. Peat O'Neill** was probably conceived in Cuba and recently trekked in Kyrgyzstan's Turkestan Range. The author of *Travel Writing: A Guide to Research, Writing and Selling* published by Writer's Digest Books, she is on the news staff of the *Washington Post*, and also teaches travel and nature writing on the Internet through UCLA-Extension. A deadline traveler, she's just barely made the gate for countless airplane, boat, train and bus departures.

*"Travel through life and you won't get stuck."*

**Johanna O'Sullivan** is an environmental activist. As Natural Resource Chair for the Suffolk County League of Woman Voters and other "watchdog" organizations, she provides non-pollution solutions for solid waste reduction, groundwater preservation and eliminating harmful pesticides. She was designated 'Mother Theresa in plain clothes' by the people who love her.

*"It is far better to give than it is to receive."*

**Linda Packer**'s first professional article was about a trip she took to Mexico in the '60s; it was published in the 'Club News' section of an *Archie* comic book when she was 10. Since that time she has continued to write about travel, and is actually getting a regular paycheck for it as Editor in Chief of *Travel Your Way* magazine. She lives in Chicago with her husband and their massive collection of Sondheim CDs.

**453**

*"Journeying is the key to unlocking our only true conundrum: the world."*

**Susan Parker** is an actress, singer-songwriter who has sung everything from rock to opera to the national anthem for Pittsburgh Pirate baseball games. She has worked in film and television and has written and recorded jingles for TV/radio commercials. She is currently storming the musical theatre world.

*"Don't go to discover the world—go to discover yourself."*

**Robert Young Pelton** has led a very adventurous life in over 75 of the world's wildest and remote countries. Along the way, he has survived a terrorist bomb attack, shelling, attacks by rebels, car accidents, muggings, illness, attacks by killer bees, and even a plane crash in the central highlands of Kalimantan. Best known for his highly acclaimed *The World's Most Dangerous Places*, RYP is also the author of *Borneo* (Fielding Worldwide), *Come Back Alive* (Doubleday) and an upcoming autobiography also for Doubleday. He is Publisher of Fielding Worldwide and Editor-at-Large for *Blue* magazine.

*"Adventure is the flame that makes us burn brightly. Knowledge and courage are the tinder and match."*

**Robert Ragaini,** before becoming a full-time writer, spent his time running from one New York recording studio to another singing such classic TV and radio jingles as "Reach out and touch someone," "Get a piece of the rock," "Folgers in your cup," "You deserve a break today at McDonalds," and the still popular, "tum ta tum Tums." Now he just runs from country to country.

*"Don't look back, they're gainin' on ya."*

**David Redhill** is a Singapore-born Australian of Anglo-Russian descent. His writing and photography has appeared in *The Sydney Morning Herald*, *The Australian*, *The London Times*, *The Guardian* and *La Vanguardia*. He has led a questionable professional history in business suits, sarongs and ski boots in over 50 countries, oscillating between responsible career paths and hand-to-mouth freelancing.

His favorite quote: a concerned friend's *"It all sounds like fun, mate—but where's it all going?"* He's still figuring that one out.

**Marcia Reynolds,** coach, speaker and author of *Being in the Zone: The Secrets of Performance Excellence* and *Golf in the Zone: Mastering the Mental Game,* travels to many of her speaking engagements by RV, and provides life coaching to clients around the world by cell phone. She can be reached at 602-954-9030, Marcia@covisioning.com, or at www.covisioning.com.

*"If you choose the road less traveled, be sure to take your four-wheel drive."*

**Mary Roach** has traveled to all seven continents, yet to this day she cannot remember to order special meals. She has written about her travels for *Salon, Islands, Conde Nast Traveler, Health, Vogue* and *American Way*. She lives in San Francisco with her husband Ed and their three pieces of luggage.

*"When I'm far away from home, I take comfort in looking up at the moon and knowing that the people I love are looking up at the very same moon. And then I realize that the time zones are all wacked and it's actually noon back home, and then I have another beer and go to bed."*

**Hank Rosenfeld** is a folk journalist, Mediatrician©, and light comedian living in Santa Monica, CA. He has written humor for radio stations across America, plays for small audiences in LA and NY, Minneapolis, Amsterdam and Leipzig, and stories for *The Realist, Spy* and assorted literary journals. Hank has lived on a pirate radio ship off the coast of Israel called "THE VOICE OF PEACE," and has been arrested for robbing the National Bank of Greece in Athens.

*"'We're all angels and we're all only here a little while. That's the fuck of life.' —Told to me by a homeless man in New York City on West 34th Street and 8th Avenue."*

**Spencer Rumsey** was born in Wilmington, Delaware, a state noted for its lack of width and depth. He is currently an editor in *Newsday*'s op-ed section. His articles have appeared in *The Rising Nepal* and the *New York Post*, to name a few.

*"The deepest experience cannot be packaged."*

**Swami Dyhan Santosh** became a 'Peace Warrior' upon re-birth into his present body. Between beach meditations in San Francisco and writing inspirational short stories, 'Santosh' is actively involved in making global peace a believable reality. His brainchild, the "World Peace and Technology Tour" aspires to travel around the planet in a fleet of busses during the millennium, promoting goodwill and demonstrating technology to liberate the masses. Visit the non-profit Peace Tour web site at www.peacetour.org, and don't forget to sign up for your free personalized email at www.peacetour.com

*"World peace begins with inner peace within each and every one of us."*

**Mark Schwartz** was losing his hair gradually in New Jersey and Missouri before irrevocably misplacing it somewhere in southern Mexico. Fortunately, a love for Iberophonics and mambo grew in its stead, and he now writes about world music for *Rhythm Music*, *VIBE*, and *Jazziz* magazines, and has appeared on National Public Radio.

*"With an ISDN connection, a good set of speakers, and a takeout menu, we can now see, hear and savor the world without ever leaving the comfort of our homes. God save us all."*

**Anik See** has been traveling on bicycles since her father unscrewed the training wheels. She is the bicycling editor of *Big World* magazine, has been referred to as "an angry Gen X" poetry and prose writer and is a food researcher and recipe developer in real life. She lives, bikes and eats in Toronto.

*"When one jumps over the edge, one is bound to land somewhere."*
—D.H. Lawrence

**Eric Seyfarth** has worked as a desk-bound editor and writer for the past 15 years. The benefits were nice, dental insurance was good, and the paychecks were nearly regular. But the annoying little voice telling him to get Out There would not be quiet. So he and his wife recently quit their perfectly good jobs, sold everything, and hit the road for two years of international travel. Seyfarth is currently working on a book about music of the world in a dozen countries entitled *At the Speed of Sound: Around the Globe in Search of World Music*. He no longer has dental insurance. 'On the Trail of the Hadza' appeared in *Blue*.

*"There is no such thing as place, only people who make it so."*

**Bill Shein** is a comedian and writer living, inexplicably, in Washington, DC. His career as a humorist began in 1990 purely out of desperation: After graduating from Tufts University with a degree in American history, he faced a tight job market in which very few history companies were hiring. In addition to writing *Buzzsaw*, a daily humor column for America Online, and running a comedy web site at http://www.witcity.com, Bill helps train humor writers in emerging democracies in the fine art of poking fun at the powers-that-be. He also frequently embellishes his biography with entirely fabricated items, often involving the so-called "training of humor writers in emerging democracies in the fine art of poking fun at the powers-that-be."

*"Travel the world. Meet interesting people. Do new things. And let a warm smile come across your face as you write about your adventures and gleefully deduct the entire cost."*

**456**

**Abby Sinnott** is a collector of foreign textures, light, sounds and colors. She has traveled extensively throughout Europe and is currently planning to flee her home country and head for a sweating jungle in South America. A medical writer by day, she writes fiction whenever she has a spare moment and plans one day to start her own magazine.

*"The further I traveled, the closer I got to home."*

**Douglas Smith** has mapped and interpreted the geology of the western-central Baja Californian desert for scientific publications (and fun!) for the past fifteen years. He is currently a research professor in Tennessee, and is involved in restoring natural habitat to disturbed rivers.

*"Travel alone for extended periods in the wilderness. Turn off your spinning, racing, 9-to-5, TeeVee-saturated mind. Slow down. Look around. Existentialism Happens!"*

**Marilyn Hope Smulyan** is a 50-year-old writer with a passion for the outdoors and natural history. She particularly loves to travel by bike and has toured extensively in the United States and Canada. Her most recent article, 'Bicycling to the Top of the World,' about a solo trip up to the Arctic Circle in Canada, appeared in the Summer 1998 issue of *Maiden Voyages*. She lives in San Francisco.

*"Immersing myself in nature, every sense is acutely aware. I notice everything and nothing. Every moment is a dare."*

**Randal Thatcher** grew up, bought a Camaro, and went off to college. Seven years later, he graduated with a 4-year degree and went straight to work in the corporate arena. He was driving on the 'fast track' with a full tank ... but an empty soul. So, after a short but brilliant business career, he quit, bought a backpack, and traveled the world with his wife. Now he's writing, traveling, and playing bluegrass banjo with no regrets.

*"Whenever my smile goes missing, it's time to pack a bag and go off in search of it."*

**Phil Trupp** is an award-winning author of more than a dozen books, and a contributor to *Smithsonian, Reader's Digest* and *Caribbean Travel & Life*, among others. He was one of the first Americans reporting from Castro's Cuba. A NOAA Aquanaut and Explorers Club Fellow, his writing ranges from exploration to the arts, and "the liberation of all things journalistic." His latest book, *Sea of Dreamers* (Fulcrum) was published in fall 1998.

*"The magic of discovery is to see with new eyes."*

**Annalisa Layton Valentine** will publish her first book in 1999. Be on the watch-out for *Fool Me Twice*, a true middle-life adventure story. After a career in molecular biology and raising a family, Annalisa learned to dive, became a PADI Instructor, shed her possessions and became a sailor. While sailing the Red Sea, she was captured twice; once by the Eritrean Army, and once again in a far more insidious manner. She jumped ship in Oman and fled to India, only to be deported to Germany, of all places.

*"It is easier to ask forgiveness than permission."*

**Cindy Lee Van Dover** is a former Pilot-in-Command of the deep-diving research submarine ALVIN. Her research took her to mountain ranges miles below the surface of the sea where she studied the biology of its more exotic denizens. On shore, she shares her knowledge with students at the College of William & Mary. This excerpt is from *Deep-Ocean Journeys: Discovering New Life at the Bottom of the Sea* (Addison-Wesley 1996), an autobiographical account of her career as a deep-sea scientist and the forty-ninth person—and the only woman—ever to qualify as a navy-certified Pilot-in-Command of the deep-diving research submarine ALVIN.

*"You might have to work to get where no one else goes, but it's worth it."*

**Simon Winchester**, after an unpromising start as a geologist in East Africa, drifted into journalism in northern England, becoming a full-time foreign correspondent in 1970. He has reported—for *The Guardian* and the *London Sunday Times*—from almost everywhere, except Peru and the Hamptons. Since 1994 he has worked freelance, and prefers writing books. His latest, *The Professor and the Madman* (HarperCollins), became a national bestseller, suggesting that freelance writing and long-term survival may not necessarily be mutually exclusive.

**Becky Youman** and **Bryan Estep** maintain that any resemblance to Goofus is purely incidental. Currently based in Santiago, they are writing *Open Road's Chile Guide* to be published in April 1999. They also contribute to the *Santiago News Review*, *Big World*, and *Transitions Abroad* among other periodicals. In addition to their current stint in Chile, they have also called Brazil, Argentina, and Mexico home.

*"Don't call us jalepeño breath. We're eating habeñeros."*

**458**

**Steve Zikman** is the co-author of the forthcoming bestselling series book *Chicken Soup for the Traveler's Soul* with Jack Canfield and Mark Victor Hanson. His book, *The Power of Travel* will be available in June, 1999 from Penguin Putnam. Steve is a trained Labyrinth facilitator and the president of The Power of Travel™ Seminars & Services, providing individuals, corporations and organizations with the inner preparation and motivational momentum to enhance, enrich and expand their experience of travel, be it business or pleasure.

*"Follow what you love and it will take you where you need to go"*
—Natalie Goldberg

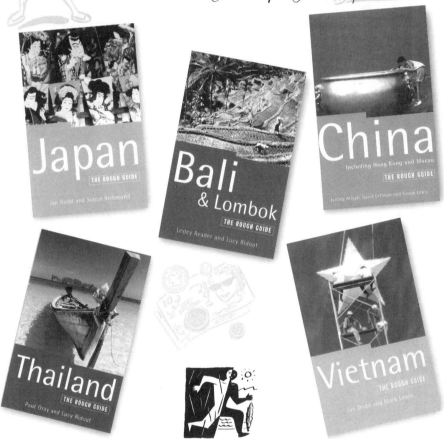